CANADIAN LANGUAGE POLICIES
IN COMPARATIVE PERSPECTIVE

Canadian Language Policies in Comparative Perspective

EDITED BY

MICHAEL A. MORRIS

McGill-Queen's University Press

Montreal & Kingston • London • Ithaca

© McGill-Queen's University Press 2010
ISBN 978-0-7735-3705-7 (cloth)
ISBN 978-0-7735-3706-4 (paper)

Legal deposit second quarter 2010
Bibliothèque nationale du Québec

Printed in Canada on acid-free paper that is 100% ancient forest free (100% post-consumer recycled), processed chlorine free.

This book has been published with the help of a grant from Clemson University.

McGill-Queen's University Press acknowledges the support of the Canada Council for the Arts for our publishing program. We also acknowledge the financial support of the Government of Canada through the Canada Book Fund for our publishing activities.

Library and Archives Canada Cataloguing in Publication

Canadian language policies in comparative perspective / edited by Michael A. Morris.

Based on papers originally presented at the 18th World Congress of the International Political Science Association, Québec, Québec, Aug. 1–5, 2000.

Includes bibliographical references and index.
ISBN 978-0-7735-3705-7 (bound)
ISBN 978-0-7735-3706-4 (pbk)

1. Language policy – Canada – Congresses. 2. Language policy – Congresses. I. Morris, Michael A. II. International Political Science Association. World Congress (18th: 2000: Québec, Québec)

P119.32.C3C355 2010   306.44'971   C2010-900667-4

This book was typeset by Interscript in 10/13 Sabon.

Contents

Figures, Maps, and Tables   vii

Preface   xi
Michael A. Morris

Contributors   xiii

Introduction: Comparing Perspectives on Canadian Language
Policies   3
Michael A. Morris

PART ONE PERSPECTIVES AND OVERVIEWS

Introduction to Part One   17
William F. Mackey and Michael A. Morris

1   History and Origins of Language Policies in Canada   18
William F. Mackey

2   Comparing Language Policies   67
William F. Mackey

3   Evaluating Language Policies   120
William F. Mackey

PART TWO INTERNATIONAL PERSPECTIVES

Introduction to Part Two   161
Michael A. Morris

4   The Language Issue in the United States, Canada, and Quebec:
Some Comparative Aspects   166
Jacques Maurais

5   The Danger of Denial of Languages: An Eastern European-Canadian
    Comparison   179
    Yaroslav Bilinsky

6   Canada's Domestic French-Speaking Groups and the International
    Francophonie Compared   206
    Jürgen Erfurt

PART THREE NON-LINGUISTIC PERSPECTIVES

Introduction to Part Three   243
Michael A. Morris

7   Linguistic Issues and Immigration in Quebec: Relating the "Cultural
    Communities" to the "Quebec Nation" and the French Language   246
    Louise Fontaine

8   Canadian Federal Policies on Bilingualism, Multiculturalism, and
    Immigrant Language Training: Comparisons and Interaction   267
    Eve Haque

9   Canada's Official Languages in the Provinces of Quebec and Ontario:
    A Demographic Comparison   297
    Michel Paillé

PART FOUR GROUP PERSPECTIVES

Introduction to Part Four   329
Michael A. Morris

10 Language Policy in Ontario: From the Recognition of Linguistic
    Rights to the Free-Market Policy   333
    Normand Labrie

11 The End of the Language Crisis in Quebec: Comparative
    Implications   344
    Pierre Anctil

Synthesis and Conclusion   369
Michael A. Morris

References   385

Index   421

Figures, Maps, and Tables

FIGURES

1.1 Comparison through five thematic perspectives   11
1.2 Comparison through the interactive policy process   13
9.1 Numbers of persons in Quebec knowing English only and knowing English and French among those with English as the mother tongue   305
9.2 Distribution (percentage) of knowledge of French and English among population whose mother tongue is neither French nor English, Quebec, 1971 and 2001   308
9.3 Language most often spoken at home in Quebec among persons with a mother tongue other than English or French   316
9.4 Distribution (percentage) of language used most often at home among population whose mother tongue is neither French nor English, Quebec, 1971 and 2001   319

MAPS

1 Population by mother tongue: Canada, the provinces, and the territories, 2001   xvi
5.1 The Russian language in three Baltic states (in percentages)   181
5.2 Ukrainian versus Russian as the native language in Ukraine (in percentages)   195

Figures, Maps, and Tables

TABLES

7.1 How the "we" and the "other" are categorized in official discourse, in relation to the name changes of the government ministry: a chronology   250

9.1 Population by mother tongue, Quebec, 1971 and 2001   299

9.2 Population by mother tongue, Ontario, 1971 and 2001   299

9.3 Population by mother tongue, Canada, 1971 and 2001   299

9.4 Distribution (percentage) of knowledge of French and English by mother tongue, Quebec, 1971   301

9.5 Distribution (percentage) of knowledge of French and English by mother tongue, Ontario, 1971   301

9.6 Distribution (percentage) of knowledge of French and English by mother tongue, Quebec, 2001   303

9.7 Distribution (percentage) of knowledge of French and English by mother tongue, Ontario, 2001   303

9.8 Knowledge of French and English by mother tongue should the Ontarian distribution be applied to Quebec: absolute differences with census, Quebec, 1971   306

9.9 Knowledge of French and English by mother tongue should the Ontarian distribution be applied to Quebec: absolute differences with census, Quebec, 2001   307

9.10 Knowledge of French and English by mother tongue should the Ontarian distribution of 1971 be applied to Quebec in 2001: absolute differences with census, Quebec, 2001   308

9.11 Distribution (percentage) of language used most often at home by mother tongue, Quebec, 1971   311

9.12 Distribution (percentage) of language used most often at home by mother tongue, Ontario, 1971   311

9.13 Distribution (percentage) of language used most often at home by mother tongue, Quebec, 2001   313

9.14 Distribution (percentage) of language used most often at home by mother tongue, Ontario, 2001   313

9.15 Language used most often at home by mother tongue should the Ontarian distribution be applied to Quebec: absolute differences with census, Quebec, 1971   317

9.16 Language used most often at home by mother tongue should the Ontarian distribution be applied to Quebec: absolute differences with census, Quebec, 2001   318

9.17   Language used most often at home by mother tongue should the
       Ontarian distribution of 1971 be applied to Quebec in 2001:
       absolute differences with census, Quebec, 2001   320
11.1   Mother tongues, province of Quebec (percentages)   356
11.2   Mother tongues, Montreal (merged city) (percentages)   356
11.3   Knowledge of French and English among immigrants admitted to
       Quebec, 2001–5 (percentages)   357
11.4   Evolution of the French language, 1996 and 2001
       (percentages)   358
11.5   Levels of bilingualism, 1996 and 2001 (percentages)   359
11.6   The evolution of Canadian and Quebec language policies as com-
       pared to immigration policies, from the 1960s to the 1990s   366
11.7   Factors leading to a resolution of linguistic tensions in Quebec,
       from the 1960s to the 1990s   367

Preface

MICHAEL A. MORRIS

For Canada, language issues have been at the centre of national political life for decades – so much so that they have played and promise to continue to play a decisive role in determining the unity of the country. Numerous groups, the provinces, and the federal government all have distinctive interests and approaches to language questions and national unity. William F. Mackey, one of the contributors to this book, has succinctly summed up the importance of language issues for Canada: "No country has invested more in language policy than has Canada, and particularly Quebec" (Mackey, 1984, xi). France stands out in language promotion but not in language policy, that is, language laws and rights, including provisions for official language minorities.

The long-standing importance of language issues for Canada has attracted global attention in terms of both the lessons that the Canadian experience might be able to offer others and those learned elsewhere that might be relevant for Canada. From a positive perspective, Canada may be regarded as a laboratory for comparison of language policies, since multiple policies exist for the promotion of one version or another of cultural and linguistic diversity. For example, a recent study identified thirteen Canadian language policies: one for each of the ten provinces, two for the two (now three) territories, and one for the federal government (Corbeil, 1997). On the negative side, the coexistence of so many language policies has tended to increase areas of potential friction, in spite of some shared objectives. While all of the policies seek in one way or another to promote the identity of the political unit in question, a variety of specific measures in support of provincial and national identities have often not easily been compatible with one another.

Comparisons are invidious when made casually or to prove a case. For example, a misleading argument about Canadian language policies frequently repeated in the United States is that multiple policies in support of cultural and linguistic diversity threaten national unity. Suffice it to say that such allegations blur cause and effect: threats to national unity in Canada have multiple causes, and language policies can have positive results.

Because of the high stakes involved in language policies, comparisons will be made, but unfortunately, they often are ill-informed and misleading, as the example just cited demonstrates. The challenge is to make careful, judicious comparisons. Some sound groundwork for systematic comparison has been laid in the relevant literature. It is the intention of this book to build on this research in developing more systematic comparative approaches to Canadian language policies.

NOTE

This book is a sequel to an earlier publication in French: Michael A. Morris, ed., *Les politiques linguistiques canadiennes: Approches comparées* (Paris: L'Harmattan, 2003).

Contributors

PIERRE ANCTIL obtained a PhD in social anthropology at the New School for Social Research in New York in 1980 and completed a post-doctoral fellowship at the Jewish Studies Department of McGill University in 1988–91. He held several administrative positions in the Quebec government between 1993 and 2004 and was later director of the Institute of Canadian Studies at the University of Ottawa. He is currently a Killam Fellow in the Department of History at the University of Ottawa. Professor Anctil has written several books on the Montreal Jewish community, including *Le rendez-vous manqué: les Juifs de Montréal face au Québec de l'entre-deux-guerres* (1988), *Tur malka: flâneries sur les cimes de l'histoire juive montréalaise* (1997), and *Saint-Laurent, Montreal's Main* (2002). He has also translated into French the memoirs of Yiddish-Canadian writers Israël Medresh, Simon Belkin, and Hirsch Wolofsky between 1997 and 2001.

YAROSLAV BILINSKY was an associate of the Russian Studies Research Center at Harvard in the years 1956–58 and received his doctorate from Princeton University in 1958. He taught political science at Douglass College of Rutgers University from 1958 to 1961 and then at the University of Delaware from 1961 until his retirement in 2002, when he was awarded the title of Professor Emeritus. He has also been a visiting professor at the University of Pennsylvania and Columbia University. His publications include five books and monographs and sixty-two articles. He is also the co-author, with the late sociologist Tonü Parming, of the two-volume, 725-page research report *The Helsinki Watch Committees in the Soviet Republics: Implications for the Soviet Nationality Question, March 31, 1980*, which has been published on the website of the National Council for Eurasian and East European Research, www.nceeer.org. About half a dozen of his publications relate to linguistic topics.

JÜRGEN ERFURT is a full professor holding the chair in Romance linguistics at the University of Frankfurt am Main, Germany. He specializes in sociolinguistics, language policy, language change, and linguistic minorities in Eastern and Western Europe and in Canada. He has published numerous books and articles in these areas, most recently three books in 2008, including Gabriele Budach, Jürgen Erfurt, and Melanie Kunkel, eds., *Écoles plurilingues – multilingual schools: Konzepte, Institutionen und Akteure. Internationale Perspektiven*. He is the co-editor (founder and head of the Editorial Committee) of the journal *Grenzgänge. Beiträge zu einer modernen Romanistik*, an interdisciplinary journal of the linguistics, literature, and history of Romance cultures, and also co-editor of the journal *Osnabrücker Beiträge zur Sprachtheorie*, which is devoted to general linguistics.

LOUISE FONTAINE received a doctorate in political science from Université Laval in Quebec City in 1990 and is currently teaching at Université Sainte-Anne in Nova Scotia. She has published articles on immigration and ethnic nationalism, public administration, and political sociology, including relations between the state and ethnic groups in Belgium and Canada. Her book *Un labyrinthe carré comme un cercle* analyzes transformations in Quebec politics relating to cultural communities. From 1998 to 2001 she was secretary general of the International Society for the Sociology of Religion (SISR), for which she organized various international conferences.

EVE HAQUE is an assistant professor in the Department of Languages, Literatures and Linguistics at York University in Toronto. Her research interests include language policy and planning, ethnolinguistic nationalism, immigrant language training, and issues related to language, multiculturalism, and nationalism. Her publications cover questions related to language, multiculturalism, nationalism, and immigration, and she is currently working on a study of the Royal Commission on Bilingualism and Biculturalism for the University of Toronto Press.

NORMAND LABRIE (PhD in linguistics, Université Laval, Quebec) is associate dean, Research and Graduate Studies, at the Ontario Institute for Studies in Education of the University of Toronto (OISE/UT), and a full professor at the Centre for Franco-Ontarian Studies. He specializes in sociolinguistics, language policy, and the study of linguistic minorities in Canada and Europe and has published numerous books and articles in these areas.

WILLIAM FRANCIS MACKEY (MA, Harvard; *docteur-ès-lettres*, Geneva; fellow of the Royal Society of Canada and the Royal Academy of Belgium; *chevalier de l'Ordre national du Québec*) is the author of two dozen books and some two hundred articles on language policy, bilingualism, sociolinguistics, and language education. He has been a language policy adviser to governments in Canada, Ireland, and Australia and a member of governmental language commissions. Dr Mackey was senior lecturer at the University of London from 1948 to 1951 and founding director (1968–71) of the International Center for Research on Bilingualism at Université Laval, where he is now emeritus professor.

JACQUES MAURAIS holds degrees from Laval and Cambridge universities, and before his retirement, he was research director at the Office québécois de la langue française in Quebec City. He is the former coordinator (2002–6) of the sociolinguistic network of the university branch of the Francophonie, the international organization that brings together French-speaking countries around the world. He has published numerous works on sociolinguistics and language policy, including a book co-edited with Michael Morris: *Languages in a Globalising World* (Cambridge University Press, 2003).

MICHAEL A. MORRIS is professor of political science at Clemson University, South Carolina, where he also holds a joint appointment as professor of languages. He received an MA in Hispanic studies from the University of Madrid/Middlebury College and an MA and a PhD in international relations from the School of Advanced International Studies of Johns Hopkins University. Dr Morris has published four books of sole authorship and numerous monographs and articles, as well as edited volumes on various topics of international affairs. With Jacques Maurais, he co-edited *Languages in a Globalising World* (Cambridge University Press, 2003).

MICHEL PAILLÉ is a demographer with degrees from the universities of Montreal and Pennsylvania. Before his retirement, he worked for twenty-four years with the Conseil de la langue française (1980–2002) and the Office québécois de la langue française (OQLF; 2002–4). He is a former president (1989–93) of the Association des démographes du Québec and has authored numerous articles in specialized Canadian and European journals on various aspects of demolinguistics in Quebec and Canada. From 2004 to 2008 he was associate researcher for the Hector-Fabre Chair at the Université du Québec à Montréal. He still regularly publishes with the OQLF, *L'Action nationale,* and the *Bulletin d'histoire politique.*

Map 1 Population by mother tongue: Canada, the provinces, and the territories, 2001

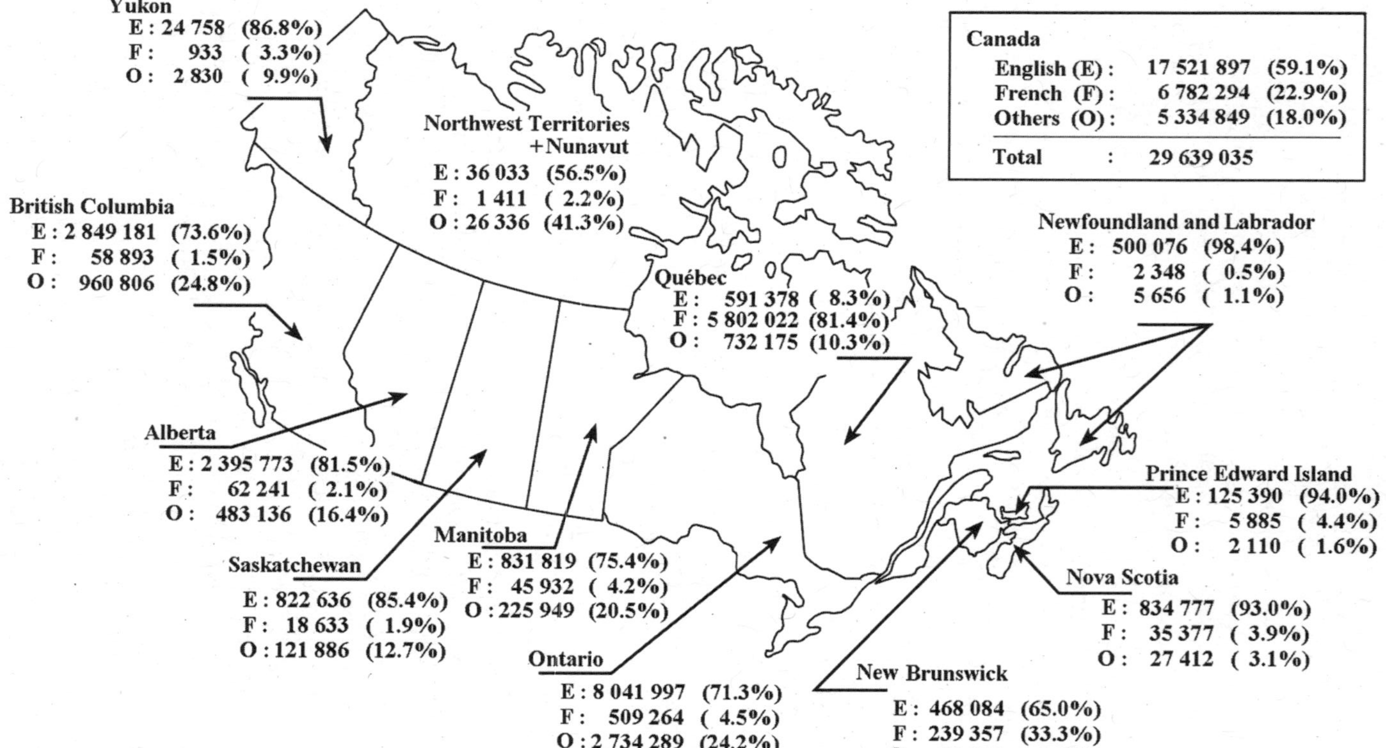

SOURCE: L. Marmen and J.P. Corbeil, *New Canadian Perspectives: Languages in Canada: 2001 Census* (Ottawa: Canadian Heritage and Statistics Canada, 2004), table A.1; original map in French from M.A. Morris, ed., *Les politiques linguistiques canadiennes: Approches comparées* (Paris: L'Harmattan, 2003), 5.

CANADIAN LANGUAGE POLICIES
IN COMPARATIVE PERSPECTIVE

Comparing Perspectives on Canadian Language Policies

MICHAEL A. MORRIS

Comparison of language policies, whether domestic or international, highlights the similarities and differences of each. On this basis, a comparative perspective can identify best and worst practices, as well as those in between, across numerous cases. Systematic contrasts essentially raise the bar for evaluation by examining a gamut of practices. Self-evaluation of a case on its own and in isolation can be useful, but evaluation is more reliable when a practice is contrasted with other cases.

A textbook on comparative politics provides a clear, powerful justification for the application of a comparative approach across disciplines and countries. As Martin Slann has observed, "The rapid and accelerating growth and pervasiveness of communication technology and the globalization of the world economy have made the exposure to and understanding of different political cultures more useful than ever before. The study of comparative politics enables the student to maximize an appreciation of societies that are distinct from and often in opposition to our own values. There is no longer the possibility of remaining aloof from or the luxury of remaining ignorant of the other countries with which we share this planet" (Slann, 2004, ix).

A recent study examined a related subject, immigration and diversity in schools in Quebec, from a comparative perspective and provided an explicit justification for this (McAndrew, 2001, 21). What was missing, however, was a systematic comparative approach to Canadian language policies. Such comparisons have been few, scattered, and unsystematic. I substantiate this assertion later in this chapter as well as in the introductions to each of the subsequent parts of this book.

A distinction that also helps describe the literature is between comparative, partly comparative, and non-comparative analyses. Comparative studies, as noted, have been few, scattered, and unsystematic. At the same time, a substantial number of publications have been partly comparative in nature, in that they either point toward full-blown comparisons or provide useful information for supporting systematic comparison. This characterization does not impute a comparative intention to such authors but, rather, is limited to the observation that they prepare the way for eventual systematic comparison. Non-comparative works neither involve nor prepare the way for comparison and hence are not of interest here.

While the finding that the literature is not systematically comparative is critical in nature, the scope of the critique provided in this book is fairly limited. We do not indict the literature as such but instead appreciate and aspire to build on and extend the few comparative works, as well as the more numerous partly comparative ones. Our desire is to develop and promote systematic comparison of Canadian language policies.

An initial step toward such comparison is first to appreciate some key problems. Three obstacles – complexity, multidisciplinarity, and diversity – complicate systematic comparison of Canadian language policies.

First, while language policy comparisons can be very useful, they are not tidy. The nature and function of language permeate everything in human society, while language policy aspires to shape its use. The resulting ongoing tug and pull between language use and language policy makes for a complex, changing situation. Language policy therefore faces formidable, complex obstacles to achieve its ends. Comparisons must cope with a similar complex reality. For example, specifying what is distinctive and what is shared between different language policies, while useful, is not straightforward. Comparisons that purport to capture their socially dynamic setting need to explore and assess multiple aspects of language policies from various angles. This book relies on multiple perspectives in order to emphasize the importance of regarding the language use–language policy relationship from different angles.

Second, language policy comparisons are necessarily multidisciplinary in character. Such policies involve different emphases over time, including public policy, economics, geopolitics, law, and sociolinguistics. Comparisons contrasting different policies also must capture this multidisciplinary reality. A comparative, multidisciplinary approach is demanding; it is addressed here in two ways. First, the authors have a wide range of disciplinary expertise. For details, see the section on the contributors which appears earlier in the volume. The diversity of personal orientations and approaches helps reflect the dynamism of multidisciplinary reality. And second, all the authors, in their ongoing research on language policy, have adopted a multidisciplinary approach. Original disciplinary boundaries have been blurred as they have necessarily had to cope with a complex subject.

A third problem in any systematic comparison of language policies is that the very diversity of perspectives implicit in a comparative approach makes it difficult to integrate scattered lessons and findings. This inherent difficulty is addressed here in several ways. Ongoing communications between all the authors have helped promote integration of the various approaches. As well, the formulation of some approaches to systematic comparison, discussed later in this chapter, provides a framework for making complementary comparisons. My summation at the end of the volume also synthesizes and extends conclusions from the various parts and chapters of the book.

STEPS TOWARD THE SYSTEMATIC COMPARISON OF CANADIAN LANGUAGE POLICIES

Having identified some obstacles and suggested how they can be managed, we can now undertake a systematic comparison on a more positive footing. Six steps or measures can provide a framework for systematic comparison.

Step One: A Structured Survey of the Relevant Literature

Since a few previous works about Canadian language policies have been explicitly comparative in nature, attention will focus on them, with only summary attention being given to publications with a more tangential comparative focus. In order to further refine our focus on the relevant literature, the many linguistic analyses of Canadian language policies will not be included here. Linguistic analysis can certainly impact on policy, as when different kinds of changes in language use are documented, and authors in the subsequent chapters rely on these findings as appropriate. But here our focus is on policy comparison, which is addressed more squarely through policy-related studies rather than linguistic analysis. Further sharpening our focus, we do not aspire to be comprehensive or exhaustive in our survey but, rather, more modestly to represent major lines of comparison. The emphasis here, then, is on a synthesis of the literature that in some way or another has dealt broadly with Canadian language policies in comparative perspective. More specific literature surveys are provided in the individual introductions to the main sections of the book.

The origins of federal language policy did reflect the importance of comparison, even though the subsequent literature followed up only unevenly on this initial effort. Comparison was among the first preoccupations of the Royal Commission on Bilingualism and Biculturalism's Research Division, as witnessed by the numerous studies of the major officially bilingual countries (see the various volumes published by the commission, 1963–70). Details are provided later in this volume; see especially chapters 2, by William Mackey, and 8, by Eve Haque. Results of these studies were used to formulate the commission's recommendations, which became the foundation of the first Official Languages Act. That is why almost a quarter of its text is devoted to the implementation of bilingual districts, a notion taken from the language policy of Finland, which had created them in 1922, but eventually rejected in Canada.

Corbeil (1997) identifies thirteen Canadian language policies, although he narrows this number down somewhat in acknowledging that eight are implicit in nature while five are explicit. The explicit language policies are defined by an overall body of legislation in which one law plays a central role and various other laws and regulations expand on the objectives set forth in the fundamental law. The implicit policies involve ad hoc and sporadic involvement in language questions, which may have considerable practical importance but do not embody the sustained effort to manage language issues evident in the explicit cases. For example, chapter 10, by Normand Labrie, deals with the language policy and practice of the province of Ontario, which are mostly implicit but nevertheless have had a sustained adverse effect on a minority language group (Franco-Ontarians).

Three of the five explicit Canadian language policies are of particular interest here: those of the provinces of New Brunswick and Quebec and the federal government. The other two (those of the two, now three, territories) are interesting, but up to now have had much less of a domestic and international impact. While a definitive judgment about the territorial language policies would be premature in light of fairly recent changes, they are addressed in several chapters as well as in the conclusion.

All three of the explicit language policies selected for attention here have their ardent supporters, yet each is controversial as well. To one degree or another, they all promote the use of French, although this emphasis has not sufficed to eliminate areas of friction between them, not least because some anglophone groups would prefer no governmental measures promoting French. Since the geographical scope, governing principles, and constituencies of each of the language policies are different, promotion of harmony and cooperation between them is a challenge.

While there is an extensive literature about both federal language policy and that of the province of Quebec, these policies have not generally been compared to one another, nor has their interaction been assessed systematically. Federal and provincial language policies on occasion have been compared in several ways, but these comparisons have been scattered and few.

A few examples are cited below of works that involve the comparison of provincial and/or federal language policy.

Barbara Burnaby (1996) catalogues and describes the various language policies in Canada but does not compare them to each other or to other countries. Similarly, Richard Bourhis, in the collection he edited (1984), examines the impact of Quebec's 1977 Charter of the French Language from multiple perspectives, but the comparisons are scattered and only loosely related to one another. His introductory chapter compares language planning in Quebec with that of other multilingual societies; chapter 7, by Taylor and Dubé-Simard, compares anglophone and francophone attitudes toward the Charter of the French Language; and chapter 10, by John Mallea, compares minority language education in Quebec and anglophone Canada. In an edited journal issue, Bourhis (1994) assembled contributions that survey various Canadian language policies and language communities, but comparisons between them are largely limited to some brief passages in Bourhis's introductory article. Similarly, Edwards (1993/94) surveys Canadian language policies and makes comparisons, although in very brief fashion.

José Woehrling (1995) is primarily interested in Quebec's language policy, but this interest has led him to broader comparisons. He compares federal language policy to Quebec's language policy with regard to their respective impact on francophones and anglophones in Quebec as well as on francophones outside Quebec. He concludes that while there are some complementarities, their divergencies are greater since federal language policy emphasizes reciprocity between language groups throughout the country via bilingualism, which tends to prejudice French, while Quebec favours francophones within the province. Another comparison he has made (Woehrling, 1993) involves the potential impact of North American free trade on Quebec's language legislation, which in some ways he fears could involve constraints on the province.

In a later article, Woehrling (2005) returns to the theme of conflict and complementarity between Quebec's language policy and that of the federal government. The contrast focuses solely on the legislation of each jurisdiction without examining their relationship to groups or non-linguistic issues (the subject of Parts 3 and 4 in this book). Woehrling's articles, while careful, share the characteristic of much of the literature in focusing somewhat narrowly on one kind of comparison. Michael Macmillan (1998) also surveys the legislative history of explicit Canadian language policies with particular emphasis on the emergence and evolution of language rights (1998).

KEY LEGISLATIVE LANDMARKS IN CANADIAN LANGUAGE POLICIES

A brief summary of the guiding principles for the most explicit Canadian language policies provides the background for this survey of the literature. The centrepiece of federal language legislation is the Official Languages Law of Canada of 1969, which declares English and French to be the official languages of the country and promotes bilingualism across the entire country, including in Quebec, the only province with a French-speaking majority. This law was updated and extended in 1988. As federal legislation, it is national in scope, but at the same time it is limited in applying only to matters under federal jurisdiction, such as the provision of certain services in French and English and support for bilingualism. In Canadian constitutional practice, the various provinces have ample scope to legislate language issues, including the areas of culture and education.

The governing principles of the federal approach have been referred to as "institutional bilingualism," which obliges the government to address the relatively narrow aim of serving the public in one or the other of the official languages, rather than trying to meet the much more ambitious goal of promoting bilingualism among the population at large. The aim was, rather, to free citizens from the burden of having to become individually bilingual. It follows that language is regarded as a matter of personal preference. Consequently, while federal language policy promotes bilingual services, it does not seek to interfere in personal decisions involving language and education. Federal policy regards this approach as fair in promoting reciprocity in all provinces as well as enshrining equality before the law. Critics have described this free-market approach as being ultimately biased in favour of the majority language of the country, English, at the expense of French.

Federal promotion of bilingual services has been paired with support for multiculturalism. While these two policies are not necessarily contradictory, the generally low number of French speakers outside the province of Quebec does tend to strengthen emphasis on multiculturalism at the expense of bilingualism (Carey, 1997). In response to declining numbers of francophone speakers in all provinces outside Quebec save New Brunswick, successive Quebec governments have felt all the more compelled to promote French within the province. Eve Haque, in chapter 8 of this volume, compares federal multicultural, immigration, and immigrant language-training policies.

Quebec's key language law is the Charter of the French Language of 1977. A number of language laws preceded this legislation, and the charter has been subsequently modified through provincial legislation, including some changes in response to federal constitutional challenges to certain provisions. The charter is a landmark document in squarely embodying a territorial approach to language policy. A number of rights for anglophone speakers are recognized in the province, but otherwise French is regarded as the sole official language, and numerous measures are taken to promote the use of French throughout the province. This approach has been called "functional bilingualism" in that English is frequently used and to some extent protected, but French is promoted as the main language of the province, including among recent immigrants (the territoriality principle).

The centrepiece of language legislation in New Brunswick is the Official Languages Law of 1969. This declares both English and French to be official languages, making New Brunswick the sole officially bilingual province in the country. Although the anglophone and francophone populations in the province tend to be concentrated in different geographical areas, Quebec's territoriality approach has not been followed. Instead, the governing principles of the province's language policy resemble those of the federal government. That is, bilingualism is encouraged throughout the province in contrast to the unilingual territorial approach of Quebec.

In this book, Canadian language policies are faulted in different ways. For example, authors call attention to shortcomings of federal language policy (Haque in chapter 8 and Labrie in chapter 10) and provincial language policies (Fontaine in chapter 7, Paillé in chapter 9, and also Labrie in chapter 10). Successes of both federal and provincial language policies are also recognized here. In chapter 11 Pierre Anctil is most explicit congratulating the various actors for ending the language crisis in Quebec, but other authors from varying perspectives recognize federal and provincial achievements.

Step Two: The Distinctive Contributions of Each Chapter of This Book

This general introduction sets forth strengths and limitations of the comparative approach to Canadian language policies. In the introduction to each of the subsequent parts of the book, each chapter in that part is briefly summarized in order to show how it relates to the part of the book in which it falls, including how the chapter develops the relevant comparison. The introductions also address the distinctive contributions of each chapter.

Step Three: The Identification of Systematic Comparative Research

What are implications for comparative research implied by each chapter? Since the comparative approach is so promising and yet has been relatively

neglected, this book will, it is hoped, encourage comparative work. The initial application of the first two steps points toward systematic comparative
research (step three). The very diversity of views in this book (step one)
suggests avenues for research. In essence, multiple perspectives help policy-
makers as well as linguistic groups in coping with a complex reality.

Step Four: The Systematic Comparison of Canadian Language
Policies through Five Thematic Perspectives

Patterns emerge in the literature, giving it a certain structure converging or
clustering around recurring themes. Each of these themes broadly shares
the strengths and weaknesses of the literature as a whole; that is, sporadic
contributions have been made toward systematic comparison, but the actual
comparative works are few and fairly narrow in scope.

The structure of the literature as it stands is our point of reference. Our
concern is how each cluster can be more comparative. The chapters in this
book address each cluster from a comparative perspective. This book identifies and systematically assesses five kinds of thematic perspectives comparing
Canadian language policies: Part One examines historical and policy perspectives; Part Two, international perspectives; Part Three, non-linguistic perspectives; and Part Four, group perspectives. Figure 1.1 demonstrates that all the
thematic perspectives overlap and interact with one another, thereby contributing to systematic comparison by analyzing Canadian language policies from
different yet complementary angles. A brief rationale for each perspective is
indicated below. These five perspectives highlight the extent and limits of
comparison in the relevant literature. To the extent that previous publications
in the area of Canadian language policies have involved comparisons at all,
they usually have dealt predominantly with only one of the five perspectives
identified here. It may be concluded that a systematic attempt to compare
Canadian language policies is lacking, and this book seeks to fill this void. At
the same time, it is because of the contributions of the existing literature that
a more systematic comparative approach is now feasible.

The five thematic perspectives portrayed graphically in figure 1.2 satisfy
basic requirements for systematic comparison. Each perspective constitutes
a major way of organizing and looking at language policy. In addition, each
is validated in that it reflects a major cluster in the literature. In this chapter
and in subsequent parts of this book, the existing literature is organized
around each of these perspectives, suggesting their importance individually
and jointly. Reliance on multiple perspectives addresses the need to assess
multidisciplinary, multi-faceted language policy from varying angles.

Figure 1.1
Comparison through five thematic perspectives

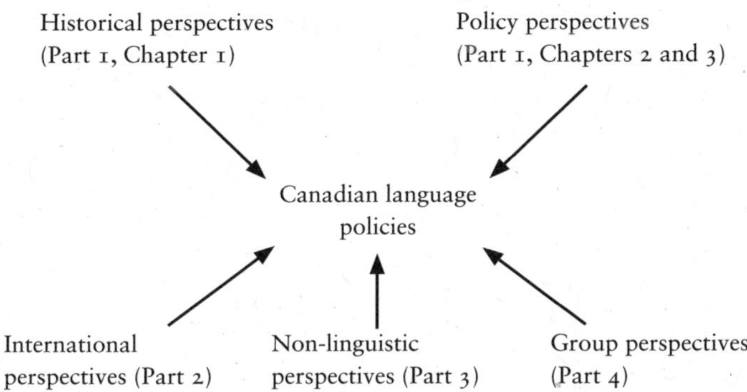

NOTE: The interdisciplinary, complex nature of language policy suggests that various complementary kinds of comparison will capture reality more than a single comparison. Figure 1.1 presents all the comparisons included in this book and how each focuses on Canadian language policies. This schema is simplified, since the five perspectives overlap with one another and are also impacted upon by Canadian language policies.

A recent comparative article on language policy by Kenneth McRae (2007) may be used as a test case to judge the usefulness of our five thematic perspectives. This article by a Canadian is an example of systematic comparison of language policy in four democratic countries that recognize two or more legally equal official languages (Belgium, Canada, Finland, and Switzerland). While the comparative approach McRae relies on is of interest here, new insights about Canada are few inasmuch as the reference point for comparisons is Finland.

The comparative categories McRae relies on provide a useful benchmark for comparison with our own categories or perspectives, however. He begins with the historical foundations for language pluralism in order to provide the context for language policy comparisons (Part One of our book). He then proceeds to compare three selected social structural dimensions. These are the size, stability, and geographical distribution of language groups (approximately our Part Four), the interface of language divisions with other social cleavages (roughly corresponding to our Part Three), and foreign influences on domestic language situations (related to our Part Two). The close correspondence of the comparative categories between the reference article and our approach reinforces our view that each of our perspectives is important and reflects a considerable portion of language reality. Language use is so complex that comparative categories can vary, but it is significant that certain categories recur in the literature, reflecting their innate importance. Our five perspectives are flexible and broad enough to encompass the relevant literature while viewing policy from multiple angles.

Step Five: The Systematic Comparison of Canadian Language Policies
through the Interactive Policy Process

Steps one to four add structure and specificity to comparisons, although systematic comparison is still handicapped by the notoriously fluid and seemingly erratic nature of the policy process. Canada's multiple language policies have been formulated, implemented, and evaluated by governmental bodies at different levels and places over lengthy periods of time. In addition, the historical and policy records of languages in Canada and other countries are enormous. Hence, any kind of systematic comparison of Canadian language policies either with each other or with international counterparts seems to be a formidable task.

Step five presents a schema for facilitating systematic comparison through the interactive policy process. Figure 1.2 illustrates the dynamic, interactive sequence of the policy process. First, policy may be seen as structured and sequential. There is a logical sequence of policy stages from formulation to implementation and then compliance, followed by reaction and evaluation and eventual modification. The sequential order of these policy stages is represented by arrows, progressing steadily from the formulation stage in the upper left-hand corner around the rectangle in clockwise direction and returning again to formulation because of modification. This rationalistic way of looking at figure 1.2 is useful in order to appreciate the multiple sequential stages and aspects of the policy process.

This rational portrayal of the policy process simplifies counterpart models in the political science literature (one such model has nine stages in the policy process), while focusing on language policy in comparative perspective. Since this model reflects consensus in the literature about the nature of the policy process in general and relates to language policy in particular, it serves as a point of reference for the authors in developing their respective chapters.

At the same time, the policy process is much less tidy in practice, as indicated by the numerous oblique arrows in the figure. For example, because of the interactive nature of the policy process, evaluation may precede implementation. Similarly, implementation (e.g., by governmental "language police"), compliance, and public reaction may be evaluated independently (e.g., by Quebec's Estates-General; see Commission des États généraux, 2001). Such fluid processes, involving changing patterns of interaction among policy stages, may result in hard-to-predict modifications or amendments to policy (as in the successive amendments to the Quebec language charter between the 1980s and the present, for example).

It follows that the policy process has fluid as well as rationalistic characteristics and that the balance between them varies over time. The resulting

Figure 1.2
Comparison through the interactive policy process

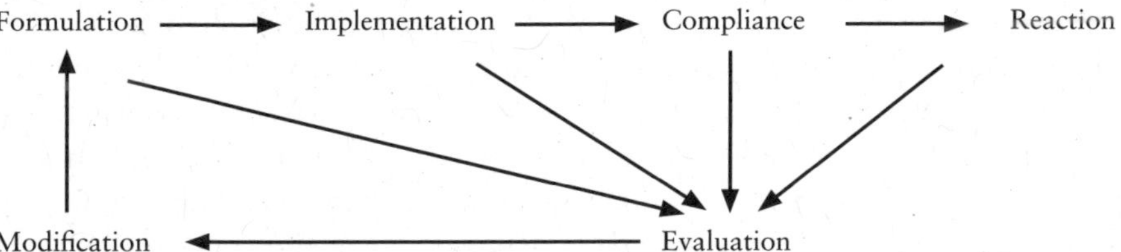

NOTE: This model reflects rationalistic as well as fluid aspects of the policy process. While the complexity of the policy process limits possibilities for systematic comparison, the advantages of comparison counsel as systematic an approach as possible. Policy similarities and differences illustrate comparison through the interactive policy process. The model implies similarities shared by policies ranging from language policy to health and defence policies. At the same time, the policy model is sufficiently flexible to reflect distinctive aspects of policy in each issue area. For example, formulation of a language policy is distinctive since special factors must drive such an event because language policy is not an innate characteristic of nationhood, as is an army. Such distinctiveness of language policy is likely to lead to comparison and interaction with other language policies (Reaction). Reaction can also occur through the *reaction* of the people who have been affected by its *implementation* and *compliance* having been given an outlet through such ad hoc institutions as the Quebec États-généraux, whose evaluation, submitted to the powers that be, results in the *modification* and *reformulation* of such policies as the language charter of Quebec (Commission des États-généraux, 2001).

dynamic nature of the process limits just how systematic analysis can be, but the advantages of a comparative perspective counsel bringing this analysis to bear as much and as systematically as possible.

Inasmuch as the chapters in this book all deal with Canadian language policy comparisons, they necessarily address the policy process as portrayed in figure 1.2. There is a difference of emphasis and orientation in each chapter. Chapter 1, by William Mackey, provides the historical background, which is relevant for both policy and thematic comparisons. Chapters 2 and 3, also by Mackey, analyze each of the components in figure 1.2 in detail, with reliance on many Canadian and other examples. Chapter 8, by Eve Haque, particularly focuses on the formulation stage of Canadian federal language policy but also notes continuities in this policy and makes comparisons with provincial language policies. Pierre Anctil, in chapter 11, focuses more on the latter stages of the policy process (implementation and evaluation), but he too relies on historical evidence in assessing the policy formulation stage.

Step Six: The Methodologies Appropriate to the Subject Matter of Specific Chapters

Steps one to five establish a framework for systematic comparison without imposing a uniform methodology on the authors. In view of the multidisciplinary, multi-faceted nature of language policy, it is unlikely that a single methodology could guide research throughout the field. At the same time, sophisticated methodologies do exist that are relevant, which authors have been encouraged to rely on as the subject matter of each chapter dictates. For example, Mackey elaborates a method for comparing language policies, which he illustrates through numerous Canadian and other international examples (chapter 2 and 3). Jürgen Erfurt and Normand Labrie (chapters 6 and 10) rely in part on discourse analysis. In chapter 9 Michel Paillé develops a methodology for comparing demographic trends in two Canadian provinces over time.

Step six therefore complements the framework for systematic comparison described in steps one to five. Various methodologies build on and extend the common framework orienting this book. The conclusions in the final chapter synthesize and extend findings related to steps 1–6 presented in the various chapters of this book.

PART ONE

Perspectives and Overviews

Introduction to Part One

WILLIAM F. MACKEY AND MICHAEL A. MORRIS

It is impossible to understand Canadian language policy in ignorance of the past that created it, for it is a continuation of centuries of conflict, competition, and compromise between two of the great world languages and the powers that propagated them within the ever-changing contexts of their domains; this is the perspective of chapter 1. These contexts comprise all the constituents of society, since they have to do with its most essential component – intercommunication; that is, language – without which society cannot exist. When public policy is applied to language, it touches both the essence of social behaviour and the most innate acquisition of individuals: the instrument of their thought, speech, and integration into families and communities. That is why language permeates every pore of society and why any interference in its workings can have such far-reaching and sometimes unintended consequences.

It is not surprising that questions of language affect every human and social science and their multiple subspecialties with their various conflicting theories and schools of thought, each with its own in-group terms for talking about language – familiar words with restricted meanings and invented words with familiar meanings. Compounding this complexity is the fact that an outsider often remains unsure of the direction of the discourse and the changing levels of generality in the argument. This is especially true in interdisciplinary discourse such as the one we are now attempting.

The chapters in this book cover a number of comparative perspectives but not all of them. Yet they treat not only Canadian language policy from a comparative perspective but also comparative language policy from a Canadian perspective; this is the focus of chapter 2. History and comparison are the prerequisites of any evaluation of a language policy; this is the subject of chapter 3.

1

The History and Origins
of Language Policies in Canada

WILLIAM F. MACKEY

The basic determinants of Canadian language policies are intertwined with the rise of French and English as world languages and especially with almost a millennium of intermittent conflicts and accommodations between France and England.[1] To understand these policies, and possibly to evaluate them, it is necessary to chronicle changes in the relative policy potential of these two languages in relation to those turning points in history that have most affected them. One can then study policy patterns of success and failure. One can, for example, analyze the results of a stable policy of language promotion prevailing through victory and defeat, thanks to the power of cultural preponderance and persuasion over military and economic superiority. For while language is a basic component of culture, some cultures value it more than others.

Language policy is also an expression of the relative value placed on a language by the society that engendered it and on its degree of cohesion with the people who speak it, their land, their religion, and their past. We can compare these policy-related values, for example, not only as they differ between England and France but also as they diverged between Republican France and French Canada. Language in French Canada had been intimately linked with the preservation of the religion of its people (*la langue, gardienne de la foi*) and the patrimony of its past (*notre maître, le passé*).

We are indeed constrained by the past in our study of French and English language policies.[2] But how far back must we go? The farther the better, if we take the advice of that long-time statesman and sometime historian Winston Churchill to the effect that the farther we look back, the better we can see what lies ahead. For a good understanding of the dynamics of

To assist the reader, an outline of this chapter is provided in appendix 1 (57–8).

French and English language policies, we had better go back to the time when the official language of England was not English but French.

Since we are telling what is, in effect, two interlinked stories of action, reaction, and interaction, with plots and subplots, as it were, we are faced with the question of what comes before what. Our solution will be, as far as possible, to put the cause before the effect and political motives before policy decisions. That is why, for instance, we place Quebec's language claims before federal policy decisions.

In the final analysis, language policies depend on those who make them. States do not make policies; people do. And what they do depends on their perception of the present and their vision of the future. Their politically motivated short-term solutions can generate long-term problems; and their long-term solutions can fall victim to the laws of unintended consequences. For example, a language-related immigration policy may generate long-term race-related conflict. That is why we cannot ignore the visions and decisions of policy makers such as Francis I of France, Edward III of England, Castlereagh, Channing, Durham, Laurier, Henri Bourassa, Pearson, Trudeau, and René Lévesque – to name only these.

In the pages that follow, we will therefore examine the determinants of language policies in terms of contact, competition, conflict, and accommodation between French and English: first in Europe, then in North America, and finally in Canada. In Europe, contact was so close as to maintain French as the official language of England until the slow emergence of modern English three centuries later. While in France, from the time of Francis I onwards, French became an official language and the international language of Europe long before it was to become the national language. In North America the conflict between France and England was an extension of what it was in Europe. The competition between French and English, however, did not come to an end when New France fell under British rule. In Canada this competition between a French America and a British dominion occasioned the making of language policies at all levels of governance. It provided the basis for Quebec's language claims, resulting in federal language laws, those of other provinces, and the counterclaims of the First Nations.

Meanwhile, as Canada's Anglo-French hegemony was being diluted through centuries of massive immigration from all quarters of the globe, the character of the country became less and less English and French and more and more multi-ethnic and multicultural. Policies had to be developed to reflect this new reality. On all these policy-related events, hundreds of volumes have been published; only the highlights can be mentioned in the few pages that follow.

ENGLISH AND FRENCH IN EUROPE

French as the Official Language of England

The history of language policy in England goes back to the Norman Conquest[3] of 1066, after which the European character of the island was forged through the massive, systematic, and thorough expropriation of Anglo-Saxon lands by French-speaking Norman knights. This takeover also included the lands of the Anglo-Saxon church, whose famous monasteries had maintained a centuries-long written tradition. Many of the twenty thousand or so Norman knights who replaced the Anglo-Saxon landed gentry also held on to their other landholdings and related allegiances in France, thus constituting a powerful binational upper class. Since they did not speak the language of their new land, however, they had to depend on a few bilingual middlemen to convey their orders to their new Anglo-Saxon subjects.[4] For almost three centuries (1066–1362) French remained the official language of England while sharing with Latin (as it did in France) certain higher functions as the language of learning and of the law, a practice that persisted in England until 1713.

Meanwhile, succeeding generations of bilingual speakers, unschooled in their mother tongue, were transforming their speech into a virtually new language, having unloaded their cumbersome and redundant grammatical inflections while taking on a treasure of new words from their Norman and former Scandinavian overlords and the Latin of their educators. For the new English tongue was no longer an inflected language like Anglo-Saxon or French but an analytic one whose structure favoured the absorption of foreign words and the creation of new ones.[5]

The Emergence of English (1360–1660)

This new tongue emerged slowly as the official language of England. Long before its demise, its ancestral Anglo-Saxon component had enjoyed a lengthy literary tradition that predated that of French by more than a century. By the seventh century, English monasteries, with their productive scriptoria, had become Europe's leading centres of learning.[6] Indeed, it was from them that Charlemagne was to recruit leaders of the cultural renaissance of medieval Europe. After England had fallen under Norman rule, these monasteries were placed under the control of Norman, French-speaking clergy, the replacements of whom were often recruited from the Continent, since their binational allegiance was also that of the nobility.

Although the level of binational allegiance started declining in the 1260s, it created long-lasting intergenerational conflicts within families with landholdings on both sides of the Channel. These disputes over land escalated into conflicts between the English side and the French side of the families and eventually into difference between English and French. When, for example, one of these Anglo-French landowners became king of England, he remained, by virtue of his French landholdings, an unwilling vassal of the king of France. The problem was compounded by complex family interrelationships, which generated claims and counterclaims to the throne. The consequent centuries-long conflicts remained unresolved. Notable was the one that caused the Hundred Years War, begun in 1337 to decide whether a grandson or a nephew had the more legitimate claim to the throne of France.[7] Even after a century of war, the claim remained unresolved. In the meantime, it had generated generations of cultural prejudice, intensifying during periods of war and even extending to the colonies in the New World.

The increasing enmity resulted in slow but progressive downgrading of French in England. In 1362 Edward III decreed that English be used in the courts. By 1388 the powerful guilds were issuing their reports no longer in French or Latin but in English. This growing status gave assurance to authors, who by the 1380s were venturing away from Latin, French, or Italian to write, as did Chaucer, in the "King's English." Although the first printing presses specialized in satisfying the demand for the Latin classics, they eventually became the most powerful medium for the diffusion of written English. From 1360 to 1660 there was a slow but steady development in the status of English. Not until 1489, however, did it officially become the exclusive language of Parliament. And only in 1647 was a movement initiated to replace all laws written in French with English ones. Yet, as was the case in France, the official language had not yet become a national language.

French as an Official and International Language

At the end of the Hundred Years War, France was not yet the unified and centralized state it was to become. Although French had been developing a national literature, Latin continued to serve as the language of learning and official records – that is, until the advent of Francis I, who, early in his career, had expected to be named emperor of the Holy Roman Empire, where the working and official language was Latin. When the post went to Charles V of Spain, the two monarchs became bitter and lifelong rivals. Their clash of arms became a conflict of languages. The aim and later obsession of Francis I was to dislodge Latin, the symbol of the empire, from its privileged position as the European language of law and diplomacy.

Beginning in 1539 at Villers-Cotterêts, the king decreed that henceforth, within his kingdom, court records would no longer be kept exclusively in Latin. And all those who owed him allegiance were expected to address him in his language. From then on, French continued to expand as a language of public administration in France, while the king and his successors were relentlessly promoting it as a language of diplomacy in Europe – and with remarkable success, since this policy of promotion became a permanent doctrine of the French foreign office.[8]

One of the crucial achievements of this policy happened in 1648 at the watershed treaties of Westphalia, which broke the religious, political, and linguistic monopoly of the Holy Roman Empire, that loose federation of some thousand semi-autonomous principalities which was no more an empire than it was holy or Roman.[9] The treaties affirmed the sanctity of national borders and the 1555 (Augsburg) principle of territoriality in religion (*cujus regio, ejus religio*) and later in language (*cujus regio, ejus lingua*). Although this was the time when Spanish had become the alternative language of diplomacy, at Westphalia France overcame the Castilian opposition and had French recognized as the alternative to Latin, which still remained the language of record.[10]

Meanwhile, with the founding of the Académie française in 1634, a policy was in place to make written French as official and as standardized as Latin.[11] As such, it would have no rival as a language of diplomacy. It would also become unrivalled as the language of learning and the international language of the European elite. The prestige of French began to surpass that of France. For even in defeat, negotiations and consequent treaties were exclusively in French, as was the case, for example, at the end of the Seven Years War in 1763 and at the dismemberment of the Napoleonic empire in Vienna in 1815. Here Britain entered the Congress of Vienna not only as the chief victor but also as the leading European power, backed up by its vast empire. Yet it did not, as expected, impose its language.

Britain shared with Austria a desire to ensure peace and stability in Europe, while Russia insisted on compensation for having liberated so much of Europe from French control. France, in defeat, sought to protect as many of its interests as it could, including the status of its language. In this context, the imposition of English, in the view of Lord Castlereagh, the British foreign secretary, would have disrupted not only the negotiations but also the workings of the diplomatic corps. It would also have been violently opposed not only by France but also by Russia, for whom French was the internal working language of many of its ministries and particularly of its foreign office. For the British foreign office, language had never been a main preoccupation. The English people had become accustomed to serve under monarchs with little or no English, from the French Henrys to the German Georges and, in between, a Dutch William of Orange.[12] Not that everyone was delighted with the exclusivity of French in diplomacy. In fact, there appeared in the final version of the Treaty of Vienna a penultimate provision (article 20) stating that its use of French should not be interpreted as a precedent.

A decade later came the famed "Canning Instructions." Contrary to the pragmatism of his predecessor, the new British foreign secretary, Lord Canning, seemed to have come to the realization that negotiating in one's own language could become an asset. So in 1826 he issued detailed orders to all British diplomats to make English the language of all treaties and covenants to which Britain was a party. These orders became famous in succeeding decades for being so often repeated and so seldom obeyed. The latest reissuance of the Instructions is dated 1923, attesting to the fact that the British and other diplomats continued drafting their covenants in French.

For after the dismemberment of the Napoleonic empire, the international use of French did not, as expected, decline; in fact, it flourished as never before. For through centuries of use and development, the language had acquired a momentum of its own, independent of the fortunes of its homeland. Since it was taken for granted as the international language, its use increased in the same measure as did the multiplicity of contacts in a rapidly interconnecting world, with its proliferation of conventions, conferences, associations, and all manner of international organizations too numerous to mention, ranging from the International Postal Union to the epoch-making Hague and Geneva Conventions.

It was only after the appearance of the United States on the international scene that English began to emerge as an alternative language of diplomacy. The practice goes back to the Founding Fathers and their opportunistic Treaty of Amity with France in 1778. The American colonists, not having a professional diplomatic corps, insisted on copies of documents their people understood.[13] After the First World War had come to an end, it was expected that the peace treaty would appear exclusively in French, as was the custom. And the French president, Clemenceau (a Breton), insisted that the custom be maintained. But the British prime minister, Lloyd-George (a Welshman), and the American president, Woodrow Wilson (a former professor of English), both demurred. Their reasons were neither patriotism nor love of the English language but a stated policy that in liberal democracies the people should have access to treaties that affect them – to "open covenants openly arrived at." The eventual appearance of the treaty in both French and English *ex equo* had far-reaching consequences. It marked the end of French exclusivity as the international language of diplomacy. And since the first twenty-six articles of the treaty became the Covenant of the League of Nations, English had achieved a fortiori the status of an official international language on a par with French. While French did maintain its international prestige, English, with its millions of speakers in all quarters of the globe, continued to expand as an international language.

After the Second World War this period of Anglo-French hegemony came to an end. The international status of French – and to a lesser extent that of English – were both diluted by the presence at the peace table of other big powers. The relevant meetings took place in San Francisco at the founding of the United Nations. At the table, in addition to the American, British, and French delegations, were the representatives of the other big winners, Russia and China, along with the envoys of other nations, notably those of Latin America.[14] An intractable deadlock on the choice of an official language was finally broken by a motion of the Russian spokesman (Molotov) to the effect that English, French, Russian, Chinese, and Spanish should all be the official languages of the conference. The motion carried, leading eventually to these languages becoming the official languages of the United Nations.[15] Although this decision put an end to the period of Anglo-French hegemony, the working languages continued to be English and French (with the later addition of Spanish in the General Assembly).

All things considered, this was another victory for France's policy of language promotion. And there were more to come. Subsequently, French was to figure as an official language in all the European treaties, conventions, and organizations. It became an official language of the Council of Europe and the de facto administrative language of the European Union. Yet here again, the watering down of its primacy continued, as the EU admitted more and more countries, each insisting on official recognition of its own national language. The European constitution, agreed to in October 2004, which a former French president, Valéry Giscard d'Estaing, had painfully forged, was turned down by the French people in June the following year.[16]

French and English as National Languages

While French in the seventeenth century was expanding abroad as an international language, at home it remained unknown to the majority of the French population. As in England, this was a population of mostly illiterate labourers and peasants attached to the land and to its local speech, whose forms varied from one parish to the next, becoming gradually unintelligible beyond walking distance.[17] This geolinguistic pattern remained virtually unchanged even after France and England had evolved from agglomerations of duchies into unified nation-states. The first major impulse toward forging a national language came, not from a self-centred state, but from an outreaching reformed Church in the form of the Protestant Reformation. Its aim was to place the word of God directly into the hands of the people in a language they could understand. Sacred texts and commentaries thereon were published in the written forms of the major European languages: the enduring King James Bible in English, the influential works of Calvin in French, and much more. Although the Reform movements attracted millions of adherents, the written texts were available only to those who could read them. So the Reformation had a vested interest in increasing the number of people capable of reading their mother tongue. Aided by the zeal of the converted and the productivity of the new printing presses, there was consequently a surge of literacy in England and France.[18]

Nevertheless, by the eighteenth century, most of the populations of France and England remained illiterate. It took a second impulse to reactivate the spread of the national language. In France this impulse arose as a by-product of the French Revolution. Its constituent assembly having declared the language of power to be that of the people (*la langue républicaine*), its Convention of 1790 subsumed it in its Déclaration des droits de l'homme et du citoyen, particularly Article XI, the free communication of opinions and ideas (*la libre communication des opinions et des idées*). In theory, this principle meant that, within the confines of the nation-state, everybody should be able to understand everybody else. Since no one knew the extent to which such was the case, the Convention commissioned a nationwide investigation of the citizenry's knowledge of the national language. The task was entrusted to Abbé Henri Grégoire. It took him three years to complete, and it turned out to be one of the most extensive sociolinguistic surveys ever undertaken. When Grégoire reported his findings to the Convention in 1793, it came as a sobering revelation to the assembled ideologues: less than half the population of some twenty-two million French citizens could speak the national language, and only three out of twenty could write it. It seemed astonishing that a language which was spoken throughout Europe and well-known abroad should be so little known at home. In order to empower the population with a knowledge of the national language, a policy of mass literacy was proposed, along with urgent and stringent measures for the

propagation in all the provinces of the French language through the diffusion of a standard grammar and dictionary, along with books, newspapers,
and popular songs.[19] Most important for the future was to school the young
in the national language. The école nationale movement, directed centrally
from Paris, did indeed raise the level of literacy. Yet it did not eliminate
the spoken regiolects. What emerged was a widespread diglossia whereby
Parisian French was superimposed as the national acrolect – the dialect of
literacy, power, and prestige.

However, what did more than the French Revolution for the diffusion
of French was the Industrial Revolution and its aftermath. It was imported
from England, where it was having similar effects upon the diffusion of
the national language. The displacement of land-bound peasants into urban
centres and their transformation into industrial workers, coupled with the
gathering together from different regions of craftsmen and tradesmen into
large factories, created a class of wage earners who had to use a common
language to communicate. Compulsory military service and the general mobilization of troops in times of conflict, notably the wars of 1870–71 and
1914–18, did much to dilute remaining regional dialect differences. New
networks of roads and, later, railways linking the periphery to the centre
also accelerated the interflow of goods, services, and people, all of which
aided the diffusion of the French of Paris. These changes also favoured
the exchange of information printed in the standard national language
– books, newspapers, magazines, and school texts. The code books to the
standard language – grammars and dictionaries, big and small – also fell
into the hands of all who could read.[20] The infrastructures of the Industrial
Revolution helped propagate the standard forms of the national language,
not only in France and England but in all quarters of the globe where French
and English were written, so that everyone who could read could understand anyone who wrote. This high degree of standardization, coupled with
rich and growing vocabularies, made these languages the most fitting for official purposes; it is not surprising that half the world's sovereign states still
use them as de facto official languages.

FRENCH AND ENGLISH IN NORTH AMERICA

One of the main determinants of language policy is the relationship between
land and language. It can affect the extent to which principles of territoriality and personality may apply. Patterns of settlement, when they overlap,
have been the sources of conflict. This has been the case for the French and
English colonization of North America.

Patterns of Settlement

The French and English settlers came to North America as newcomers to a
New World. Their enduring Old World rivalries led to territorial conflicts
and eventually to linguistic ones as well.

FRENCH SETTLEMENTS

The implantation of the French language in North America came half a century after Canada had been discovered and claimed for the French throne.
The first settlement was Port-Royal in 1605, which did not endure as well as
those of Quebec in 1608, Ville-Marie (Montreal) in 1642, and a number of
more rural seigneuries and parishes along the St Lawrence valley. Out of this
heartland came more parishes to serve new settlers, following the French
explorers as they adventured deeper into the continent: one in the Red River
valley (Manitoba) in 1720 and another on the Great Plains (Saskatchewan)
in 1759, at a time when the first Acadian settlements were being dismembered
by the British. Even after New France had fallen to the British, the colonization of the continent out of the French Canadian heartland did not come to
a halt. Settlers from Quebec arrived in what is now Alberta in 1780 and on
the Pacific Coast in 1800. And even after France had sold off its vast holdings west of the Mississippi to the United States in the Louisiana Purchase
of 1803, the French colonization of North America continued, with new
parishes in Detroit (1803), Grand Rapids (1820), Missouri (1828), Illinois
(1832), Kansas (1860), all united in 1863 under an archdiocese in Chicago.
As new generations graduated from parish schools, institutions of higher
learning were established to accommodate them. Colleges were founded in
Manitoba (1903), Alberta (1913), and Saskatchewan (1917), and also publishing houses, weekly newspapers, and benevolent associations.

These far-flung settlements were not as isolated as they may seem. They
actually constituted a network, which in 1937 was coordinated by a permanent secretariat in Quebec City (Le Conseil de la vie française en Amérique).
Its documentation service would compile the most reliable statistics on the
place and number of French-speakers in North America. It later was able to
get support from the Quebec government, which, as late as the 1940s, had
maintained a ministry of colonization.[21]

In sum, over a period of more than three centuries, the first truly international modern language was planted on North American soil, one with
a wide and deep written tradition – a well-standardized medium capable of
serving the needs of any modern state. During this period its spoken and written forms had spread from the east coast to the west coast of the continent,

mostly from its heartland in the St Lawrence valley. This expansion could not endure: immigration from France having ceased after the British conquest, direct immigration from Britain and English-speaking North America began to affect Canada's demographic patterns.

ENGLISH SETTLEMENTS

The oft-told tales of the first English settlements in the New World, from the early arrival in Virginia to the landing of the Pilgrim Fathers, are too familiar to need recounting. The two relevant events whose consequences fashioned Canadian language policies were the ceding of New France to the British and the aftermath of the American War of Independence.

The source and symbol of the first was the dramatic, hard-fought battle of the Plains of Abraham at Quebec on the morning of the 13th of September 1759, which left the generals on opposing sides dead. In the space of a few hours, New France fell under British rule. Although the local militia did subsequently defeat the British army at the battle of Sainte-Foy (1760), any hope of reinforcements from France vanished in the spring when the long-awaited supply ships from Europe turned out to be, not French, but British.[22] At the time, the French population of Canada was about 65,000, as opposed to some 9,000 British, including the Scots who had settled in Acadia (Nova Scotia) after France had ceded it to Britain in 1713 at the Treaty of Utrecht (in exchange for some trading posts in India).

The second relevant event was the American Revolution, which indirectly changed Canada's demographic balance. It was not the revolution itself but its aftermath that proved decisive. Since within each of the rebelling colonies the decision to separate from Britain was far from unanimous, those who chose to remain within the empire were persecuted by the separatist majority to the extent that they had to seek refuge in areas still under the control of the Crown, notably in what is now maritime and central Canada. They settled in such numbers that new jurisdictions had to be created to accommodate them: New Brunswick in 1784 and Upper Canada in 1791. This eventual intake of some hundred thousand English-speaking, Protestant British subjects completely unbalanced the French-English demographic ratio: from 7 to 1 to 7 to 10. It created a dominant British base which, in years to come, was to convert Canada into an English-speaking country. Adding to this base were the waves of direct migration from Britain fuelled by the policy of imperial preference and coupled with the influx during the 1840s of tens of thousands of Irish immigrants fleeing the famine in their homeland. Only through its solidarity and a superior birth rate was French able to maintain its demographic status. By 1870 the ratio was, out of a

Canadian population of 3.5 million, 1 million French-speakers and 2 million English-speakers. This ratio was maintained until the Great Depression, after which the birth rate in French Canada began to decline.[23]

Sources of Conflict and Accommodation

Conflicts inherent to the changing patterns of settlement began to manifest themselves as Canada evolved from a collection of colonies to a more independent state. Notwithstanding the vastness of the country, people of different languages, races, and religions began occupying the same living spaces, creating multi-segmented societies. Conflicts of race and religion became associated with conflicts of language and vice versa, their relative importance changing from place to place and from time to time.

At the time when accommodations of federation were being mooted, the primacy of religion had been such that many politicians conceived the population of their country as being composed of two important groups, Protestants and Catholics, the latter being subdivided into French and English. This conception fashioned the accommodations and entitlements in the act of confederation, creating permanent federal and provincial institutions. These institutions, established at a time when Canada was in its most formative years, were founded along religious lines. For example, to conform to the federal constitution (the British North America Act of 1867), a Quebec law was passed in 1869 to provide Protestants with full control over their own school systems, which were to operate exclusively in English. The same religious dichotomy was applied to all other Quebec institutions – hospitals, colleges, social services, and the press – with separate English and French newspapers, such as the leading Quebec daily *L'Action catholique,* which reflected the views of the Catholic hierarchy. Over time, however, these faith-based institutions were to become less and less relevant, as language replaced religion as the prime social indicator. Even in Quebec such sacrosanct dichotomies as the Protestant and Catholic school boards were to be replaced by linguistic ones.

Since distinctions neither of religion nor of language coincided with provincial boundaries, all provinces had to accommodate minorities, the weaker ones having to rely on federal protection. French Canada extended far beyond the boundaries of Quebec, and so-called English Canada included large English-speaking minorities in Montreal, the Eastern Townships, the North Shore of the St Lawrence, and part of the Gaspé Peninsula. Many of the post-Confederation problems in Canada had to do with such provincial minorities. In the Maritime provinces, a growing Acadian population, having resurged from the infamous deportation of their forebears, began to assert their linguistic distinctiveness. In western Canada the first French settlers had been in the majority only until they were joined by more and more English ones, who eventually became the dominant majority. The latter had to accommodate them, not because of any understanding of an historical French-English compact, but simply because of their numbers and their precedence.[24]

As for the Native populations, treaties between individual tribes and the British Crown, begun in 1781, multiplied. Meanwhile, some aboriginals had intermarried with the early French settlers, producing the hybrid population of Métis, who continued to live on the lands of their Native ancestors. These same lands were to be inundated by a wave of post-Confederation English-speaking immigrants, who had been given title to them. The French-speaking Métis rebelled in 1869–70 and again in 1885 to save their ancestral holdings in what would become Manitoba and Saskatchewan. In 1885 an army sent by the central government in the east crushed the uprising; its leader, Louis Riel, was tried and hanged for treason. And in 1890 a law was enacted in Manitoba eliminating French as an official language.

These events created a feeling of mutual and long-lasting antipathy between French and English populations throughout Canada. They occurred at a time when thousands of immigrants from Britain were given free land to cultivate. Some brought with them not only their language, culture, and traditions but also their internecine hostilities, ethnic prejudices, and sectarian malice, handed down from one generation to the next. Every 12th of July, for example, the public could witness the Protestant Boys parading down the main streets of Canadian cities to celebrate the victory of William of Orange over the Irish Catholics in 1690.

Between 1900 and 1950 the teaching of French was abolished in the public schools of nearly all the provinces of English Canada. French was, however, maintained at the college level as an elective subject. In the universities, professors of French language and literature were recruited, not from French Canada, but mostly from England and their assistants from France. They rarely missed an occasion to warn their permanently monolingual students not to contaminate their would-be accent through contact with their French-speaking compatriots. The "two solitudes" had by now split Canada from the Pacific to the Atlantic, passing right through the middle of metropolitan Montreal.

By 1930 the French population of Canada was struggling simply for the recognition of "the French fact in America." At the federal level, French had been progressively ignored. No matter what the political party in power, in a twenty-strong Cabinet, there was seldom more than one French Canadian, often considered the "Quebec lieutenant." In the Canadian public service, French Canadian representation had fallen from 22 per cent in 1918 to 13 per cent in 1946. Minor concessions came slowly from the federal administration in the form of such symbols as bilingual currency and postage stamps. It took a decade-long struggle to have the national air carrier, Trans-Canada Airlines, change its name to the more bilingual Air Canada. That this was considered a great concession to French-speakers is a measure of the perceived inequality of the two official languages.

Within the province of Quebec, little had changed. It remained deeply Catholic, mostly rural, and increasingly isolated. Its commerce and its cities were dominated by an important English-speaking minority integrated with British, American, and Ontario interests. In the First World War, French Canadians were reluctant to fight on the side of the British; in the Second World War, sympathies were split between Vichy France and the Free French, exiled in Britain. Yet thousands of young men left rural Quebec to join the Canadian forces, while the women flocked to good-paying jobs in urban factories. Both returned after the war, not to the farms, but to the cities, creating a new urban French-speaking proletariat, which began to organize into trade unions. By 1948 they had launched, in the mining town of Asbestos, their first major strike, a perceptive analysis of which, by a future Canadian prime minister, Pierre Elliot Trudeau, documented how profoundly Quebec was changing.[25] This was a population to be reckoned with; it had to be accommodated.

Outside Quebec, the end of the war had brought certain willingness for rapprochement in the context of a growing desire for a distinct Canadian identity. In 1947 Canadian citizenship became distinct from the status of British subject. In 1955 a Canadian Citizenship Branch was created within the public service. New citizens were required to have a working knowledge of English or French and a smattering of Canadian history and civics. It was the beginning of a period of *bonne entente*. Provinces began slowly revoking parts of their anti-French legislation. In 1944, for example, Ontario withdrew its unfair Regulation 17 (see below). Some of the English-speaking elite started to consider French a good thing for Canada, and a bicultural country a possible inoculation against the increasingly aggressive marketing of American mass culture.

FRENCH AND ENGLISH AS CANADIAN LANGUAGES

As the notion of a national identity began to take hold, so did the perception of French and English as not being the exclusive property of the mother countries. This perception was given credence by the phenomenal productivity of Canadian writers, particularly in Quebec. While Canadian literature became a respectable academic specialty, universities through-out Canada added courses in Quebec literature to their list of offerings. At the same time, dozens of Canadian linguistic reference works became available – glossaries, dictionaries, language atlases, word banks, and philo-logical studies on the evolution of French and English in different parts of the country. Eventually, the Quebec and Canadian governments took on a long-term funding commitment for the production of a standard national dictionary through such enterprises as the *Trésor de la langue française* and the Canadian Bilingual Dictionary Project.

These commitments to the languages were justified by their governments' involvement in the making of language policies. These policies had taken a very long time to evolve to the point where one could ask: what counts as *the* language? In fact, one can trace the origins of these policies back to the time when Britain had to face a new population of French-speaking sub-jects. From there, the long road from the birth of Canadian language policy to the accommodation of a multicultural democracy is marked by many milestones: new constitutions, language laws, royal commissions, and the language-related legislation of the central government and of the provinces, particularly Quebec.

The Birth of Canadian Language Policies

From the beginning, Canadian language policy was tributary to acts of accom-modation: from the basic Quebec Act of 1774 to the liberal Constitutional Act of 1791, through the inept Act of Union of 1840, and culminating in the British North America Act of 1867. These legal instruments owe their basic principles to the fact that when France and England settled North America, they were already mature nation-states. They had much more experience in subjugating minorities than in accommodating them. They were centralizing powers, and they naturally continued to centralize their possessions in the New World. New France was an extension of the realm of the Sun King, and British North America was ruled through the Colonial Office in London. These two major European powers had been intermittently at war for more than two centuries when New France fell under British rule.

Almost overnight Britain was faced with the governance of a large popu-lation the status of whose language was greater than that of its own, as the language of the 1763 treaty confirming the British victory was to demon-strate. More difficult to accept than the French language, however, was the religious allegiance of the new subjects to Rome and their unwillingness to recognize a Protestant king as head of the official religion.

A decade later Britain began to witness a growing revolt in more and more of its North American colonies and the prospect of losing all its holdings in the New World. It was assumed that there were those in Quebec who would be happy to have the Battle of the Plains of Abraham refought in their favour, at a time when the Americans were asking them to join the revolution. Decisive would be the policy of the most influential sector of the French Canadian population: their Catholic hierarchy. For them, to undo the past was to choose between a far-away, bankrupt France and a new, nearby, secular Protestant English-speaking power. In this context, a British guarantee of protection of their religion, language, and customs seemed in 1774 to be the wise choice.[26] Two decades later this decision must have seemed providential in light of the treatment reserved for the Church and its provincial clergy during the French Revolution: French Canada had eschewed anti-royalist revolutions in both France and America in exchange for legal protection of its integrity and existence. This legal document, the Quebec Act of 1774, is basic to an understanding of the history of Canadian language policy. It has been interpreted as being essentially an ethnogenic treaty – a pact between peoples – one whose leitmotif would colour the course of Canadian history, since it implicitly seemed to accept the French Canadian population and their descendants as a distinct people (race or nation) – distinct by their origins, religion, land, and language. The implication of this pact was to become a constant component in all subsequent constitutional matters affecting French Canada – in the Constitutional Act, the Durham Report, the Confederation debates, the Quiet Revolution, and the separatist ideologies.

First was the ethnic component. In his famous report of 1839 on his investigation into the causes of the rebellions of 1837–38, Lord Durham concluded that the fundamental conflict in Canada was "a struggle not of principle, but of races" and that the only solution was its elimination through assimilation. Some thirty years later, at the Confederation debates, Georges Cartier would counter, "We could not do away with the distinction of race ... the idea of the unity of races was a utopia" (17 February 1865). A generation later the solution was, according to Henri Bourassa, the most ardent nationalist of his day, "a duality of races, each with Canada as its fatherland."[27] This concept of duality regularly reappeared in documents on language policy. For example, the first mandate of the Royal Commission on Bilingualism and Biculturalism was to report on the status of the "two founding races," later amended to the more politically correct "founding peoples."[28]

The second component was religion. While Protestant Britain and Catholic France were colonizing North America, a fierce, religion-instigated war involving "Protestant" and "Catholic" armies was ravaging the whole of Europe, the Thirty Years War (1618–48). From this perspective, the implicit recognition of Catholicism in the Quebec Act was all the more remarkable. This recognition was later extended in the Constitutional Act of 1791, whereby Catholics in Canada were given the right to vote and also to hold office, a franchise forbidden to Catholics in Britain. Even in the twentieth century the primacy of religion over language was publicly proclaimed: "Let us fight for our language in order the better to protect our faith."[29] And this at a time when French-speaking bishops were still creating English-speaking parishes to serve the descendents of Irish immigrants, a testimony to the primacy of religion over language. It seems likely that, had the settlers in Quebec been mostly French Protestants, the history of Canadian language policy would have been quite different.

Third was the territorial imperative – the importance of having a land of one's own. The rebels of French-speaking Lower Canada did join those in English-speaking Upper Canada in 1837 to obtain for themselves a fully representative government, putting both of them together in a single province in the Act of Union of 1840. But this did not turn out to be a viable solution for the "two nations warring within the bosom of a single state," which Lord Durham found upon his arrival in Canada. It is true that he and his superior, British prime minister William Pitt, had toyed with the idea of a French state within the British Empire. But they also understood that, with memories of the Napoleonic menace still fresh in British minds, such a proposal would have been politically untenable in England.[30] Their solution proved equally untenable in Canada.

The union of Upper and Lower Canada produced neither coordination nor assimilation. Although the rebels from both Canadas had achieved the representative government for which they had fought, their elected representatives voted mostly for bills concerning their own side. The union soon devolved into an ineffectual, semi-federation, dependent on double majorities, dual premierships, twinned ministries, double two-party systems, and rotating capitals. The experience provided a strong motivation to create a federation. Its formation in 1867 broke the union deadlock by putting the two dominant groups back into their own territory, while maintaining the fundamentals of the traditional pact between them. Yet the motivations for joining Confederation varied between regions. While the Maritime colonies were attracted to commerce, the west needed links with other British colonies in the face of the unrelenting expansion of the United States westward and northward, proclaiming as its northwest border the 54th parallel of latitude, adjoining Russian-held territory, and beyond, after it purchased all of Alaska from Czar Alexander II. It would thus have deprived British North America of access to the Pacific. In the Canadian west, Manitoba was the first to join Confederation in 1870, followed by British Columbia in 1871 and Prince Edward Island in 1873; Saskatchewan and Alberta became provinces in 1905. Thus was created a country that stretched from the Atlantic to the Pacific and whose constitution remained the British North America Act. Despite its name, the British took no part in the negotiations which produced this act. It was drafted mostly by representatives of French Lower Canada and English Upper Canada, who regarded it as a pact, as did the British Parliament, which ratified it. Not so the other colonies. Even the founding ones from the Maritimes rather regarded the resulting union as a geopolitical and economic one, as did the provinces which joined later. Yet those who considered Confederation as a pact did not see it in the same light: for the English, it was an instrument of unity and fusion; for the French, it was an assurance of diversity and cooperation. These differences were to become sources of policy conflicts for many years to come.

The Evolution of Language Policy in Quebec

After Confederation, the objective of French Canada was to maximize its position within federal institutions, according to its vision of Canada as a federation of two founding peoples with two equal languages reflected in an official nationwide bilingualism. But this vision became more and more illusory. The French fact was largely ignored by English Canada, and the burden of bilingualism was carried almost entirely by the native-born speakers of French.

Between the two world wars, direct immigration of French-speakers from Europe had come to an end – this at a time when the French Canadian birth rate was beginning to fall below the level of renewal (from the highest in Canada to the lowest). Outside Quebec and Acadia, succeeding generations of French Canadians were no longer speaking French at home. In this context, it appeared that French could not survive in a free competition of languages in North America. French Canada turned to its government for help.

In the Quebec heartland the policy began to drift away from the promotion of official bilingualism in Canada to the primacy of French in Quebec. After the death of the old regime in 1959, this changing policy could be read in the slogans of the political parties that came to power, from *Maître chez-nous* (Lesage, 1960) to *Égalité ou indépendance* (Johnson, 1966) to *Un Québec souverain* (Lévesque, 1976).

From the outset, it was evident that the notion of being masters in one's own house applied to Quebec. As a policy-generating principle, its implementation would put an end to what was left of the notion of French America and its association with the old regime. The notion and its ideology had long been maintained as a loose association of French-speaking Catholic dioceses and far-flung isolated parishes scattered throughout the Canadian and American West. Quebec's policy of linguistic territoriality and its national territorial identity of the French Canadian heartland led to the provincialization of French identities outside Quebec. Soon Canada became aware of the Fransaskois, the Franco-Colombiens, the Franco-Manitobains, the Franco-Ontariens, and others who joined the Acadians in promoting a policy of bilingualism, which Quebec had abandoned in favour of a provincial policy of French unilingualism. Yet they understood that while an aggressive Quebec gave weight to a federal policy of official bilingualism, an independent Quebec could weaken it. Meanwhile, each could militate, as a minority, within its respective provincial jurisdiction. Even after the association of all these provincial French Canadian minorities was created in 1975, with federal help, as the Fédération des francophones hors Québec, their combined political power could not outweigh that of Quebec, which was then undergoing a profound cultural, political, and institutional revolution.

The Quiet Revolution began in 1960, after the fall of the old regime, marked by the death of its long-time leader, Maurice Duplessis. To implement its agenda, the new regime had to overcome three monopolies, social, economic, and political – that of the Church over society, that of the English over business, and that of the federal government's centralization of political power. Consequently, in the space of a few years, all sectors of Quebec society had been transformed. All the social monopolies of the Church were taken over by a non-sectarian bureaucracy. In 1964, for example, education policy was taken out of the hands of the denominational Comité catholique du Conseil de l'instruction publique and Comité protestant du Conseil de l'instruction publique and transferred to a newly created ministry of education.

The main objective of the new elite was not the propagation of their religion but the survival of their language. One of their first acts was the creation in 1961 of a French Language Bureau (L'Office de la langue française), which led in 1967 to a language-promotion act (Loi pour promouvoir la langue française au Québec, or Bill 63) targeting the immigrant and English-speaking population.[31] This was followed by the creation in 1968 of a commission of inquiry into the current situation of the French language in Quebec (the Gendron Commission).

Meanwhile, the assorted associations and movements promoting the idea of an independent Quebec were merging into a full-fledged political party, the Parti Québécois. These movements represented a wide spectrum of political opinion – some anti-clerical liberals, some left-leaning socialists, and a few militant extremist groups, one of which, Le Front de libération du Québec, advocated and practised outright terrorism, in the form of bombs placed in mailboxes, kidnapping, and murder, notably that of a cabinet minister in the Robert Bourassa government in 1970. The Quebec premier was consequently advised to call upon the powers of the federal government to help combat the terrorism. Whereupon the Canadian prime minister, Pierre Elliot Trudeau, invoked the seldom-used War Measures Act, temporarily suspending civil liberties, while the Canadian army occupied Quebec to eliminate the terrorists. These events, to be remembered as the October Crisis, shook the entire country, awaking the rest of Canada to the seriousness of Quebec's aspirations.

Language policy continued to dominate the legislative agenda; a sequence of bills and amendments, each more comprehensive or aggressive than the preceding, tested the reactions of the public. Some of these were directed at the immigrant population. Tens of thousands of immigrants from all quarters of the globe had now come to Quebec. Some 90 per cent of those settling in Montreal sent their children to the English schools, even though most of them had neither English nor French as their home language. In this context, immigration did not seem to favour the survival of French in Quebec.[32] Consequently the government attempted to legislate the language of instruction in favour of the use of French. Bill 22 (1974), which made French Quebec's official language, also restricted the right to attend an English school to those capable of passing a test of competence in the language. This legislation did not, however, satisfy the public; nor did the bill as a whole. They were expecting something more comprehensive.

The public got their wish in Bill 101, after the newly elected separatist Parti Québécois took power under the charismatic René Lévesque. Based on some of the findings and recommendations of the Gendron Commission (1968–72) and tabled on the 26th of August 1977 as the Charter of the French Language, this bill turned out to be possibly one of the most comprehensive pieces of language legislation ever enacted. Under its 213 articles it covered such areas as: the status of French as the official language of Quebec; basic language rights; the language of the law and of legislation, civil administration, public and semi-public agencies, professional bodies, labour relations, and business and commerce; the legality of contracts; education; and Native affairs. It also created a number of important public agencies and services for administering the law, including an advisory council, a French language board, and services for the promotion of French in business, commerce, and industry, commissions on place names and terminology, punitive measures, translation services, transitional provisions, and implementation schedules.[33]

It is true that circumstances have dictated periodic amendments to the Charter.[34] Yet it eventually remained above party politics and thus stood the test of time, enduring as part and parcel of the Quebec identity for more than a quarter-century.[35] In 1983 the Quebec government invited proposals for possible changes to the Charter from the general public, including those who felt they were adversely affected by it. Modifications affecting out-of-province English-speaking children were consequently enacted. In 1988, to conform to a Supreme Court ruling on freedom of expression to the effect that the exclusion of all languages other than French in commercial signage was deemed unlawful, an amendment permitted the use of other languages, including English, along with French as the dominant language (Bill 178).

In 1980 a referendum on independence was called by the governing Parti Québécois. Some 60 per cent of the population voted against sovereignty. The overwhelming rejection came largely from the English-speaking population coupled with the ethnic communities. Yet a second referendum on 30 October 1995 resulted in a virtual tie (Yes: 49.89 per cent and No: 50.21 per cent).

Quebec's birth rate had by now fallen below the replacement level, and the outlook was discouraging; the number of children under the age of five with French as their mother tongue had fallen by 66,000 between the years 1996 and 2001. By the year 2006, notwithstanding the sudden surge in the birth rate, the French mother-tongue population had declined to below 80 per cent for the whole of Quebec; in Montreal, its metropolis, at less than 50 per cent, it had actually become a minority, according to the official 2008 assessments in *Rapport sur l'évolution de la situation linguistique au Québec, 2002–2007* (Quebec: Office québécois de la langue française). The future of the French language would now have to depend largely on a successful policy of immigrant integration. This would include a two-fold objective: the assimilation of all immigrants through an all-French school system and special language courses and control of Quebec's own immigration policy. Since mass immigration from French-speaking Europe had come to an end, the only choice left was immigration from non-European countries. The consequent flow of immigration from Africa, the Caribbean, and the Middle East would transform the traditional ethnic character of Quebec, placing the concept of "two founding peoples" in political jeopardy. So that by the turn of this century, of the four original components of French Canadian identity, two (ethnic origin and religion) no longer held. Preservation of the other two (land and language) had henceforth become proportionately more important.

Periodic assessments of the successes and failures of the language policy became part of a process of adjustment to a rapidly changing society. In

1996, for example, there appeared an internal inter-ministerial report on the situation of French, along with the publication of *Le français langue commune: enjeu de la société québécoise: Un bilan de la situation du français au Québec* (Quebec: Ministère de la culture et des communications). These assessments became increasingly comprehensive. The 2008 report, for example, contained detailed and fully documented chapters on language demography, the language of education from kindergarten to university, the language usage of immigrants, and French in the workplace, in business, in consumer products, and in the media. It also assessed the level and quality of language usage.

From the year 2000 came the reports of the Estates-General (Commission des États-généraux) and their findings on the remarkable achievements of the French language charter. The findings were a measure of how far Quebec had come since those of Lord Durham a century and a half earlier. Although the culture, ethnicity, and religiosity had indeed changed, the land and the language remained intact. The rationale for a sovereign Quebec now rested more than ever on the fact that the common community language of its residents was French.

More and more of these French-speaking residents were non-European newcomers, numerous enough to change the face and traditional culture of Quebec society. What this shift entailed for public policy became rather too much for many of the most militant *Québécois de souche,* and they made known to the media what they felt about the exotic customs of the newcomers and their foreign religious practices. They noticed, for example, that within the city of Montreal, some sixty new mosques had appeared. A sense of no longer belonging to the homeland they had known and loved, coupled with a fear of becoming a powerless minority in their own land, created an identity crisis so intense that by 2006 it prompted the government to appoint a high-level commission of inquiry. It was co-chaired by an eminent Canadian philosopher, Charles Taylor, and a well-respected Quebec historian, Gérard Bouchard. Their research revealed the breath and depth of resentment of so many of the 3,500 who attended the hearings and open forums. The report, however, which was released on 22 May 2008 was not what these plaintiffs had expected, for it justified the government's policy of inclusiveness while condemning the marginalization and stereotyping of the 130,000 or so Muslims (of all stripes) and other visible minorities who had recently made Quebec their home. The report recommended that all Quebec citizens respect the rights of these newcomers and support their integration in a spirit of reciprocity and equality, while also maintaining the secular ideals of Quebec's Quiet Revolution.

Federal Language Policies

Federal language policies have been reactions to the grievances of French Canada, especially those of Quebec. They are often seen as conceptual artifacts composed of traditional principles and political expediency. They are not limited exclusively to language laws; they also appear in the form of ministerial declarations, administrative directives, constitutional provisions, and juridical rulings. They result from a dynamic of reaction and interaction between circumstances and principles, public opinion and political will, and provincial politicians and federal ministries. As instruments of accommodation, federal language policies have evolved by successive approximation toward the traditional Canadian ideals of peace, order, and good government. They have done so by combining the hindsight of experience with some foresight gained from one's own mistakes and those of others. We can see this evolution in the contents of the following sequence.

1960   Quebec's Quiet Revolution begins

1963   creation of the Royal Commission on Bilingualism and Biculturalism (henceforth the B and B Commission)

1964   creation of a federal language bureau to bilingualize the Public Service

1965   the alarming preliminary report of the B and B Commission

1966   the Pearson Declaration ("Canada is a bilingual country")

1967   appearance of the first volume of the B and B report (the final one would appear in 1970)

1968   the founding of the Parti Québécois

1968   (17 October) the Trudeau Declaration ("Federal bilingualism not to change the merit system")

1969   the first Official Languages Act

1969   the launching of the bilingual premium for federal civil servants (a 15 per cent salary add-on)

1970   the first report on bilingual districts

1972   the Drury Declaration (C.M. Drury, as Treasury Board president, responsible for language policy implementation, presents to the public service its goals and timetable, e.g. 25,000 new bilingual posts by the end of 1978)

1972   the Coulombe Report (policies for the bilingualization of the public service)

1973   (29 June) Parliament adopts policies for a bilingual public service

1975   the second report on bilingual districts

1976   the Bibeau Report (external study on the results of the bilingualiza-
       tion policies)
1976   the Gens de l'air crisis (Quebec pilots and air traffic controllers insist
       on the right to use French over Quebec airspace, citing the Official
       Languages Act, article 2; their claim was ratified in 1979)
1977   the Pépin-Robarts Task Force on Canadian Unity
1982   the patriation of the Constitution (After losing its veto right, Quebec
       refuses to ratify it)
1982   the Canadian Charter of Rights and Freedoms (sections 16–22 de-
       voted to French and English as official languages)
1987   the Meech Lake Accord (entrenching minority rights; to be ratified
       by the provincial legislatures by 1990)
1988   the Second Official Languages Act
1990   the demise of the Meech Lake Accord when Manitoba refuses to
       ratify it and Newfoundland suddenly withdraws its prior ratification
1994   new regulations on bilingual services to the public
2003   action plan for use of official languages (two years in the making)
2004   new official language policy directives

Instead of analyzing the details of all these policy-related events, it would
seem preferable to concentrate on a few of the most representative and
significant, which would be the Royal Commission on Bilingualism and
Biculturalism, the first Official Languages Act, the bilingual districts adventure, bilingualizing the public service, and the second Official Languages Act.

THE ROYAL COMMISSION ON BILINGUALISM AND BICULTURALISM
Also known as the Laurendeau-Dunton Commission, after its co-chairmen,
this inquiry ranks as one of those monumental problem-solving and policy-
generating projects that mark Canadian political history for generations to
come. It belongs in the company of other historic commissions such as the
ones on federal-provincial relations (the Rowell-Sirois Commission), on
Canadian unity (the Pépin-Robarts Task Force), and on Indian Affairs (the
Erasmus Commission). It was appointed by a newly elected federal prime
minister (and Nobel laureate), Lester Pearson, who sensed the rising tide of
a language-related Quebec separatism. His advisers neither understood its
cause nor knew what to do about it. The problem seemed sufficiently grave
to warrant the appointment of a royal commission of inquiry. Its mandate
would be "to report on the existing state of bilingualism and biculturalism
in Canada and to recommend what steps should be taken to develop the
Canadian Confederation on the basis of equal partnerships between the two

founding races." Great pains were taken to make sure that the commission was representative, both linguistically and geographically. Under the bilingual co-chairmanship of newspaper editor André Laurendeau and university president Davidson Dunton were ten commissioners from different parts of the country: five English-speaking citizens, including a Ukrainian professor of linguistics from the west, and five French-speaking citizens, including a Polish professor of French literature from the east.

Although the commission had to labour for seven years, what its members found after ten months of inquiry seemed alarming enough to report immediately. After a series of nationwide hearings, public meetings, and formal briefs from all sectors of society, they decided in 1965 to come out with an urgent preliminary report. Its basic message was that Canada was passing through "the greatest crisis in its history." Its immediate effect was to make the public aware that there was a problem, and people tried to rectify it, or at least to understand it. Many national organizations – public, private, and volunteer – engaged in bilingualizing their services. The very word "bilingualism," which had before rarely been heard or read, began to fill the media and soon became part of the everyday vocabulary.

Meanwhile, the commission's research branch, under political science professor Michael Oliver, was working on some 160 research projects, mostly with the help of the social and political science departments of Canadian universities. Its international division, under political scientist Kenneth McRae, commissioned studies from abroad, in collaboration with foreign scholars working in officially bilingual countries, notably Belgium, Switzerland, Finland, and South Africa.

On the basis of all these voluminous research reports, coupled with the findings from dozens of official hearings and hundreds of formal briefs, the commission produced, between 1967 and 1970, six books of its long-awaited final report. The problems of constitutional and juridical reform planned for inclusion in the final volumes of a ten-volume study were deemed sufficiently large and time-consuming to warrant a separate inquiry, which in effect was launched a few years later. The final report appeared therefore as six books: Book 1 (recognition and protection of French and English as official languages), Book 2 (education), Book 3 (the work world: volume 1, the private sector; volume 2, the public sector), Book 4 (other ethnic groups), and in a single volume, Book 5 (the national capital) with Book 6 (voluntary associations). As for the recommendations their most general ones were:

1 English and French as *de facto* official languages throughout Canada
2 French as the language of work in Quebec

3 reform of the federal public service along bilingual lines
4 special schools for French and English official minorities and the nation-wide teaching of their languages
5 development of a cultural policy reflecting Canada's ethnic diversity

These recommendations generated a series of laws and regulations, some of which required for their implementation the preparation of periodic reports, such as those concerning bilingual districts, the public service, and notably the annual reports of the Commissioner of Official Languages.

THE FIRST OFFICIAL LANGUAGES ACT
The government could not afford to wait for the completion of the commission's final report before acting. On the basis of its first book, it enacted, on 9 July 1969, an Official Languages Act, which comprised forty-one articles in ten areas:

1 the status of French and English as official languages in all institutions under federal jurisdiction (art. 2)
2 procedures for their use in all official documents (arts. 3–7)
3 establishing the validity of texts in French and English (art. 8)
4 language obligations of ministries, judicial and quasi-judicial administrative bodies, and Crown corporations (arts. 9–11)
5 after every decennial census, with the collaboration of each provincial government, to create bilingual districts in places where the number of speakers of the minority official language (at least 10 per cent) would warrant (arts. 12–18)
6 creation of an independent Commissioner of Official Languages with extensive powers and the necessary staff and facilities for an ongoing supervision over the implantation of language laws and compliance thereto, reporting annually to the governor general and directly to Parliament; tenure, seven years (renewable) (arts. 19–34)
7 Power of the governor-in-council to issue regulations to ensure compliance with the language laws in the conduct of government affairs (art. 35)
8 basic terms and their meanings – "mother-tongue," "official language," "Crown corporationm" and others (arts. 36–8)
9 modification of the law on regulations; must certify with the clerk of the Privy Council copies in both official languages (art. 39)
10 implementation: time limits for ministries, government offices, and nominations and promotions of relevant personnel by the Public Service Commission (arts. 40–1)[36]

The implementation of these articles placed an added burden on all government bodies, Crown corporations, and especially the Treasury Board, which was entrusted with their administration. Especially frustrating were the attempts to create bilingual districts and, over the years, the long-term task of making the public service bilingual.

THE BILINGUAL DISTRICTS ADVENTURE

The Official Languages Act provided for French communities outside Quebec and English ones inside that province to be identified and authorized as bilingual districts before obtaining federal (and hopefully provincial) services in their language. Identifying and mapping such districts was to be the task of a special extra-governmental commission (a Bilingual Districts Advisory Board) appointed by law after each decennial census on the basis of which the districts could be authorized (10 per cent in an area to be delimited by the board). These areas, to be constructed out of the small census divisions, did not need to correspond to existing boundaries of any kind. Yet most communities received the majority of their services from municipalities under provincial control. So a bilingual district could only be meaningful if the provincial government committed itself to offering its services and those of some of its municipalities in the two official languages. This requirement meant that the board had to meet with the population of each potential bilingual district to receive their application, but also with the premiers of each province to obtain a commitment. Most community leaders were delighted that the federal government would devote the time, trouble, and expense to providing them in their home language services they had no trouble obtaining in their language of work. Most provincial and municipal governments, however, were reluctant to go along.

The first board (the Duhamel Commission), appointed immediately after the law appeared, had to make do with the latest available census figures, which were then almost a decade old. Nevertheless, it hastened to create bilingual districts by maximizing the provisions of the law. Since the French population of New Brunswick was above 10 per cent, as was the English population of Quebec, both rated as bilingual districts. Consequently, Quebec so strongly objected with its apparently downgraded status that the report was shelved, the impending next decennial census providing a handy pretext.

The second board (chaired by political scientist Paul Fox) was, in 1971, more cautiously appointed. Like the B and B Commission itself, it was equally balanced along linguistic and regional lines, and it interpreted the law quite differently, if not always unanimously. Several of the commissioners were less concerned with the letter of the law on bilingual districts than in justifying their raison d'être as instruments for redressing a linguistic imbalance. After they had visited all of Canada's qualified official language minorities, it became evident that while the French ones bemoaned the past, the English ones feared the future. The meetings with the premiers of all the provinces netted only two who were keen on bilingual districts – the most bilingual (New Brunswick) and the least bilingual (Newfoundland). The English ones were indifferent, and the French one (Quebec) was categorically opposed, claiming language management as its exclusive jurisdiction. The then-fractured board more or less agreed to maximize the areas of qualified French minorities outside Quebec in exchange for minimizing those of English minorities, all of whom were inside Quebec. This approach meant that the home riding of the then Canadian prime minister would not qualify for federal bilingual services, nor would that of the English-speaking Montrealer who, on 21 November 1975, had to present the proposal to Parliament. This outcome was the death knell of federal bilingual districts. No more were suggested, even if it meant contravening the law, as indeed happened when, after the following census, Prime Minister Trudeau refused to appoint the bilingual districts board as stipulated in the law.[37] Henceforth, bilingual services were determined by administrative criteria, such as significant demand, the nature of the post, and services to the travelling public at airports, border crossings, train stations, and the like.[38]

In retrospect, one can see that the trouble with this provision of the Official Languages Act was fourfold:

1 It was an attempt to apply an arbitrary territoriality to the principle of personal preference.
2 While the English minorities had always been served in their language, the French minorities that the law was designed to serve were both bilingual and diglossic, since even if their home language was unilingual French, their outside language had to be that of the environment that provided their livelihood. Changing these diglossic habits would require an investment in behaviour modification.
3 Since these communities were part of a most mobile population, they were not permanently attached to the land they lived on. Yet according to the law, bilingual districts were permanent; they could be added but not taken away, even though between censuses the minorities may have disappeared.
4 In multi-ethnic communities, raising one ethnic group, albeit an official one, to a special status could transform a town's sense of ethnic equality to one of inter-ethnic conflict, as was indeed the case, for example, in

Bonnyville, Alberta, after the town was visited by the second Bilingual Districts Advisory Board.

BILINGUALIZING THE PUBLIC SERVICE

By the mid-twentieth century, Canada was reputed to have developed one of the world's most competent and dedicated civil services; it would soon be challenged to become also one of the most bilingual. The challenge was the prospect of bilingualizing a bureaucracy of some half a million people (including Crown corporations and the military), most of them adult mono-lingual speakers of English. How this challenge was handled is a fascinating story that remains to be told. On the one hand, there was an innovative and politically motivated language law; on the other, a powerful and well-entrenched bureaucracy.

The challenge first appeared in the Pearson Declaration of 1966 demand-ing public servants to become bilingual and to supply services in the language of the client, while maintaining the right to do their work in the language of their choice. From the point of view of the powerful and highly union-ized Public Service Alliance, this was an unprecedented imposition, since it required the mastering of a new skill that civil servants had not been con-tracted to perform. So the alliance forced the government to negotiate (see the Drury Declaration of 1972). Eventually, it succeeded in having this future skill transferred from a personal to a government responsibility – and at gov-ernment expense, since civil servants now had to be paid to study what was for them a foreign language or one that they may have studied in college but never really learned. Because the mastery of a new working language was so unexpectedly different from that of other work skills that the public service had taught, the upshot was that an increasing number of public servants were spending more and more of their working hours in language study (see the Bibeau Report below). By 1992 the time devoted annually to language training, through the federal language bureau alone had risen to more than two million working hours, not counting the hours spent in the extensive language training programs operated by various federal ministries. We can get a rough idea of how this outcome had come about by looking at two key studies: an internal policy document (the Coulombe Report) and an external evaluation of its implementation (the Bibeau Report).

The Coulombe Report. The Treasury Board, to whom this expensive under-taking was appropriately entrusted, was faced with the monumental task of creating a bilingual public service. It therefore appointed a task force to determine how this should be done. The answer came in seventeen volumes in the form of the Coulombe Report (1967–72) (Pierre E. Coulombe, Stewart Beaty, Monique Hébert, Marcel Pilfoud, et al.). It is in this report that we can find the sources of the federal policies on bilingual recruitment, levels of language competence, regulations on bilingualism, use of official languages in intercommunication, the role of the language bureau in training public servants, bilingualism in the Secretariat of State, the French language potential of the workforce, French language work units, the identification and evaluation of bilingual posts, the interrelation between the ministries and the translation bureau, balanced participation, bicultural training, and research.

To comply with the principle of parity, the language training services had to be offered in both French and English. In practice, however, the types and levels of second-language competence were not comparable; the needs were not the same. Not only were native French-speaking civil servants far fewer in number, but most had already been in the habit of working in English. What they needed for career advancement was to improve their skills in writing their reports and correspondence in English. So the federal language bureau had also to provide English language programs to meet their needs.

A few of these bilingual services had admittedly already been established. The oldest was the Translation Bureau, founded in 1934 (although translation services themselves predate Confederation). In 1958 it added a simultaneous interpretation component. However, after the passage of the Official Languages Act, its staff increased exponentially. Between its founding date and 1984, the number of translating staff had grown from about a hundred to some two thousand. As for the French language units, they had been created in 1970 to accommodate mostly newcomers who worked only in French. After involving some 28,000 public servants, the units were abandoned as "an unworkable obstacle to career advancement." A system of language categorization was established by which civil service posts were placed firstly into four basic categories: bilingual, either English or French, English-essential, and French-essential. The bilingual category was cross-classified by skill: oral, reading, and writing. Each was further rated by level of competence: basic, intermediate, and superior. How all this worked in practice remained to be seen. As problems mounted, the Treasury Board, now under Jean Chrétien, decided to find out by commissioning an outside independent inquiry, to be directed by a professor of language education, Gilles Bibeau.

The Bibeau Report. The burden of implementing the language policy fell eventually upon the shoulder of individual public servants, who often found it excessive. So did some of their supervisors, who had to meet the impossible targets of their political masters, coupled with complaints from the public.

These were some of the questions addressed by the outside investigation commissioned by the Treasury Board. The results appeared in 1976 as An Independent Study of Language Training in the Public Service (Gilles Bibeau, W.F. Mackey, Raymond Leblanc, H.P. Edwards, et al.), known as the Bibeau Report. Its twelve volumes covered such areas as language-training programs, measurement criteria, the language of work, the psychosocial dimensions, and testimonials from deputy-ministers and program administrators.

It turned out to be a critical report that the government was unhappy to receive and reluctant to distribute. The findings documented the unusual increase in the number of public service personnel. This was due not only to the army of language instructors required but also to substitutes for the language learners while they attended language classes. Since an oral method was being used, it was felt that small classes of less than a half-dozen would increase talking time; it also increased the number of instructors. Most of them were young and inexperienced native speakers of French, fresh out of college, facing middle-aged managers required to produce oral contortions of which they were incapable. Few of the instructors had teaching qualifications, and few stayed long enough to accumulate teaching experience. Those who did were promoted out of class into administrative positions. Most took advantage of their civil service status to obtain, by design, transfers to other ministries, sometimes to positions more in keeping with their post-secondary training. Within a few years, the turnover had been such that the percentage of native speakers of French in the workforce of federal departments had considerably increased.

Meanwhile, within most branches of government, many types of duplication were needed to enable administrators to take their language leaves. These ranged from a few hours a week to a full year sabbatical. It is true that some of the older cadres were exempt from the language requirement, but since the quotas still applied to their departments, they were often grandfathered into gradual redundancy, as they bemoaned the performance of replacements who were more bilingual than competent. Some did admittedly return from language leave with a conversational knowledge of French, but few were able to work in the language or write their reports in it. Many found that they had so little use for their new language that they were actually forgetting what they had learned. Whereupon private tutors were hired to converse with them in their offices for a few hours a week, lest they fail to maintain the level of bilingual competence required of their post.

Those responsible for the bilingualization of the public service had been desperate to find a surefire method that would make people bilingual in the shortest time. Over the years, they went through any number of fashionable methods and questionable quick fixes, ranging from subconscious suggestion to total immersion. Failure was attributed to too little teaching time. So the programs were further expanded on the questionable premise that the more teaching you do, the more learning you get.[39] In sum, much of the language training had been inept, inefficient, and unaccountable.

A NEW OFFICIAL LANGUAGES ACT
All the foregoing internal and external reports, coupled with the results of court challenges to the Official Languages Act of 1969 and almost a decade of experience in implementing it, provided a wealth of material for a thorough language policy review. This undertaking took two years and culminated in a new Official Languages Act (1988, enacted 1 April; effective 1 July).

Although the new act incorporated articles of the 1969 document, it was more comprehensive and better structured. Its twelve parts covered the following:

1 language use in Parliament
2 public documents, executive directives, treaties, and agreements
3 languages of the courts and of the administration of justice
4 communication with the public
5 language of work in federal institutions
  (Provisions in the foregoing five parts to have precedence over past and future acts of Parliament, with the exception of the Charter of Human Rights.)
6 participation in the public service
7 role of the Treasury Board in policy implementation (as of 1972)
8 role of the Secretariat of State in language promotion: the learning, acceptance, and appreciation of French and English in Canada
9 duties of the Commissioner of Official Languages (as of 1969)
10 language rights
11 role of the Public Service Human Resources Agency
12 amendments to the Criminal Code stipulating the right to be tried in the official language of one's choice

The most significant major differences between this act and its predecessor were that the first concentrated on providing bilingual services, whereas the second added another and equally onerous dimension: language promotion. One may now ask whether these two pieces of language policy legislation achieved their main objectives.

1 External bilingual services: as seen in the annual reports (1971–2005) of the Commissioner of Official Languages, the relatively small number of practices that had to be adjusted or situations that had to be rectified in services to the public is a measure of the degree of compliance with the language laws.
2 Balanced participation: the level of native French-speakers in the public service had grown from a low of 13 per cent to a high of 27 per cent by 1995, equivalent to their percentage of the Canadian population.
3 Freedom of language choice: in almost all French-speaking and English-speaking areas across Canada it was now taken for granted that one could expect to be served by the federal government in the official language of one's choice.

Yet the most widespread achievements go beyond the letter of the language law. They concern the consequent changes in the behaviour and attitudes of the population. Although the general public unfortunately remained unaware of the details of these considerable language policy achievements (for the media, small incremental improvements do not make big headlines), the growing bilingual job requirement of Crown corporations and government agencies alerted parents to the sort of language competence to be expected when their children entered the job market. Within a few years of the first federal language regulations, thousands of parents in English Canada were having their children schooled exclusively in French within the new French immersion classes of their schools. Even in the west, where its teaching had been outlawed, the French language was being transfigured from a liability into an asset.

In most parts of Canada many of the traditional grievances of French-speaking minorities had been rectified, as French and English now enjoyed equal status before the law. Yet tensions between English Canada and French Quebec endured, since federal support of active minorities remained at variance with certain provincial language policies.

Provincial Language Policies

What are the determinants of provincial language policies? It would seem that the farther one gets from the main French-speaking concentration in Quebec, the fewer the provincial provisions for the French language. But the differences may have less to do with distance than with numbers and less with numbers than with proportions. Although Ontario has twice as many French-speakers as New Brunswick, their official status is lower. This discrepancy seems to be because they account for less than one-fifteenth of Ontario's population but about one-third of New Brunswick's. Soon after Confederation, thousands of British immigrants overwhelmed the demographic ratio in favour of English. In the west, as soon as they were given control of their own affairs, governments began to establish English-only policies, as they did, for example, in Manitoba in 1890 and in the North-West Territories in 1894. As a result of the massive British immigration, demographic patterns had changed from a replica of Quebec to a duplicate of Ontario – dominated by a English-speaking Protestant majority. The language, culture, and traditions of this majority were to determine the language policies of succeeding generations. In 1913 Ontario passed a law (Regulation 17) making English the only language of instruction after the third grade. It forbade the teaching of French in public schools and discouraged its use elsewhere, and that at a time when 20 per cent of the population were French-speaking. Ontario abrogated its much-criticized Regulation 17 only in 1944. It created French primary and secondary schools in 1968, followed by bilingual districts and French language school boards. In 1987 appeared the Ontario French Language Services Act. Pressure from the federal government's language policies had become a major determinant of provincial ones.

Another determinant of provincial language policy had been the terms under which a province entered Confederation and whether it considered it a pact or an alliance. Manitoba is a case in point. From 1835 all of its settled area was governed by the Council of Assiniboia and its successors, wherein French and English functioned as official languages. In the late 1860s, when there was talk of joining Canada, the leader of the dominant French-speaking Métis population, Louis Riel, drew up a list of rights as conditions for joining; these included the maintenance of French and English as official languages. These provisions (sec. 23) became part of the Manitoba Act of 1870, ratified by the British parliament in 1871, whereby Manitoba became part of Canada. Twenty years later, when the growing population of English-speaking settlers had become the majority, they abrogated these language provisions through their own Manitoba Act of 1890. Although overruled by the Supreme Court of Canada in 1892 and again in 1901, the English-only policy prevailed. In 1916, for example, English was declared the sole official language, following the repeal of the Laurier-Greenway agreement of 1896, whereby teaching in ethnic languages was permitted after regular school hours. In the context of the new Canadian language policies of the late twentieth century, however, the Supreme Court was asked for another ruling on the matter. In 1985 it declared the 1890

Manitoba Act to be invalid, along with all the 4,500 provincial laws that had been enacted thereafter. These had to be re-enacted in their certified French versions. In 1952 the Public Schools Act had specified English as the language of instruction during the school day; after hours, the teaching of other languages, including French, was permitted, along with their use in religious instruction. By 1994, however, Franco-Manitobans had finally obtained their own French school division.

Farther west, where French Canadians comprised an even smaller proportion of the population, their language was largely ignored, regardless of the fact that the provinces of Saskatchewan and Alberta had been carved out of an area (the North-West Territories) where since 1878 French had had equal status with English, a status maintained when the provinces were admitted into the Confederation. Thereafter, however, the legislation became aggressively pro-English, all other languages being either discounted or repressed. In 1892 English had become the sole language of record and of public schooling. Only after 1967, under pressure from the federal government, were meaningful concessions made to the official minorities.

In Saskatchewan, after it entered Confederation in 1905, English became the sole language of instruction. This policy was re-enacted in 1929 and again in 1931. After 1967, however, some French (an hour a day) was allowed in school, increased in 1974, and an Official Minority Language Office was created in 1980; these services were later extended to heritage and Native languages.

When Alberta entered Confederation in 1905, it officially maintained the bilingual tradition of the area. In practice, however, it became exclusively English-speaking. By 1915 it had outlawed all other languages for use in school. Even as late as 1988, under the Alberta Language Act, no official documents were allowed in a language other than English; the purpose was to pre-empt the imposition of a federally sponsored institutional bilingualism. In school, however, the use of French was permitted, especially after the appearance in 1969 of the federal Official Languages Act – as indeed was the case in other provinces. The Alberta Schools Act of 1969 permitted French schooling where numbers warranted, these being determined by school boards, whose members were mostly English-speaking.

Still farther west, in British Columbia, English also dominated. French was considered a school subject, along with a number of other languages, including the Asian and Native ones that dominated the daily lives of an increasingly cosmopolitan population.

The only province whose language policies matched those of the federal ones was New Brunswick. When the federal Official Languages Act appeared in 1969, New Brunswick enacted its own version the same year (on 18 April). It was followed in 1976 by further language legislation and in 1981 by the Act Recognizing the Equality of the Two Official Linguistic Communities of New Brunswick – in a province which, in 1871, had abolished funding for French schools.

In Nova Scotia and Prince Edward Island, where teaching in French had been prohibited in 1864 and 1854 respectively, new language regulations addressed the aspirations of Acadian populations for their own schools. In Newfoundland there was a lingering disappointment that the province's Acadian Port-au-Port Peninsula did not become, as had been expected, a federal bilingual district.

While Quebec had adopted a language policy based on the principle of territoriality, it is significant that in all other provinces, French Canadian communities (with no state of their own) kept claiming their ethnic origin as a marker of distinctive identity, protected by a federal law based on the principle of personality. The publication in 1978 by the federally sponsored Fédération des francophones hors Québec of the English version of its voluminous survey of the situation of French minorities outside Quebec, under the title *The Heirs of Lord Durham: Memoirs of a Vanishing People*, alerted the Canadian public to the plight of francophones in each province. It established a rationale for placing the struggle for the survival of French minorities throughout Canada on a national political level. In two abundantly documented volumes confirming the thesis that the higher the concentration, the slower had been the assimilation of French minorities, it demonstrated how these closed collectivities had been subject to domination, assimilation, and conflict with provincial laws because most citizens did not accept the special status accorded at the federal level. This discrimination was most evident in the field of education.

It would be erroneous, however, to put all these provincial anti-French laws in the same political basket. The rationale for many of them had to do more with religion than with language. Some of the lawmakers had been self-proclaimed, traditional anti-Catholics; others were secular liberals who held that religion was not the business of the state. French separate schools were essentially Catholic institutions, many of them bilingual and open to all. As the only residential schools in some areas, they were also frequented by the children of English-speaking Catholics to be schooled in their religion. It was because these schools were sectarian that they were so often denied public funding, not always because they were French. When Quebec began to appear as a more secular and cosmopolitan society, any sort of overt anti-French legislation became increasingly unacceptable.

First Nations and Second Languages

As an aftermath of Confederation, all lands still occupied by First Nations fell under federal jurisdiction. Through a sequence of Indian Acts (1876–86), the political autonomy of aboriginals was abolished, and they became, in effect, wards of the state. The federal policy was to civilize and assimilate them. This objective was accomplished mainly through a system of residential schools whereby school-aged children from different Native groups were taken from their homes and schooled in the dominant colonial language. Generations later, when their descendants were now allowed to promote their ancestral tongue, many had first to learn it as a second language.

Of the fifty or so Native Canadian languages, none had figured on the agenda of federal or provincial governments. The Indian Affairs Branch (the oldest one in the federal bureaucracy) would have nothing to do with aboriginal languages: they belonged in a museum. And it was indeed only in the National Museum of Canada where they were recorded, analyzed, and preserved by a staff of linguistic anthropologists, successively under Edward Sapir, Marius Barbeau, Jacques Rousseau, and their followers.

Languages of the First Nations were not part of the mandate of the Laurendeau-Dunton Commission. Neither did they figure in the subsequent official language acts or in the patriated constitution of 1982, although post hoc attempts were made to subsume Native language rights under the "cultural heritage" clause (sec. 27) or the one on the acknowledgment of treaties (sec. 3). This latter constitutional provision did admittedly provide impetus to some hundred long-outstanding Native land claims. The few that were settled resulted in a measure of cultural and linguistic autonomy of the now legitimate landowners.

Aboriginal affairs were not on the agenda of the ill-fated Meech Lake Accord, signed by provincial premiers in 1987. This lack of inclusion was to become a hidden factor in its demise when, at the 1990 deadline, Manitoba, in the person of a Native representative in the provincial legislature, refused to ratify the accord. For a serious policy agenda on the First Nations and their cultures, one would have to wait for the report of the Royal Commission on Aboriginal Peoples (1992–97). Meanwhile, people continued to debate the Trudeau Policy Statement of 1969, which proposed to: abrogate the Indian Acts; close all residential schools; redress the constitutional discrimination against aboriginals; and offer primary education in the Native languages and ancestral tongues as second languages for assimilated aboriginals.

It was not, however, at the federal level that language policy initiatives were actually taking place. In 1975 a landmark treaty, the James Bay

Agreement, was signed between Quebec, the Cree, the Inuit, and the federal government. It provided for services in Cree and in Inuktitut; Native regional school boards; teaching in the Native tongue along, with the study of French as a second language; and self-government.

A ratifying federal Law on the Cree and Naskapi of Quebec specified the right to use the Native tongue in official public assembly. In 1983 the Quebec National Assembly enacted a policy on relations with the province's aboriginal inhabitants comprising fifteen basic principles, including a legal recognition of aboriginal peoples as "distinct nations" with rights and responsibility for their own languages, which could qualify for state support. The responsibility for the implementation of the policy was entrusted in 1989 to a special Secrétariat aux affaires autochtones.[40]

In the sparsely populated north, where First Nations were still in a majority, the importance of language identity emerged, notably in the Yukon, the Northwest Territories, and, after 1999, the vast (350,000-square-kilometre) newly created Nunavut, where Inuktitut was declared an official language along with French and English. In 1988 the Yukon Language Act provided for the use of Native languages in the Legislative Assembly and created a Language Service Bureau for the preservation of aboriginal languages, which was further enhanced in the Yukon Education Act of 1990. In the Northwest Territories the Official Languages Acts of 1984 and 1988 had recognized as official languages Chipewyan, Inuktitut, Dogrib, North and South Slavey, Gwich'in, and Cree, along with French and English, their use to be administered by an Office of Language Commissioners. After 1995 the federal government allocated millions for the preservation and promotion of these languages. The actual work of language policy development, however, was done largely by non-governmental organizations such as the Métis National Council, the Inuit Tapirisat, the Federation of Saskatchewan Indian Nations, and bodies for the study and promotion of specific languages.

Policies of Multiculturalism

Of all the federal language policies, the western provinces were most receptive to those related to multiculturalism, since they reflected the multi-ethnic makeup of their populations. Indeed, this factor had not been forgotten in the haste to create a bilingual Canada, for the second half of the mandate of the Laurendeau-Dunton Commission was to account for "the contributions made by other ethnic groups to the cultural enrichment of Canada, and the measures that should be taken to safeguard that contribution." As an assurance that

these "other ethnic groups" would not be neglected, two of the commissioners, both foreign-born, were chosen from these groups. For it had become
evident that the ratio of these groups was increasing, relative to that of
Canadians of British and French origin. In fact, since Confederation, it had
quadrupled: from 8 to 37 per cent between 1871 and 1991. At the same
time, the population of British origin had proportionately declined by half,
from 60 to 36 per cent, while that of French origin had diminished by a fifth
(from 31 to 26 per cent).[41]

After accepting the final report of the Laurendeau-Dunton Commission,
the prime minister in 1971 announced a policy of multiculturalism. The stated objectives were to enrich Canadian culture, to promote fair play for all,
and to instill pride in one's identity, in an atmosphere of non-discrimination.
Grouping immigrants simply by country of origin was a conscious attempt
to avoid the skin-colour classifications of the United States and Britain.
While the classification of citizens by religion was avoided, there was some
attempt to recognize faith-based identity claims. This was an endeavour to
accommodate greater and greater diversity within the Canadian Charter of
Rights and Freedoms while avoiding the politicization of race, religion, or
ethnicity. It was an overt policy of non-assimilation, promoting cultural and,
possibly, language maintenance. To counter a consequent tendency toward
fragmentation and conflict, the policy stressed ethnic harmony as a main
objective, by means of inter-ethnic contact through the medium of one of
Canada's official languages.

Most western provinces reacted favourably to the policy, enacting comparable legislation of their own. In 1973 appeared the Saskatchewan
Multiculturalism Act. But it was not until 1988 that the federal government
enacted its own Multicultural Act, proclaiming ethnic diversity as the hall-
mark of Canadian society. Federal funding was to be provided to promote
heritage languages and cultures, to ensure that aboriginal rights were protected, and to guarantee freedom from discrimination and provide equality
of opportunity to all. From these objectives we can deduce that, although
language is the strongest element of cultural identity, it would not be considered its *sine qua non*; yet the policy did open the door for the use of heritage and aboriginal languages as media of school instruction.

CONCLUSION

In retrospect, if we look at how Canada has evolved from colony to nation,
from a British dominion to a bilingual federation and a multicultural country, we can trace the relative weights of language and culture in Canadian

identity in the origins of its heads of state: from Confederation until after the Second World War, the governors general were all British aristocrats (dukes, earls, viscounts, and barons); from 1952 on, they were all Canadians, starting with Vincent Massey and alternating between celebrated English- and French-speaking public figures. After the Multicultural Act, some were foreign-born immigrants or neo-Canadians from ethnic minorities, symbolizing the multi-ethnic character of the population.

As a progressive liberal democracy, Quebec could no longer remain isolated from the rising tide of Canadian cosmopolitanism. Indeed, it is one of those sad ironies of history that, having left the protective arms of a powerful universal Church to build the first French-speaking secular polity within anglophone North America, Quebec society should now have to accommodate other languages and other religions.[42] By the end of the millennium, the two traditional pillars of French Canadian identity, faith-based nationalism (*la langue, gardienne de la foi*) and ethnic irredentism (*notre maître, le passé*) had ceded to the pragmatic policies of language-based inclusiveness and progressive cultural accommodation (see Jocelyn Létourneau, *Passer à l'avenir* [Montreal: Boréal, 2000]).

Looking back, we see the growing importance of language as becoming independent from ethnicity and religion, while remaining attached to the collective memories of the founding peoples and their descendents who brought to Canada the fruits of two of the greatest Old World civilizations. Nevertheless, it must be remembered that the French and the English have been in competition for almost a millennium, during which time their languages have often been proxy to their conflicting interests. Although both languages have spread to all quarters of the globe, only in Canada have they shared so fully the burdens of a modern industrial state. Canada has also been the catchments of overflowing populations – no longer those of the traditional homelands but now those of countries from all continents. The consequent cultural entropy has been part of the price to pay for the survival and spread of these two great languages. Their future and that of their language policies will be determined by the extent to which they drift apart or cling together in the rising tide of an increasingly cosmopolitan culture.

APPENDIX 1: AN OVERVIEW OF THE CHAPTER

English and French in Europe
   French as the Official Language of England
   The Emergence of English (1360–1660)

    French as an Official and International Language
    French and English as National Languages
French and English in North America
    Patterns of Settlement
        French Settlements
        English Settlements
    Sources of Conflict and Accommodation
French and English as Canadian Languages
    The Birth of Canadian Language Policies
    The Evolution of Language Policy in Quebec
    Federal Language Policies
        The Royal Commission on Bilingualism and Biculturalism
        The First Official Languages Act
        The Bilingual Districts Adventure
        Bilingualizing The Public Service
        A New Official Languages Act
    Provincial Language Policies
    First Nations and Second Languages
    Policies of Multiculturalism
Conclusion

APPENDIX 2: SELECTED READINGS

A bibliography of each of the sections covered in this chapter would be too vast to include and too onerous to use. For example, one key reference to the development of French, Ferdinand Brunot's *Histoire de la langue française des origines à 1900*, appears in several large volumes. For an overall view of the domains covered in this chapter, the following works might suffice.

On the Making of French and English

Balibar, Renée. 1985. *L'institution du français: essais sur le colinguisme des Carolingiens à la République*. Paris: Presses universitaires de France. For an English summary, see the review in the *Journal of the History of European Ideas* 13 (1991): 125–31.

Jespersen, Otto. 1967. *Growth and Structure of the English Language*. 9th ed. Oxford, Blackwell. This is a classic: one of the most readable short histories on the development of English, having endured since its first appearance in 1928.]

Lodge, Anthony. 1993. *French: From Dialect to Standard*, London: Routledge.

McKnight, George H. 1928. *Modern English in the Making*. New York and London: Appleton-Century. Of the dozens of works on the history of English, old and new, this is the one devoted most to its fashioning as a standard language.

On the New World Language Communities

Edwards, John, ed. 1998. *Language in Canada*. Cambridge: Cambridge University Press. Contains chapters on French, English, and other languages in each of the provinces, on Canadian varieties of English and French, policies of official bilingualism and multiculturalism, Canadian duality, education, and language teaching.

Louder, Dean R., and Eric Waddell, eds. 1993. *French America*. Baton Rouge: Louisiana State University Press. Or the original: *Du continent perdu à l'archipel retrouvé* (Québec: Presses de l'Université Laval, 1983). Contains chapters on Quebec, Ontario, the Canadian west, the Métis, British Columbia (Malliarville), Acadian migrations, New Brunswick, Newfoundland, New England, the American west, Missouri, Louisiana (Acadiana), East Texas Cajuns, population mobility, and ethnic identity.

On the Languages of the First Nations

Collis, Dermot Ronán F., ed. 1990. *Arctic Languages: An Awakening*, Paris: Unesco.

Maurais, Jacques, ed. 1996. *Quebec's Aboriginal Languages: History, Planning, and Development*. Clevedon: Multilingual Matters. Begins with a substantial survey of the aboriginal languages of the Americas, followed by chapters on the demolinguistics and geolinguistics of Quebec's aboriginal languages, their degrees of standardization, and the federal and Quebec policies concerning them. Includes selected grammatical sketches of Mohawk, Montagnais, and Inuktitut and a series of enlightening perspectives on their own languages by Native speakers of Algonquin, Atikamekw, Cree, Huron, Inuktitut, Micmac, Montagnais, and Naskapi. Ends with an abundant bibliography and detailed index.

On Components of Language Policy in Canada

Bourhis, Richard Y., ed. 1984. *Conflict and Language Planning in Quebec*. Clevedon: Multilingual Matters. Contains chapters on language planning, terminology, Francization, social classes, business, intergroup relations, cross-cultural communication, minority language education, and Anglo-Quebec, plus a chronology of selected historical and linguistic events and the complete English text of Quebec's Charter of the French Language.

Corbeil, Jean-Claude. 2007. *L'embarras des langues: origine, conception et évolution de la politique linguistique québécoise*. Montreal: Éditions Québec Amérique. The most comprehensive account of the origins and development of language policy in French Canada. Ranges from the dialects and diglossia of the first colonists to the language problems of contemporary Quebec. Covers some fifty topics (e.g., contact with English after 1760, current policy issues on usage and standardization), all well-structured into parts, chapters, and sections. The first part treats the rationale and findings of the Quebec and federal language commissions and the crises over language laws. The second part, on contemporary Quebec under the Charter of the French Language, covers the basic principles and evolution of the Charter and its successes and failures. The third, more theoretical part groups such topics as federal language policies, bilingualism, terminology, and relations with the standard French of France. Particularly useful is the final part and its seventy pages of documentation. These include appendices highlighting the various language laws, statistics on language use, and immigration, followed by a bibliography of language laws, a substantial chronology of relevant events from 1957 to 2007, more than a hundred basic references, and an index of important names and issues.

Mackey, William F. 1978. *Le bilinguisme canadien: bibliographie analytique et guide du chercheur*. CIRB Publication B-75. Québec: Centre international de recherche sur le bilinguisme. Contains separate chapters on each of the ten dimensions of Canadian language policy: linguistic, demographic, political, economic, juridical, administrative, social, geographic, cultural and ethnic, with corresponding references (some 4,000 in all); also sections on standardization and sociolinguistic surveys and a glossary of terms; includes the complete texts of: Canada's Official Languages Act, New Brunswick's Official Languages Act, and Quebec's Official Language Act.

Some Key Documents in Chronological Order

Hart, Gerald E. 1891. *The Quebec Act of 1774*. Montreal, Gazette Printing Co. Includes enlightening extracts from British parliamentary debates on the bill before it was finally enacted.

Lord Durham's Report. 1960. Edited with an introduction by G.M. Craig. The Carleton Library, no. 1. Toronto: McClelland and Stewart.

Royal Commission on Bilingualism and Biculturalism [Laurendeau-Dunton Commission]. 1965. *Preliminary Report*. Ottawa: Queen's Printer.

– 1967–70. *Report*. 6 vols. Ottawa: Queen's Printer.

Commission of Inquiry on the Position of the French Language and on Language Rights in Quebec. 1972. *Report*. [Gendron Report]. 3 vols. Quebec: Éditeur officiel.

Sheppard, Claude-Armand. 1971. *The Law of Languages in Canada*. Ottawa: Information Canada.

Bilingual Districts Advisory Board [First]. 1971. *Recommendations*. Ottawa: Information Canada.

Bilingual Districts Advisory Board [Second]. 1975. *Report*. Ottawa: Information Canada.

La Charte de la langue française. 2002. Quebec: Éditeur officiel. The French Language Charter, including Bill 104 and all prior amendments.

The Official Languages Act: Annotated Version. 1992. Ottawa: Supply and Services.

Languages Commissioner of the Northwest Territories. 1993. *Eight Official Languages: Meeting the Challenge*. Yellowknife: Office of the Languages Commissioner. First annual report and subsequent annual reports.

Official Languages Regulations on Services to the Public: Synoptic Table. 1994. Ottawa: Treasury Board.

Commission sur la situation de la langue française au Québec. 1996. *Le français, langue commune: enjeu de la société québécoise*. Quebec: Éditeur officiel.

Commission des États généraux sur la situation et l'avenir du français au Québec. 2001. *Le français, langue pour tout le monde* Quebec: Éditeur officiel.

Annual Reports, 1970 to Date

Commissioner of Official Languages. *Annual Report*. Ottawa: Public Works and Government Services.

Secretary of State. *Official Languages*. Ottawa: Supply and Services.

Treasury Board. *Official Languages in Federal Institutions*. Ottawa: Supply and Services.

NOTES

1 A special thanks to Jacques Maurais for lending his expertise to the betterment of this text and my gratitude to Grant D. McConnell and to my wife, Ilonka Schmidt Mackey, for their critical reading of the manuscript.

2 As we examine the evolution of these policies, we can evaluate the extent to which they have profited from the lessons of history or heeded Santayana's dictum "Those who do not remember the past are condemned to repeat it."

3 A few decades earlier, however, there had been a French Norman presence at the court of Edward the Confessor.

4 A document dated 8 October 1258, the Provisions of Oxford of Henry III, was probably the first bilingual public declaration ever issued in both French and English.

5 For native speakers of English, Anglo-Saxon had become a foreign language – as much so as Dutch or Icelandic.

6 Especially in the seventh and eight centuries and during the literary renewal of
Alfred the Great, a memorable intermission between the Viking invasions and
the conquests by Danes and Norwegians. The latter were gradually integrating
England into a Scandinavian empire, a destiny diverted by the Norman Conquest,
which integrated England into a wider Europe, where it remained thereafter.

7 Edward III of England was the grandson of Philip III of France, whose nephew
was Philip of Valois, who claimed the throne of France as Philip VI.

8 For a brief sketch of its development, see "La politique linguistique dans
l'évolution d'un État-nation," in *Langues et sociétés en contact*, ed. Pierre Martel
and Jacques Maurais (Tübingen: Max Niemeyer Verlag, 1993), 611–70.

9 The emperor was forced to make separate concessions to the Protestant powers
assembled at Osnabrück and, some thirty miles away in Münster, to the Catholic
powers, which included France.

10 After Westphalia, fewer and fewer European treaties appeared exclusively in Latin,
and where that language predominated, the supporting documents were generally
in French (e.g., Ryswick in 1692). Some appeared *ex equo* with Latin (e.g., Utrecht
in 1713) or with Spanish (e.g., Pyrenees in 1659 and Nijmegen in 1678). More and
more were drawn up exclusively in French (e.g., Aix-la-Chapelle in 1668 and 1748,
Ratstadt in 1714, Vienna in 1736, Paris in 1763 and 1783, and all subsequent
European treaties until the early twentieth century).

11 It is true that there had also existed a number of projects for an English language
academy, dating back to the one commissioned in 1617 by James I from Edmund
Bolton. Dozens of serious proposals continued to be made, some associated with
the Royal Society, others originating from such influential figures as Addison, Swift,
Dryden, Defoe, and Adams. The last, writing in 1780 from Amsterdam, suggested
an American academy so that the United States be the first in having an institution for "refining, correcting and improving the English language." Such a proposal, however, had already been made earlier, in the *Royal American Magazine* of
January 1774. All these plans for an English academy, however, came to naught.

12 In England, whose monarchs never seemed formally to have renounced their
claim to the French throne (even after it had ceased to exist), French lived on as
a language within the aristocracy, most enduringly in their medieval customs and
rituals, such as that of royal assent to legislation: *Le roi le veut* (to a public bill),
Soit fait comme il est désiré (to a private bill), *Le roi s'avisera* (to signify a refusal),
and so on. French also remained a component of the whimsical anachronisms
of aristocratic pageantry, as illustrated in mottos of their coats-of-arms: *Honni
soit qui mal y pense, Dieu et mon droit*, and the like. Their French counterparts,
however, adhered to Latin, as exemplified in the motto on the shield of Louis XIV –
Deo favente haud pluribus impar – perpetuated on the escutcheon of what became
the first French-language university in the Americas founded during his reign at
Quebec by the first bishop of New France, François Montmorency de Laval.

13 While condescending to accommodate the language of the Americans, France maintained its language as the official one: "déclarant que le présent traité a été rédigé et arrêté en langue française." The same reservations were subsequently added by France to the English version of covenants with the United States. After 1800, however, on the insistence of the American State Department, all treaties with France were drafted in English and French on the basis of the equality of both languages.

14 Most countries except France had agreed on English as the working language. Yet France, in the person of Georges Bidault, insisted that it should be French. Others countered that if any language other than English be used, it should be their own. Latin America proposed English, French, and Spanish. China wanted languages to be official according to the function each performed, insisting that a distinction be made between official languages and de facto working languages.

15 The UN Charter stated (art. 111): "The present charter, of which the Chinese, French, Russian, English and Spanish texts are equally authentic, shall remain deposited in the Archives of the Government of the United States of America."

16 For a comparative appraisal, see "Conflicting Languages in a United Europe," *Sociolinguistica* 15 (2001): 1–18.

17 The master of classical French, the author Jean Racine, complained that at a hundred leagues from Paris he could not make himself understood. This problem was not surprising in a country where most of the inhabitants, particularly the large peasant population, lived out their lives completely unaware of the very existence of other provinces and their people. The same situation applied to England at the time.

18 For a good overview of the development of national literacy in France, see F. Furet and J. Ozouf, *Lire et écrire: L'alphabétisation des Français, de Calvin à Jules Ferry* (Paris: Éditions de Minuit, 1977).

19 For the complete text of the Grégoire Report, see the appendix to Michel de Certeau, Dominique Julia, and Jacques Revel, *Une politique de la langue : La Révolution française et les patois* (Paris: Gallimard, 1975).

20 Indeed, this was the period in which appeared the great multi-volume standard dictionaries of the French and English languages. Most notable was the French dictionary of Émile Littré (1863–73) and that of Pierre Larousse (1868–1876), the English dictionary of Noah Webster (1828) in the United States, and Murray's *English Dictionary on Historical Principles* in Britain, which grew into the monumental *Oxford English Dictionary* (1879-1932). It is true that a century earlier there had been official glossaries such as the *Dictionnaire de l'Académie française* and grammars such as the *Éléments de grammaire française* (1790) of Abbé Charles François Llomond, which was later made official during the French Revolution. And in England there was the equally inadequate and subjective dictionary of 1755 compiled by Samuel Johnson. But their influence was hardly comparable to that of the products of the great lexicographers and grammarians of the nineteenth and twentieth centuries.

21 Created in 1890 by Honoré Mercier to deflect the exodus of unemployed French Canadian workers to the mill towns of New England. The plan of his deputy minister, the Abbé Labelle, was to colonize the north country of Quebec and Ontario, thus creating a French-speaking corridor between Acadia and the Canadian west. This could have become a political reality only two decades earlier if, upon the addition of a bilingual Manitoba to Confederation, its claims to its eastern hinterland had been heeded: lands between James Bay and Lake Superior.

22 One of the most significant battles of the century, *la Conquête* has become part and parcel of Quebec consciousness (as hinted in the province's motto, *Je me souviens*). So much was this the case that its 250th anniversary re-enactment in 2009, long planned by the mayor of Quebec City and the federal administration of the Plains of Abraham (the National Battlefields Commission), had to be cancelled under pressure from the sovereigntist Réseau de résistance des Québécois, which threatened to disrupt such a "celebration" over the "graves of our ancestors." For a full and fascinating account of the genesis of this historical battle and its amazing aftermath, read Joyce Carrol, *Wolfe & Montcalm* (Toronto: Firefly Books, 2004), or the French version published in Montreal by Éditions de l'Homme in 2006.

23 Compare Jacques Henripin, *La population canadienne au début du 18e siècle,* Cahier 22 (Paris: INED, 1954), with Jacques Henripin, E. Lapierre-Adamcyk, and P. Festy, *La fin de la revanche des berceaux* (Montreal: Presses de l'Université de Montréal, 1974).

24 The colony at Fort Garry (at the confluence of the Red and Assiniboine rivers) had established a good working relationship between the French Canadian, Montreal-based fur traders, the English-speaking personnel of the trading post of the Hudson's Bay Company (which owned all the land), the Scottish settlers, the Natives, and the French-speaking Métis.

25 See Pierre Elliot Trudeau, ed., *La grève de l'amiante: Une étape de la révolution industrielle au Québec* (Montreal: Éditions du Jour, 1970).

26 For a wider perspective, see Philip Lawson, *The Imperial Challenge: Quebec and Britain in the Age of the American Revolution* (Montreal: McGill-Queen's University Press, 1989).

27 See J. Levitt, ed., *Henri Bourassa on Imperialism and Biculturalism, 1900–1918* (Toronto: Copp Clark, 1970), 107.

28 But not historically correct, for the original text used the word "race" with the same meaning it had had in all the preceding Canadian political documents, that is, in the genetic sense applied simply to people of common ancestry, collective memories, and cultural practices. After the Second World War and the horrors of its Holocaust, the word's wider anthropomorphic meaning was the more frequent in the media, where it was usually associated with genocide, repressive discrimination, and "visible minorities."

29 "Mais si nous voulons défendre notre patrimoine intellectuel qui est celui de toute
   la race française, nous devons le faire selon l'ordre harmonieux, nos devoirs sociaux et de notre vocation providentielle. Nous luttons pas seulement pour garder
   la langue, ou *la langue et la foi*: luttons pour la langue *afin de mieux garder la
   foi* " (Henri Bourassa, *La langue, gardienne de la foi* [Montreal: Bibliothèque de
   l'Action française, 1918], 51).

30 John George Lambton, Earl of Durham, was in his twenties when Napoleon
   threatened to invade Britain.

31 Passed only in 1969, after a number of modifications following strong protests
   against the free choice of school language.

32 This attitude was reflected in the popular thinking of the time, as reflected, for
   example, in the Quebec order-in-council 136, which appeared in *La Gazette officielle du Québec* 103 (20 March 1971), and the document "Le Québec ne veut plus
   d'immigrants" (Quebec: Ministère des communications, 12 October 1971).

33 For the complete text in English, see Richard Y. Bourhis, ed., *Conflict and Language
   Planning in Quebec* (Clevedon, UK: Multilingual Matters, 1984), 262–84.

34 The excluding clauses of the bill whereby only laws issued in French would be official were brought to the attention of the Supreme Court of Canada, which considered them illegal, ruling in 1979 that the law should appear in both French and
   English, both versions being official.

35 See Pierre Bouchard and Richard Y. Bourhis, eds., *L'aménagement linguistique
   au Québec: 25 ans d'application de la Charte de la langue française*, in *Revue
   d'aménagement linguistique: Terminogramme*, autumn 2002 (Quebec: Les
   Publications du Québec, Office québécois de la langue française).

36 For the complete texts, see William F. Mackey, *Le bilinguisme canadien: bibliographie analytique et guide du chercheur*, CIRB Publication B-75 (Quebec, 1978) :
   Canada's Official Languages Act (564–77), New Brunswick's Official Language Act
   (583–4), and Quebec's Charter of the French Language (585–603).

37 In the meantime, some provinces, particularly Ontario, were creating their own bilingual districts.

38 To understand why bilingual districts, which worked in Finland, could not do so
   in Canada, see Kenneth D. McRae, "Bilingual Languages Districts in Finland and
   Canada: Adventures in the Transplanting of an Institution," *Canadian Public Policy*
   4 (1978): 331–51.

39 To understand how certain types of language teaching can actually be counter-
   productive, see William F. Mackey, *Language Teaching Analysis* (London:
   Longman, 1965); American ed.(1967), with successive updated translations in
   France (1972), Russia (1975), Japan (1979), and China (1990).

40 In 1988 the federal Secretariat of State had advocated the creation of a National
   Institute of Aboriginal Languages.

41 See Charles Castonguay, "The Fading Canadian Duality," in *Language in Canada*, ed. John Edwards (Cambridge: Cambridge University Press, 1998), 36–60.

42 Read the report of the Conseil des relations interculturelles to Quebec's minister of citizens' relations and immigration, "Laicity and Religious Diversity: Quebec's Approach," in the Metropolis Research and Policy Review of the *Journal of International Migration and Integration* 6, no. 2 (2005): 291–326.

2

Comparing Language Policies

WILLIAM F. MACKEY

Before adopting a methodology that can have such far-reaching consequences for language policy comparison, one must face some basic language-related questions.

Who owns the language? Although a language as an operating code can belong to those who create it, a human language – that anonymous and monumental work of uncounted generations – can only belong to those who use it. It does not belong to the state.

Who makes the policy? The state has no monopoly on language policy.[1] Any group of people whose existence depends on the use of language may control the forms of their language, its functions, and the domains of its use within its own institutions: families, markets, churches, schools, hospitals, and assorted social, business, or political associations.[2] The choice may depend on how the languages are affected by the policies of the various jurisdictions under which the institution must live and on how these jurisdictions have taken each of the languages into account.

How does policy affect language? Public policy can include the selection of a single language variety as the language of power while legalizing its use and rewarding its users. It can exclude all other varieties and languages by restricting their use and penalizing their users. Between the two extremes of state lingualism and official linguacide exist policies of different types and degrees of accommodation ranging from linguistic laissez-faire to official language promotion. These are parameters that any program of language policy analysis and comparison must take into account, since they affect the forms and functions of a language within systems of social communication.

Why, where, for whom, and for what? Why was the policy needed? Since motives – real and alleged – generate language policies, they are part and

---

1 To assist the reader, an outline of this chapter is provided in the appendix (112–14).

parcel of any analysis or comparison. Where does the policy apply? Across the country or in designated areas, such as ethnic enclaves or bilingual districts? For whose benefit was the policy intended? For the majority group, for a minority with special status, for all minorities, or for the entire population? For what purpose? What was the policy meant to achieve? National unity, cultural integration, cultural diversity, or other objectives?

Such motives, objectives, and decisions are the main components in the creation of language policies and must consequently be accounted for in any program of policy analysis and comparison. A good number of these policy-directed questions are addressed in the chapters to come: forms, functions, and domains of language use (Maurais); territorial and personality principles in the dynamics of identity (Bilinsky); changing patterns of identity and language promotion (Fontaine); language use and the integration of immigrants (Paillé); linguistic ethnicity in a globalizing national economy (Labrie); effects of immigration on language policies (Haque); the linguistic status of Canada in the French-speaking world (Erfurt); and the relationship of Quebec's language policy to social peace (Anctil). Their relevance will become increasingly evident as this chapter unfolds.

PROBLEMATICS

This chapter is also an attempt to advance solutions to the three problems in language policy comparison posed by Morris: (1) the "need to assess multiple aspects of language policy from various angles" and the consequent vagueness and lack of rigour in comparisons based on different data or presented from different perspectives, (2) the "multidisciplinary reality" of language policy and the "disciplinary orientation" of language policy discourse, and (3) the "effort to integrate scattered lessons and findings within common types or patterns."

The first of these problems is attributable to the lack of a common analytic framework. The second is inherent to the essentially arbitrary and a priori division of knowledge into self-contained academic disciplines, each fragmented by competing dogmas expressed in different in-group metalects. It is hardly surprising if so much discipline-oriented discourse has produced so few problem-oriented solutions. The third problem, that of integration, arises from the lack of any standard units of comparison compounded by the absence of a common terminology (Sartori, Riggs, and Teune, 1975).

In the last analysis, these problems exist because language permeates society; indeed, there can be no society without language and no language without society. That is why language comes within the purview of so many disciplines: in interpersonal interaction (psychology), in social institutions (sociology), in political institutions (political science), in populations (demography), in territories (geography), in cultures (anthropology), in legal systems (law), and in markets (economics). Within these disciplines, those whose main concerns are language-related have created such subdisciplines as psycholinguistics, sociolinguistics, glottopolitics, demolinguistics, geolinguistics, and ethnolinguistics, which remain discipline-oriented in as much as each simply applies the theoretical artifacts of its discipline to language-related data (Ricento, 2006). Some of this work has been co-opted by the expanding science of linguistics and loosely grouped under the umbrella of "the language sciences," which embraces "applied linguistics" and its discipline-oriented subspecialty of "language planning."

Yet language policy has been central to none of these disciplines, for the very strength of an academic discipline in advancing the frontiers of knowledge through its many subdisciplines and their ever-narrowing specialties may become a weakness when any one of them is called upon to solve the wide-ranging problems of language policy. In sum, while the motives and objectives of language users may be marginal to most academic disciplines, they are central to the study of language policy (Mackey, 2006).

MULTIDISCIPLINARY BECOMES INTERDISCIPLINARY

Multidisciplinary treatments of language policy rarely reveal a complete picture. As a problem-oriented body, however, a language commission may have to forge interdisciplinary solutions out of a mass of multidisciplinary material. Heterogeneous data and analyses from different disciplines must eventually be structured into something coherent and relevant to language policy. That is why the success of language commissions has depended so largely upon their judicious use of more problem-oriented approaches to the making and maintenance of language policy. It is helpful when the appointees are simply citizens of good judgment, unbeholden to the concerns of any academic discipline, while keeping many of them on tap but none on top.[3] Although such ad hoc language commissions can forge a better interdisciplinary instrument, they can hardly show the changing, time-dependent dynamics between unstable language policy components, ranging from the political to the symbolic (Loubier, 2008). That is why permanent bodies for managing language policies have become necessary.

The problem-oriented experience and extensive research of some of these language commissions will guide us as we attempt to compare the effects of motives, objectives, and decisions on the forms, functions, and systems of language in society. We begin, therefore, with the basic problems of comparison.

THE COMPARATIVE METHOD

It has been declared, "One of the supreme intellectual achievements of the 19th Century" (Kimball, 2003, 347). For it was by means of the comparative method that some of the greatest scientific advances of our time have been achieved, notably in biology and linguistics: from the origin of species to the genetic code; from the ancestry of language families to the typology of language universals.[4]

The comparative method is tributary to the scientific approach to the study of nature. It rests on the two main pillars of the scientific method: observation and interpretation. A field of knowledge is advanced by cumulative increments in the scope, accuracy, and verifiability of relevant observations coupled with ongoing analysis, classification, and modelling necessary for a correct interpretation of the phenomena. One observes clusters of formal similarities and differences, relates them to specific functions, and interprets their significance by comparison with what has been established or, by experimentation, through differences between sets of data. Since the forms and functions vary in space and time, observations are made for purposes of comparison in different places and at different periods. Thus it was found that forms and functions evolve in different ways in different places to produce a multiplicity of different systems. The method is applicable to both evolutionary biology and comparative linguistics: so much so that since the 1980s there has been a concerted effort (e.g., from Hoenigswald and Wiener, 1987, to López-García, 2005) toward the forging of a common methodology. This includes the application of the root-branch model, the sequencing of regular correspondences, such as those between, for example, the Romance and Germanic languages (e.g., Lat. /p/ = Eng. /f/, Lat. /t/ = Eng. /th/: Lat. pater = Eng. father), the phenomenon of convergent emergence, and the like.

Rigorous applications of this method has revealed unlikely affinities not at all evident through use of the descriptive method, no matter how thorough the analysis. Take, for example, the discovery that such disparate languages as English, Kurdish, Yiddish, and Lithuanian, though mutually incomprehensible, have a common (Indo-European) ancestor – fundamentally different from that of Arabic and Hebrew or Somali and Berber, which, though likewise different, belong to the same (Semito-Hamitic) family.

To what extent is such a method applicable to the study of language policy? Before we attempt to answer this question, it is necessary to compare the comparisons, to see how they were able to lead to such remarkable discoveries. What is it in language, biology, and other fields of observation that has made systematic comparison so rewarding? Is there something akin to this element in the components of language policy? If so, what should we be comparing? What types of meaningful comparisons are possible? How comparable are the components?

What Are We Comparing?

What we compare depends on why and determines how we compare. The purpose of the classical comparative method was one motivated by the search for origins. The method was to classify, compare, and sequence time variations in the discrete units of codes (such as phonemes and morphemes) and their internal functions within closed systems. Through a painstaking process of progressive approximation, this study could produce a proven lineage. Thus were established stable, self-regulating correspondences. To what extent is such a method applicable to the comparison of language policies?

The answer depends on what is covered by the policy. It is imperative to appreciate what this is before one can know exactly what to compare. One must likewise understand what a policy comprises, its limits and potential for command and control over the life of languages. The idea of a language policy is to direct an innate human activity toward social objectives. Language policy is a multidimensional artifact coupling an attribute with an activity. Understanding the nature and essence of its two components, language and policy, and the constraints of context on its aims and content is the starting point for any analysis or comparison of its diverse practices. Since both language and policy are polysemic, it is imperative to decide which meanings we are matching. This is not an idle precaution.

THE MEANINGS OF LANGUAGE
At the outset it is important to avoid that common confusion between language (French: *language*) and a language (French: *langue*).[5] One must also distinguish between the denotation of language and its connotation, for to know what a language can connote to people is to understand the passions that a language policy can arouse in some. Connotations may be heavy with emotive associations linking family and faith, nation and culture, evolving from one generation to the next, and ranging from the utilitarian to the symbolic.

A language is therefore necessarily cumulative. Each language bears the imprint of those who have used it. This characteristic helps explain the investments expended on practices and policies for its preservation. These are especially relevant to a language with written traditions whose time value – its coinage, as it were – provides access to its storehouse of accumulated knowledge and wisdom. No policy can expect to replace this by edict (Mackey, 1976b).

Any vernacular and its forms, uses, and users may be the object of policy. Its code as a speech variety, distinct by virtue of the place or class of its users, may be formalized as a language, as opposed to its relatives, which may be rated dialects along with other low-status vernaculars. The language may be based on the usage of an elite, the writings of literary luminaries, or the speech of a ruling majority, each providing a corpus from which elements of the language may be codified and standardized ("language planning," i.e., management, *aménagement*).

Language planning is an instrument of language policy, since it can make a language fit for the uses of power: control, status, and prestige (Mackey, 1979a). For some languages it may be the indispensable prerequisite to their eventual diffusion. Yet it is not within the power of the makers or keepers of the code to determine either the extent of its use or the behaviour of its users (Baldauf and Kaplan, 2003). That is the purview of policy. Language policy operates at the intersection between what makes a group of people a society (language) and what makes it function as such (politics). The former is an inherited system; the latter is the practice of power. Consequently, the first question to ask about the language policy of any jurisdiction is: Who has the power and ability to make choices where language is concerned; who, for example, decides on the languages of education? Whose choices will prevail are matters of politics (Joseph, 2006).

THE MEANINGS OF POLICY

Arguments justifying interests, desires, advantage, or expediency can define a policy and result in a course of action toward stated objectives.[6] When the course of action concerns a language, achieving its objectives may assume some control over its forms, its uses, and its users. Language policy is the influence of power over language. The power may be political, economic, demographic, social, cultural, or ideological, each weighing unequally upon the language at different times and in different places. Some of these forces may be interrelated, interdependent, and cumulative; demographic majorities, for example, can alter political systems, while economic elites can control them. The ideologies of militant minorities can promote policies favouring their languages.

The sum of these powers can have a cumulative and multiplier effect, to such an extent that, if they all support the same language, it will have little need for the protection of an overt language policy. If English-speakers are at once the most numerous, richest, best educated, and most productive in the United States, they may have little need for laws telling them when or where to use their language and to whom (González and Melis, 2001).

Yet as producers of goods and services, they have an economic interest in attracting and keeping customers, many of whom (over 40 million in the United States in 2000) have home languages other than English.

In comparing language policies, we have been dealing not so much with closed systems as with open ones, not with internal functions of language but with external ones, as observed in its functions within society. Language policy has been less concerned with language origins than with language survival. It is concerned with the life expectancy of languages and with what can be done about it. To this end, a language policy may admittedly have to take into account the state of the code (e.g., its lexicon) in addition to its corpus of available writings. This process of language management may be an indispensable component of a policy for the preservation, restoration, elaboration, modernization, or other adaptations of a language that are needed to make it fit for the societal functions which the policy intends it to fulfill (see the section on forms below and Kaplan and Baldauf, 1997). Quebec's language policies, for example, have provided for the management of the language (e.g., arts. 188 and 189 of the Charter of the French Language).

One can also compare institutions, ranging from the family to the sovereign state, as to the purposes of their policies. Even the smallest institutions such as the family may adopt a policy aimed at perpetuating the language of their forebears through methods like those that have seemingly succeeded elsewhere.[7] These are not the same purposes as those of a business or multinational corporation motivated by such objectives as customer satisfaction, product safety, and compliance with the liability laws of different countries. These policy purposes may again be different from those of a sovereign state bent on solving its problems of language by seeing how others have done so.[8] One of these purposes may be to attenuate the power and influence of the majority over the minority, where power may be economic, demographic, political, social, or ideological. In the final analysis, in comparing language policies, we are dissecting human purposes and decisions about a form of behaviour indispensable to the survival of society.

Types of Comparison

Comparisons may differ according to the time frame, scope, and contents of the policies. The period covered may be the present, the recent past, or a specific point or stretch of time. One may also attempt to compare two or more policies according to the range of language-related areas they cover within the limits of their respective jurisdictions: for example, the scope of language policies of two sovereign states (country comparisons). Finally, one may analyze and compare, in whole or in part, the content of the language policies as they affect each language and its forms, functions, and users.

TIME FRAMES

The classical comparative method comprised two basic time-related types of comparison: the diachronic (points in time) and the synchronic (forms observed at the same time in different places). The first dominated the nineteenth century in its search for origins; the second rose to prominence in the twentieth century in its quest for universals. They are not, however, mutually exclusive. In practice, they have sometimes been combined into what became known as the historico-comparative method (Hock, 1991). Applied to language policy comparison, this method can show us how changing contexts over time have fashioned each of the policies, revealing where some succeed and others fail. Each policy may sometimes be analyzed as a sequence of successive approximations to some form of social accommodation. One could thus compare different stages in the making of Canadian federal policy as it evolved from one of language accommodation to one of language promotion.

Comparison may be based on two places at two points in time, as Michel Paillé has done in his diachronic comparison of official language minority populations in Quebec and Ontario in 1971 and 2001 (chapter 9). These studies share some of the best criteria for valid comparison: relevant measurements. Yet they are not direct measures of language policy as such but, rather, of the sine qua non of language survival: the number of language users. Contrariwise, the diachronic parts of chapters 7 and 10 focus directly on the language policies of a single province, explaining how they have changed over a given stretch of time. These include Louise Fontaine's study of identity politics in Quebec during the 1960s and 1970s (chapter 7) and Normand Labrie's more general perspective on Ontario's language policies during the twentieth century (chapter 10).

One could apply these measures diachronically to evaluate the development of Canadian language policy as it has affected more and more domains of official language use, from bilingual postage in the 1920s, to bilingual currency in the 1930s, to bilingual Crown corporations in the 1950s (when the Canadian flag carrier, Trans-Canada Airlines, was renamed Air Canada), to other domains in the 1960s, culminating in the Official Languages Act of 1969. Such diachronic studies can be enlightening in so far as they can reveal not only how policies have changed but why. Longitudinal comparison helps one understand the rationale of past decisions on language policy. It can also enable one to apply to the comparisons the counterfactual logic of hindsight: What would have happened if nothing had been done? What other ways were available to achieve the language policy's objectives? And what would have happened if, at that fork in the road, one had taken the other path?

SCOPE

Language policies differ so widely in their range of coverage that this factor itself can become an object of comparison, not only of the number of languages covered but also of the amount and importance of protection provided for each of them. This may range from almost nothing to almost everything to do with the public use of language. So how wide is the coverage of each policy? How many languages, with how many provisions?

How Many Languages and Which Ones? If we compare sovereign states (country comparisons), we are likely to find in each of them more languages in use than are covered in the country's language policies – some 6,500 in less than two hundred countries. We often find the same few languages (mostly English, French, Spanish, and Portuguese), which are official or co-official with a limited number of regional tongues. Yet these are not always the everyday speech of the majority of the people. So how many of these tongues are included in each language policy and to what extent? In Canada, along with English and French, the jurisdiction of Nunavut in the Eastern Arctic, which covers an area the size of Europe, has included Inuktitut as an official language, while the vast region of the Western Arctic has added Cree, Chipewyan, Tlicho, and Slavey as official languages.

How Many Provisions for Each? One might imagine that language policies would provide many provisions for the use of the official language. Yet some policies consist merely of a constitutional declaration on the official status of a language, while others comprise an elaborate charter covering the forms of the language, its domains of use, and the language behaviour of its users.

In Canada, although the central government covers more territory and more languages, the scope of its language policy is limited mostly to domains under federal jurisdiction. Quebec, however, within a more limited territory but a wider range of language-related jurisdictions was able to enact and maintain a language policy with maximum coverage, including the language itself, its uses, its users, and most domains of their public activities, from the medium of schooling to the language of work and play. Since this policy has been flexible enough to make way for some corrective action and fine tuning, its adaptation and maintenance through periodical revisions and amendments over a quarter-century have also been the object of comparison (Bouchard and Bourhis, 2002).

As for non-official languages, Canada's central government, under the framework of official bilingualism, promotes all the languages of its citizens, albeit within the narrow limits of its jurisdiction. This policy covers the aboriginal languages of Canada's First Nations, the heritage languages of its early settlers, and especially the languages of its official French and English regional minorities. Although the official language of Quebec is French, its language policies have always included provisions for its traditional and once-dominant English-speaking minorities. Within its Charter of the French Language it also provides exemptions to enable the public use and maintenance of its main aboriginal languages and their respective nations (art. 88 and 95). More specific accommodations are introduced in periodic nation-to-nation agreements with the aboriginal communities (Trudel, 1996).

CONTENT: THEMATIC COMPARISON
Each of the components of a language policy may become the object of comparison. The method used depends on the order of analysis and the consequent area of expertise required. One can distinguish three orders of analysis as they relate to the forms, function, or systems of intercommunication.

Forms. A policy may specify not only a language variety that counts as the language but also its forms: from the way it is written to the words it contains. Such policies may vary in both time and place. In Canada one could compare, for example, policies on the writing of official Inuktitut in the Eastern Arctic with those in the Western Arctic (Collis, 1990; Dorais, 1994). One could also analyze the difference in policies on standards and norms of usage in various provinces, notably with language management norms and practices in Quebec (Bédard and Maurais, 1983; Maurais, 1999). And one can compare the latter with those of other French-speaking countries.

Comparative studies on the management of official languages can be found in the growing literature on language reform (Fodor and Hagège, 1983–94) and language planning (Kaplan and Baldauf, 1997). There are also the publications of 622 research centres that produce occasional reports on the standardization, modernization, and enhancement of some four hundred languages in 125 countries (Domínguez and López, 1995).

Functions. Societal functions within their different domains of use are most amenable to systematic comparison – not only their number but also their modality. These functions might include education, signage, legislation, public administration, city bylaws, labelling, instructions on customer products, and much more. One can, for example, compare the language policies of different countries as they affect the use of languages in education (McConnell and Roberge, 1994). One can also compare signage regulations and practices in different countries (Leclerc, 1989). There have been a number of diachronic studies on language legislation in Canada and abroad (Sheppard, 1971). Comparisons of municipal language policies and their regulation of language functions have also been the object of international conferences (Herberts and Turi, 1999).

Language Users in Social Systems. The leading themes of some of the following chapters may be considered under this heading. They deal with different communities of speakers (group comparisons) and different language-related institutions (institutional comparisons).

These also include language policies that are tributary to more general policies on human rights and the application of principles of equity concerning the users of different languages, either as individuals or as groups. Since the founding of the United Nations, there has been a marked increase in the number of international covenants, conventions, and accords on the treatment of language minorities. Some have been in effect long enough to invite some comparative evaluation and assessment.

Questions of Comparability

At the outset it would be helpful to bear in mind the standard caveat against comparing "apples and oranges" by mixing categories and levels. Between two language policies what is comparable and what is not? What is it in language policy that affects its comparability? We can isolate a couple of obvious variables: (1) the structure, size, and status of the relevant institutions and policymaking bodies and (2) the nature of the policy components.

THE STRUCTURE OF INSTITUTIONS

These may include institutions within sovereign states, autonomous regions, provinces, corporations, non-governmental organizations, supranational bodies, local governments, private institutions, and the like. Before comparing them, we have to establish their structure and the extent of their jurisdiction, their relative size and status, and the focus of the institutional comparison.

Jurisdiction. The comparability of language policies in sovereign states depends on the relation between their political structures and areas of jurisdiction. In the first place, there is likely to be some incompatibility between nation-states and federations. The first may have complete jurisdiction over language policy; the second may have none at all. So to classify language policies simply by their presence in the constitutions of sovereign states can be quite misleading. Such classification leads, for example, to the placing of Cameroon and Canada in the same category on the grounds that both their constitutions declare English and French to be their official languages. These are hardly meaningful comparisons.

To conclude that Canada and France each has its own language policy while the United States has none is to ignore the place of language policy in political structure.[9] The United States has no official language for the simple reason that jurisdiction over language was intentionally not included in its federal constitution, which states that all authority not specifically allocated to the central government belongs to the states, and this includes matters of culture and hence language and custom. And although the US constitution does specify the right of the citizen to an elementary education, which is language-related, it imposes its implementation as the responsibility of the states. This arrangement seemed a good idea at the time, with so many isolated colonies with different cultural, religious, and linguistic differences to maintain. It came about after much consideration and debate, which one can follow in the Federalist Papers.[10] The idea may be just as valid today. Indeed, it has resurfaced in a new incarnation as the principle of subsidiarity within the European Union's constitutional debates (Mackey, 2001).

Size and Status. Does a polity the size of the United States or the European Union have the same policy options as smaller states such as Antigua or Andorra? What is the influence of size differential on language policy potential? Is the policy of Nauru (whose size and population are that of an urban suburb) comparable to that of India? Size may indeed matter in country comparisons of language policy (Alesina and Spolaore, 2003). In the 1980s both Ireland and the Netherlands were able to achieve the sort of social consensus of which larger countries such as Italy have been incapable.

One may then ask to what extend the sovereign state holds sovereignty over language (Mackey, 1991). And to what extent is the sovereign state the basic unit of language policy comparison? Should we not simply compare the language policies of those who make them in institutions (public and private) where they exist in national, intranational, international, and multinational bodies, or in transnational treaties such as the one between Belgium and the Netherlands on the standardization of Dutch (Willemyns, 1983)?

Focus of Comparison. If the focus is not the country but the language, one can compare how its status may vary in countries of different sizes and political structures. This approach has been attempted for a number of poly-centric languages, including English (Clyne, 1989; Herriman and Bernaby, 1996). Or the focus may be on education. When language policy relates to education, it matters that in some countries such as France education is controlled by the central government and in other countries such as Canada and the United States it is a regional or local responsibility, while in still other countries it is a private or institutional one (McConnell and Roberge, 1994).

In the United States nothing prevents a municipality from having its own official language, as was indeed the case in Dade County, Florida, (including Miami) between 1973 and 1980, when Spanish enjoyed the status of an official language (Beebe and Mackey, 1990). The city had to serve members of its official minority in their own language, but the firms that hired them could forbid them to use it in the workplace. Private firms were free to make their own policy, within the law of equal opportunity employment, whereby firms were compelled to hire visible minorities – but not audible ones.

QUANTIFICATION OF COMPONENTS

Quantification is crucial to language policy that has to do with difference of degree in language forms, functions, and behaviour. Measurement is important both in the making of language policies and in comparing and evaluating them. The policy has to take into account the significant degrees of difference between the languages and language varieties, between the uses of these languages and their users. In comparing language policies, one must therefore take into account differences in both policy components and language components, discussed in the second and third sections of this chapter (82ff.). By quantifying differences in feasibility, cost benefit, and compliance, it may be possible to evaluate the different policies (see chapter 3). In sum, policies must deal with differences between the forms and functions of languages and language varieties and with the extent to which these differences determine the behaviour of those for whom the policies are intended. The types and tools, however, vary between language forms, language functions, and language behaviour.

Language Forms. Language policy can affect both the code and the corpus of a language. The code of each language is composed of its significant sounds, its structures, and its vocabulary. Between languages, the difference in these components is mostly a matter of degree. Difference between their significant sounds (phonemes) has been measured through techniques of comparative phonometrics, such as vectorial phonology (e.g., Mackey, 1974). Differences between their structures (morphology and syntax) have been subject to the measurements of inter-lingual distance (e.g., Mackey, 1971; 1976a, chaps. 10

and 11). Differences between vocabularies and their size, range, coverage, availability, and frequency distribution have been the object of numerous lexicometric studies (Dale and Reichert, 1957). Such quantitative studies have been used to predict the degree of inter-comprehension between speakers of two different languages or language varieties (Huot, 1980). There have been studies on the degree of difference between the numerous varieties of widespread and genetically related languages (e.g., Goebl, 1984). Some direct tests of inter-intelligibility have also been developed (Casad, 1974).

For the vocabulary, a distinction must be made between lexical potential (as measured in the range and size of dictionaries, glossaries, and the like) and that fraction of the lexicon which is coded in the minds of the language users to whom the policy is addressed: the words available to them (competence) and the ones they actually use (performance) (see the section on patterns below, 79ff.). As for the corpus, measurements are made and updated, in each domain of use, of the number and diffusion of publications in different media: print, audiovisual, and electronic (bibliometrics). The corpus of a language can determine the choice of medium of communication and instruction in different domains and at different levels. If a language has little or nothing in print in the field of science, for example, it can hardly become the medium of science education at the secondary or tertiary levels (e.g., Tsunoda, 1983). And since there is more science available in some languages than in others, a national language policy may be incapable of controlling the choice of language in advanced studies (e.g. Ammon and McConnell, 2002).

Language Functions. Language policies can specify which languages can function in different domains of society – government, education, public administration, signage, and the like. Some languages may have more functions than others. These can be quantified and compared: comparative language dynamics (Mackey, 2000b). One can list, weigh, and count the functions in each domain in which a language must or may be used (McConnell, 1991). A method measuring some hundred language functions within eight public domains has been applied to establish the degree of language vitality of the constitutional and minority languages of India, Western Europe, West Africa, and China (McConnell and Gendron, 1993-1998). These are, in effect, synchronic measures of comparative language policy potential. Or one can take a single function in a domain and level therein and compare the extent to which it exists in policy and performance in a given language at different times and places. By adding to the number and distribution of domains under its jurisdiction, the state can legislate and increase the use of its official language. It can do so through its administrative apparatus. Yet it cannot succeed unless the language itself is capable of functioning within these domains, as can be measured by the potential of the relevant domain-oriented corpus. The extent to which a language policy can change the language of a social function within a domain is a measure of its success (see chapter 3).

Language Behaviour. Quantifying the effects of a language policy on the language behaviour of groups and individuals requires a different sort of methodology: that of the sociolinguistic survey. In measuring the effects and potential of a language policy on different groups, one must first take into account their number, geographical distribution, relative wealth, cohesion, degrees of identity, and extraterritoriality. The value of any measurement of these policy determinants will of course depend on the quality of the surveys and of their methodology.

A language policy may be based on measurable population proportions, locating, for example, areas where official minorities may have the right to certain services in their home language. Directives for supplying these services are often couched in such vague terms as "significant demand," "if numbers warrant," and the like, the meanings of which must be quantified by those responsible for policy implementation. But the few tools they are given for the task are quite often limited or inadequate. Most are derived from census data based on answers to questions assumed to mean the same thing to all respondents at all times and in all locations. While this assumption may hold true for most questions, it may not apply to questions about language competence and language behaviours and the corresponding responses; yet these are digitized in the same way as are the answers to questions on age, sex, place of birth, home ownership, and the like. But questions such as "Can you maintain a conversation in English and French?" may not have the same connotation in Vancouver as they do in Montreal, a difference that one can confirm in Statistics Canada's ongoing inter-census analysis of response variance (Mackey and Cartwright, 1979).

Interpretation and comparison of results may be complicated by the fact that some groups are bound together less by the languages they speak than by where they live, where they come from, or their faith and its language. It is understandable therefore that there are more ethnic groups in the world than there are languages (Dalby, 2000).

Such comparisons become meaningful in so far as they explain the making and maintenance of a language policy or the generality of its existence in comparable contexts. They begin to lose significance outside the ever-changing conditions within which they are motivated and maintained. It is true that progress in all fields of scientific endeavour has been associated with the quantification of components. This has also been the experience in language-related areas of research (Mackey, 2002). It remains to be seen whether the comparative study of language policy will follow this trend.

Part of the problem is that phenomena related to languages and their uses and users are continually changing in different ways and at different rates in different places. Motives, objectives, decisions, and their causes and consequences are part and parcel of a language policy that in turn generates changes in the content and direction of languages and their use. In the last analysis, we are comparing motives, objectives, and decisions concerning the forms, functions, and users of languages.

COMPARING THE POLICY COMPONENTS

The current context of language policy is one of multilingual states and multi-state languages. While the world's 6,500 documented languages are housed in less than two hundred states, three-quarters of these states, accounting for half the world's population, share ten official languages. Most (some 95 per cent) of the other languages have less than 5 per cent of the world's population. Some 1,500 of these languages have less than a thousand speakers. Many of these languages, with no young speakers, are becoming extinct – at the rate of two a month (Crystal, 2000). And the rate has been increasing exponentially since the sixteenth century as a result of the rise of nation-states, overseas empires, and the decimation of indigenous populations through war, famine, disease, conquest, acculturation, urbanization, and increases in the range and intensity of intercommunication. Yet each language is directly or indirectly accounted for in some sort of overt, covert, or attributed language policy – be it one of assimilation, interdiction, neglect, indifference, tolerance, promotion, or revival – by individuals, institutions, states, or groups of states.

If language policy has to do with decisions on the use of a language, it cannot be limited to the sovereign state (Kaplan and Baldauf, 1997). Indeed, such decisions on language use can range all the way from the interpersonal to the international, from the plurilingual family to the multinational organization. Parents and grandparents can insist that their language be used in their home, outside of which a different language may prevail. In the European Union all the official languages of its more than two dozen member states may be officially respected, yet it must of necessity establish the working languages of its agencies and administration (Mackey, 2001). Its policy on language competence ("mother tongue plus two"), whereby EU citizens learn two foreign languages, however, produced some unintended consequences. By 2009, according to a Eurobarometer survey, Europeans under twenty-five were five times more likely to speak English as a foreign language as they were French or German. If one adds the native speakers of English, some 60 per cent of young Europeans can speak English "well or very well." Since many of these go on to university, at home or abroad, while European universities become consciously cosmopolitan, English becomes the default language that most students understand, so that it begins to function as a European academic language (Ammon and McConnell, 2002). Likewise in the media: most of Europe's major dailies, at great expense, have created English electronic editions, which become interlinked into a European news network.[11]

Meanwhile, European policy-makers faced with the prospect of a culturally impoverished Europe, with its great literary patrimonies left unshared, have attempted to reverse these practices in order to save the principle. For example, the European Federation of National Institutions for Language, albeit without the agreement of the Dutch and Scandinavians, wants to disallow English from being chosen as the first foreign language on the grounds that it leads to *Anderthalbsprachigkeit* (mother tongue plus one and a half) (Blanke and Scharnhorst, 2007).

Although some language policies have stood the test of time, language policy is not inherently permanent, for the same policy that represented a liberation for one generation may become a burden to the next. Language situations change from one generation to another and even perceptively between decades or within interrelated jurisdictions. Policies may have to adapt to such changes. That is why culturally segmented societies are continuously involved in language policy discussion in response to the necessary and ongoing policy adjustments to changes in their divided interests (McRae, 1983–98).

Language policies that fail to account for changes in sociolinguistic situations or the political emergence of linguistic irredentism may be doomed to failure. The value of adopting the requirements of a powerful political union may come to outweigh that of linguistic and internal hegemony, so that a policy of interdiction may evolve into one of tolerance. In mid-2004, for example, the Turkish parliament, in the hope of admission to the European Union, approved laws enabling its Kurds for the first time to teach their language in privately run courses. Language conflicts do not always decrease over time. They may increase as other values such as income, education, and ethnicity coalesce with those of a distinct language. Just where language rates in the hierarchy of these values is a matter of prime concern in the modification of a language policy.

Yet language policy is not only about language. Its raison d'être may be inferred as a subtext, since language often poses as a proxy for something else – religion, race, class, or ethnicity (Blackledge, 2005). In Quebec before the Quiet Revolution, when religion was most valued, both endogamy and the consequent transmission of French from one generation to the next were associated with the preservation of the faith (*la langue, gardienne de la foi*). Social policy on human or minority rights may subsume a language policy component. The constitutional right of US citizens to a primary education, for example, may subsume a duty of the providers (i.e., the states) to do so in a language the children understand. In comparing the policy components of language policies, one must analyze the interplay between their motives, objectives, and decisions.

Motives

The motives may be political, cultural, or economic, and the consequent policies may be directed at both the users and non-users of the language or at the language itself (its codification, enrichment, implantation, and maintenance).

POLITICAL MOTIVES

In studying the relation between language and political power, one must distinguish between the power of attraction and the power of control, between control through a common language and the use of language as a proxy for something else. And finally, language policy can be the embodiment of political ideology – national unity, independence, regional autonomy, irredentism, or the liberalisation of a language long suppressed by policies of centralization.

Language policy may be motivated not only by ideology but also by reaction against insecurity or inequality, or by a need to establish a separate identity or a desire to impress a favourable image upon others. It may also be a means to unite a community or a state, as it did in the case of Republican France. It may be the prerequisite for administrative control, territorial integrity, extraterritorial influence, or economic advantage. Policies of language survival or revival may be the causes or consequences of political irredentism.

The interplay of these motives within a particular social, demographic, and cultural context determines the development and implementation of a language policy. Quebec's language policy, for example, evolved during a decade of dilemma (1960–70), within a growing consciousness of a context that included an ever-falling birth rate, the anglicization of its immigrants, and a lack of high-wage French-speakers in an English-dominated workplace. All these forces coincided with the rise of a secularized middle class with increasing social prestige and self-regard.

A language policy may, in the hands of an ethnic group or cultural elite, in reality be used as an instrument of political power. The real intention of the policy may be political, social, economic, or ideological (Weinstein, 1987). In practice, knowledge and self-interest may be one and the same. A language policy may be used to propagate a patriotic belief in ethnic superiority at the expense of other languages and cultures (Bordieu, 1991). Yet the resulting elitism may be an unintended consequence of the *dirigisme* needed to bring liberty, equality, and fraternity to the people (Shiffman, 2002). During the French Revolution, the centralist Jacobin faction, after seizing power, began to view the remarkable differences between the language of the upper classes (French) and the speech of the people (the regional patois) as a relic of the a*ncien r*égime and an obstacle to intercommunication between the citizen and the state. The obvious remedy was a language policy whereby the central state should appropriate the language of power and give it to the people (De Certeau, Julia, and Revel, 1975).

CULTURAL MOTIVES

Yet what about the hundreds of other languages that no state has chosen to nurture? Some of these have become the purview of non-governmental institutions. Language-oriented learned societies (funds and foundations in England, Japan, and the Unites States) have adopted a policy of preservation for the sake of the language itself (Hagège, 2002). The policy is based on a rationale of four considerations: moral (possible loss of accumulated collective experience), scientific (loss of linguistic knowledge), economic (cost of social peace), and aesthetic (beauty in diversity) (Mülhäusler, 2000). It is a policy based on a perception of morality, aesthetics, and society wherein the very existence of a code constitutes an unalloyed good (Edwards, 2002). To preserve these tongues, many have been developed as written languages, regardless of their viability (McConnell, 1991). This confusion between language survival and literacy fails to account for the fact that most languages have survived through intergenerational transmission by word of mouth. Their survival has always depended, not on literacy, but on orality. It may sometimes be better to keep the ancestral language as a living tongue than kill it in an attempt to make it into what it is not. Forcing its survival to depend on turning speakers into writers might also be inefficient at a time when oral recordings have become cheaper than printed books and the ubiquitous cellphone has made distance irrelevant.

Compounding the confusion is the lack of distinction between code and corpus, between a language as a record of the way the human mind has been able to express its conception of the world and as a collection of language users whose only function becomes the use of the language (Kibbe, 2003). Some of them might prefer to become literate in a language of widespread and upward mobility, for the implementation of such a policy often implies some intervention in the lives of disadvantaged peoples whose native tongue may be one of their liabilities (Ryan and Terborg, 2003). That people should serve their ancestral tongue is a policy that goes beyond the preservation of endangered species. If it is the official language, its fate may become intertwined with that of the nation-state, even to the extent that the language may sometimes seem to be more important than anything else (Klinkenberg, 2001).

In some countries, language policy, particularly as it affects schooling, has been a by-product of cultural and religious ideologies (Gonzáles and Melis, 2001). The power and prestige of certain languages in specific areas of culture has determined policies on the acquisition and use of these languages. French was long a prerequisite for diplomacy, German for science, Italian for art, and English for business, science, and technology (Ammon and McConnell, 2002). Arabic was the language of Islam; Latin that of Catholicism, which in turn had been associated with the survival of French in Canada and the revival of Irish in Ireland. Maintenance of aboriginal languages through mother-tongue literacy has long been the policy of Christian missionaries (Ostler and Rudes, 2000).

Finally, in comparing the cultural components of language policies, one has to account for differences in education policy, cultural identity, and norm conformity. Does the implementation of an education policy account for differences in cultural values? Is social learning more valued than formal education? Does the culture value identity over education? Is its norm of success different? Does the language policy implementation account for different degrees of tolerance of deviation from the norm? Does the tolerance extend to differences in religion?

ECONOMIC MOTIVES

While the purpose of a religion may be to save souls, that of a business is to turn a profit. Profits are made by supplying a demand. If what is supplied is language-related, as it is in service industries, profits are made by matching, at the lowest cost, the language of supply to that of demand. A demand from one country may be satisfied profitably by another if the language of service is the same. This, for example, became the practice toward the end of the past century. American service providers began moving their supply source offshore through firms in countries such as India, where a competence in English, combined with an abundance of lower-paid skilled workers, ensured a reliable supply of services. Profits also depend on increasing the demand. People in the business of supplying proprietary software, for example, have done so only for languages that could increase their profits.[12]

Finally, there is the language of the workforce. It may be in the interest of businesses to enable language minorities to work for them. Private enterprises in Quebec have maintained language policies aimed at the integration of French into the North American economy (Guillotte, 1987; Vaillancourt and Carpentier, 1989). Some economists have argued that bilingualism has been beneficial to the economy (Grin, 1996). Others have pointed out that only monolingualism can ensure the stability of the workforce and hence its competitiveness. The most stable and dependable workforce in Canada had long been in Quebec. Any evidence of instability has been cause for alarm, as witnessed by the prospect of losing the province's young doctors , when in late 2006 the Quebec Medical Association released the results of a survey wherein some 20 per cent of them stated their intention to move their practice outside Quebec within the next five years.

Objectives

Achieving language-related goals may have indirect consequences other than the intended ones when different language groups are treated according to different principles. It is necessary to compare these principles and their types of politicization.

POLICIES FOR WHOM AND FOR WHAT?

Depending on the consequences, this basic question may generate a multitude of others. Is the policy directed toward speakers of national or indigenous languages (such as Basque and Breton in Europe or Quechua and Cree in North America)? Or does it cover minority speakers of leading immigrant languages such as French, Spanish, German, Italian, Chinese, Hindi, and Arabic? Policies addressed to beneficiaries of a language policy may require criteria of identification (Jernudd and Neustupný, 1987). If the policy affects all members of a group, it may also require guidelines for the management of conflict between collective rights and individual rights: for example, between ethnic rights and women's rights or between the right to belong and the right to disassociate. Does the policy imply the right to use one's language in public, or does it also include a right to one's own institutions – schools, hospitals, and services – or to a stake in each of them? To what extent is the policy domain-related?

THE POLITICIZATION OF PRINCIPLES

Policies about a language may be governed by the right to use it. This may have devolved from accepted principles or from simple expediency. These can include simply the normative principles of justice, which may require the political protection of languages, either in the context of collective rights or as a derivative of more universal individual rights (De Schutter, 2007). These principles include the primacy of the person, that of the state, that of the people, and that of the divinity. They are often the same as the founding principles of the political system governing the users of the language – federal democracies, nation-states, theocracies (Kymlicka and Patten, 2003).

Language rights may be part of a system of rights and duties. Rights may be inherited or acquired. Inherited rights are related to such features as race, sex, and other genetic and personal traits over which one has no control. Acquired rights relate to culture, religion, and language, the practice of which one can modify during the course of a lifetime. These rights may be inherent or attributive. Inherent rights refer to what nobody can alter (such as one's place of birth), as opposed to attributive rights (such as citizenship), which may be conferred. These rights may also be individual or collective. Several may become language-related, such as an individual's citizenship being dependent on competence in the official language or a language group's right to levy taxes for the promotion of its language. Which principles govern the right to be different and the extent to which a liberal democracy should recognize differences and accommodate conflicting identities? This question was brought to the fore and hotly debated in 2007 in Quebec at the hearings of the Bouchard-Taylor Commission on reasonable accommodation (Taylor, 1994; Bouchard and Taylor, 2008). It was argued that in order to recognize some groups and not others, one had first to discriminate between the worthy and the unworthy ones. The political exploitation of such conflict-promoting differences may be forestalled if the grievances are brought into the open, fully debated, and competently assessed (Harvey, 2009). Special accommodation for some groups, reasonable and positive as it may seem at the time, can lead to different sorts of entrenched institutionalized discrimination, saddling the rapidly converging multicultural societies and the mobile polysocial populations of modern states with policies impossible to implement. Witness the ongoing political conflicts in Quebec between individual and collective rights, between women's rights and those of religions, and between language rights and citizenship. Fundamental disagreements on the precedence of such rights have become part of the platforms of political parties.

Principles based on the primacy of the person, of the state, or of the people appear in language policy as the principles of personality, territoriality, or ethnicity. These cannot always be applied uniformly throughout the state, as attested in the creation of bilingual districts.[13] In addition to these two overriding principles based on personal freedom as opposed to territorial integrity, language policy may be structured according to other principles relating to the individual, the institution, or the group. One of these is the ethnicity principle, according to which persons have the official right to function in the language of the group, culture, or community with which they identify (Kloss, 1965). The functions themselves, however, may sometimes be restricted, as in the case of religious affiliation, for example. Yet these groupings may create, within the state, ethnic entities with legal status enabling them to attract adherents with little or no knowledge of the language that had first warranted juridical recognition of the groups. This legal status can even become extraterritorial in that all adherents, no matter where they live, have the right to be ruled by the laws of the ethnic entity to which they belong. This principle was the basis of a system that governed the Ottoman Empire after the Byzantine capital fell under Turkish rule.

CONFLICTING OBJECTIVES

The more goals a language policy aims to achieve, the greater the chance of overlap and conflict. Some goals will be quite general: equalization of status, separatism, national identity, and the like (Ager, 2001). Others may be more specific, having to do with such concerns as the mobility of the workforce, social justice, schooling in one's home language, public signage, and so on. Some language policies may have as their special concern the language itself and the need for planning its future. Some of these goals may fail to coincide with more general national policy, often leading to conflicts between individual and collective rights (Le Grand, 2003).

Maintaining the freedom of the individual as a national objective may be incompatible with the autonomy of ethnic groups whose customs comprise the subservience of certain individuals (e.g., women) to the ancestral culture of the collectivity, even though the intended goal may have been the maintenance of regional languages and cultures.[14]

Language policies that are not consistent with national goals tend to produce conflict within the power structure of the state (Mackey, 1979b). Within the state, the policy of one of its institutions may be different from that of the area in which it operates. This discrepancy has been especially evident in the enduring conflict between the state and the church. While the state may decree that all citizens be literate in its official language, the church sees a need for mother-tongue literacy to help children to learn and remember their prayers and to read the word of God in their own language.[15] If a state lacks resources to educate the majority of its citizens, should it get involved in minority language education? Or should each minority have its share of the limited resources? To what extent does the state finance a language for its own sake? What are the costs in terms of basic education? Is each family aware of the trade-off? Is their choice made under elite or group pressure?

Decisions

Most sovereign states maintain some sort of central or regional (overt or implied) language policy (Leclerc, 1994). In analyzing these documents and their juridical implications, the following questions are relevant.

COMPARING POLICY ENACTMENTS

Who holds jurisdiction over language policy? Which language has its own territory? Are language rights territorial, individual, or collective? Does one language minority have more rights than the majority, or can its language rights be subsumed? Do group rights include control of educational institutions? Who settles the conflicts between group rights that are inherent and those that are attributive? Are language rights limited to intra-national minorities, or are they extended to extra-national (e.g., immigrant) populations? What duties do minority language rights impose upon members of the majority language group? It is within the context of such rights and principles, coupled with a degree of altruism or self-interest, that one can compare policies of promotion, imposition, interdiction, tolerance, and accommodation (Le Grand, 2003).

Promotion and Imposition. In some countries, the national language is so important that vast sums of money may be expended to promote it at home and abroad. The promotion is unrelated to the size of the state, for it is equally practised on behalf of regional languages (such as Basque, Catalan, and Irish) as it is for those with the highest prestige (such as French, English, and German) (Mackey, 1987; Ammon, 2000). A national language may be even imposed as a prerequisite to the right of citizenship. Since 2004, for example, foreigners qualifying to apply for British citizenship have first to pass tests of proficiency in one of the national languages (English, Welsh, or Scots Gaelic).

Interdiction. This policy may take the form of territorial confinement (linguism), negative discrimination (linguicism), or complete eradication (linguicide). Such were the policies of interdiction of Welsh in England under Henry VIII and of Catalan in France under Louis XIV. They were extended in Republican France to all regional languages and language varieties with the exception of Parisian French. They succeeded in eliminating these regional tongues from the public domains, but not without resistance, notably from the speakers of Breton (Piriou, 1971) and Alsatian (Philip, 1975).

Tolerance. As opposed to nation-states, federations have been more amenable to policies of linguistic tolerance. Many federations have been founded on principles of acknowledged diversity, as was, for example, the United States (*e pluribus unum*), which left cultural concerns to its composite states while practising an informal pragmatic approach at the federal level. The European Union has made the protection of language minorities a criterion for membership. Such protection has long been a concern of the Organization for Security and Cooperation in Europe.

Accommodation. In some federations a strong central government can protect language rights throughout the country. The existence of nationwide political parties, coupled with central control of fiscal and economic policy, helps promote a balance between individual, collective, and territorial rights. Yet in countries with multi-party systems and no overlapping cross-country memberships, no one party may be able to govern alone, for the population may be multiply segmented by class, economy, religion, and ideology. Accommodation can then only be reached by mutual agreement, taking into account social structure, behaviour patterns, inter-group attitudes, political cultures, and traditions of interrelationship between the people and their elites. Such are the types of pluralism that have determined the evolution of language policy in Belgium, Finland, Austria, and Switzerland (McRae, 1983–98).

Basic contracts between the state and its minorities may conform to the Universal Declaration of Human Rights of 1948, the European Convention on Human Rights of 1949, or to a country's constitution (Kallen, 2003). The European Charter of Regional and Minority Languages, fifteen years in the making, was launched in 1992, yet by the end of the year 2000, it had been ratified by only eleven of the forty-one member states of the Council of Europe, half of them having already signed up (Woehrling, 2001, 159–82). Under persistent internal and external pressure, even strongly centralized states can be accommodating to the users of its minority languages.[16]

Obtaining such rights, however, can become highly politicized, especially when it involves getting back anything of which one has been unjustly deprived. Losers have long memories.[17] The disposed and oppressed of the past can become the oppressors of the present by treating others as they themselves were treated. Such retribution can poison the politics of irredentism, as the ethnic violence of living memory bears witness. The treatment of Germans in the Sudetenland is a case in point. And in contemporary Pakistan there have been attempts by the Jamal-el-Islami faction to replace school English with the language of the Koran. The greatly shrunken boundaries of Austro-Hungary after two world wars left Hungarian-speaking minorities all over central Europe. Attempts to recover them include basic laws whereby the nation is defined as embracing all ethnic speakers, no matter where they live. For example, Hungary's "Preference Law" of 2001 provided these extraterritorial speakers with access to work permits, identity cards, education, and welfare benefits. Since such clauses contravened the basic principles of the European Union, they had to be rescinded before Hungary could be admitted in 2004.

One must also ask how the language policy deals with the pressures coming from different forces within a language group: ideology (for an ethnic state with its own language), activism (mobilization of the population to agitate for language rights with social reform), elitism (union of language activists with local power brokers), and networks (extraterritorial groupings of language minorities). Where does the impulse for change originate – from the centre or the periphery, from theoretical constructs or popular consensus?

CHANGING LANGUAGE POLICIES

Many language policy objectives evolve over time, outlasting the interests of the generation that initiated them. They may have been the results of a striving toward the implementation of principles such as liberty, equality, national unity, economic development, pluralism, or the aspirations of the people. The evolution of Canadian language policy, for example, might be viewed as a sequence of successive approximations to a formula of accommodation that has never reached a completely satisfactory outcome. It may be studied as a case of management of change, about which so much was written at the turn of the twenty-first century. Ongoing changes to be taken into account include the death of old speakers and the lack of young ones; the imperceptible shift in stages of bilingualism, from incipient to residual; the growing dependence on speakers of another language for one's goods, services, or employment; and the effects of long-term contact with dominant cultural, economic, or political forces, including the absorption of their conceptual universe, vocabulary, and terminologies.

Over time, therefore, the direction of a language policy may have to adjust to shifts in the dominant social paradigm – from that of the welfare state to that of a risk society, from a model of free-market competition to one of ecological protection, from the primacy of the sovereign state to that of the level playing field fashioned by the globalization of production and consumption. Authoritarian and centralized regimes can differ from democracies and federations in the ability to take all these factors into account. Some democracies are more flexible in the adjustment of language boundaries and the application of pluralistic language models. Finland's language policies have been among the most flexible (McRae, 2007). It will be admittedly difficult for policy-makers to notice all these intertwined and evolving dimensions of language use, especially when their thinking is blurred by the global glare of an all-pervasive reductionist economic ideology fuelled by an unquestioning belief in the utopia of liberty in a free world market. In such an ideological context it is easy to forget the dictum of Lacordaire – *Entre le fort et le faible, c'est la liberté qui opprime* – and to sideline a multitude of data waiting to speak truth to the power of dogma.

COMPARING THE LANGUAGE COMPONENTS

The demand for national languages greatly increased during the twentieth century as a result of the tripling in the number of sovereign states from 60 to 195 (Mackey, 2003). Because the supply of languages still outnumbered the demand by an average factor of thirty to one, a limited number of possible national languages or dialects had to be selected for special treatment (Breton, 1998). This included modernization, reform, renewal, and fusion of language varieties, followed by ongoing programs of expansion and maintenance. Raising the chosen language variety to the level of a standard written code capable of meeting the many needs of a modern sovereign state has involved normalizing or simplifying the grammar, rationalizing the spelling, standardizing the terminology, and modernizing and enriching the lexicon through adaptation and neology, albeit within the constraints of the structures of the language being adapted (Mackey, 1953).

One of the main differences between Quebec's language policies and the federal ones is that the latter are limited to language promotion while the former also put the state into the business of language development. Quebec's charter provides for the development and diffusion of the French language. It permits the maintenance of a sizable full-time bureaucracy devoted to standardizing terminologies and place names and to the creation of new words to meet the changing needs of the language. Words, such as *courriel* (e-mail) and *dépanneur* (after-hours grocery), that did not exist before are now part and parcel of the French language.

Language development has also been integral to the policies on newly official Canadian languages, such as Inuktitut and Cree. Since such languages have nothing comparable to the vast resources of French, they have much further to go, starting with the way the standard language is written (its script and orthography). For the methods and techniques they need for development, we must look beyond their borders.

Forms

Policies differ in the extent to which they deal with the forms of the language – its identification, standardization, and development.

IDENTIFICATION

What variety of speech is considered as the language? Which varieties are excluded and why? How should conflicts with them and between their users be managed? Answers to these questions can determine the content of a policy's language component. What counts as a language depends largely on who decides.[18] The facetious definition by Marshal Lyautey of a language as being a dialect with an army and a navy is a sad commentary on the relation between language and power. To call a language a dialect can be a form of political warfare. The same powers that can fashion a language as a symbol of cultural and political hegemony can manipulate its official status. The very act of legislating a language as "official" lends it an exclusive symbolic power (Bordieu, 1991). For case studies of this kind of manipulation in countries such as Croatia, Ireland, and Cyprus, see Dedaić and Nelson (2003).

In manipulating the identity of an official language, one can distinguish between policies of integration, which minimize difference, and policies of differentiation, which maximize them. Under politically centralized regimes, languages such as Catalan, Kurdish, Corsican, and Piedmontese have been classed as dialects. What counts as a language within a state depends on what counts as the language of the state. Where that language is the dialect of the centre of power and prestige, all of its varieties tend to be rated as dialects; policies of territorial nationalism tend to reduce the number of languages by subsuming them as varieties of the national language.[19] A variety may be upgraded or downgraded following changes in the power structure. In the language census of India, for example, grouped under the Bihari language were four "mother tongues" in 1901, five in 1921, nine in 1951, and twenty-four in 1961. Then Bihari and other languages were lumped together as Hindustani and later under Hindi, the official language of India. Yet outside India some of these "dialects" have rated as national languages, as is the case of Bhojpuri in Mauritius.

Contrariwise, minor regional differences have often been elevated to national symbols, such as those of Czech and Slovak, spoken Serbian and Croatian, and Italian and Corsican – not to mention the minor graphic differences in French that safeguard national identities in Quebec, Belgium, Switzerland, and France (Pohl, 1986–87). Linguistically, however, there is no reason why Parisian should be more French than Gascon, other than Paris having become the centre of political power (Gendron, 2007).

Accelerating levels of intercommunication between the Arctic peoples, through satellite broadcasting, cellphones, and the Internet, may in the long run result in a degree of spoken dialect levelling, as indeed has occurred in France, England, Canada, and the United States.[20] Yet once these languages become official, it is the written norm that carries the weight of the law. Since the late 1950s the Northern Coordination Research Centre in Ottawa has been working towards a future spelling unification of Canadian Arctic and Greenlandic languages. Language policies affecting aboriginal languages, none of whose varieties have benefited from a spoken norm, let alone a written one, have been faced with problems of acceptance, consensus, and compliance. Within a multi-dialectal planning group, it seems that single written forms of words and their spellings are accepted only in so far as they conform to the usage of each member. Years of consensus building may result in a language that is little used by an increasingly diglossic population whose literacy had become dependent on schooling in a language of wider communication, while the spoken varieties remained a continuum of mutually modifying practices.

Where schooling has always been in the home language, however, the grouping into a uniform written language can strengthen it. Such a policy of language integration can be seen as an effort to construct a counterweight to powerful neighbouring languages such as French and English. This was the case, for example, with the Flemish of Belgium, where in 1980 a treaty with the Netherlands (Nederlandse Taalunie) enacted a common international norm for written Dutch.

In comparing language policies as to their choice of language variety, one must ask whether its viability had been taken into account. Was the life expectancy of the language or language variety a factor? According to what threshold of survival (e.g., no young speakers)? What level of viability would justify public support?

STANDARDIZATION

It is hard to imagine how a modern state could function without at least one standard language to ensure the rule of law and the education of its citizens, whether that language be the speech of the majority, of a ruling minority (an acrolect), of a favoured region (a regiolect), or of a social class (a sociolect) or, as is often the case, the language of a faraway colonial power (an exolect). Half the world's sovereign states maintain an exolect as an official language, usually one with a long-standing and widely recognized written standard, such as French, English, Spanish, and Arabic.

The value of a standard is its uniformity, permanence, and inviolability – or the perception thereof. No one expects the metric system to be invalidated by the fall of a French government. The same is true of a standard language, whose permanence and resilience may depend on institutions that outlive their members. These bodies may take the form of academies,[21] branches of government, or quasi-official societies or enterprises that function as keepers of the code and managers of its adaptation to changing circumstances, while maintaining its symbols of national identity. On the selection and elaboration of a dominant speech variety, much has been written within the linguistic subdiscipline of "language planning," especially on the standardization of script, spelling, grammar, and vocabulary.

The Politics of Script. To the Eurocentric mind, it might seem unthinkable that one should specify the script in which an official language should be written. In the Quebec Charter of the French Language, it was sufficient to specify French as the official language. For Canada's aboriginal populations, however, the way some of their languages will be written is of great import. While the Mohawk, Montagnais, and Mi'kmaq (Micmac) use the Roman alphabet, the Inuit, Cree, and Naskapi write in syllabics, as do the inhabitants of the new territory state of Nunavut. The language of these last, however, has also been written in Roman script in Labrador and Greenland. The differences are profound and the arguments powerful – profound because they are not only conflicts between different alphabets (Roman, Cyrillic, and Semitic) but choices between different ways of writing the spoken word: alphabetically, syllabically, or pictorially; powerful because they oppose the force of logic to the weight of tradition.[22]

Having easily and successfully mastered one of the world's most efficient writing systems, with a literacy rate of 100 per cent, why should the Inuit switch to a less efficient and more cumbersome system (Dorais, 1994)? Their logic-based system goes back to the 1840s, when a Wesleyan Methodist missionary, James Evans, set out to devise a writing system suitable to the polysynthetic, agglutinative languages he encountered in Canada. To be efficient, it had to be quick and easy to learn, quick to execute, and easy to read. His successful shorthand-like syllabic script was first applied to Cree. It was later propagated through the Arctic by an Anglican, James Peck. In 1976 it was formalized as the standard script by the Canadian Inuit Tapirisat. It is true that other missionaries had devised other, albeit less-efficient, writing systems adapted to the new languages they encountered. In the seventeenth century, for example, Chrétien Le Clerq had devised a hieroglyphic system to help the Mi'kmaq learn their catechism, a system that lasted until the end of the eighteenth century.

Where a script is associated with other identity markers such as religion or race, it may count as a separate language. What separates Serbian from Croatian is not so much the spoken word but the way it is written, the former in Cyrillic, the latter in Roman letters. It also helps if one writes the language in a different direction. Spoken Yiddish may have been a medieval middle German dialect; writing it in Hebrew script helped make it a distinct language (Fishman, 1991).

In some countries an official script may be elevated to a component of a nation's constitution. The constitution of India, for example, specifies that its official language is Hindi as written in the semi-syllabic script of the sacred Sanskrit texts, that is, in *devanāgari* (*deva* = divine).[23] This specification is understandable in a country whose written languages share dozens of different scripts. Some thirty of these languages use more than a single script; a few appear in as many as five different forms of writing. All this to accommodate over a billion people claiming more than a thousand mother tongues.

The Territoriality of Orthography. The fact that nations may adopt the same script does not mean that they use it in the same way.[24] While using the alphabet in the writing of the national language, countries vary greatly in the logic and coherence of their orthography.

These inconsistent and inefficient orthographic practices were applied to hundreds of non-European languages by the European missionaries who first reduced them to writing. These orthographies proved difficult to dislodge after post-independence language policies were enacted (LePage, 1964). There were two reasons for this problem: first, the already literate elite had a vested interest in retaining the colonial orthographies, and second, those who favoured the maintenance of association with their former colonial masters came into conflict with those who wanted to maximize their national distinctiveness. The policy conflict was particularly heated in countries where the vernacular was an unstandardized and unstable Creole, based on Portuguese, Dutch, Spanish, English, or French. Haiti and the new Republic of the Seychelles provide good examples (Schieffelin and Doucet, 1994). Into this conflict entered the mass literacy movements that followed the UNESCO declaration of the human right to primary education in the mother tongue. Funded by international agencies and non-governmental foundations, experts were expedited to standardize vernaculars for use in schooling. Their consulting linguists inevitably favoured the development of orthographies based on phonological principles (one letter per phoneme) using analogues of the anatomically standardized alphabetic symbols of the International Phonetic Alphabet. The letters were therefore based on the Western-oriented Roman alphabet, the configurations of which belied its ancient Mesopotamian pictographic origins. While Saussure's principle (*l'arbitraire du signe*) that all signs are arbitrary still held, the symbols representing the signs were not equally appropriate.

The more successful they had been in bringing such literacy to the new peoples, the less successful would they be in implanting policies of spelling reform based on consistent phonological principles. Although literacy acts as an asset to language survival, it can also serve as an impediment to policies of language reform, because orthographies become symbols of the territorial, cultural, and national identities of sovereign states (Pohl, 1986–87). To alter the form in which a nation's cultural patrimony exists has been tantamount to tampering with a sacred text. Witness, for example, the centuries-long failures of the most authoritative policies for modest changes to some of the quite obvious and ridiculous anomalies in the spelling of English and French. And in German all efforts to try to de-capitalize the common noun – the *kleinschreiben* policy –have failed. At the same time the successful alphabetization of hundreds of aboriginal languages along phonological principles has endowed them with some of the world's most consistent orthographies – albeit with low levels of literacy. Policy-wise, it would seem that the less that had been written in the language, the greater the potential for an efficient standard orthography.

DEVELOPMENT

The Lexicon. Although the code of a language is most intimately associated with its closed and compact systems of phonology and grammar, it is the open system of its ever-changing lexicon over which a language policy may exercise the most control. The purpose of the policy may be to see that the language gets the words it needs to fill its required functions. Its main concern may be the development of a national language: distinct, authentic, and self-sufficient.

This goal may require a policy of purification, such as the de-anglicization of French in Canada or the de-castilianization of Catalan in Spain (López, 2007).

For fully developed languages such as the official European languages, the first concern has been with national standards. Some of these, including French, English, Spanish, and German, are also polycentric, being the national languages of different sovereign states (Clyne, 1989). There is therefore a restriction in the extent to which deviation from international norms is beneficial (Mackey, 1987).

Policies concerned with the development and maintenance of a language may find it necessary to provide the means for expanding its lexicon in order to meet the increasing needs of a society in constant economical and cultural change. Such augmentation is needed even for languages with more words than can be used.[25] Quebec's language policy, for example, provided for a number of government agencies to manage changes in language usage, including the neologies in public and private publications. These agencies comprised, notably, a French language board, a terminology commission, and an open word bank. Official decisions on terminology, when enacted, were publicly posted in the official gazette. In France, however, new terms were first submitted to the Haut Comité de la langue française, a branch of the prime minister's office, and if approved, were later ratified by law. Such a modern and dynamic language as French in Quebec and France must keep hundreds of lexicographers busy at updating the vocabulary.

One can imagine, therefore, the enormity of the task of putting the lexicon of any of the official Canadian aboriginal languages on a par with that of English or French. Complicating the task are fundamental differences in linguistic structure (Mackey, 1953). Most of these languages being polysynthetic, what counts as a word is not the same as in European languages. It may even be equivalent to a sentence, since subject, verb, and attribute may be simple affixes to a word, so that names for the artifacts of Western civilization have first to be reconceptualized. Doing so has proven easier within the concrete world of science, engineering, medicine, and technology than in the abstract world of law and politics, with its notions of human and property rights. Some aboriginal languages offer many resources for creative lexicon development. The Inuit Cultural Institute at Eskimo Point has spent decades on the development of political, social, and scientific terminologies (published in *Uqaqta*, the institute's house journal).

The structure of other aboriginal languages is open to direct borrowing from other languages, including French and English. In some tribes the degree of acculturation has been so high that half of their everyday vocabulary

has been imported within living memory. It has been said that certain aboriginal languages have to be creolized before they can serve the needs of the
modern world.

The Corpus. Once the new language is properly coded, it must be put to use
by expanding its corpus of available writings while increasing the number
of readers, writers, and speakers in order to implant it as the language of
the nation. A prime example of the process can be seen in the elaboration
of a variable trade jargon (Bazaar Malay) into the national language of
Indonesia. The same language planning processes apply to policies of language survival, revival, and reform (Fodor and Hagège, 1983–94).[26]

In the area of corpus development most aboriginal languages do not enjoy
the advantages of some regional or minor languages with long literary traditions, languages such as Icelandic, Catalan, and Yiddish, for example, whose
literary corpus lends them both autonomy and legitimacy (Fishman, 1991).
In Nunavut, for example, the production of dictionaries, glossaries, books,
and magazines in Inuktitut has been promoted for decades, but it will be a
long time before this official language can replace English or French as a
medium of secondary and post-secondary education. The same can be said
for official aboriginal languages in the Canadian Northwest (Cree, Tlicho,
Kutchin, Slavey, and Chipewyan). Meanwhile the aboriginal populations
continue to be schooled in English or French, giving access to a corpus sufficient to attain the highest levels of learning. As a result, the population
had to become diglossic, using the prestige language for some functions (administration, commerce, and secondary education) and the Native language
for others (home, community, and primary schooling). In spite of the high
ideological status bestowed on the Native tongue, the economic well-being
and development of these populations may continue to depend on the use
of a prestige language.

Yet no matter what the policy, its viability depends on the context in
which the language is used. If it is little used, it is soon forgotten. Ultimately,
it is the people who use the language who determine its usefulness, and
hence its vitality and status (Mackey, 1976b).

Functions

The prestige of a language is a function of how much it has been used, for
what, by whom, and for how long. A long history of being used for most
purposes in the most important domains of society enhances the status of
a language.

DOMAINS OF USE

Language use is most amenable to language policy, especially within domains that can be regulated – the courts, the military, the schools, public administration, and the like. In which institutions of the state, therefore, is the other language (or languages) to function and to what extent – in education, public administration, the legislature, the courts? Is the presence of both languages governed by the principle of parity? Is there a bilingual bureaucratic infrastructure to make this possible? Policies will differ as to the domains in which a language may, must, or may not be used. For example, the Quebec Charter of the French Language stipulates that French must be used in most domains and that English may be used in some domains (e.g., certain schools) in specified circumstances. Under Canadian language policy, however, either French or English may be used in areas under federal jurisdiction, where services are provided in both languages according to personal preference (Corbeil, 1987).

In unregulated domains, the main determinants of language use have been the cohesion of kith and kin (family and friends) and the need to communicate outside the home for one's survival or well-being (McConnell and Gendron, 1993–98). These two basic impulses interact within language boundaries and beyond the cultural horizons of their inhabitants. In the political context they become the territorial and communicative imperatives that determine the implementation and outcome of a language policy (Mackey, 2001). These in turn depend on the status, function, and prestige of each of the languages.[27]

The distinction between prestige, function, and status is like the difference between past, present, and future. The interplay between them is both cyclical and cumulative. The prestige of a language increases its status, which in turn multiplies its functions, which increase its prestige, reinforces its status, and so forth (Mackey, 1989). The prestige of Latin, for example, maintained its status and function as the language of learning in Europe for centuries after the fall of the Roman Empire. After French gained its status as the official language of Quebec, it could not have performed its functions in all the domains of modern life without the prestige of a corpus accumulated by the language over hundreds of years. It is because of such prestige that so many former colonies have maintained the official status of the imperial languages of their colonial masters, giving the educated elite of these new states access to an immense corpus of information, knowledge, and power. In most African states this language is French (16), English (13), Portuguese (4), or Spanish (1). Some states maintain, along with the colonial language, Arabic and/or an African tongue as official languages. In addition, some states accord a regional status to their most important languages. Nigeria, for example, has 15 of these national languages; South Africa, 11; and Senegal, 6.[28]

To raise the status of one of these national languages, one must add to its functions.[29] Each function may mean the elaboration of a corpus. The prerequisite is a standard writing system and a relevant lexicon, which implies the development of a normative terminology. Changing the language of the law, for example, from English or French to a language such as Inuktitut, Wolof, or Sinhalese can be a monumental task (Cooray, 1985). In England and France the changeover from Latin was the work of many generations (Mackey, 1994a).

STATUS AND FUNCTION

Each societal function affected by a language policy may carry a directive on the use of the official language. May it be used or must it be used? The answer may depend on whether the use is internal or external. According to Quebec's language policy, for example, certain English institutions may use English and French internally but must be prepared to serve the public in French. Or the uses may be specified in regulations covering such functions as administrative directives, official letters, advertising, sales, and services (Bouchard and Bourhis, 2002). Some provisions on language use in some countries may also be subsumed in policies of wider import, such as those affecting public safety and consumer protection. Compliance appears in such directives as owners' manuals, directions for the use of medicines, equipment, and household appliances, public signs, and safety signals.

The fact that a language may or must be used does not mean that it will be. Except at the most rudimentary level, a language without lore can hardly function as the language of learning. No language can function beyond the level of its development. One must ask, therefore, to what extent the policy provides for the development of the language to a level consistent with its attributed functions. What corpus does it have, or how will one be developed and managed?

Patterns

Language policy depends on the geolinguistic and sociolinguistic contexts in which it must operate within the demographic and identity patterns of the populations and their degree of interdependence and belonging.

DEMOGRAPHIC PATTERNS

The geographical configurations of countries are rarely congruent with language boundaries, so that one nation's dominant language may be its neighbour's minority dialect, as with, for example, German-speakers in Belgium, France, and Italy. Or two countries may share the same minority language when the boundary between them splits a speech community in two, as is the case where Basque and Catalan straddle the French border. The mobility, intermingling, and partition of populations, especially during the past centuries, has increased the number of minority languages.[30] All languages, no matter how great the total number of their speakers, rate as minority languages somewhere in the world, along with indigenous, trans-national, colonial, and immigrant languages. Borders are becoming a legacy of the past. They seldom suit everyone who must live within them; the problem is to find policies that make most people feel at home.

If the many languages of the world reflect great diversity, the same can also be said for the relatively few states that harbour them. Sovereign states vary widely in size, shape, wealth, cultural diversity, population, and political system. The interplay of these variations determines the potential and feasibility of language policies. The territoriality afforded by large countries, coupled with their population mobility, may make language conflict more tractable than in small countries where face-to-face encounters are more probable. Countries such as Canada, the United States, Russia, and India have the potential to accommodate a number of viable, partly autonomous entities (Alesina and Spolaore, 2003). How they do so depends on their political structure and dominant ideology. States with federal structures where culture and education are under the jurisdiction of partly autonomous provinces have language policy potentials different from those of states where such matters are under central control.

In the past century the tendency has been, not for the fusion of states (as exemplified by the reunion of the two Germanys and the two Yemens), but toward their division into self-determined sovereign states. Yet there may be a limit to the number of languages even a large state can accommodate (Mackey, 1991). The constitution of India has been able to endow several states with a distinct official language, but it has left dozens of other languages without status. As for the newly created smallest countries, their viability has already become increasingly dependent on the free flow of goods and commodities and upon the protection of supra-national institutions whose number has also increased during the past century. Such bodies, as well, can only function in a limited number of languages. For each community covered by a language policy, one must therefore ascertain the number of speakers of each language and their location, distribution, territoriality, and extraterritoriality.

Number. How many speakers of each language does the policy cover? That depends on who counts as a speaker (Mackey, 2003). Counts based on mother tongue ("language first acquired") are not always the same as those on "language spoken." In Canada, according to the 2001 census, 59 per cent of the population claimed English as their mother tongue, while it was the language most often used for almost 68 per cent (Statistics Canada, 2002).

The regional bilinguality of the population must also be accounted for in relation to its diglossic behaviour; otherwise bilingual services based on mother tongue may be instituted in areas where they may never be used. For such areas, language laws often stipulate vague numerical quotas couched in such phrases as "where numbers warrant" or "sufficient demand" or more specifically as mother-tongue percentages, as was the case for the proposed bilingual districts in Canada and in Finland (McRae, 1978).

Location. Speakers of the same language may live together within areas differing widely in size and population, forming patterns of language distribution not always contiguous with political boundaries within the state. A template of these superimposed on a country's political map reveals both the spread and number of different groups that may in some way have to be accommodated. The North American language area, for example, was occupied by three European colonial powers, which displaced hundreds of Native American languages. Although each created separate federations (Mexico, the United States, and Canada), their frontiers were not international or intra-national language boundaries. Subsequently and especially over the past two centuries, millions of increasingly mobile immigrants have transformed North American population patterns (Mackey, 2004).

Distribution. The problems of language policy provisions for widely scattered and small, isolated populations are different from those of populations concentrated in big cities, as attested, for example, by the difficulties of establishing bilingual districts in a vast country such as Canada (McRae, 1978). Although ethnolinguistic nucleation is a characteristic of all multilingual cities, policies differ widely in their tolerance for ethnic segregation or its promotion (Mackey, 1985, 2000a). In some cities, people of the same language have their own quarters with their own public institutions, as has long been the case with the English-speaking population of Montreal. Yet if the national policy is based on proportion rather than number, a small rural population may have more language services than their more numerous urban compatriots with a smaller proportion of the total population of a large city. Although Europe's seemingly large Muslim population of 12 million is a relatively small percentage of the 375 million total, concentration in a few cities has motivated policies of restriction, such as symbolic interdiction of the headscarf in public schools and of the importation of spouses for arranged marriages.

Territoriality. In traditional societies, be they agricultural, pastoral, or nomadic, land has been linked to survival, since it ensured both life and a living. Three concepts of territoriality have affected language policy: the primacy of the people (ethnicity), the primacy of God (religion), and the primacy of the state (nationalism). The ethnic territoriality of antiquity ceded to the religious territoriality of the late Middle Ages (*cujus regio, ejus religio*) to the national territoriality of the modern age (*cujus regio, ejus lingua*) (Cornish, 1936). Yet policies based on each of these principles have persisted in Africa, the Middle East, and Europe. Their coexistence has been the source of fundamental and intractable conflict. Linking land and language, however, can be the basis of a policy of accommodation. Failure to do so may spell the difference between peace and lasting conflict. Notorious in this respect was the redrawing of the map of Europe after the First World War. The flagrant injustices – vengeful, opportunistic, and perfunctory – of the cartography of peace resulted in a patchwork of countries, which in Central Europe and the Middle East left a third of the population with the status of language minorities. The lasting consequences darkened the history of the past century, bequeathing a legacy of conflicts that have remained unresolved.

In sovereign states with two or more official languages, there is always the question of deciding to whom the policy applies – to all citizens no matter where they live or to some citizens depending on where they live. In other words, does the citizen adapt to the language of the locality (the principle of territoriality), or does the state accommodate the language of the citizen (the principle of personality)? If a bilingual state invests in bilingual services on demand, it may choose to limit these to places where such demand exists (Cartwright, 1977). The remapping of an area can enhance language rights or it can eliminate them, as did the merging in 2002 of some sixty Quebec municipalities, some with English-speaking majorities, into cities with large French-speaking majorities, thus eliminating their bilingual status (Bouchard and Bourhis, 2002). A backlash of de-mergers in 2006 returned the control of some municipalities to their English-speaking majorities.

Extraterritoriality: *The Power of the Diaspora.* Different types of geolinguistic segmentation may generate different language policies, both at home and abroad. Intersections of land and language boundaries create territorial patterns of demolinguistic split, overlap, overflow, diffusion, or fragmentation that divide communities speaking the same language or implant them in larger populations speaking a different language. The resulting language communities turn out to be binational, transnational, multinational, international, or intra-national (Mackey, 1988). These different geolinguistic patterns determine language policies such as those affecting Basque in Spain and France (split), Dutch and French in Belgium (overlap), German in northern Italy (overflow), Chinese in Southeast Asia (diffusion), Native languages in North America (fragmentation), and French in western Canada (implantation). Some of these implanted communities can interact and coalesce into diaspora with more natives abroad than residents at home, maintaining, through a common language, permanent intergenerational links between persons and places. Corsicans, Hungarians, and Armenians, to name only a few, are among the better known (Jaffe, 1999). Some have become powerful and wealthy enough to affect the policies of their native land. They can remain free from the best and worse consequences of their policies back home, while promoting in their host country a relevant foreign policy, often contrary to its own self-interest.[31]

IDENTITY PATTERNS

Language policies may have to take such realities into account, especially in countries with increasingly plurilingual admixtures and multiple identities. In such countries, not only do people belong to a number of different groups for different purposes, but they belong to each with a different degree of intensity, both as regards commitment and investment. Identity becomes dependent on the structure of the community, its stratification, the degrees of differentiation, and group solidarity. One must therefore distinguish between the types of identities and their dynamics.

Types. Language identities in mixed populations have ranged from the conflictual to the integrative. In the case of conflictual identities, conflict and confusion are equally likely in mixed populations living in an atmosphere of Herdian nationalism. Identifying a language with a people has engendered long-lasting policies extending beyond the borders of the state (Breton, 1998). The effects have been especially dramatic for speech communities living in disputed borderlands. In Alsace and Lorraine, for example, the identity crisis suffered by the inhabitants between 1870 and 1914 has been well documented and vividly illustrated in the works of such regional writers as Hans Arp, Iwan Goll, and Maurice Barrès (Bendrath, 2003; Mackey, 1993).

With cases of integrative identities, different allegiances may sometimes be merged into a hierarchy of belonging or dispersed among different language groups as circumstances warrant. Identity hierarchies may be ascendant (e.g., first a Montrealer, secondly a Quebecer, and thirdly a Canadian) or, inversely, top-down (a Canadian first, etc.) (Oakes, 2001).

Circumstantial identities depend on the language groups with which the persons must associate, through marriage, employment, schooling, or spare-time activities (Djité, 2006). They may include diglossic identities imposed by the structure of a bilingual community, whereby people belong to one language group for some social functions such as work and sports and to another for other functions such as schooling and religion. The type of language policy appropriate for such populations may depend on their bilinguality, whether only the elites are bilingual, the majority, the minority, or both. If the entire population is bilingual, a policy of providing services in both languages may be more symbolic than functional. If their situation is one of stable diglossia with bilingualism, it remains redundant as long as people keep on using each language for its own purposes. Changing these purposes becomes an exercise in behaviour modification and results in a decrease in the bilinguality of succeeding generations (Mackey, 2002).

In immigrant populations, language policy may have to adapt to different stages of assimilation – from incipient to progressive bilingualism and then to integral bilingualism, diglossia, or residual bilingualism (Mackey, 2005). At any one of these stages the immigrant population may be faced with a policy of language transfer (assimilation) or one of language maintenance (multiculturalism). While the first is typical of the US federal policies, the second is associated with the Canadian multicultural policies.

In addition to the association of people with a language are the differences in the number of links between their language and their ancestry, culture, race, and religion. Each of these may override any amount of language loyalty. But each may also thrive independent of language in varying levels of adherence, as attested by the millions of people who boast Irish ancestry (notably on the 17th of March), and celebrate it in complete ignorance of the Irish language. Yet the practice of a common language with everything linked to it may comprise a legitimate ethnic identity: one people, one language, one religion, and one culture, to the exclusion of all others. These practices forge mutually re-enforcing bonds of belonging that can make language conflicts intractable.

These language-related bondings help explain why the large number of languages (some 6,500) is surpassed by an even larger number of ethnicities (more than 13,000) (Dalby, 2000). Just as a religion may be practised in different ethnicities, any language or language variety can be associated with several ethnic or tribal groups, each with its own ancestry, history, culture, customs, and religious practices. Some 200 African languages, for example, are shared by some 3,000 ethnic groups totalling a population of more than 700 million people segmented into some fifty-five sovereign states. In most of these sovereign states there has been a latent, enduring, and sometimes intractable conflict between ethnic and national identities. In some countries (e.g., Rwanda) ethnic identity has become an evil that has to be outlawed, since it has led, and could again lead, to ethnic cleansing and genocide. Yet national identities and linguistic nationalism whose theoretical underpinnings go as far back as Johann Herder (1744–1803) have provided explanations of the great identity crises and genocidal disasters of our age (Myhill, 2006). When people emigrate, as they do in increasing numbers, only the strongest components of their ethnicity may survive. Emigrants may be more attached to what they believe than to where they were born or where they live. Their host country may have to accommodate both their religion and the language in which they practise it.

It may therefore be necessary for a language policy to accommodate to degrees of ethnicity ranging from a vague consciousness of identity to an all-pervading pattern of social behaviour, dominated by religious practice, endogamy, ethnic attitude, value scales, learning tradition, and codes of interpersonal and intergroup interaction.

Dynamics. In the evolution of identities, perceptions of commonality that bind together a society and each of its institutions – family, school, church, and a multiplicity of associated interest groups – are by their nature impermanent. They evolve over time at a rate and intensity determined by changes in the surrounding economic, political, and social contexts (Schmidt, 2000). Identity is also the story a society tells about itself, often including that of its struggle to become a nation. In Quebec this story began to change after the Quiet Revolution, and consequently, a Quebec identity had to be reconstructed (Létourneau, 2000). The contexts of settlement may favour the development of bilingual identities such as those that evolved in North America – Norwegian-Americans, Italian-Canadians, Pennsylvania-Germans, Franco-Ontarians, and many more (Ureland, 2001; Mackey, 2004). Language policy may have to take account of changes in these double identities.[32]

Language identities may also become politicized. Language differences may be a leading justification for a political party (e.g., the Bloc québécois in the Canadian Parliament). They may also be exploited to advance a political agenda – conservatism, socialism, irredentism (Calvet, 1999). Some plurilingual societies are dominated by an uncertain sense of belonging to different societal groupings with vague boundaries and mutually modifying practices. This very vagueness can be exploited to favour any grouping or "-ism." A sense of belonging can thus be manipulated in favour of one language group, under the banner of national or ethnic identity. As a result, an increasingly heterogeneous population can be placed in an unwelcome dilemma, splitting families, friends, and associates.[33]

In any language minority, native-born or immigrant, language policy depends on its own degree of politicization. Its dominant faction may at times be headed by a charismatic leader or professional ethnic, leading a militant minority within a minority, whose activities, sometimes intimidating, can produce effects greater than the numbers would warrant. The activities of rival factions can often be observed in a judicious sampling of the ethnic press. In multinational states, language policy may depend on political ideology – nationalism, liberalism, or communism. For Marxist regimes, the operative factors have not been linguistic, ethnic, or cultural but, rather, the conflicts between social and economic classes. China, the former Yugoslavia, and the USSR, accorded formal linguistic and territorial recognition to ethnic populations, large and small, in the form of autonomous regions, republics, provinces, communes, and boroughs. These concessions were often top-down ideological decisions taken on behalf of the presumed beneficiaries.

In a process of legitimization, sovereign states and their components have been increasingly interactive, the state becoming more proactive in regulating its national and international economy, thus making all else, including language, subservient to what it perceives as the public interest (Habermas, 1975). When decisions are taken on behalf of any language community, the question arises about the legitimacy of the representation. What counts for a legitimate representation of the language community? Is there division between native-language speakers and non-speakers, between second-language speakers and would-be speakers? Are the claims of each of these groups legitimate?

For makers of language policy, multilingual societies can also pose important questions of classification. Who counts as a language user? Who decides? Who identifies whom in this continuum of parameters with differing degrees of belonging, belief, and behaviour? Is self-identity the solution, and if so, how will it operate? Does the right to be culturally different from the majority suppose the right to be the same? Does categorization of people by language and culture penalize the bilinguals who belong to two different cultures? For answers, people have turned to the courts.[34]

DEGREES OF BELONGING AND DEPENDENCE

Degrees of Belonging. One of the thorniest problems in devising a language policy is to find out who belongs where and to avoid putting people in

permanent categories where they do not belong and refuse to enter. People
have been classed by ethnic origin, mother tongue, main home language, language best-known, language most used. Policies based on assumptions that
everyone wants to keep the ancestral tongue or that those living in the same
place will speak the same language or that they will shift to the speech of
the majority have often turned out to be ill-founded and untenable. People
may react badly to authorities who brand them with unwanted labels that
stick to them for the rest of their lives. One of these is a person's ethnicity; it
is essentially a construct that may or may not include the forms or functions
of a distinct language (Fought, 2006; Zelinsky, 2001).

Within the borders of a single sovereign state, the multiplicity, complexity,
and dynamics of belonging may vary greatly from one area to another. In isolated, quasi-tribal areas, belonging may be simple, stable, and all-pervasive;
in the large cities it may be complex, unstable, and multi-dimensional. With
the worldwide acceleration in the mobility of populations, the identity of
land and language becomes less and less tenable (Maurais and Morris,
2003). Such is especially the case in countries where most people no longer
live in the places where they were born but in large plurilingual cities whose
populations have become increasingly heterogeneous (Mackey, 2000a).[35]
This process occurs when rich countries with retiring and unreplenished
populations are beholden to poor countries with many young people eager
to get in. It is not surprising that societies with such admixtures of diverse
and changing identities should lend themselves less and less to policies based
on traditional Cartesian categories and more to the fractals of complexity
theory, whereby, within an apparent homogeneity, a number of small differences emerge and coalesce into new and dynamic entities: language-related
movements, ethnic revolts, and new elites (Mackey, 1994b; Gladwell, 2002).

Adherence to each of these multiple belongings is far from equal, lending
to each relevant language a different degree of support. For some speakers of an ancestral tongue, the language may represent everything that was
first seen, felt, heard, and thought in the intimacy of their homes, to the
extent that the language takes on an inherent value with its own right to
survival. Maori, for example, as the ancestral tongue of the first inhabitants,
thus developed into the symbol of a cultural and political revolt culminating
with its enactment in 1957 as an official language of New Zealand. When
a common language is all that is left after other markers of distinction,
such as creed and culture, have vanished, it takes on an added degree of
importance – as, indeed, it did in Quebec after the Quiet Revolution. The
degree of language loyalty may correlate with the stages of assimilation in
some immigrant groups, but not for all languages or for all communities, as

comparisons of Italian communities in Montreal, Toronto, and Vancouver have demonstrated. Language policy must account for degrees of language loyalty ranging from a vague association to an intense commitment to the fortunes of the language.

Degrees of Dependence. Language policy comparison must also take into account the economic, cultural, and political development of each constituency affected by the give-and-take of the policy. In terms of economic dependence, a self-sufficient community is better placed to maintain the status of its own language than is one that must use another language in order to survive and prosper. Subservient populations have long been brought into rich countries to do work their own citizens dislike. The workers, many illiterate, have come from countries with impoverished rural areas. In the United States of the early twentieth century these were Sicilians. In the west the workers were Mexican or Chinese. In the east they were Puerto Ricans, especially between 1950 and 1990. No policy protected the languages of these workers. On the contrary, they were expected to adapt and assimilate. Their economic advancement depended on their mastery of English, since they had no economy of their own to promote their culture (Huebner and Davis, 1999).

With regard to political development, language minorities experienced in self-government and political affairs are more likely to obtain and maintain equitable language policies. In this context, it is enlightening to compare the language policies of the former constituencies of the Habsburg Empire with those of the former components of the Russian and Ottoman empires, heirs to a different political heritage. The Habsburg Empire was a *Rechtsstaat*, one that is based on the rule of law, a crucial element in the creation of a democratic state; this legacy, having survived intervening dictatorial regimes, facilitated a transition to democracy. Such was the case, for example, in Hungary, Slovenia, Poland, and the Czech Republic, which by the end of the millennium had become independent and successful states with their own laws and official languages.

In terms of cultural autonomy, literate and educated groups are more likely to obtain policies that favour their language. In contradistinction to the waves of Hispanic immigrants who preceded them to the United States, those in the first wave of Cuban refugees were hardly *braceros* (labourers). As members of the displaced Cuban business and professional elite, they were in a position to create their own economy and social services, including schools and banks, and through political action to obtain, in 1973, official status for their language in the Florida county in which most had settled

(Beebe and Mackey, 1990). After the influx of the less-cultivated second wave, however, this status was revoked through the Dade County Anti-Bilingual Ordinance (80/128) of 1980 and later by the state's constitutional referendum (the 11th amendment) in 1988, whereby English was declared the official language of Florida. Other states followed suit. For example, at the federal election of 7 November 2006 the majority of Arizona's voters supported the ballot proposition to make English the official language of their state.

CONCLUSION

In sum, comparing policies is not like comparing languages: since policies are not interrelated and evolving systems of systems, they cannot share the typologies of language. Yet they must share the same contexts of their social environment. It is only within these contexts – historical, ethnic, geographic, ideological, economic, cultural, and political – that a language policy can be evaluated.

APPENDIX: AN OVERVIEW OF THE CHAPTER

Introduction
Problematics
Multidisciplinary Becomes Interdisciplanary
The Comparative Method
  What Are We Comparing?
    The Meanings of Language
    The Meanings of Policy
  Types of Comparison
    Time Frames
    Scope
      How Many Languages and Which Ones?
      How Many Provisions for Each?
    Content: Thematic Comparison
      Forms
      Functions
      Language Users in Social Systems
  Questions of Comparability
    The Structure of Institutions
      Jurisdiction

Size and Status
Focus of Comparison
Quantification of Components
Language Forms
Language Functions
Language Behaviour
Comparing the Policy Components
Motives
Political Motives
Cultural Motives
Economic Motives
Objectives
Policies for Whom and for What?
The Politicization of Principles
Conflicting Objectives
Decisions
Comparing Policy Enactments
Promotion and Imposition
Interdiction
Tolerance
Accommodation
Changing Language Policies
Comparing the Language Components
Forms
Identification
Standardization
The Politics of Script
The Territoriality of Orthography
Development
The Lexicon
The Corpus
Functions
Domains of Use
Status and Function
Patterns
Demographic Patterns
Number
Location
Distribution
Territoriality

    Extraterritoriality: The Power of the Diaspora
  Identity Patterns
    Types
    Dynamics
  Degrees of Belonging and Dependence
    Degrees of Belonging
    Degrees of Dependence
Conclusion

NOTES

1 Except perhaps under a thought-controlling totalitarian regime with a policy to exclude all languages save one of its own making, such as the fictional "Newspeak" of the Orwellian state.

2 A family, for example, motivated by an attachment to its ancestral tongue, may decide to use it as the exclusive language of the home. Or it may embrace as an objective the survival of more than one language by adopting its own formula of home bilingualism, such as the Grammont policy of *une personne; une langue* (Mackey, 2005).

3 In this respect, it is enlightening to compare the workings of the Canadian federal (Laurendeau-Dunton) commission and those of the more focused Quebec (Gendron) commission in the use each made of its respective research division. It is likewise instructive to compare the failed attempt of the first Bilingual Districts Advisory Board in applying the letter of the law with the equally unsuccessful adventures of the more politicized second board in interpreting its intent (McRae, 1978).

4 Modern linguistics was really an outgrowth of comparative philology, whose data were largely corpus-oriented. For reasons of scientific rigour, a new "science of linguistics" restricted its orientation to the description of codes. It was only in the middle of the past century that university departments of linguistics started to proliferate, especially in the United States, and the few universities (such as Harvard) that already had departments of "comparative philology" began to change their names to "linguistics" (Hoenigswald, 1973).

5 The former refers to any code (biological, electronic, chemical, visual, or acoustic). It includes that sociobiological, innate, or acquired trait of a species (from hives of bees to pods of whales) essential to the species' social survival. For there can be no society without language and no language without society – animal or human. Human language, however, is a specific system of conceptual symbols (French: *langue*), a code of intercommunication and conduct within and between generations of people associated in groups ranging from families to nations. It is a unique

segmentation and codification of a group's conceptual universe, and as such, it is the most inclusive component of the group's culture and the most exclusive marker of its identity (Mackey, 1985).

6 The meanings of "policy," however, have been progressively distorted by appendages of convenience. When spin doctors rebrand themselves as "policy analysts," the word becomes part of a euphemism for their stock-in-trade, propaganda. Since the turn of the century, the word seems to have joined the ranks of what Uwe Pörksen has called *plastische Wörter* (plastic words), whose meanings can be moulded to suit the purpose of the user ("Don't ask why. It's corporate policy.").

7 To promote comparison of home language policies, the *Bilingual Family Newsletter* has been issued by Multilingual Matters for more than a quarter-century.

8 To this end, the research division of the Canadian Royal Commission on Bilingualism and Biculturalism (Laurendeau-Dunton Commission) added a comparative studies department which eventually produced voluminous, and as yet unpublished, reports on the language policies of officially bilingual countries, notably Belgium, Finland, Switzerland, and South Africa.

9 Leclerc's inventories (1989 and 1994) treat US language policies as those of its constituent states, cities, and other jurisdictions where such policies, if any, are to be found. Canadian federal and provincial language policies can be easily compared with those of over 350 other jurisdictions by visiting the website of CIRAL (Centre international de recherche en aménagement linguistique). The policy descriptions include regular updates, one of the latest appearing in mid-2009.

10 Particularly Papers 17 (Alexander Hamilton) and 56 (James Madison), which explain why local administration of cultural matters and public morality is most fitting for the governance of a heterogeneous people with different religions and cultures, who have settled in separate regions to practise their own customs and ways of life. The idea of moral federalism of this type goes back, perhaps, to an act of the English Parliament, of which some of the Founders or their forebears were undoubtedly cognizant. It was the Act of Toleration (1689), whereby decisions on religion-related matters were left to the discretion of local administrations. It was such a principle that enabled about half the states to have their own language policies, although not all have been equally tolerant of language diversity. Even at the federal level, in times of war and perceived threats, politicians have practised the politics of fear, where calculated scares become policy components exploiting inherent fears of the unknown (languages included) coupled with ignorance of comparable probabilities, thereby consolidating control over public attitudes and behaviour.

11 This expansion of English is not attributable to a British policy of English language promotion. On the contrary, save for a minority of militant pro-Europeans, there has been a relative indifference to European affairs and, in spite of an increase in the cosmopolitanism of the population, a decline in the study of foreign languages.

(In 2003 the foreign language requirement was dropped in England and Wales for pupils over fourteen.)

12 Operating systems were provided in 2004 by Microsoft for some thirty profitable languages; other languages, such as Quechua in 2006, were added as they became profitable. These did not include languages such as Welsh, Basque, Icelandic, and Hungarian or any of the hundreds of other written languages.

13 The policy may permit the application of the personality principle in certain limited and well-specified areas of use, as was the case in certain parts of the Austro-Hungarian Empire – covering a dozen national languages – where the use of German or Czech became optional in certain regional courts, school councils, and electoral districts (Lukas, 1908).

14 The Canadian policy of self-determination subsumes such collective rights, including a code of written laws in the local language. In 2003, for example, the Tlicho nation, after half a century of negotiating with the federal and provincial governments, was accorded (on 23 August) its own part of the Canadian Northwest (an area the size of Switzerland), with jurisdiction over its language, culture, and economy.

15 Such a conflict between language policies helps explain the vacillations in Spain's treatment of the Native American nations that fell under its imperial rule. The policy of the state was military conquest, subjugation, conversion, submission, and castilianization. Since the process required the collaboration of the church, the Council of the Indies in 1523 accorded the Crown the right to propose its own candidates for church posts and to pay their salaries. While the objective of the Crown was castilianization, that of the church was conversion, which meant maintenance of the Native languages. And by 1580, in the Laws of the Indies, the church was able to insert a stipulation whereby, to qualify for duty, future friars had to study the indigenous language of the area to which they were posted. Meanwhile, in 1562 the Council of Trent had made Latin the exclusive and compulsory language of the Catholic liturgy.

16 In order even to create a federation, the languages of their component peoples may have to be accorded official recognition. For example, agreement on a provisional constitution for postwar Iraq was only reached after the Kurdish language was accorded official status along with Arabic. Language protection of Kurdish is also a condition for Turkey's eventual admission to the European Union. In 2003 some three hundred Moroccan schools launched the teaching of Tawazight, the regional Berber tongue; it was scheduled to become available to all schools by the year 2013.

17 Yet irredental language movements have long been ignored by nation-states; their proponents are brushed aside as unrealistic complainers "Steaming up a lamentation of an ancient tale of wrong / A tale of little meaning, though the words are strong" – that is, until they become politicized and some of their most extreme factions remain intractable.

18 In 1492, when Queen Isabel of Castile, while showing the bishop of Ávila her copy
    of the first Spanish grammar (dedicated to her by its author, Antonio de Nebrija),
    asked what it was good for, he reportedly replied that it could be an instrument for
    building an empire in which the word of the monarch could be heeded throughout
    her realms.

19 Many regional varieties of vulgar Latin sprung up over the centuries in all regions
    of Italy and other parts of Europe covered by the Roman Empire. Any one of these
    could have become a national language. Those that did were classed as languages,
    downgrading those that did not as merely derivative or corrupt dialects of the stan-
    dard national language (Coluzzi, 2008).

20 Eskimo (Inuktitut) used to be seen as a language. Yet with the advent of territorial
    self-determination, its dialects could be considered as distinct languages – in the
    Eastern Arctic, Ualinirmiut (with three dialects); in Labrador, Laapatuamiut; in
    Keewatin, Kivallirmiut (five dialects); in the Central Arctic, Qitirmiut (two dia-
    lects); and in the Western Arctic, Ualinirmiut (three dialects) – all distinct from
    Alaskan (Iñunpiactun) and Greenlandic (Kalaallutut).

21 After the founding of the first academies, the Italian Accademia della Crusca
    (1582) and the Académie française (1635), others followed suit, for the standard-
    ization of Spanish (1713), Swedish (1786), Hungarian (1830), Basque (1918),
    Hebrew (1953), and other languages. There have even been academies for each
    contending variety, as has been the case for Norwegian and Arabic. In the past
    century, quasi-official bodies were founded for the standardization of more than
    a hundred languages, including Turkish, Greek, Frisian, and Dutch, to name only
    these (Fodor and Hagège, 1983–94).

22 A stroke of the pen to represent a syllable is more efficient than the forming of the
    configurations of two letters to achieve the same results. For a simple presentation
    of the history and geography of the different scripts, see Rogers, 2005.

23 After the separation of the Muslim north, it became a political necessity to specify
    a script that excluded both the Urdu variety, written in the Arabic script of the
    Koran, and also Hindustani, scripted in the Roman alphabet of the Christian West.
    Compare this policy with the Soviet policy of alphabetization (Sebba, 2006).

24 While English is claimed as a national language in Britain, the United States, and
    Canada, minor spelling differences between them, plus a few odd words and ex-
    pressions, may be all that remains to mark their national distinctiveness. This lack
    of difference poses a problem for Canadian policy-makers who may wish to show
    the Americans that they are not British and the British that they are not Americans.

25 The rate of growth in the lexicon of these languages (hundreds of words a year in
    the case of English) coupled with their rate of diffusion, frequency, range, avail-
    ability, and coverage, may also differ from one country to the next. In this respect,
    American English is seen as more dynamic that British English.

26 These processes created for each of the languages a demand for its own lexicographers, grammarians, and other specialists in the language sciences. To coordinate their work, agencies had to be created in places such as Catalonia, Quebec, Ireland, Belgium, and Friesland, to name only these. The Basque government even created a ministry of language policy reflecting the relative importance accorded to a distinct language as an instrument of political identity.

27 The status (from Latin: *stare* = to stand) of a language – its standing, as it were – may be established by custom, consensus, or law. Its functions (from Latin: *facere* = to do) – what one does with it; that is, its actual use – may vary in mode, degree, and intensity according to the competence and performance of its users. Its prestige (from Latin: *prestigium* = impression) – what one sees in it – depends on what it has to show: its corpus of writings, for example, which can be seen in the world's great libraries, and its book and media markets, representing what has been done and what can be done with the language.

28 Both these status categories – "official" and "national" – exclude hundreds of minority languages whose recognition can only depend on a state's compliance with international conventions, such as the UN Declaration of the Rights of Persons Belonging to National, Ethnic, Religious or Language Minorities (art. 27, 1994), on anti-discrimination policies or special language status, or through cultural policies promoting diversity within a context of population mobility and globalization.

29 The difference between domain and function is the distinction between "where" and "for what," between place and purpose, between institutions and activities.

30 A Kurdish population of some 30 million speakers, for example, is partitioned between Iraq, Iran, Syria, and Turkey, where they have had the status of a "non-people."

31 In 2007 the Armenian-American lobby had its century-old case against Turkey, a crucial US ally, placed on the agenda of the American Congress. The Croatian diaspora, after masterminding and financing (at over $30 million) a separatist agenda in its homeland, was accorded in 1991 extraterritorial voting rights and parliamentary representation (10 out of the 120 seats). In some federations such activities have become illegal. In 2004 Hungary had to put an end to them in order to gain admission to the European Union.

32 In the long run it may have to accommodate to the emergence of new identities resulting from the fusion or fission of different language communities (A, B, C, etc.) either by amalgamation (A + B > C), division (A > B + C), incorporation (A + B > A), or proliferation (A > ABCD). For example, part of the English-speaking population of Montreal, linguistically unqualified for jobs in the public sector and unhappy with its new minority status, instead of emigrating to English-speaking provinces, decided in 1998 to group together as the Greater Quebec Movement, whose policy was linguistic assimilation into the French-speaking majority through such means as having their children schooled in French.

33 In 2003 the Quebec National Assembly unanimously confirmed that Quebec
was a "nation." That same week of 30 October the federal Parliament in Ottawa
voted that it was not. In 2006 the latter body changed its mind after the new
Conservative minority government, on 27 November, upstaged the separatist Bloc
québécois by moving that Quebec be recognized as a nation "within Canada." All
parties voted in favour – albeit somewhat grudgingly, with 16 No votes. Since aboriginal tribes had also been recognized as nations, no one seemed sure what it all
meant (see note 6 on plastic words). Although the bill changed very little in fact, it
proved to have been an astute political master stroke whose electoral consequences
were felt even within the separatist heartland of the Bloc, where less than a year
later, on 17 September, the most unilingual French-speaking riding in the country
voted overwhelmingly Conservative in the federal by-election of 2007.

34 In Quebec, for example, when the provincial administration in 1988 deprived the
city of Rosemère of its bilingual status, on the basis that its English mother-tongue
population had fallen below the required 50 per cent, the new categorization was
challenged in court. After studying the case, the court ordered that the status be
reinstated on the grounds that the state had no right to categorize citizens permanently on the basis of such arbitrary criteria and inflexible rules, which deprive
people of the right of multiple association, since "a person can be part English and
part French, and successively more one than the other" (*Alliance for Language
Communities vs H.G. Québec*, 1990, RSQ 2622, Reeves). Meanwhile, the government itself remained under continuous pressure from militant language groups to
apply the letter of the law.

35 By the year 2000 at least a quarter of the population was foreign-born in the
largest cities of North America and Europe, including Toronto, Vancouver, and
New York. Population projections of 57 per cent foreign-born by 2017 were made
for Rotterdam. In that city, as well as in San Francisco and other rich cities, about
half the school population had a home language other than the one in which
they were being taught. During the same period, researchers were able to identify 350 different languages in the homes of London's schoolchildren (Baker and
Eversely, 2000).

3

Evaluating Language Policies

WILLIAM F. MACKEY

The foregoing chapter addressed the question of how and why one language policy can be different from another; the present chapter discusses if and when one policy can be better than another. Although comparison is not necessarily evaluative, evaluation is inherently so. Impartial evaluation is dependent upon an understanding of the nature, origins, and limits of a language policy, coupled with an adherence to the relative prerequisites of objectivity.

At the outset, any evaluation of policies poses three major problems: rejection of the ideologies and premises on which the policy is based, disagreement with its underlying motives and objectives, and supposing the implementation of a policy to be the policy itself. If we cannot circumvent or surmount these barriers by discounting them at the outset, our analysis may unwittingly become a proxy for the evaluation of different political regimes. How can this happen? It depends on the extent to which an objective evaluation of a policy is coloured by each of these determinants: ideology, motives and objectives, policy and practice.

Ideologies may determine language policies (Blommaert, 1999). Initially, through the written word and a sacred text, writing appeared as a gift from the gods (*devas*).[1] It was associated with the foundations of most organized religions. The sacred text was kept in holy places; their priests were its readers, interpreters, teachers, and leaders of an elite literate class and protectors of its ideology (Ali, 2002).

Loyalty to the nation-state and its dominant language did not always supplant a faithful adherence to a national or universal church (Cornish, 1936). In some countries there was no contradiction between loyalty to the Vatican

---

[1] To assist the reader, an outline of this chapter is provided in the appendix (156–7).

and loyalty to the maintenance of an ancestral tongue. The loyalties were complementary: one could support the other in a sort of symbiosis between religion and language. This was often the foundation of language policy. One thinks for example of officially Catholic countries such as pre-revolutionary France, Poland, Spain, and much of French Canada before Quebec's Quiet Revolution, where language was seen as a guardian of religion.

Evaluating a policy in which the purpose of language preservation is the maintenance of one's faith becomes an entirely different proposition after that faith has been abandoned. Official religions became incompatible with the creation of the secular nation-state. Some of these states then turned to secular ideologies such as linguistic nationalism, dialectic materialism, and democratic liberalism. The last began to dominate most of the twentieth century's new democracies (Mackey, 1975).

Canada experienced two such world views: religious nationalism and liberal internationalism. The first was dominant in Quebec until the middle of the past century; the second was shared thereafter by the whole of Canada and its provinces, adhering to the principles of international conventions on human rights, the protection of minorities, and freedom of expression. Nevertheless, these remained ancillary to the principles upon which the country itself was founded and to the political and social motives of those who espoused them.

With regard to motives and objectives, while we may reject the motives of a language policy or disagree with its objectives, we do have to understand them and their interplay if we are to attempt to compare one policy with another (see the section on implementation below, 139ff.). The likelihood of the language components of any two policies being equivalent is no greater than the comparability of the ideas, attitudes, and backgrounds of the policy-makers (see the section on adaptation, 147ff.). While their thinking may be clouded by some fashionable idea or by the principles of a popular, pervasive, or reductionist ideology, one must account for the difficulty for these policy-makers to calibrate all those intertwined dimensions of a living language or to foresee its ultimate fate.

Policy and practice may also be confused. One may adhere to the ideology behind a language policy, share its motives, and agree with its objectives and yet condemn it on the basis of its performance. It is admittedly their consequences that make it possible to evaluate the extent to which different policies actually achieve their objectives. Yet one must not confuse the inherent value of a policy per se, its principles and structure with the way it is implemented and adapted.

PRINCIPLES AND STRUCTURES

Policies are mostly based on principles – directly or indirectly stated, presumed or assumed. These principles have often devolved from dominant ideologies or from systems of belief and belonging underpinning the institutions to which a policy applies. They define the nature of the institution, its raison d'être, be it the well-being of the nation or the protection of the language, culture, or religion of the people in whose interest the policy was formulated. Whether or not we acknowledge these interests is beside the point. No matter what one's own beliefs and values may be, it is only according to the principles which engendered the language policy that it can objectively be evaluated. One can deplore the principle and admire the policy as much as one can adhere to the principle and condemn the policy. Some language policies are still based on principles of nineteenth-century political romanticism, on beliefs in the soul of the people and in primitive myths about the birth of a nation. In evaluating post-colonial language policies, one must not, for example, factor in one's opinion of the theocratic Arabization of North Africa as against the Central African ethnocratic elevation of a tribal language to official status, or the democratic outing of a former colonial language in South Africa. We have to take each principle as a given, be it the principle of the parity of Canada's two founding peoples, that of the primacy of French in Quebec, or that of cultural equality. On this basis we can evaluate how well each policy is designed to achieve its objectives in relation to whatever dominant primary principles may have to be taken into account, such as freedom of speech, minority rights, or ethnic equality (Mackey, 1979). In other words, how is each language policy structured politically, juridically, and socially?

Structures of a language policy may depend on the political structure of the state and the way the policy components are apportioned within the country's power structure. The constitutions of some federations (including those of the former USSR and the former Yugoslavia) enunciate the general principles of their language policies, which the constitutions of each of their constituent republics, states, or provinces are required to apply by specifying the political status of all the languages within each jurisdiction (Mackey and Verdoodt, 1975). This approach is quite different from how language policy is structured in nation-states such as France, for example, whose policy is to maintain the exclusivity of its language and culture. Yet when such nation-states admit more foreigners than they can assimilate within a generation, the policy may not hold. While the primacy of one language is what their policy may proclaim, the parity of several cultures is what they may be constrained to accept.

The language policies of officially bilingual sovereign states are also dependent on their political structure: Canada's, with its open bilingual federalism, is different, for example, from that of Belgium, with its principles of strict cultural autonomy and watertight parallelism (Domenichilli, 1999).

In terms of juridical structure, these policies, when applied by the state, may be overtly specified in the laws of institutions, or they may be implied in its regulations. Laws proclaiming freedom of expression in the language of one's choice, however, may be meaningless if few people understand the language. They may simply mean that the stronger languages become more powerful at the expense of the weaker ones, unless the latter are sufficiently well protected by the law.

The law is concerned not only with rights but with duties as well, since the corollary of the language liberty of some is the linguistic obligation of others. The freedom of one is the burden of the other. Although the burden may be distributed by the institution in such a way as to minimize the resistance of those who must bear it, the means has to be provided to implement the acknowledged principles, if conflict is to be avoided.

Achieving this end implies a juridical structure of interrelated language principles, rights, duties, means, and objectives. The acceptance of principles engenders the recognition of language rights, creating corresponding duties, which, in turn, suppose the use of means to attain objectives compatible with the principles. Since these objectives, rights, duties, and principles will not always be found in a single document, it is necessary that the totality of the language laws and regulations operant at any one time be analyzed as a unit, if the juridical structure of the language policy is to be understood. Otherwise, any inherent conflict-causing contradictions may not become evident. Some of these contradictions may be the results of development. When a language policy evolves over a period of years within different levels in the administrative hierarchy of the institution, new laws and regulations enacted to solve one difficulty may create other problems in the application of principles that have already been taken for granted. A glance at the federal structure of language regulations in Canada will serve as a case in point.

In 1963, for example, the principle of parity between the French and English languages was established in the Canadian Parliament. Only the declaration of this principle, coupled with some ideological directives, was first furnished by the policy-makers, leaving the specifics to government departments and ministries with the responsibility of establishing policy objectives. In the absence of any uniform competence criteria, the ministries confined themselves to juridical and numerical ones: so many bilinguals of a certain skill for a given date, place, and time to fill jobs of a specific category.

With regard to social structure, the application of such language policy objectives and their underlying principles can have profound effects upon the restructuring of the workforce now required to conform to the expectations of the public. In Canada the hiring of government personnel became subject to the principle of parity between French-speaking and English-speaking applicants. Their subsequent behaviour in the workplace was now governed by the equality of both French and English as working languages. Save for the unilingualism of the newly created French-language units, the right of civil servants to work in the official language of their choice supposed not only a corresponding obligation to know both these languages but also a consequent duty of the government to supply its unilingual officials with the means of becoming bilingual. This policy of a bilingual public service involved the bilingualization of a wide variety of professional skills in different work environments within all branches of government departments, including the highly technical ones.

Within these political, juridical, and social structures and according to their governing principles, one can analyze and compare language policies as to their justification, the consistency of their requirements, the feasibility of their directives, and the cost of their components relative to their benefits.

Justification

It is on the basis of their founding principles that language policies can be comparatively justified. These principles, as we have seen, may devolve from a system of values that can include such concepts as natural law, norms of justice, civil liberties, and human rights, including those of citizens to use a language without prejudice. These, however, may have to be reconciled with the right of the state to national cohesion in accordance with certain *droits acquis* within its political structure. The latter could even become the dominant principle – the raison d'être of the policy. For example, the alarm set off in 1965 by the preliminary report of a Canadian royal commission to the effect that the country was falling apart instigated an avalanche of hearings, briefs, reports, research projects, recommendations, and enactments resulting in the 1969 Official Languages Act. One can now ask: to what extent was all this effort justified in order to keep Canada together? For example, one of the policy objectives was the integration of all language-related services. Since achieving this goal presumed the adhesion and collaboration of all the provinces, which were no longer forthcoming, this component of the federal language policy ended in failure (see chapter 1). It was also seen as counterproductive, especially in areas with long-standing patterns of diglossic coexistence, in which a laissez-faire policy of leaving well enough alone might have been preferable. Such a policy, however, would not have been justified for Quebec, where application of the principles of the Quiet Revolution led logically to the primacy of French.

One cannot assume, however, that the language policies of those states that have one are of equal relative importance to their respective national objectives. Some, such the Irish and the Basques, have devoted the highest percentage of their national budgets to the promotion of the ancestral tongue, albeit without the success of others such as Quebec and Catalonia (see the discussion of cost versus benefit below).

In justifying Canadian language policies in greater detail, one has to look at the extent to which the objectives are functional. What is the relation, for example, between competence objectives and the actual requirements of bilingual posts? These posts may admittedly have been created on the basis of public demand for services or the need for intercommunication within the public service. If neither of these needs, however, requires second-language competence and the demand is non-existent or insufficient to maintain those newly acquired language skills, the language directive and consequent outlay may be difficult to justify.

The fact that language policy directives are justified in principle does not mean that they cannot be countered by other principles (the question of consistency is further discussed in the next section). For example, Canadian official language policy was confronted with the principle posed by the Public Service Commission of Canada in 1971 whereby any member in no need of a new language skill in his or her work had no right to use public funds to acquire it.[2] Even so, the commission questioned whether the extent of bilingualization of the federal bureaucracy was sufficient to enable it to serve the public in both languages.

Consistency

Some language policies are more consistent than others – consistent within their own structures (internally) and consistent with other policies to which their adherents are subject (externally).

INTERNAL CONSISTENCY

Within its own structures, a language policy functions as a system of interrelationships between principles and practices, rights and duties, aims and means. Within such a system there may exist inherent contradictions. In Canada these became evident from the very beginnings of federal language

policy development. At the outset, there was an evident contradiction between de jure and de facto equality of the two official languages, between
the language rights of the citizen and those of the public servant, between
the responsibilities of government departments and the compulsory bilingualization of their personnel, and between the duties and obligations of
management.

The result was a collection of language programs, each with its own objectives, some of them contradictory. The aim of a bilingual public service,
for example, could only be attained by discounting the primacy of the merit
principle upon which the public service was founded. Compulsory bilingualization also contravened the contractual protection of the unionized
public servant against post hoc bureaucratic directives.

As the official federal language policies came into force in the 1960s and
1970s, their drawbacks came to the fore. For example, nearly all federal documents had been drafted in English, yet they could now not become official
until the French versions were supplied. This requirement was legally binding. Moreover, the application of the principle of personality and consequent
language rights of the public servants and those of the public they served led
to an inherent contradiction in the juridical structure of the language policy.
It gave cause for potential conflict among public servants with rights to work
in the language of their choice: when a public servant speaking one language
communicates with a colleague speaking the other language, at least one
of the parties may have to forego the right to be addressed in the language
of personal preference – unless, of course, both agree to function within a
regimen of receptive bilingualism. Furthermore, the right of the employee
to work in one language implies a duty on the part of the employer and an
obligation on the part of the administration to place its staff in situations
permitting them to work in the language of their own choosing.

With a view to meeting these seemingly contradictory requirements while
respecting the principle of institutional bilingualism, a system of quotas was
established for bilingual public servants.[3] Because different posts required different types and degrees of bilingualism, however, the quotas had to be set
up according to categories of bilingualism.[4] These categories depended on
the needs of the population as they were variously interpreted by each of the
ministries and branches of government according to the provisions of the language law, particularly in respect to article 9, section 2, which dealt with public needs and requirements.[5] The result was that the official minorities could
not be served equally well in all areas and for all their needs and requirements.
In sum, an initial lack of balance between rights and duties can lead to the ac-
cumulation of internal inconsistencies as a language policy evolves.

EXTERNAL CONSISTENCY

This is the sort of thing most people will notice. First, how does the policy affect the political principles underpinning the basic laws of the state? To what extent, for example, does a constitution based on the freedom of the individual give people the choice either to keep their language and culture or to abandon them?

Second, the policy may affect different jurisdictions in different ways. The economic policy of a municipality may run counter to the language policy of the state. In 2004, for example, the municipality of Greater Montreal launched an economic policy aimed at making the city a cosmopolitan, bilingual metropolis open to enterprises from all over the globe. Yet it had to make sure that, in conformity with Quebec's language charter, these enterprises functioned in French. This restriction was soon pointed out in briefs presented to the Office de consultation publique de Montréal. The business-friendly municipal policy seemed to have more in common with the federal policy of multiculturalism within a framework of official bilingualism. But this policy was seen in Quebec as a recipe for cultural entropy and as a promotion of a global culture that could efface its national identity. Even though the business community considered compliance with the language charter to be an irritant to the city's economic development, any municipal policy of linguistic laissez-faire was in direct contravention of Quebec's policy on the *francisation des entreprises*, for one could hardly oblige a business to switch to French as a working language while at the same time promoting language equality and freedom of choice. Permitting English to become the language of business in Montreal would indicate to the citizens of French Quebec that their home language was in some way deficient, even detrimental, to their own economy (Roy, 2004).

There was also a lack of consistency within the same social space, between Quebec's language policies and those of the federal government. Many of these can be traced back to differences in the basic concepts of "majority" and "minority." French is the majority language in Quebec; English the official minority language. French is the official minority language in Canada; English the majority language. The promotion of Canada's official minority languages according to the principle of parity applies to official minorities both outside Quebec (French) and inside Quebec (English), but here language promotion infringes on areas of exclusive provincial jurisdiction. Although French is Quebec's majority language, English in Quebec is not considered a "minority" language since it is dominant in Canada and in North America, in which context French rates as a minority language in need of all the promotion and protection it can muster (Legault, 1992).

Moreover, according to a clarification by the United Nations Human Rights Commission on 31 March 1993, its covenant covers only minorities within sovereign states, not those within any of its constituent provinces.[6]

These inconsistencies have been largely responsible for the demise of several policy initiatives, including that of the federal policy on bilingual districts and many other cases that have not come to the fore. For example, all service corporations in Quebec must comply with its language laws on the primacy of French; Crown corporations throughout Canada conform to federal language laws governed by the principle of language parity. The consequent conflict becomes most evident in areas of public signage. The Shawville fiasco is a case in point. In this Quebec town in the 1990s a filling station of Petro-Canada (then a Crown corporation) applied its federal corporate regulations on bilingual signage. Contrary to repeated Quebec court injunctions, it had no federal authorization to do otherwise. After years of legal wrangling between 1998 and 2004 and much embarrassment, the case finally petered out in bureaucratic fatigue. Such conflicts would not have emerged under a constitution of asymmetrical federalism, whereby federal institutions in Quebec would conform to provincial regulations promoting the primacy of French in Quebec.

Feasibility

The comparative feasibility of language policies is subject to the laws of probability within different contexts of control. The extent to which any institution has control over its means of intercommunication – the code and use of its language – is a measure of the feasibility of its language policies. In a country with no control over the language behaviour of its citizens, any language policy it may have is subject to the same sort of forces that govern free markets and open societies. These forces may determine the fate of any language, even that of the greatest. When one contemplates the much-heralded fears for the fate of French, one of the world's most prestigious languages, one can understand the concern over the probable survival within North America of dozens of other languages with fewer speakers and still fewer readers (Mackey, 2004).

Since a language is not the property of the state, there is a limit to what a country's language policy can do in determining the fate of any of its languages. These limits vary greatly between states and also between languages, and they have to be taken into account in any evaluation of a language policy. The comparative successes and failures, for example, of Catalan and Basque or of Hebrew and Irish cannot be attributed exclusively to the countries' language policies. A language policy can be objectively evaluated only within, and not beyond, the limits of its possibilities. In other words, how feasible is it?

It may not be feasible to make one language equal to another in all respects (policies of language equality), but it may be possible to make it equal in some respects. The latter may be achieved by standardizing the language's code and enriching its corpus (developmental policies) or by reinstating the function of an ancestral tongue in a society that has abandoned it (policies of language revival). Yet in many cases, the only thing that one can reasonably expect is to prevent a language from dying out without a legacy of what it was (language conservation). These policies may coexist at different levels within the same jurisdiction.

POLICIES OF LANGUAGE EQUALITY

Scientifically speaking, all languages are equal. That is, all languages and language varieties are equally worthy of scientific analysis. Indeed, this is the premise that underpins modern scientific linguistics. And yet, after a stroll through the aisles of any academic library and an examination of its reference shelves, it becomes evident that one can do more with some languages than with others. This sort of inequality, though seemingly unfair, must have an impact on any language policy.

A second sort of inequality has to do with the relative number of speakers – that is, with language minorities. Yet all languages are minority languages somewhere in the world, even the great world languages: English in Cameroon, French in Canada, Spanish in the United States, German in Belgium, Chinese outside China, and thousands of other languages distributed unequally among the countries of the world – all this for the simple reason that the boundaries between languages do not coincide with the boundaries between states. So that majority languages in some countries may appear elsewhere as minority or even moribund languages. Most of the world's minority languages, however, are nowhere the majority languages of any state. The fact that a minority language in one country may be the majority language next door is an element in establishing its language policy, as was for example, the status of Swedish in Finland and that of English in Quebec. It also has to do with the power and prestige of each language, its demographic, economical, cultural, and ideological attraction, the literacy of the two populations, and the similarity of their languages.

Yet many policy declarations on the equality of two languages remain, while the intended beneficiaries of such policies see the same inequalities live on. These inequalities, which seem to be a constant in plurilingual federations, can arouse permanent feelings of injustice. Rational solutions are often impossible and juridical ones ineffective. Can one modify the language behaviour of people in order to justify the existence of a bilingual post? Can the language practices of bilinguals be changed by offering them bilingual services?

How are these contradictory concepts of equality accounted for in different language policies? Often through the fiction of juridical equality, if not by different degrees of juridical inequality. Yet legislating language equality is often ineffective because the law is ill-equipped to abstract all the mutually modifying practices of the verbal behaviour of people. The law can deal with language only to the extent that is juridically manageable: that is, objectively and quantitatively. Yet many language components remain essentially qualitative. Many speakers belong in varying degrees and at different times to two or more language groups. Language equality is either an unattainable ideal or a juridical fiction (Bastarache, 1991).

Juridical language equality and inequality open the door to policies of linguistic reciprocity: if some of my people overlap on your land and yours on mine, then I will treat your lot as you treat mine. So, for example, French in Ontario should be treated as is English in Quebec and vice versa (see chapter 9). The problem with such a policy is its feasibility. Are the language minorities really comparable? Some may admittedly have been at some point in the past. Yet over the past two centuries, they may have diverged ethnically, culturally, and economically. How uniform and unified is each minority? Are they unified or "divided by the same language," to quote George Bernard Shaw's characterization of the United States and England? Since a language minority as a community develops customs of diglossic behaviour, to what extent is it feasible to change these habits? This was another of the difficulties confronting some of the proposed bilingual districts provided for in the first federal official language act, which turned out to be unfeasible. Likewise, to have expected the English diplomatic corps, who had for centuries transacted in French, to suddenly revert to English, as the post-Napoleonic language policy of the British Foreign Office required (the Canning Instructions) proved entirely unfeasible.

On the other hand, the reason why it was entirely feasible for Quebec's language policy to have French-speakers work in French is that so many of them had already done so (see the Gendron Report). And the language charter was to ensure that they would continue to do so, while preventing a growing minority from having to work in English. At the federal level, however, more and more people were being required to work in both languages, since the policy of language equality required the federal government to serve the public equally well in English and French, even though the vast majority of public servants could speak only English. When one realizes the number of years it takes a monolingual adult to acquire a professional speaking and writing mastery of a new language, one wonders how feasible it was to expect a monolingual public servant to attain such an objective by taking language courses. This policy objective was not based on feasibility studies of any kind. It is true, however, that the Laurendeau-Dunton commissioners had indeed been conscious of this problem: they even addressed it in their volume on the work world (volume 3) and again in their recommendations. In recommendation 10, for example, the commission proposed that the federal bureaucracy begin implementing the use of the most feasible level of bilingualism: enhancing a reading knowledge of the other language, which many college-educated public servants had already begun to acquire, followed by training in oral comprehension. This recommendation was ignored when the public service began defining its language objectives in 1970; the first and primary objective became the ability to speak both languages,[7] notwithstanding the fact that the Canadian Parliament on 23 June 1970 had accepted the commission's recommendations in their entirety.

DEVELOPMENTAL POLICIES

Much has been written on language development, especially during the past half-century. The writings appear under a variety of different rubrics such as "language planning," "language management" (*aménagement*), and even "language engineering" (Laforge, 1987; Maurais, 1987). These terms are often taken to be synonymous with language policy. For some recent examples, see Spolsky (2004) and Kaplan and Baldauf (1997).

The reason for the continuing confusion is that the first impetus for such studies was provided by the post-colonial creation of new states, with their problems of development, including that of their national languages (LePage, 1964). Many of the proposed developmental plans were the fruits of the new funding policies of philanthropic foundations in North America and Europe. Their funding addressed the language problems of developing nations; it also provided a boost to the ongoing work of linguistic anthropologists and Christian missionaries, who for centuries had been developing tribal languages as part of their policies for the propagation of their faith in the home language of the faithful and literacy in their mother tongue. With so much support for research and so many undeveloped languages, academic studies, independent of language politics, began to proliferate to an extent that they were sometimes grouped under the literature of an academic subdiscipline. Indeed, such academic studies of language development were now undertaken for their own sake or for that of the language itself.

One rationale for these studies seemed to be that until a language was properly developed, it could not fulfil any new functions attributed to it by a language policy. It was as if the *mots d'ordre* were "Develop the language, and the policy will follow" – "Build it, and they will come."

Language development is a long and ongoing process of standardizing the code and enriching the corpus, with no guarantee of the extent to which these will be used. The extensive literature on language planning supplies abundant examples of success and failure. One of the most notable examples of success was the development of a Bazaar Malay jargon into the national language of Indonesia. Such successes, however, are far outnumbered by the failures, for no matter how complete the planning, how efficient the code, the results are useless unless they are used, as the many recorded failures of spelling reform policies for English, French, and German can amply attest.

One of the reasons for the failures is the difficulty of changing the ingrained habits of a population. Each community, by its very nature, must have had some means of communication in one or more languages. So any newly developed language component may first have to replace an existing one. In communities with official language minorities some activities, however, must take place in the majority language. Some of the people must of necessity become bilingual and also, according to their needs, diglossic – using different languages for different purposes, such as writing, shopping, and schooling. Changing these diglossic habits involves the modification of ingrained habits of human behaviour (Mackey, 1989). If a person is in the habit of using one language for writing and reading and another for conversation with friends and family, the fact that a written form of the home language has been developed will not of itself make that person write in it.

LANGUAGE REVIVAL AND SURVIVAL

Since policies of language revival meet with such wide-ranging differences of success, it is worthwhile analyzing the reasons why some fail while others succeed. If, for example, one examines the history of the remarkable revival of Hebrew as the mother tongue of the citizens of a young and modern state, what becomes evident is that its institutions, including the army, the schools, and the synagogues, in which language is acquired and used are controlled by a population intent on the application of the country's language policy and eager to make it succeed. Another population with a high degree of social, economic, and political independence – that of the Republic of Ireland, a long-established English possession – could hardly expect to make its ancestral Celtic tongue replace the usual everyday language of its population. Yet considering the odds against such a transformation, one must credit the modest revival of Irish as the official and second language of the citizens of the republic as a vindication of its persistent language policy.

In the case of Canada, one may ask whether such achievements are likely for the few dozen First Nations the promotion of whose languages may be part of a national policy. The outcome will depend on the relative weight of variables affecting the populations who still speak these moribund languages and their commitment to reviving them. Some of these variables have to do with the relative status of the languages, the type of language behaviour of their speakers, the complementarity and redundancy of their dialects, and the dynamics of dialect levelling and diffusion. The feasibility of a policy of language revival depends largely on the vitality and life expectancy of at least one of the language's dialects and the bilinguality of its population. Such languages may range from those with few, if any, monolingual speakers to those of isolated communities with a majority of monolingual speakers. Reviving the use of these languages is quite different from reviving the use of French among official minorities outside Quebec. In the case of Canada's aboriginal languages, the challenge is to provide them with stable functions; the priority has been to provide these languages with the functions of a standard written language. For a few languages, such as Inuktitut, for example, this has been achieved for a few functions but not for all those of the wider community, where English or French continues to be used. In other cases, reducing the language to writing and supplying it with dictionaries and grammars have done little to modify language behaviour, especially that of already literate adults. Once a person can read, world languages such as English or French can offer more than a tribal language can provide. Reading and writing these world languages have been the priorities of provincial education policies in the social advancement of their aboriginals – albeit to the detriment of their tribal languages.

The size and territoriality of the language community may also be a determining factor in the feasibility of a policy of language survival. Sometimes, the smaller the language group and the more isolated its territory, the greater its chances of survival (Wurm, 2002). Then there is the question of priority. Does the policy favour languages whose revitalization is most likely over those on the verge of extinction (Grenoble and Whaley, 2006)? Some failures of language revival policies have simply been due to the fact that by the time the code and corpus are ready for implementation, most of the remaining native speakers have died out. Does the policy therefore allocate resources proportional to the life expectancy of each language, or does it do so on the basis of the principle of language equality? In other words, are "hopeless causes" supported on a par with viable ones (Newman, 2003)?

Yet expectation is not prophecy. Unpredictable events beyond state control can change everything. Individual initiative and group militancy, coupled with unexpected geolinguistic, economic, and demographic changes, can transfigure a dying tongue into a national language. And the prevailing language policy can be evaluated according to the extent to which it adapts to such transformation. It is not through literacy but through orality, the intergenerational transmission by word-of-mouth, that most of the world's thousands of languages have survived for the past millennia. It has indeed been for want of speakers that so many of them have died. Most of these have been aboriginal or immigrant languages whose few remaining speakers were isolated from those who spoke their language. Anything that brings same-language speakers together can add to the survival of their language. A new way of doing so appeared during the last decades of the past century through the creation of same-language web-communities, webloggers, and chat rooms with as few as a dozen speakers. Yet the large number of these small widely scattered same-language groups could add up to a large number of people, forming the multilingual segment of the statistical "long-tail" of the world's Internet population. Some institutions, as part of their language policy, promoted the formation of groups who can use their language, as did, for example, the ministry of language policy of the Basque government.

The probability of such promotion occurring for all of the thousand languages with only a few remaining adult speakers is indeed slim. The fact remains that languages have been dying at the rate of about two a month (Crystal, 2000). Many will disappear without a trace. The fate of moribund tongues is of little concern to the states that contain them, and their speakers, as subjects or citizens, are expected to adopt one of the national languages. Nor does the general public mourn the loss of languages other than their own.

There are those, however, for whom the death of a unique language is akin to the loss of a species, a diminution of the diversity of life and culture (Duchêne and Heller, 2007). They may not be able to reverse the process of its obsolescence, but they can incite governmental and non-governmental organizations into adapting policies of language conservation to preserve for posterity a picture of each language by establishing the best possible record of its code and corpus.

LANGUAGE CONSERVATION

That the revival of a language may be a lost cause does not mean that it should disappear from human memory. It may be regarded as part of a nation's patrimony, and its conservation can become a matter of policy.

Like so many of the world's aboriginal languages, Canada's Native languages have been declining ever since the country was occupied by European settlers. Under Confederation, the remaining Native peoples became wards of the state – "Give us your land, and we'll take care of your people." Their physical well-being became the duty of the Indian Affairs Branch; their languages and cultures the responsibility of the National Museum, wherein a few notable anthropological linguists (such as Edward Sapir and Marius Barbeau) laboured to rescue Canada's Native languages from oblivion (see chapter 1).

The education policies of the provinces, however, excluded Native languages, as did the departments of most universities. One would have imagined that before a universe of some six thousand unofficial languages, graduate students in linguistics could hardly be at a loss for original and useful research topics. The contrary has been the case: less than 5 per cent of doctoral dissertations in linguistics have been devoted to endangered languages.[8] Nearly all others were about some of the minutiae of linguistic theory. This aberration is directly attributable to the much-hyped shift in fashion from descriptive to theoretical linguistics during the latter half of the past century. It was as if professional linguists, for fear of being taken for mere polyglots, had remained proudly monolingual. They seemed more at home in their offices than in the field, more comfortable in cyberspace than with illiterate speakers of a dying language. Ironically, however, cyberspace became part of the solution to the conservation of languages. It was inconvenient and time-consuming for academics to devote themselves to the recording of dying languages. It was much more convenient to train their native speakers in linguistic field methods while trying to obtain ongoing support for their work. This support would eventually come not only from granting agencies but later from foundations devoted to the conservation of the world's languages in electronic data banks such as that of the Rosetta Project. Data on each language were fed by ongoing updates directly from the field; they were centralized in such training centres as the International Institute of Linguistics (formerly the Summer Institute; www.sil.org) in Dallas.[9]

This work of language conservation has continued independent of the universities. These languages may admittedly never be developed into national ones, but they can be recorded and archived as part of the patrimony of human culture. Language policy, like all politics, being the art of the possible, the conservation of the code and corpus of these languages may be all that is feasible.

In sum, in comparing the feasibility of policies of language equality, development, survival, revival, and conservation, we have asked such questions as the following. To what extent are the objectives attainable? It is one thing, for example, to require public officials to become fluent in two languages; it is quite another thing to convert a tenured unilingual bureaucracy into a bilingual one, for in adult language learning, some objectives are not attainable, others are partly so, and still others may be reached by certain persons but not by others. Are the objectives of the policy operational? That is, are they specific enough to bring about the required changes in language behaviour? Even though the policy is feasible, the next question would be: is it worth it?

Cost versus Benefit

One can evaluate and compare the costs of different language policies relative to their benefits. The costs are not only monetary; they are also political, administrative, social, and cultural. They can affect the goodwill, efficiency, and morale of institutions. Benefits may include not only the diffusion, enhancement, and enrichment of a language but also peace, order, and justice in a society.

The relation between the cost and the benefit of a language policy depends on the value scale of those for whom the policy was intended: its beneficiaries. They may value their language more than their economy or their social and academic standing. For example, the language policy of Ireland during the 1960s provided for primary education in Irish. That children schooled in Irish were consequently two years behind their English-educated counterparts seemed a small price to pay for the extension of Irish as a medium of schooling (Macnamara, 1967).

In Canada during the same period, following the alarming preliminary report of the Laurendeau-Dunton Commission, no price seemed too high for keeping the country from falling apart. Yet even when the need is urgent and cost is no object, it helps to know what the cost is in relation to the benefits, if only to improve the efficiency of the undertaking. As in all emergencies, there was bound to be unwitting waste and cost overruns. The launching costs of Canada's policy of official institutional bilingualism turned out to be enormous. The initial and ongoing need for staff training and replacement resulted in some expensive duplication and redundancy. It involved a massive and abrupt increase in government personnel in an effort to bilingualize the federal public service. New people had to be hired to fill posts designated as bilingual, with some consequent disruption in the workforce. When managers were away on language leave, there was an inevitable decrease in efficiency and output. In 1992, for example, the time spent on language learning at or through the facilities of the Central Language Bureau was aggregated at about two million working hours (see chapter 1). This figure did not include the hundreds of hours that each ministry, department, or Crown corporation spent on its own language requirements.

This enormous cost in time and money expended on the lengthy language training of personnel had to be measured against improvements in their performance after their return to work. Did they use their new skills in their work? How well and how often? Did their language skills improve with use? Were they maintained? If they remained unused or forgotten, what benefit was derived from investing more resources on skill maintenance?

There was also the cost of a sharp increase in the number of official translators. By 1984 the staff of the long-established Translation Bureau had grown from a few hundred language workers to more that two thousand. Although many translated documents remained unread, the principle of parity required that both French and English versions appear simultaneously. In retrospect, this level of non-functional symbolic duplication seemed almost acceptable when compared to what would be required a decade later by the European Union, some of whose documents had to appear in a dozen languages redundantly addressed to people in the habit of working in one of the major European languages (Mackey, 2001). By the year 2007, the number of official EU languages had risen to twenty-three, with a cost of some billion and a half dollars to translate more than a million pages of text and interpret the babel of some ten thousand meetings.

In countries where the policy is one of language development, the cost versus the benefit is of a different order, especially if the language in question has hitherto been diffused only by word of mouth. In illiterate multilingual societies, the cost of code standardization and corpus production can far outweigh that of literacy in an available second language (Thorburn, 1971). At one point, the planners and producers may even outnumber the potential consumers. The time value of a policy must also be factored in. For some languages whose development has depended on different funding agencies, or various advisers therein, decades have been wasted on doing, undoing, and redoing the systems of standardization. By the time the orthography, lexicon, and corpus have been standardized for some languages, there may be no one left to use them.

A country's language policy may at times become subservient to its economic policy, especially when the benefits of foreign investment are concerned, for the cost-benefit equations of the investors may have to be accommodated. Foreign direct investment has favoured free and open societies: the fewer the rules, the faster the growth. Compliance may affect growth, as a brake, a hindrance, or an obstacle. The more of these there are, the slower the growth and the greater the costs in relation to the benefits. Likewise for labour policy: in June 2006, for example, Quebec had finally to give Ontario access to its labour market in answer to the demand from Quebec's building industry for more construction workers.

The cost-benefit ratio of a policy may therefore be evaluated as a trade-off in time, money, efficiency, and equality: between cultural control and economic dependence, between political opposition and language imposition, between ethnic heritage and national identity, between the doctrine of linguism and the creed of kinship. Since much of this trade-off is a matter of degree, it helps if the components of comparison can be quantified. To calculate the cost versus the benefit of a policy or of its components, one needs to obtain relevant quantitative data for at least two points in time and possibly cumulative data for the intervening period. Admittedly, some costs cannot be aggregated into a single figure, yet they can be separately grouped as budget items, increases in personnel, losses in productivity, litigation, and out-migration. Benefits may be measured as achievements of policy objectives by means of before-and-after comparisons. The more specific the objective, the better its attainment can be quantified. For example, the percentages of pupils schooled in each language can be compared; so can changes in the use of each language in each of its social and official domains. In signage policy one can, for example, compare the street signs of a given area at two points in time. Sources for "before" data include the studies and research reports prepared for language commissions prior to the development of a language policy: for example, the voluminous data to be found in the research reports, studies, and briefs prepared for the federal Laurendeau-Dunton Commission or data from Quebec's Gendron inquiry. Sources for "after" data include the periodical reports of agencies responsible for policy management: for example, the annual and occasional reports of the Office of the Commissioner for Official Language and, for Quebec, the reports of the Office québécois de la langue française and the Commission de surveillance and its successive reincarnations.

What one can do with the results of such a cost-benefit analysis depends on its time frame. Long-term intergenerational studies on language shift and language transfer may confirm or disprove the justification of different language policy components (see chapter 9). Short-term cost-benefit studies may help improve policy implementation in, for example, the efficiency of public service programs of bilingualization through different methods of language acquisition or behaviour modification (Mackey, 1978). By coupling such evaluations with a rigorous counterfactual analysis of the likely cost of the alternatives, one may conclude that doing something was better than doing nothing. Sometimes the most costly policy on a language conflict is to ignore it (see chapter 5).

In sum, different language policies may be evaluated and compared as to their justification, consistency, feasibility, and cost versus benefit. Few policies may rank high in all these criteria. Yet it will become evident that in each of these aspects some policies are better than others. They can be appreciated only with regard to the scope of the policy and its dynamics of adaptation. One must ponder the extent to which a flawless but limited policy is better or worse than a somewhat flawed but wide-ranging one.

IMPLEMENTATION

It is important to keep separate the evaluation of the structure of a language policy from that of its implementation. The objectives of a policy may be laudable but its implementation a failure. Yet failures of implementation are not necessarily permanent. Given enough time, the policy objectives may eventually be reached. Not all of them are likely to be achieved at the same time, in the same place, and to the same extent.

For these reasons, implementation is often the more difficult undertaking to initiate and the more expensive to maintain: *vouloir qui veut; implante qui peut.* Since it may require ongoing management of change in both the forms and functions of a language, the policy may have to provide for a permanent bureaucracy to that effect – as have, indeed, Canada's and Quebec's language laws. Separate sections of these language agencies are equipped to manage different policy components. That is why it is preferable to examine one policy component at a time, for its implementation depends on whether it has to do with language form, language function, or language behaviour.

Language Form. In evaluating the scope of different language policies, we find few that extend to the actual forms and usage of their official languages. While Canada's federal language policies do not require the control of English and French as Canadian languages, the management of Quebec's official language is a crucial component of its language policy. Its Charter of the French Language provides for subsequent additions and amendments specifying the role of its policy implementation agencies in managing the way in which the language is used. For example, the amendment of 12 June 2002 (Bill 104) requires monitoring not only language status, function, and behaviour but also language usage (art. 160). It stipulates that the Office québécois de la langue française submit every five years to the minister responsible for the implementation of the charter an assessment of "l'usage et au statut de la langue française ainsi qu'aux comportements et attitudes des groupes linguistiques."[10]

The extent to which new forms are successfully added to a language code and old forms deleted differs greatly from one policy to the next. It depends largely on the language attitudes of the public and on the entrenchment of their habits. Eliminating old but needless forms (e.g., anglicisms in French) may be more difficult than implanting new words that fill an obvious need. To eliminate words such as "cute," "smart," and "tough" from everyday spoken usage was more difficult than the rapid switch from "email" to *courriel*. Success in lexical implantation also depends on the immediacy of the needs.

If a modern, developing, industrial or post-industrial society in North America is to be expected to operate in French, it must be given the means to do so. New concepts and technologies that are continually coming in with English labels require immediate standard equivalents in French before the borrowed labels, such as "blogger," "browser," and "chat room," become the norm.[11] This response requires quick, open, and widespread online access to up-to-date word banks such as those of the Office québécois de la langue française, which stores the results of terminological research and development such as, for example, its online *Grand dictionnaire terminologique* and results of the project on the Aménagement de la terminologie française de l'informatique (Laplante, 2005). To this end, a Quebec government website has been open to the public: www.olf.gouv.qc.ca/resources/bibliotheque/dictionnaires/internet.

Language Functions. To the extent that one controls an activity, one may change the language in which it takes place. If a provincial government controls education, it can decree the language of public schooling. If it controls the licensing of public cinemas, it can legislate on the language of their films, as, indeed, Quebec had done in its Loi sur le cinéma, enacted during the avalanche of American movies in the 1980s.[12] If a government's jurisdiction includes contract law, it can define the legality of contracts according to the language in which they are written. Yet it has little control over the language in which contracts are drawn up, no matter what the language policy, for this process often results from an unpredictable sequence of oral interpersonal interactions.

The rate at which long-standing relationships between language and function can be altered depends on the extent to which the latter is subject to command and control. If a language functions as the language of liturgy, for example, the implantation of a new language or the elimination of an old one can be a matter of edict. It took less time to switch the language of Catholic liturgy throughout the world from Latin to the vernacular than it did to implant a new language of business in Quebec.

Language Behaviour. Language policy implantation is often an exercise in behaviour modification, particularly changes in the language used for specific purposes. Since the 1980s a vast literature has appeared on the management of change in institutions; it includes, however, little, if anything, on the modification of language behaviour. Making people change their everyday habits of intercommunication from one language to another is difficult, even within populations where everyone knows two languages. In Canadian cities with bilingual populations, the highly bilingual tend to use the language most people understand; others will use the language they know best. If one language is to function as both the official and usual language, as is French in Quebec, it is those less-bilingual English-speakers whose language behaviour will have to be the most modified in order to comply with the law. Therefore, in evaluating the implementation of language policies, one has to gauge the level of compliance to the policy in relation to its consequences.

Compliance

Compliance is one measure of a policy's impact. It can also be viewed as a ratio between the cost of enforcement and the degree of adherence (see the discussion of cost versus benefit above). In evaluating and comparing language policies, one examines how each policy provides for compliance to its regulations. Who has the authority to apply them, and how have they been applied? Who bears the burden of compliance: the institutions or the public? What penalties are provided for non-compliance? What is the role of the beneficiaries in the implementation of the language policy? The answers will depend on whether we are talking about the mechanisms of compliance or the methods used.

MECHANISMS

Policies differ in the structures they create to ensure compliance to their regulations. In Canada the Official Languages Act provides for an extra-governmental ombudsman responsible only to Parliament; in Quebec compliance is in the hands of the government bureaucracy within different agencies under a cabinet minister responsible for the implementation of the language law.

The role of the federal Commissioner of Official Languages, however, is not only that of an ombudsman who reacts to complaints (about a thousand a year to date) and dispenses information. It is also a proactive role that includes supervision, liaison, language promotion, preventative intervention, and monitoring the respect for language rights. For example, in May 2006, the commissioner publicized a lack of compliance of federal agencies in Quebec for their failure to provide services in English. The supervision includes the auditing of outlays by federal institutions for language policy compliance. The liaison involves ongoing interaction, at all levels of government, with management committees, parliamentarians, and government departments, especially those concerned with citizenship, immigration, health, and transport. This liaison operates not only at the federal level but within each region of Canada wherein the Office of the Commissioner maintains a liaison staff, who keep contact with local, non-governmental, and community associations. The commissioner can then intervene at points where new laws, regulations, or policies are being developed. In this way, the role of the commissioner in Canadian society has continually expanded since the post was created. Finally, the commissioner has the duty to appeal to the courts where needed to ensure compliance with the language policy. All these activities are reported annually to Parliament and to the governor general by the commissioner, whose publication division also puts out relevant monographs and research reports in addition to maintaining a website.

In Quebec the Charter of the French Language provided for an entirely different mechanism to ensure application, analysis, and compliance. By 1982, when the policy was fully operational, this consisted of four bodies: the Office de la langue française (staff, 350; budget, $14.5 million), the Conseil de la langue française (staff, 35; budget, $2.1 million), the Commission de protection de la langue française[13] (staff, 40; budget, $1.2 million), and the Commission de toponymie. Also, there were two appeal boards, one for businesses and the other for schools, each with a staff of three and a combined budget of about a quarter million (Blouin, 1983).

These mechanisms of compliance for both the federal and Quebec policies (with the possible exception of the Quebec appeal boards) were kept fully occupied during the first few decades of their existence. That so many complaints (many trivial, multiple, even spiteful) should be given so much time and attention can testify to the value of both these mechanisms as being more than adequate.

METHODS

How these mechanisms of compliance are actually used may depend on the people who use them; their style and methods of operation may consequently affect the results. For the federal policy, much depended on the personality of the commissioner; for the Quebec policy, it depended more on the background of the bureaucracy. The commissioner's post was occupied at various times by a number of different celebrities, ranging from active academics to retired judges. Some promoted methods of intimidating militancy;

others preferred the approach of quiet persuasion. The tenures of some are memorable, and their annual reports provide some worthwhile and even entertaining reading.

In Quebec the initial problem was to find the appropriate staff for the new language agencies. Fortunately, this demand coincided with an increased supply of educated personnel. The remarkable achievements of Quebec's Quiet Revolution, with its urgent need to establish a competent state bureaucracy, had been partly attributable to the availability of an educated clergy, former clergy, and former seminarians after the dramatic fall in the number of religious vocations. For example, the second chairman of the Conseil de la langue française and three of the five men on the executive of the Commission de surveillance were all former priests. Like the generation who implemented the new order in Quebec, they were men with a mission, educated in seminaries and classical colleges and now devoted to a career of service to the new state. Many, after a stint in the newly created ENAP (École nationale d'administration publique) were eager to lend their missionary zeal to the implementation of the new language laws. Their clientele could count some six million speakers of French, who were now permitted, and often encouraged, to report to the agency any infractions to the language regulations. Some 14,000 complaints were lodged during its first six years. For each, a separate file was created and duly submitted for study by one of the six inspectors. That less than two dozen of these thousands of complaints resulted in indictments is a tribute to the judiciousness of this personnel.

The authors of the charter had supposed that most complaints would be about workplace discrimination against French monolingual speakers. Fewer were made than expected, and fewer still were judged legitimate, save for those involving branches of certain corporations headquarted in the United States and subject to American law. The most obvious were the signage practices of American franchises that had trademarked bits of the English language in their company logos. Nevertheless, the two *commissions d'appel* providing for institutional compliance had less to do than expected (Blouin, 1983).

In rural and traditionally English-speaking communities, however, small family businesses felt particularly vulnerable, especially when regulations on the use of French in the workplace were extended to small firms (under fifty workers). The rationale for such an extension was that such firms accounted for a third of Quebec's workforce and that only some 20 per cent of English-speaking Montrealers used French as their language of work (Conseil, 2005). Problems in complying with the language laws were compounded by a confusion between institutional and individual bilingualism. Was the burden of compliance to be borne by the institution or by its members? At issue, for example, was whether English community hospitals in urban centres could offer services in French without requiring their doctors and nurses to be professionally fluent in that language. French-language hospitals had a similar obligation imposed by the ministry of health to supply services in English on demand. The principle was enacted into law in December 1986 as a statutory obligation (Bill 142). It was not based on identity but on language preference, whereby any citizen, regardless of home language, could demand to be served in English. This requirement was later incorporated into a more general law including social services (Bill 120), which generated subsequent ministerial directives. One of these, Services de santé et services sociaux de langue anglaise (22 October 1990), lists some 250 service agencies (about a third of the total) with a statutory duty to offer social services in English. It went so far beyond the areas usually covered already by established English-language institutions that it was sometimes characterized as a policy of *rebilingualisation* (Legault, 1992, 127).

Consequences

One can evaluate the consequences of a language policy only in retrospect: after a reasonable lapse of time, one can benefit from the hindsight of history. After watching federal and provincial language policies evolve in Canada over the past half-century, one can see how well their consequences have confirmed their intent. One can look at data from diachronic studies or compare synchronic ones. Quantified data can be compared using intergenerational studies of language use (see chapter 9). The value to the policy-makers of such diachronic comparisons is that they can provide occasions for improvements in certain components or provisions of a language policy and, if need be, for the re-enactment or amendment of language laws. Examples are the Official Languages Act of 1988 and the successive amendments to the Quebec Charter of the French Language (see chapter 1). Nevertheless, while many consequences may or may not warrant change, others may be beyond rectification.

INTENDED CONSEQUENCES

When we look back at the implementation of both the Quebec and the federal language policies over the past quarter-century, it would seem that most of the intended consequences conform to what the policy-makers had in mind. In Quebec in 1974 the main policy objective was to make French the common and usual language of Quebec society; by 2006 there remained few public activities that did not take place in French, while something like a linguistic equilibrium had been established whereby English had become, in public, a de jure minority language (Bouchard and Bourhis, 2002). Outside Quebec, thanks to the implementation during the same period of a federal policy of institutional bilingualism, one could be expected to be served in French by federal agencies within areas of their remit. The face of Canada as a bilingual federation had become evident; so had that of Quebec as a French society.[14]

UNINTENDED CONSEQUENCES

Since language is so tightly interwoven within the fabric of society, language policy is not devoid of social consequences, sometimes unforeseen or unintended (Laponce, 1989). For Quebec's language policy these included the reactions of English-speaking populations at home and abroad. Many English-speaking people began leaving Quebec at an ever-increasing rate, which reached as high as five thousand a year; between 1991 and 1996, according to Statistics Canada, there were 24,125 such departures. Yet those who remained seemed to realize, for the most part, the justification of the Charter of the French Language (see chapter 11). Nevertheless, they sometimes resented its methods of implementation (Caldwell, 2002). They accepted many of the protections provided by the charter in matters of schooling, particularly article 73, whereby parents were permitted to send their children to be schooled in English, provided that either of them or one of their children was a Canadian citizen educated in English in Canada. At the same time, the Quebec English-language system (including the former Protestant school boards) added hours at all levels to the teaching of the French language. Yet their competence in French as a working language, even at the college level, was not comparable to that of the rising French-speaking immigrant population. It remained insufficient for work in the monolingual public service of Quebec, with the effect that the English minority therein was permanently under-represented (Chambers, 1992, 27).

Consequently, some English-speakers, placing the well-being of the individual citizen over that of the English language, began to promote the abolition of their separate schools in favour of a single common school open to all, regardless of mother tongue. By 1999 this initiative had taken form as on off-shoot of the opposition Equality Party under the name of the Greater Quebec Movement. But not all English-speakers were willing to abandon their *droits acquis*; the movement was opposed by well-entrenched English institutions: the universities, colleges, and school and hospital administrations. Indeed, it had never been the expressed intention of Quebec's language policy developers to make French the home language of its three-quarters of a million English-speakers.

Nevertheless, the language of schooling was crucial to the demographic status of French in Quebec, the fertility of whose population had fallen below replacement level. The replacement of French-speakers could now come only from the outside: the shortfall could be filled only through a substantial increase in the number of French-speaking immigrants. This supposed control not only of education but also of immigration policy came at a time when Quebec was receiving less than 15 per cent of Canadian immigrants,[15] while it accounted for a quarter of Canada's population. After obtaining from the federal government the control of its own immigration policy, Quebec was able to admit thousands of French-speaking immigrants, coming not from France but mostly from former French possessions in Africa and the Caribbean. Although many non-French-speaking immigrants from other parts of the world were admitted, their children had to be schooled in French and not, as in the past, in either English or French.

Before the charter, most immigrants to Quebec, almost 90 per cent of whom settled in the Montreal area, had sent their children to English schools. They could now no longer do so; as early as 1991–92, 76 per cent of the immigrant children were studying in French (Paillé, 2002, 54). Consequently, a quarter-century after the enactment of the charter, some 100,000 living in Quebec by 2001 (a quarter of them Quebec-born; out-migrants and deceased excluded) had received their education in French in Quebec while they were children (Paillé, 2002, 60). By 2001, some 45 per cent had French as their working language in the city of Montreal (Conseil, 2005). Within one generation (1971–2001), French as a home language had almost doubled (from 9.3 per cent to 19.7 per cent) (see chapter 9). This shift did not account, however, for that quarter of Quebec's foreign-born immigrants who had already left, most of them within less than two years (Forget, 2004). Nevertheless, in Montreal, 10 per cent of whose population by the year 2001 was foreign-born, third-language speakers (representing more than 150 different languages) now outnumbered (by 10 to 8) the native speakers of English. Another unforeseen consequence of these policies, after a generation of French-speaking immigration, was a profound modification of the character of traditional French Canadian society in Quebec. It also affected the interpretation of the doctrine of the pact between Canada's two founding peoples (see chapter 1).

The implementation of federal language policy also experienced some unintended consequences. Some of its components were dependent for their implementation on the collaboration of the provinces, which was ensured at the time when the policy was in the making. Subsequent changes in provincial politics, however, resulted in the revocation of these promises, making it impossible to implement the policies on which they were based. Consequently, any federal policy on community language services was interpreted by most provinces as an infringement on their jurisdiction. That is another reason why the implementation of the federal bilingual districts policy was doomed to failure. Even preliminary suggestions of their possible creation were sometimes counterproductive, as, for example, in the case of the Bonnyville contretemps (see chapter 1). To these unintended consequences one could add many of the attempts to make the public service bilingual.

ADAPTATION

Language policies are solutions to problems arising in social circumstances at certain times and at given places. These policies can consequently become outdated through changes in the society for which they were originally fashioned. So when circumstances change, policies may need to adapt. Some policies, however, are more adaptable than others; some of the most adaptable have also been the most enduring.

If, for example, we compare the language policies of Canada with those of Quebec, we find that although both have adapted to changing circumstances, they have not done so in the same way and to the same extent. There are two reasons: first, the mechanisms of adaptation are not the same; second, the procedures are different. These differences have determined the level and extent of adaptation, both structural and social.

Structural Modification

This type of modification includes changes in the policy itself (policy amendments) and in the way it is applied (management procedures).

POLICY AMENDMENTS
These have to do with the content of the policy. Examples for Canada include the restructuring of the Official Languages Act; for Quebec, the succession of bills on amendments to the Charter of the French Language. For the latter, the changes were instigated through different procedural mechanisms: recommendations of its statutory advisory board, public opinion surveys, academic consultations, and assorted court challenges and amendments following federal intervention, particularly after the patriation in 1982 of the Canadian Constitution. For Canada's language policies, they have often

been initiatives of the Treasury Board, functioning through ad hoc committees and task forces with defined mandates.

In practice, Canada's mechanism has been more ponderous than Quebec's. The federal one must overcome several hurdles before the recommendations of its task forces appear on Parliament's legislative agenda, where they may be ranked far from the top. In Quebec, however, the permanent advisory board reports directly to a designated cabinet minister, who can fast-track new bills through the National Assembly, where language questions are always politically important.

MANAGEMENT PROCEDURES

These concern the workings of the institution responsible for implementing a language policy. They include the creation and abolition of administrative departments and additions and reductions to language bureaucracies for purposes of increasing their efficiency or decreasing their budget.

In Canada a quarter-century of changes in management procedures were needed to attain, by successive approximations, the objectives of federal language policies. For example, recommendations from the Bibeau and Coulombe task forces resulted in major changes, such as the creation and later abolition of the French language units. Further examples may be found under the section on bilingualizing the public service (see chapter 1).

In Quebec some management procedures were specified in its Charter of the French Language. During its implementation, however, the need to modify these procedures or create new ones became evident. Some were the work of inter-ministerial committees; others emanated from within the bureaucracy itself. Changes were also initiated by reactions of the public, particularly those of the "new minority" as represented by long-established English-speaking institutions. Others were occasioned by the need to comply with the judgments of the courts on a number of contested procedures.

Social Accommodation

The extent of any social accommodation to a language policy depends on the type of society for which it was intended. In societies such as Quebec before its Quiet Revolution, within its rural, traditional, and faith-based communities, little if anything ever changed, and policies remained stable. Since then, Quebec has undergone profound and accelerating social changes to which policies have had to adapt. Some of these changes affected the whole of Canada, having to do with the dynamics of interaction between language and society, the understanding of which requires extensive analysis.

Social adaptation of language policies is often based on feedback from non-governmental organizations, political activists, and concerned citizens, especially at the federal level. In contradistinction to Canadian language policy management, Quebec has maintained provisions for ongoing social feedback from its internal and external advisory groups, such as the Comité ministériel permanent au développement culturel (1997) and the Estates-General on the future of French (2001) – and this in addition to the regular reports of its statutory advisory council and its outside consultants (Georgeault and Pagé, 2006). An analysis of these reports over the years reveals an increasing concern for policy adaptations to the languages and cultures of immigrants. Such concern has increased with the rapidly changing makeup of the population to whom the policy would apply: who they are (demographic adaptation) and what they do (social adaptation).

DEMOGRAPHIC ADAPTATION

To what extent has the language policy adapted to the makeup of the population to whom it will apply? From the outset, Quebec's language policy made provisions for its English-speaking and aboriginal communities. The large, well-entrenched English institutions were permitted to operate in their language, save when services to a French-speaking public had to be provided in French. As for Quebec's aboriginal languages, protection for them was provided in the Charter of the French Language (arts. 87, 88, and 95). In subsequent and more specific legislation, Quebec recognized a number of aboriginal communities within its territory as distinct nations by virtue of language, land, race, and patrimony, by the same token as the descendants of the French settlers who colonized the St Lawrence valley had considered themselves a nation. Legally and structurally, therefore, Quebec rated as a multinational society (Mackey and Verdoodt, 1975).

Yet throughout the province, especially in its cities, a rapidly growing multi-ethnic workforce had converted Quebec into a de facto multicultural society, wherein the use of French and not English as the common language made Quebec a distinct society. To maintain this language-oriented distinction while nurturing a dream of nationhood, the language policy could not be based on the creed of kinship. The Quebec government consequently added to its criteria for admission the acceptance by the immigrant of a *contrat social* that included the recognition of French as the language of public discourse, along with a number of democratic principles of equality and tolerance (Gouvernement du Québec, 1990). Quebec's population had become as cosmopolitan as that of the rest of Canada – and, indeed, of other mature industrial states whose growing economy depended on imported labour. If such a state needed new workers, it had to accommodate them; if it did not, they had to accommodate to the state. If they were no longer needed, the state had a problem: the assimilation of a multitude of first- and second-generation immigrants by schooling them in a language not that of their home. What perpetuated the problem was the fact that the immigrants were now in regular interpersonal or electronic contact with their home-land. Only a small minority could switch language and identity. A noted few, admittedly, did master their second language as well as, sometimes better than, most citizens had mastered their first.

Since the second half of the past century, Canada's foreign-born population has been increasing faster than it could possibly be assimilated. Eventually came the realization that the country no longer belonged to its two found-ing peoples. It had become a country of immigrants from all quarters of the globe, of people who had survived through adaptation – change of country, occupation, and language – and through a readiness to move from province to province and city to city in search of a better life. This phenomenon, of course, was not special to Canada. It was part of a worldwide trend: the dis-placement of people from poorer and younger developing countries to the richer and aging developed world, the wealth of whose nations had become increasingly dependent on a migrant and increasingly mobile workforce.[16]

In Quebec, however, this high and unexpected degree of mobility had placed its economy in direct competition with other provinces for the retention of its immigrant workers. If it could not offer them better economic incentives, it was yet capable of providing them with cultural ones, such as, for ex-ample, family literacy in their mother tongue, something the federal policy of multiculturalism was not capable of doing (see chapter 8). Notwithstanding an aversion to this federal policy, some accommodation of immigrant lan-guages seemed to be part of the new thinking on the renovation of Quebec's language policies (Stefanescu and Georgeault, 2005). This new approach in-cludes the substitution of mother-tongue and home-language criteria for that of language use "dans le domaine public." It would shift some half a million Quebec residents to the French side of the language ledger, while placing a comparable number outside Quebec on the English side, including the vast majority of French-speakers in western Canada. It would consequently fur-ther polarize the French Quebec/English Canada divide. Such arbitrary label-ling of people without their consent is quite different from the measuring of variations in the use of a language within its private and public domains (Paillé and Comeau, 2005). Yet such policy modifications were unlikely to stem the loss to other provinces of those French-speaking immigrants who had entered Quebec thanks to its preferential language-oriented immigration policy (Dubreuil, 2006).

Canada's immigration policy had also demanded changes in the accommodation of selected workers. The policy was designed to attract an educated workforce unlikely to become a dependent unskilled underclass. In addition to the economic opportunities, high living standards, and superior quality of life, part of the attraction offered to prospective immigrants was the maintenance of their home language and culture. It was something these professional and entrepreneurial incomers were quite capable of doing while also maintaining their stakes in their homelands and their intention to return. For many, Canada was simply a country of convenience. Consequently, the first half of the multicultural policy, aimed at maintaining the Canadian mosaic, would eventually have to be downgraded in favour of the second half, aimed at promoting inter-ethnic dialogue. In practice, this shift meant less federal funding for folklore festivals and more support for cross-cultural communication and inter-ethnic enterprises. It initiated a move toward a policy of inter-culturalism whereby the right to be different supposes a duty to work toward the common good, while the responsibilities of citizenship take precedence over ethnic adherence and extraterritorial allegiance. When strangers become neighbours, the need to live together would pre-empt the desire to be left alone.

BEHAVIORAL ADAPTATION

A language policy must also adapt to changes in the communication behaviour of the society to which it applies. Over the past few decades, these changes have been phenomenal. Indeed, they have transformed the very foundation of society: intercommunication, the crucial component of language policy. Changes in the availability, range, and expanding use of new communications media have confronted established language policies with a new reality which includes media societies, communities as networks, culture as a commodity, and languages without borders.

Media Societies. A society comes into being through the integration of the needs and interests of individuals and groups. In the past few decades, however, its evolution has had not so much to do with transforming groups into society as it has with the transformation of society into groups with different purposes, interests, values, sizes, and locations. Crucial to the causes of this transformation is the distinction between communication and intercommunication: their uses, costs, coverage, and availability. Mass communication was formerly a vertical, top-down enterprise; it has become a horizontal, multidirectional activity. Passive audiences have become active and interactive groups. Newspaper readers have become Internet writers, while the press as an institution has had to give ground to online citizen journalism. The unquestioned authority of experts has had to face the so-cialization of their expertise: established encyclopedias confront evolving wikipedias. Small language-based community radio stations have also be-come interactive, while the portable radio is used less than the ubiquitous cellphone. Broadcasters have witnessed the fragmentation of their formerly passive audiences, whose members have begun broadcasting to one another. People in the business of selling audiences to advertisers have had to find other ways of making money.[17]

All these transformations affect the meaning of community, the use of its distinct languages and language varieties, and the fate of its distinct cultures, for they modify the connotations of such traditional concepts as "speech community," "nation," "national language," "language norm," and "territoriality" – with consequences for the future of languages and lan-guage policies. A speech community may be reduced to a network. The net-work may no longer be place-dependent, as more people from farther away intercommunicate for longer periods, eventually becoming interlinked into a functioning web-community. While individuals independently create and maintain such networks, the state, as protector of its language, becomes dependent on them.

Communities as Networks. Communication creates communities. In order the better to communicate with one another, people with common interests have tended to congregate in the same place. As communication has become progressively independent of distance, communities, including speech com-munities, have become less place-dependent.

In the past, for example, one of the greatest hindrances to the maintenance of French outside Quebec and the Canadian Maritimes was the isolation of its speakers. The advent and availability of the new media of intercom-munication, permitting the growth of long-distance speech networks, helps provide the sort of cohesion they require to use and maintain their lan-guage. It also helps them act politically as a single speech community able to deal directly with the federal government. Yet each member of this speech community may at the same time belong to other web-communities and participate in their activities. These communities may be faith-based, age-based, or based on common interests in different domains, while varying in size, makeup, and activity. Between those based on common interests such as culture and religion and those based on vested interests such as business and employment, there may exist a dynamic overlap between belonging and dependence of various types, each varying in degree, duration, intensity, and commitment. These are increasingly influenced by the range and frequency of personal communication and media intercommunications, which have become almost limitless.

Examples are not hard to find. Indeed, they are hard to avoid. Witness the pervasiveness of podcasting and personal blogs – always on, open to all, and open-ended. Within three years, the number of new weblogs increased from a few hundred to almost thirty million by the year 2006, according to Technocrati, a rating agency that tracks them at the rate of fifty thousand an hour. These are also continually interlinked into blogrolls of like-minded and same-language groups. All this activity has changed the nature of the language community from one dependent on face-to-face communication to a network based on an increasingly more frequent use of telecommunication. People whose daily lives were confined to whatever was within driving distance have now the means to maintain daily contact with like-minded or same-language communities anywhere and at any time. The number of these groups and their frequency of contact and degree of commitment have been variable. So the state and its language policies have had to take into account the rapidly increasing and far-ranging poly-socialization of its population, comprised as it now is of people belonging to several networks with different purposes, located in different places, and possibly operating in different languages or language varieties.

As a token of this phenomenon, one can simply witness the behaviour of people stuck in an airport waiting room. The most voluble are likely to be the most isolated. A few are using their cellphones in one hand while operating their laptops with the other, to intercommunicate with different people in various places and possibly in different languages. This phenomenon is a far cry from the time when people confined together were constrained to bond into a transient community – a far cry, indeed, from the pilgrims of Chaucer's *Tales* or the plague-avoiding congregation of Boccaccio's *Decameron*.

Culture as a Commodity. This media revolution in world intercommunication has accelerated the globalization of markets, which in turn increases the variety of whatever may be marketable. The result has been an immense increase in the commoditization of almost everything visible and invisible, tangible and intangible, culture included; for intangible commodities can be the fruits of the imagination, demand for them manufactured, and a desire to acquire them created through aggressive advertising and mass marketing, using procedures of "creative capitalism" (Toffler and Toffler, 2006).

This sort of commercial enterprise includes the commoditization of culture, dominated by marketable products of mass entertainment that know no borders. No place or time remains for local traditional cultures, which are less often experienced and eventually forgotten. This unrelenting process has been identified as "cultural amnesia." Since culture is by its nature integrative and cumulative, any such break with its continuity bodes ill for the future of a society (Jacobs, 2004).

So much for the future of language policies that fail to adapt. Like any other top-down model of communication or command-and-control enterprise, language policy may be entering a period of diminishing returns. The activities of a formal language bureaucracy enacting directives emanating from the minds of language planners seem to be having less and less effect on the mutually modifying practices of the online discourse of the young generation and their future transmission of the language.

Languages without Borders. For the first time in history, human speech has been liberated from the constraints of time, space, and number. By the year 2008, according to the International Telecommunications Union, there were 3.3 billion subscribers to a mobile-phone service, meaning that already more than half the world's population had access. Like all systems of intercommunication, from telephone networks to stock exchanges, languages increase exponentially in value with each new user or group of users. The more these systems are used, the more they are worth. An increase in the use, through the new media, of already widespread languages multiplies their value. These are the languages preferred by anyone wanting to spread a message in a tongue that most people will understand; this preference further enhances its value. Such languages are few in number, but they are the ones chosen by thousands of bloggers who, free from state control, have created multinational virtual communities in all quarters of the globe. The size and number of such virtual communities are likely to continue to increase, since they are inversely correlated to age.[18]

On the other hand, if the medium is part of the message, its purpose being the use and propagation of a language, then the form of the text begins to take precedence over its content. Same-language groups, like isolated communities, are thus provided with a range of contacts across national and international borders, since their networks in cyberspace can link together users of the same language whoever they are and wherever they may be. They also provide bilinguals with occasions to use their other tongue, thus enhancing its value. It is to this new reality that language policies will have to adapt.

Thus augmenting the range, number, and frequency of intercommunication means a potential increase in the use of all languages. It is like the rising tide that lifts all boats, even the small ones that may survive its surge. Consequently, certain ambitious multilingual policies, such as those of Canada's Western

Arctic, may have finally become feasible. This outcome does not mean that speakers of minority languages will no longer depend on the uses of the ever-expanding languages of wider communication. It means that smaller languages are able to coexist with them within a long-term diglossic relationship. At the same time, the expanding range of intercommunication within and between same-language groups must inevitably result in an intergenerational dialect-levelling, analogous to that which fashioned national languages such as French and English as a result of the communications infrastructures of the Industrial Revolution. Already in Canada's northlands the speech of the younger generation in isolated Inuit communities has become noticeably more uniform, just as the national standards of polycentric languages become more alike as they drift towards world standards. The same applies to the widespread diasporas of reviving languages such as Basque, Irish, and Welsh, whose dynamics and well-financed language policies provide for an extensive use of the new media.

Number-wise, it is the capacity of the new media to perpetuate clan-sized same-language groups, no matter how widely scattered, that permits their languages to survive. Canadian immigrants can now maintain constant and long-lasting oral contact with family and friends in their native dialects as if they had never left home – capable of being mentally and emotively more present online than they might physically be in Canada. It is less the use of language as the communication of content than it is communion, cohesion, and the reassurance of togetherness. For the millions of immigrant families in Europe and North America whose home language would die out with the passing of the last surviving grandparent, it means a possible continuation in the use and contact with the language of the homeland, if the descendants so desire. That desire, however, cannot be taken for granted. Many third-generation immigrant youths, as online web users, have eschewed their parents' same-language groups in favour of like-minded chat rooms that echo their egocentric interests, feelings, and prejudices concerning the trivia of popular culture in an idiom without borders (Sunstein, 2007). This progressive uncoupling of land and language may eventually become as significant as its initial coupling some ten thousand years ago as a consequence of the great agricultural revolution (Bellwood and Renfrew, 2002).

CONCLUSION

Since language, that indispensable component of any society, permeates its every pore, anything that modifies its role, its uses, its forms, or its functions is likely to have some far-ranging consequences. That is why, in comparing and evaluating language policies, we are dealing with something that, although problem-oriented, is by its nature multi-dimensional. It is not the purview of any single academic discipline. Language policies can be neither compared nor evaluated without taking into account their interdisciplinary dimensions: political, cultural, and economic motives; the demography of diverse populations; the ephemeral decisions of partisan politics; the nature and status of the languages concerned; and the very principles that govern states and institutions. Although the resulting language policies may be a road map to the future, the where and the why of their very existence are dependent on the past, on the patrimony of the policy's components, their history and origins.

APPENDIX: AN OVERVIEW OF THE CHAPTER

Principles and Structures
  Justification
  Consistency
    Internal Consistency
    External Consistency
  Feasibility
    Policies of Language Equality
    Developmental Policies
    Language Revival and Survival
    Language Conservation
  Cost versus Benefit
Implementation
    Language Form
    Language Functions
    Language Behaviour
  Compliance
    Mechanisms
    Methods
  Consequences
    Intended Consequences
    Unintended Consequences
Adaptation
  Structural Modification
    Policy Amendments
    Management Procedures

Social Accommodation
   Demographic Adaptation
   Behavioral Adaptation
   Media Societies
   Communities as Networks
   Culture as a Commodity
  Languages without Borders
Conclusion

NOTES

1 Hence the Sanskrit *devanāgari*, the official script of Hindi, India's nationwide official language.

2 *Public Service Bulletin* 12 (Public Service Commission, 1971).

3 *Public Service Bulletin* 39 (Public Service Commission, 1969).

4 *Treasury Board Directive*, March 1971.

5 *Official Languages Act* (Ottawa: Queen's Printer, 1969).

6 *Constatation du Comité des droits de l'homme au titre du paragraphe 4 de l'article 5 du Protocole facultatif se rapportant au Pacte international relatif aux droits civils et politiques, quarante-septième session, concernant les communications nos. 359/1989 et 385/1989*: "les minorités visées à l'article 27 [of the covenant] sont les groupes minoritaires à l'échelle de l'État ..., et non pas des minorités dans une province. Les citoyens canadiens anglophones ne peuvent être considérés comme une minorité linguistique."

7 *Official Language Ordinance* 1 (1970): E-5.

8 Between 1997 and 2000, for example, 1,860 dissertations in linguistics were produced, of which 1,152 were in and about English (Newman, 2003); the rest were about French, Spanish, German, and other well-known languages. Few were about any of the thousands of lesser-known languages.

9 An example is the fieldwork of a Canadian-trained linguist who every few months has emailed to the institute some thousand attested items of his native tongue from his home in Cameroon.

10 To this end, a number of contributing publications has appeared, such as those by Jacques Maurais: *La norme linguistique*, followed by *L'Analyse linguistique de quatre mille courriels* (2003) and *La langue des bulletins d'information à la radio* (2005).

11 This is a major challenge: marshalling the skills of creative lexicographers, coupled with the efficient and widespread use of modern communications media, which of themselves have generated most of the novel concepts that need naming. These

appear as new English words that immediately enter online dictionaries, spreading instantly throughout the world. Some are actually acronyms for English phrases such as "What I know is…" abbreviated to "Wiki," which becomes a root morpheme for the formation of other words such as "wikipedia." Some new media terms continually change their shapes and sizes: the "web-log" of 1997, after folding into "blog," propagated as such and in 2004 became the "word of the year" of the standard *Merriam-Webster Dictionary*, with its progeny: "blogger," "blogosphere," and "blogroll." The following year "podcast" was ranked as "word of the year" by the *New Oxford American Dictionary*. It is before such words become standard English that French equivalents must become available.

12 The enactment was far less draconian than the first draft. It was in effect a compromise that permitted English-only new films to be screened in cinemas for the first six weeks, after which a French version (dubbed or subtitled) had to be provided.

13 Intermittently called the Commission de surveillance, depending on the party in power.

14 The change was evident even at the level of the ubiquitous bilingual stop signs, on which a generation of militant graphitists, at hundreds of Quebec street corners, had persisted in deleting the English half (the verb "stop"). After decades of such systematic defacement, the bilingual sign was replaced by a monolingual one bearing only the French noun *arrêt* (Leclerc, 1989).

15 Targeted at about 1 per cent of Canada's total number of inhabitants, more or less, depending on the party in power.

16 In places as diverse as the Philippines, Poland, and Mexico, as many as half the working inhabitants of the poorest villages must intermittently cross state borders to support their families at home, while maintaining constant contact with them, but without becoming citizens of their workplace.

17 Significantly, for example, in June 2006 the federal Canadian Radio-television and Telecommunications Commission was petitioned by the owner of some popular radio stations in Quebec for permission to reduce the percentage of compulsory Canadian content in his broadcasts, on the grounds that he was losing his young listeners at a rate that would soon put him out of business. It transpired, however, that his audience had simply migrated to other media, where they could pick and listen to what they wanted when they wanted it. For them, radio and its egocentric disc jockeys had become as redundant as the daily newspaper. By the year 2005, more than half the daily visits to some websites were by teenagers.

18 By 2007, for example, people under thirty were using their cellphones for messaging more than twice as often as those over fifty, according to a survey by the Pew Research Centre.

PART TWO

International Perspectives

Introduction to Part Two

MICHAEL A. MORRIS

A SURVEY OF THE LITERATURE

Canada's position as a bilingual country is embedded in federal policy, which promotes French throughout Canada. This policy contrasts with Quebec's management of French within provincial territory, including language promotion as well as language interdiction and language imposition (e.g., in Quebec any contract written in a language other than French is de jure invalid; foreign newcomers must send their children to French schools). This relatively long-standing federal-provincial contrast has generated a number of studies comparing Canada with other bilingual and multilingual countries. A commonly shared orientation of such studies is that lessons can be learned through such comparisons.

Contrasts between Canada and Europe have been most common. For example, recurring international comparisons with Canada have included Belgium, Catalonia (Spain), and Switzerland, which share to one degree or another with Quebec special language provisions for linguistic groups within specified parts of national territory. One chapter in Ball (1997) compares language policies in Belgium, Canada, and Switzerland. McRae's contrast between Belgium, Canada, Finland, and Switzerland (2007) was reviewed in chapter 2.

An analysis by Rocher and Marcotte (1997) compares language legislation in Catalonia and Quebec from a variety of perspectives and concludes that in spite of significant differences, each has had an important practical and symbolic impact. Since the Catalonia-Quebec comparison has been fairly common, it will suffice here to mention an edited book (Tremblay and Pares i Maicas, 1987), which is the most comprehensive attempt to compare these two political subdivisions of larger countries. The method used in this volume is to pair chapters on the same theme, one dealing with Catalonia and the other with Quebec. Of nineteen chapters in the book, two deal with language policy, and in accord with the pairing method, the first is on Quebec (chapter 10) and the second on Catalonia (chapter 11). A final, short chapter of conclusions does comment on the various pairings, but with language policy being but one of ten issues covered in only five pages, the language comparisons made are abrupt and superficial.

Another study (Milian i Massana, 1994) compares language rights of five countries – Belgium, Canada, Italy, Spain, and Switzerland – with particular emphasis on education. While this multiple comparison is interesting, the focus of the study is fairly narrow.

Some other kinds of European contrasts with Canada may be grouped together. Canada and Wales are contrasted, with a focus on the relationship between neo-liberal governance and language policies (Cardinal and Denault, 2006). The relationship between institutions and groups is examined from this perspective and thus is also relevant for Part Four of the present book, on group comparisons. Another interesting yet narrow comparison asks if federalism makes a difference for minority language policy in Canada and Europe (Covell, 2001).

A conference organized by Linda Cardinal addressed debates about language policies in Canada and Europe, but the collection that resulted does not contain any comprehensive comparisons (Cardinal et al., 2005). Most of the papers examine Canada or Europe separately, with a few making explicit, if narrow, comparisons, including Israel and Quebec, the Northwest Territories and the European Union, South Africa, and Gaelic in Scotland and Canada.

An edited work aspires to view Canadian language policies in a larger perspective through comparison particularly with selected European cases (Wallot, 2005, vii). One chapter is on Western European policies toward cultural and linguistic minorities (19ff.), and another is on language policy in Switzerland (39ff.), but neither topic is related to Canada; nor is there any synthesis provided in the introduction or in the concluding chapters. A chapter by Jean Laponce is comparative in orientation, with some attention given to Canada (3ff.), although the focus of the chapter is on identifying patterns relating dominant languages to minority ones. Laponce elaborates this approach in a book published in 2006, which is reviewed below.

Still another kind of language policy comparison is between Canada and its larger neighbour to the south, the United States. For example, one study reviews debates in Canada and the United States respectively about bilingualism and linguistic minorities but without comparing them (Kalantzis,

Cope, and Slade 1989, chap. 2, "The Language Question: Key Debates"). Mackey (1983) has posed the question of the extent to which the Canadian experience in language planning is applicable to the United States, which he addresses by contrasting the circumstances of both countries. Direct lessons are not formulated, but the contrast can alert policy-makers to what has worked or not in each country. A more recent study by Mackey (2003) compares bilingualism in Canada and the United States. Bourhis and Marshall (1999) also contrast similarities and differences in linguistic approaches of the United States and Canada but without examining their interaction.

An edited book by Ricento and Burnaby (1998) promises a systematic US-Canadian comparison but does not so deliver. A quotation by a reviewer on the back cover of this publication states, "It is the only collection I know of that attempts a comparative analysis of language policy in the United States and Canada within a historical-structural framework." While the chapters in the book are carefully written, the editors acknowledge in their conclusion that "few of the chapters are direct comparisons between the two countries" (Ricento and Burnaby, 1998, 331). The book is divided into five parts, each of which juxtaposes separate chapters on Canada and the United States. These are not comparisons, but merely juxtapositions.

A different kind of comparison relates Canadian language issues to North American integration. A publication by Quebec's Conseil de la langue française (Fréchette, 2001) maintains that linguistic diversity can be promoted in the context of North American integration, and for this purpose it envisages a leading role for Quebec in association with the Canadian federal government. My article on linguistic diversity in North American integration complements this earlier study (Morris, 2003).

Another language policy study is unusual in comparing support for minority languages in Canada with that of a Third World or developing country, Cameroon (Robinson, 1994; Courcy, 2008). Legislation governing the promotion of minority languages in Canada and Cameroon have some similarities, but in Cameroon English is the minority official language and more underprivileged than in Quebec, with whose language policies the comparison would have been more appropriate. Also, implementation in the Third World is greatly complicated by problems of development, including scarce resources.

A report of a commission appointed by the government of Quebec is interesting in examining provincial language policy from a comparative perspective, especially in chapter 7, on francophone and international solidarity (Commission des États généraux, 2001). Recommendations of the commission call for a more active role of the Quebec government in promoting the French language beyond the province by reinforcing ties with other francophone groups in Canada, the United States, the Americas, and the Francophonie. Linguistic cooperation with the province of New Brunswick is also proposed. It is nonetheless striking that the report makes no mention of potential collaboration with any other federal or provincial language policies in Canada for promotion of the French language.

AN OVERVIEW OF THE CHAPTERS IN PART TWO

In chapter 4, "The Language Issue in the United States, Canada, and Quebec: Some Comparative Aspects," Jacques Maurais compares language policies and practices in the United States to those in Canada and Quebec. A careful case is made that incorrect perceptions of the Canadian federal language policy and most particularly that of Quebec are common in the United States. Maurais expresses concern that such distortions are not just espoused by extreme sectors of US opinion but also are shared by others who otherwise are reasonably well-informed. He corrects misconceptions about Canadian language policies by emphasizing that Quebec's language policy is constructive in defending a francophone linguistic minority through democratic procedures from anglophone majorities in both Canada and North America, and hence it should constitute a positive comparison for others, rather than a negative one. While francophones constitute a large majority in Quebec, in this context they may be considered a regional linguistic majority.

Two contrasts in Maurais's previous work are of particular interest here since they are both scarce in the literature: multiple-country comparisons and those involving indigenous languages. Both constitute important directions for future research. Maurais edited a major work on language planning (1987), including profiles of the approaches of nine different countries to this subject. An article in the volume by Maurais himself analyzes Quebec's language planning approach, while some of the other chapters deal with countries or political subdivisions often discussed in relationship to Quebec (i.e., Belgium, Catalonia, and Finland). Another major edited work by Maurais (1992 and 1996) assesses indigenous languages within Quebec's political borders and how its governments have dealt with these languages and groups. Several of the chapters in Maurais's book are comparative in orientation.

In chapter 5 of the present book, "The Danger of Denial of Languages: An Eastern European-Canadian Comparison," Yaroslav Bilinsky develops a relatively unexplored comparison between Canadian language policies and those of the former Soviet Union and various successor states, including the

Russian federation and selected Eastern European countries. The Soviet Union long suppressed ethnic and linguistic aspirations in its component republics as well as in neighbouring communist states, a strategy that contributed to the disintegration of the Eastern bloc. In the post–Cold War era, ethnic and linguistic tensions have often continued in this vast area, leading Bilinsky to warn policy-makers about the denial of language or suppression of cultural and linguistic identity. There are degrees of denial of language, and the variety of cases surveyed allows Bilinsky to specify the implications of denial of language in varying circumstances. Canada is placed on a continuum of relative denial of languages, where these other countries are located as well, an approach that positions him to make discriminating comparisons. Inasmuch as previous comparisons with Canada have tended to be limited to relatively few countries, it is most welcome to have new kinds of linguistic comparisons. There is a need to build on this neglected field and to continue to identify still other countries with which it would be instructive to compare Canada and for which the Canadian experience would be relevant.

Chapter 6, "Canada's Domestic French-speaking Groups and the International Francophonie Compared," by Jürgen Erfurt, relies on several innovative techniques. Erfurt compares an international institution, three Canadian language policies, and domestic Canadian francophone groups. The international institution is the Francophonie, and the three Canadian entities active in this organization are the Canadian federal government and the provincial governments of New Brunswick and Quebec. Canadian French-speaking groups are related to these various actors, including their interaction.

Erfurt's approach suggests at least two new directions for research on international perspectives. While heretofore nearly all international comparisons have been country-oriented, Erfurt relates Canadian language policies to an international organization as well as to domestic-international interaction.

4

The Language Issue in the United States, Canada, and Quebec: Some Comparative Aspects

JACQUES MAURAIS

In this chapter I will make a number of comparisons between the United States, Canada, and Quebec, all of which are inspired by the language debate that has raged in the United States since, approximately, the presidency of Ronald Reagan. This debate, even if it included among its instigators a former linguist (Senator S.I. Hayakawa, of Canadian origin),[1] has been based on a certain number of false ideas. These include factual errors as well as misleading and distorted comparisons with Canada and especially with Quebec. This chapter calls attention to these distortions and errors without undertaking an exhaustive comparison between the linguistic policies of the United States, Canada, and Quebec. For a more detailed comparison of the language policies practised in the United States and Canada, the reader is invited to consult Mackey (1983); for treatments of the language policy of Quebec, see Maurais (1987 and 2003), the report of the Comité interministériel sur la situation de la langue française (1996), the report by the Commission of the Estates-General on the situation of the French language (2001), and the evaluation of the linguistic situation produced by the Office québécois de la langue française (2008).

JACQUES MAURAIS

ONE LANGUAGE, ONE NATION

An idea that underlies the action of groups such as English Only and English First is that a country should have one and only one language ("One Language, One Nation"). This concept reflects the old idea of the nation-state and hence is not new in the United States. As early as 1919, Theodore Roosevelt declared: "We have room but for one language here, and that is the English language, for we intend to see that the crucible turns our people out as Americans, of American nationality, and not as dwellers in a polyglot boarding-house" (Crawford, 1992, 59; cited by Ricento, 1996). From the linguistic point of view, this idea reflects an illusion. It is estimated that at the present time some 5,000 languages are spoken in the world,[2] while there are only about two hundred countries. Unilingualism may be found only in some micro-states.

THE ABSENCE OF AN OFFICIAL LANGUAGE

At the time of its independence, the United States did not choose an official language. This lack of choice was deliberate. Hence it should not be concluded that the United States at the time did not have a language policy.[3] In effect, liberalism or non-interventionism can be a form of language policy: "From our survey of American history, we have seen that our not having an official language was not an oversight by the authors of the Constitution, but a well-thought-through effort at language planning" (Marshall, 1986, 70).[4] From the beginning, the United States has applied a Jacobin language policy (or a free-market one in the name of competitive democracy). The result today is that English unilingualism reigns uncontested in the federal government. According to a report of the General Accounting Office, from 1990 to 1994 less than 1 per cent of the documents of the federal government were produced in languages other than English.[5] This finding led Edward M. Chen (1995), a member of American Civil Liberties Union of Northern California, to conclude: "If anything, ... language minorities are vastly under-served."

In varying degrees, all the states of the United States are unilingually English, even if only twenty-nine have declared English as their official language: Alabama (1990), Alaska (1990 and 1998), Arizona (2006), Arkansas (1987), California (1986),[6] Colorado (1988), Florida (1988), Georgia (1986 and 1996), Hawaii (1978), Idaho (2007), Illinois (1969), Indiana (1984), Iowa (2002), Kansas (2007), Kentucky (1984), Mississippi (1987), Missouri (1998), Montana (1995), Nebraska (1920), New Hampshire (1995), New York (2001), North Carolina (1987), North Dakota (1987), South Carolina (1987), South Dakota (1995), Tennessee (1984), Utah (2000), Virginia (1981 and 1996), and Wyoming (1996).[7]

The official language provision of 1988 in Arizona triggered a series of lawsuits. In 1995 the Court of Appeals of the 9th Judicial Circuit declared article 28 of the constitution of Arizona unconstitutional, adding that it was "by far the most restrictively-worded official-English law to date."[8] In 1996 the case was appealed to the Supreme Court of the United States, which in April 1998 upheld the decision of the Court of Appeals. In 2006 a milder wording on official English was introduced in the Arizona constitution. There has been no other case of annulment of a provision declaring English the official language of a state (House of Representatives, 1996).

Hawaii is theoretically bilingual, since article 15 of its constitution declares: "English and Hawaiian shall be the official languages of Hawaii, except that Hawaiian shall be required for public acts and transactions only as provided by law." In fact, Hawaii is unilingually English, a fact that the group US English understood well in including this state in its official English language list because the legal provision for Hawaiian is essentially symbolic.

In spite of what some believe, French does not have legal status in Louisiana. Nor has English any official status. Louisiana has never declared an "official language" as such. In 1812 it became the first and only state to enter the Union in which a non-English-speaking group commanded a popular majority. Because the dominance of French in Louisiana caused some concerns in Washington, Congress required the state's first constitution to safeguard the rights of English-speakers. This provision (later dropped) required that all laws and official documents be published in the language "in which the Constitution of the United States is written" – that is, in English, but *not only in English*.[9]

However, in the past some states were officially bilingual, such as California for about thirty years. Moreover, the Congress of Philadelphia in 1776 authorized the publication of its official reports in German and English, and a German version of these documents also appeared annually from 1786 to 1856. The first legislative document of Ohio, in 1772, was also published in German (Mackey, 2003). But these examples of bilingualism are rather isolated.

Puerto Rico is a special case: it is not an American state with full rights but, rather, has the status of an associated state. For a few years starting in 1990, Puerto Rico had only one official language, Spanish. But the law was subsequently amended, and this state again returned to being officially bilingual. (We will consider the case of Puerto Rico below, since it is often compared with Quebec.)

The situation is very different in Canada. Since the British conquest, bilingualism was always officially present in the federal administration, except for a short period (1840–48) when French lost its official status. The British North America Act of 1867 imposed bilingualism on the institutions of the federal Parliament and the legislature of Quebec. The provinces that were created in the west after 1867 were also officially bilingual, but in 1890 Manitoba declared itself to be unilingually English. In 1977 Quebec relied on this precedent to declare itself to be unilingually French (while still continuing to publish an unofficial English version of its laws and regulations). A reaction was not delayed: two years later the Supreme Court of Canada invalidated the entire chapter of the Charter of the French Language (commonly called Bill 101) on the language of legislation and justice and restored bilingualism. Another impact of this decision was that Manitoba again had to become officially bilingual, an outcome that can appear paradoxical insofar as French-speakers now do not constitute the principal minority, whereas at the time of the creation of this province French-speaking and English-speaking people were almost in parity. More recently, New Brunswick officially declared itself bilingual, a policy that was thereafter entrenched in the constitution of Canada. Also, it should be noted that the Northwest and Nunavut territories have English and French as official languages in addition to Native languages.

POLICIES ON ABORIGINAL LANGUAGES

Notwithstanding what has just been said about the free-market language policy and resulting English unilingualism followed by successive American governments, it should be added that the United States passed a law about aboriginal languages, whereas Canada does not have one (at least at the federal level). On 30 October 1990 the US Congress passed the Native American Languages Act, which recognizes the right to use Native languages as vehicles for teaching and gives power to the tribes, states, and territories to grant official status to these languages. In Canada only the governments of the Northwest and Nunavut territories have legislated specifically concerning aboriginal languages: the Official Languages Ordinance of 1984, which in 1988 was entrenched in the federal law on official languages. Moreover, Nunavut, which separated from the Northwest Territories in 1999, is looking at Quebec's language laws as an example and is currently in the process of writing its own official languages act, one that would give the Inuktitut language equal status with English and French. The Nunavut government contemplates making Inuktitut the working language of government by 2020. In Quebec the Charter of the French Language recognizes the right of aboriginal peoples to receive teaching in their respective languages. Since February 1983 the Quebec government has recognized the aboriginal peoples of Quebec as distinct nations. Subsequently, in March 1985, Quebec's National Assembly gave official recognition to this status (Trudel, 1992, 169–70).

RESTRICTIONS ON LANGUAGE USE

Some of the twenty-seven American states that have passed laws or constitutional amendments making English their official language have relied on these legislative provisions to adopt measures restricting the use of other languages in a way which has never been done in Quebec. And this is not a recent development. In the 1880s the Bennett Law in Wisconsin and the Edwards Law in Illinois had limited the use of German in schools (Ricento, 1996). Texas in 1890 permitted teaching of seven foreign languages, but in 1919 a law forbade any teaching of foreign languages in schools (Mackey, 2003). In the 1920s, following the Great War, about twenty midwestern states passed laws to forbid teaching of German. It was in this context that Nebraska made English its official language in 1921 (National Education Association, 1996, n.p.). Some of the US laws passed since the 1980s forbid supplying state or local services in a language other than English to clients who do not master the latter language: "by restricting the government's ability to communicate with and provide services to non-English speaking Americans, many of whom are children and elderly citizens, English-only laws deny fair and equal access to government. These limits, especially as they apply to such rights and services as voting assistance, education in a comprehensible language, health services and information, financial assistance such as social security and police protection, infringe upon important and fundamental rights" (Chen, 1995).

The constitutional modification of Arizona in 1988 had as a consequence the forbidding of state employees from communicating with clients in Spanish or Navajo (Chen, 1995). The 1980 anti-bilingualism ordinance decree of Dade County in Florida (text in Leclerc, 1989, 378–9)[12] had the effect of forbidding the distribution of bilingual materials on fire prevention, the publication of Metrorail schedules in foreign languages, the publication of Spanish-language consumer information, the provision of prenatal advice by the county hospital in Creole, funding for ethnic festivals (Chen, 1995), and even the forcing of a zoo to remove from its labels the names of its animals in scientific Latin nomenclature. In California, following the adoption in 1986 of Proposition 63, which made English the official language, several towns passed regulations limiting the number of languages that could appear in commercial announcements (Chen, 1995), notably in Monterey Park (Nunberg, 1989, 580). In this last city a bylaw was relied on to undercut bilingualism by forbidding public libraries from buying books in foreign languages (ibid.).

The adoption of so many linguistic measures has in certain cases spurred intolerance among the public. In the 1990s a bus driver forbade passengers to speak Spanish in his vehicle on the risk of eviction.[13] In Texas a judge even barred a mother from speaking Spanish to her child, saying that this practice was tantamount to "child abuse" (Chen, 1995). When the ordinance against bilingualism in Dade County, Florida, was in force, speaking Spanish in the school playground was forbidden (Nunberg, 1989, 581). In 2005 Wilson County, Tennessee, judge Barry Tatum told a Mexican woman who spoke only her native Mixteco that she should be able to speak English at a fourth-grade level within six months (and to use birth control!); if she failed to do so, he would begin the process of terminating her parental rights.[14]

In comparison, Quebec's Charter of the French Language, even in its original 1977 version (thus before constitutional challenges imposed greater flexibility), only decreed French unilingualism in a half-dozen domains (for example, commercial signage, announcements of administrative bodies, and roadway signposting). This unilingualism was accompanied by exceptions in most cases. Even when there were no exceptions, as for roadway signposting, pictograms were relied on to transmit messages easily to non-French-speakers. It would thus be false to portray the Charter of the French Language, even in its initial version, as an extremist law that tried to impose French unilingualism in all domains. Rather, it was a legislative effort to define and regulate relations between languages, especially between French and English, in Quebec – in other words to redefine the distribution of functions between these two languages. This philosophy, which underlies all of Bill 101, explains why the public administration is not barred from communicating with citizens in languages other than French. It also explains why Bill 101 and, later, Bill 142 have recognized the institutions of the English-speaking community.

Bill 142, dating from December 1986, guaranteed social and health services to the anglophone minority of Quebec in the English language outside the institutions managed by the anglophone community. Because of this bill, 254 health and social centres were then identified as having to provide services in English.[15] From the point of view of the language of services, it is important to note that Bill 101 gives rights to francophones (in its declaratory articles), while Bill 142 creates obligations for the organizations to offer services in English. In fact, Bill 142 gives rights to the English language, rather than to the anglophone community: because of this provision, both francophones and allophones can avail themselves of services in English. Moreover, Bill 142 has subsequently been integrated into Bill 120: article 15 specifies that every English-language-speaker has the right to receive health and social services in the English language (account being taken of the varying organization and resources of individual institutions); article 348 specifies by area the programs oriented to English-speakers; and according to article 508, the government is under an obligation "to specify among the institutions recognized by paragraph f of article 113 of the Charter of the French Language those who are to provide health and social services to English-speakers in the English language."

THE LEGITIMACY OF LANGUAGE POLICIES

The legitimacy that the Charter of the French Language establishes for French is not the same as that reflected in the measures passed or contemplated by the United States in the 1980s making English the official language either of the federation or of various states.

In Quebec, democratic legitimacy is at the root of Bill 101. This law was passed to correct historical injustices of which the francophone majority were the victims, especially those that were revealed when the report of the Royal Commission on Bilingualism and Biculturalism (the Laurendeau-Dunton Commission) was published in the mid-1960s. Recall that the report established that even in Quebec French-speakers ranked twelfth on the income scale, just above immigrants of Italian origin and Native Americans.

In the United States, analysts have described the English Only movement as right-wing and anti-immigrant: "The founder of US English, Michigan ophthalmologist John Tanton,[16] has long been interested in restricting immigration to the US, particularly from countries south of the border; ... financial records of US English revealed that the organization had received $680,000 between 1982 and 1989 from the Pioneer Fund, an organization dedicated to 'race betterment' through eugenics" (Ricento, 1996). In fact, before launching US English, Tanton had founded FAIR (the Federation for American Immigration Reform), which lobbied in favour of restriction on immigration (Nunberg, 1989, 579). As for English First, at its origin a project of the Committee to Protect the Family, it was founded by Larry Pratt, who also was president of the association Gun Owners of America (Draper and Jiménez, 1996; López, 1995). The English Only movement also receives support from groups such as the American Legion and the Veterans of Foreign Wars of the United States (cf. House of Representatives, 1996).

In Canada the group that has most closely resembled these American movements from the ideological point of view is without doubt the Alliance for the Preservation of English in Canada (APEC). It was APEC that was responsible from the beginning for the first of a wave of anti-bilingualism resolutions and bylaws, the 1987 resolution of Matilda township in Ontario (*La Presse*, 13 February 1990). In the wake of this resolution, the famous bylaw of Sault Ste Marie of January 1990 was passed and has since been interpreted by Franco-Ontarians as an "anti-French" bylaw.[17]

THE LINGUISTIC INTEGRATION OF IMMIGRANTS

The issue of linguistic integration of immigrants is very different in Quebec from the United States. In Quebec, at the time the Charter of the French Language was passed in 1977, barely 20 per cent of allophone students were enrolled in French schools (Maurais, 1987, 372). A quarter of a century later, the situation has been completely reversed. And let it be emphasized that official policy aims at the integration of immigrants, not their assimilation. Integration as it is practised in Quebec may be defined in the following way: "Integration is a long-term process of multi-dimensional adaptation; integration is distinct from assimilation; mastery of a common language plays a key role in the process of integration; integration is not achieved until the immigrant or his descendants participates fully in collective life, and integration implies the development of a sentiment of belonging to the host society" (Conseil, 1991, 9).

In the United States a very large proportion of immigrants learn English rapidly, even in the absence of linguistic legislation. It is generally recognized that 97 per cent of Americans speak English. In the most important linguistic minority, Spanish-speakers, 80 per cent speak English. Among first-generation Mexican Americans, 95 per cent can speak English; by the second generation, more than 50 per cent can no longer speak Spanish (Chen, 1995).

PERCEPTIONS OF THE LINGUISTIC SITUATION
IN QUEBEC

The documents of US English and English First contain many misleading statements about the linguistic situation in Quebec. For example: "Look what happened in Canada, where radical bilingualists have held power in Quebec. It is now a criminal offense for companies not to give French equal billing with English. It's doubled the paperwork load, driven up the cost of doing business and forced businesses out of the province" (English First, quoted in Pullum, 1991, 114).

Other Americans, while apparently better informed, equate the objectives pursued by the Charter of the French Language with those advocated by proposed amendments aiming at declaring English as the official language of the United States. This is the view of Geoffrey K. Pullum, who over several years contributed a chronicle in an important US linguistic journal: "The language policy of the PQ [Parti Québécois] was very much like the one being proposed under this [English Language] Amendment ... In Quebec, the francophone majority want a French First policy, and in the rest of Canada French (like its speakers) is treated with utter contempt ... English First proposes that English speakers in California should embark on a language policy exactly equivalent to the one adopted by the PQ when it attained power" (Pullum, 1991, 114–15). He then explains the policy of the Parti Québécois in the following way: "Their policy was not bilingualism but francization. They made education in English illegal except under certain very narrow circumstances, and began imposing French as the language of business" (ibid.).

It is curious to observe that opposition to the language policy in Quebec comes from two contrary points of view: for some, it is a matter of a radical bilingual policy, while for others it is a policy of extreme francization. It is necessary to reiterate what we already have mentioned: the objective of Quebec's language policy has not been to remove English but to proceed to a new redistribution of functions and reallocation of domains for each of the two languages. For too long a time, this distribution had been unfavourable to French-speakers; so this is an issue of social justice. With regard to English schools, they are open to all members of the English-Canadian community (more exactly, to all children one of whose parents has graduated from a primary school in the English language in Canada).

This is perhaps the place to quote a passage from the Statement on Linguistic Rights of the Linguistic Society of America, which lends itself to discussion: "Where linguistic discord does arise, as it has with various degrees of intensity in Belgium, Quebec, and Sri Lanka, it is generally the result of majority attempts to disadvantage or suppress a minority linguistic community, or it reflects underlying racial or religious conflicts" (LSA, 1996). Since this document refers to Quebec and not Canada, one might erroneously conclude that the oppressed minority would be the English-speakers. It is worth recalling that the Committee of Human Rights of the United Nations has expressed a quite different definition: "minorities considered in Article 27 [of the Covenant] are minority groups at the level of the state ..., and not those of minorities in a province. Canadian English-speaking citizens cannot be considered as a linguistic minority."[16]

LANGUAGE IN THE WORKPLACE

In 1994 alone there were some 120 complaints of a linguistic character brought before the US Equal Employment Opportunity Commission. A number of these complaints involved disciplinary sanctions inflicted on employees who had had conversations in a language other than English in their workplace (Chen, 1995). For example, an employee of a supermarket in Coral Gables was suspended for having spoken Spanish during his work time (Nunberg, 1989, 581). The American Civil Liberties Union tried to have a regulation revoked that imposed unilingual English on employees of a university cafeteria at the University of California at San Francisco (Nunberg, 1989, 580 n5).

Quebec's Bill 101 does not intervene in conversations between employees in their workplaces. Its objective is, rather, to impose French in institutional communications and make sure that clients who wish to be served in French can be. It allows bilingualism (that is, the use of English or another language) whenever necessary for communications with businesses outside Quebec.

LANGUAGE AND CONSUMER PROTECTION

When English was declared the official language of Florida, a clerk informed a customer that he would no longer accept cheques drawn up in Spanish for the customer's mortgage (Nunberg, 1989, 581). In the same state, activists tried to boycott McDonald restaurants that displayed bilingual menus (ibid.).

Such excesses have never occurred in the application of Bill 101. In particular, the law allows bilingualism on menus (to the extent that the version in another language does not occupy more room than the French version).

BILINGUAL EDUCATION

In the United States the debate about official English initiatives has often focused on the issue of bilingual education. In various states the announced objective of referenda demanding that English be declared the official language was to reduce, if not eliminate, public funding for education for immigrants. In the United States, bilingual education is no more than transitional bilingualism, the aim of which is to integrate immigrant children into mainstream English-language classes: "the goal of these so-called bilingual programs is to improve the English proficiency of LEP [limited-English-proficient] students so they can be mainstreamed into English-only classrooms as soon as possible." Research has shown the effectiveness of transitional bilingual education: "Most experts believe that bilingual education properly administered is an effective method of helping students make the transition to instruction in English … [T]he most comprehensive research on the subject indicates that the more extensive the instruction in the native language, the better the student performs in a variety of subjects, such as math and science, as well as English" (Chen, 1995, n19).

Bilingual teaching as such does not exist in Quebec, at least in its transitional American guise. Immersion courses in French are provided in the English-language school system. Jewish schools in Montreal even have double immersion (in French and Hebrew). Teaching in the so-called ethnic schools (Greek, Armenian, etc.) are also of a bilingual type. In the French-language schools there is reliance on intensive programs of English-language teaching, but immersion in English has recently been allowed in the curriculum. What approaches the American concept of bilingual education most closely is programs of integration provided to allophone students to make easier their transition to regular classes where teaching is given solely in French.

THE CASE OF PUERTO RICO

The supporters of US English and English First have two cases that they rely on endlessly in their discussions: Puerto Rico and Quebec. In Puerto Rico, English enjoyed co-official status with Spanish for almost a century until 1991. Then the law of 5 May 1991 proclaimed Spanish the sole official language. This law has since been abolished, so that official Spanish unilingualism lasted only a few years. In society at large on the island, nonetheless, Spanish unilingualism largely predominates. English is used mainly in the offices of the American government (Leclerc, 1992, 422–4).[17]

On reading their documents, one sees clearly that supporters of US English and English First have a stark vision of the language issue. They do not understand that on part of a territory (and, in the case of Puerto Rico, it is not even a part of national territory) it is possible to have another language serve as the common vehicle of communication. For example, a publication of English First notes: "98% of the population speaks Spanish and 20% are fluent in English." Then it immediately adds: "The one out of five Puerto Ricans who are fluent in English are served by just one English-language radio station out of the 116 on the island" (English First, 1996). After having resorted to this kind of specious argument, the authors pose the following question: "Puerto Rico: Another Quebec in the Making?"

Even the opponents of US English and English First do not seem to understand that it is not expected that everybody should know English. To come back to the case of Quebec, even the counsel of the American Civil Liberties Union of Northern California was astonished by the small proportion of Québécois who spoke English as well as French: "Twenty years ago, the rate of French speakers' acquisition of English was so slight that native born Spanish speakers in the Southwest were thirty times more likely than French-speaking Quebecois to adopt English as their dominant language …

Even today only 32% of French speakers in Quebec are bilingual in English (compared to 80% of American Hispanics)" (Chen, 1996). If the rate of bilingualism of French-speakers in Quebec was indeed 31.5 per cent in 1991, it has since risen to 36.9 per cent (2001 census); on the island of Montreal, more than half (50.6 per cent) of the francophone population was already bilingual in 1991; in 2001 their rate of bilingualism was 57.4 per cent (Office de la langue française, 2005, 26, 28). So let us dramatize what the last quotation implies: the ideal is to have English as the dominant language (if not as the mother tongue, one is tempted to add). Even a human rights watchdog seems to find that the slogan "One Nation, One Language" does not suffice and should be "One Continent, One Language." And in the framework of the inter-American economic integration process, one could well come to propose: "One Hemisphere, One Language."

The last slogan may serve as a conclusion, since it vividly illustrates the imperialist view – granted, often unconscious – that numerous Americans have about issues of language policy, even among the better intentioned. And that attitude links them to the views of all hegemonic groups.

NOTES

1 "Senator Hayakawa has often remarked that he first became concerned about this issue when he observed the polarizing effects that official bilingualism had in his native Canada " (Nunberg, 1989, 583).

2 This figure is a conservative estimate. The Ethnologue data base of the Summer Institute of Linguistics instead suggests 6,170 languages (Grimes, 1988), although the distinction between languages and dialects is not made clear.

3 Before the American War of Independence, Benjamin Franklin sardonically proposed to counter the growth of French as follows : "In a passage reminiscent of Swift's Modest Proposal, Franklin recommended that Parliament might as well pass a law that midwives in the colonies should smother every third or fourth child as to have the French check growth" (Wells, 1992, 86).

4 Exactly the opposite affirmation was found on the website of US English at http://www.us-english.org/inc/official/engplus.asp in December 1996; as a result of layout redesigning of its website, this address is no longer available.

5 To be exact, 0.065 per cent. See House of Representatives, 1996.

6 This was the well-known Proposition 63, supported by 73 per cent of voters in a 1986 referendum. In 1988 in the *Gutiérrez v. Municipal Court* case, the Court of Appeals of the 9th Judicial Circuit declared that Proposition 63 was "largely symbolic."

7 For a regularly updated list, see http://www.tlfq.ulaval.ca/axl/amnord/usa_4etats-ANGLAIS-off.htm. The list produced by US English, available at http://www.us-english.org/view/13 (online, 22 February 2009), contains errors.

8 *Yniguez v. Arizonans for Official English*, 69 F.3d 920 [9th Cir. 1995].

9 Online 24 February 2009 at http://ourworld.compuserve.com/homepages/JWCRAWFORD/can-la.htm

10 This ordinance is no longer in force.

11 Rodríguez *et al. v. Greyhound Lines, Inc., et al.*, Sacramento Superior Court No. 95, A501887.

12 *The Gazette* (Montreal), 17 February 2005, A-17. See also http://www.unitedforjustice.com/learnenglish.htm (online 4 March 2006).

13 This figure is in Legault, 1992. According to the Department of Health and Social Services, in an unpublished report entitled "Services de santé et services sociaux de langue anglaise" (22 October 1990), of a total of 858 health and social centres, 249 have been identified as having to offer services in English – that is, 29 per cent of the group.

14 Here are some extracts from a note by John Tanton reported in the magazine *Arizona Republic* in 1988: "Will the present majority peaceably hand over its political power to a group that is simply more fertile? ... Can homo contraceptivus compete with homo progenitiva [?!] if borders aren't controlled? ... Perhaps this is the first instance in which those with their pants up are going to get caught by those with their pants down! ... As whites see their power and control over their lives declining, will they simply go quietly into the night? Or will there be an explosion? ... Will Latin American migrants bring with them the tradition of the mordida (bribe), the lack of involvement in public affairs" (quoted in Ricento, 1996). See also http://ourworld.compuserve.com/homepages/JWCRAWFORD/HYTCH6.htm (online 24 February 2009).

15 Online 24 February 2009 at http://www.centrefrancophone.net/histoire/index.html.

16 Opinion of the United Nations Committee on Human Rights about paragraph 4 of article 5 of the optional Protocol relating to the International Covenant on Civil and Political Rights, 47th session, concerning communications nos. 359/1989 and 385/1989.

17 See also "Puerto Rico and Official English," online 24 February 2009 at http://ourworld.compuserve.com/homepages/JWCRAWFORD/can-pr.htm.

5

The Danger of Denial of Languages:
An Eastern European-Canadian Comparison

YAROSLAV BILINSKY

Speakers of influential languages may not understand the passionate concerns of the defenders of national languages used by only several million people each (as, for instance, in the three Baltic states) or several dozen million people (in Ukraine itself and in the Ukrainian diaspora). In Canada the insensitivity of English-speaking Canadians (anglophones) to old and new claims of their French-speaking fellow citizens (francophones) led to the establishment of language and immigration policies by the province of Quebec. Advocates of Quebec independence lost in the referendum of 1995, but only narrowly, by about 50.21 per cent against and 49.89 per cent for. Elsewhere in this volume, William F. Mackey aptly calls the result "a virtual tie" (see 38).

Canada has become more flexible over time and is truly democratic, and it will probably survive as a federation. In contrast, the more rigid and authoritarian Soviet Union imploded in 1991. It had veered toward a Russocentric course under Leonid Brezhnev and even afterward under Mikhail Gorbachev. At bottom, after World War II the USSR behaved like the Russian Empire, with a single imperial language.

In his rich historical contribution in chapter 1 of this book, Mackey has pointed out that the conflicts between francophones and anglophones in Canada involved religion and culture, with occasional outbursts of francophobia. The situation finally began changing when the Quebec nationalists gained ascendancy in the 1960s and 1970s. Some Ukrainians still remember the 30 July 1863 secret instruction of the czarist minister of the interior Petr Valuev, who served under the reform-minded czar Alexander II,

---

This chapter is dedicated to the memory of Petro Odarchenko (20 August 1903–12 March 2006), a Ukrainian literary scholar, who survived Soviet exile to Kazakhstan.

"the Liberator." Sharply reacting to the Polish uprising of 1863–64, Valuev banned a Ukrainian translation of the New Testament and all other publications in Ukrainian except belles lettres. He gave the motivation for his ban as follows: "No separate Little Russian [Ukrainian] language has [ever] existed, does exist [now], and can [ever] exist, and the dialect used by the common folk is the very same Russian language, only adulterated by the influence on it of the Polish language ... The all-Russian language is just as understandable for Little Russians as it is for Great Russians [ethnic Russians in the twenty-first century], and even more understandable than the so-called Ukrainian language, presently fabricated for them by certain Little Russians, and in particular the Poles" (cited by Senkus, 1993, 5: 553). Obviously, Valuev hated the Polish and allied Lithuanian insurgents as much as he did the Ukrainophile "separatists."

The pessimists among us will see in Valuev's sweeping ban the seeds of cultural genocide, which under Stalin culminated in full genocide (the *holodomor*, or terror-famine of 1932–33, which was combined with large-scale repression of the Ukrainian formerly rural intelligentsia in the 1930s) (Bilinsky, 1999, 149; 2003, 76).[1] Pessimists see the huge population losses in Ukraine, in both numerical (10 million) and, above all, qualitative terms, as contributing to Russification under Brezhnev's campaign to build a "Soviet people." The legacy of near-genocide and Soviet nation-building also contributed to the somewhat irresolute and vacillating language policies in independent Ukraine under Presidents Leonid Kravchuk (1991–94) and Leonid Kuchma (1994–2004). On the other hand, optimists will point out that the Ukrainian language was banned, not once or twice, but as many as 174 times. It has survived and recently has made some advances in secondary schools and universities.[2]

As for Estonia, Latvia, and Lithuania, they had been independent states between the two world wars. They were incorporated into the USSR in 1940 as a result of the Molotov-Ribbentrop Pact of 23 August 1939. All three Baltic states suffered heavy population losses of near-genocidal proportions both during and after World War II. Under the Soviet regime, the traditional ethnic composition of the two smaller states, Latvia and Estonia, was changed the most by planned immigration of ethnic Russians and Russified Belorusians and Ukrainians. Though relatively small in number, the Lithuanians, the Latvians, and above all the Estonians have had a sense of superiority toward Russian language and culture. Estonian is also the furthest removed from Russian, but Latvian and Lithuanian, too, do not belong to the family of Slavic languages, as Ukrainian does.

Map 5.1 The Russian language in the three Baltic states (in percentages)

SOURCES: CIA map "The Baltic States," Base 802244 (R00112) 6-94, from the Map Division, Morris Library, University of Delaware. Language data for Estonia, Latvia, and Lithuania from CIA, 2009, 3, accessed 22 May 2009.

NOTE: For Estonia, the number of Estonian-speakers as a percentage of all those living in the country (67.3 per cent) is followed by the counterpart Russian-language percentage (29.7 per cent). For Latvia, Latvian-speakers (58.2 per cent) are followed by Russian-speakers (37.5 per cent). The same order is observed for Lithuanian-speakers (82.0 per cent) in Lithuania, with the equivalent Russian figure being 8 per cent.

The Soviet incorporation of the Baltic states into the USSR was not recognized by the United States. The Baltic states were subsequently able to leave the Soviet Union completely without joining the pro-Russian Commonwealth of Independent States (CIS). Of the former Soviet Baltic republics, it was Lithuania that declared independence first on 11 March 1990.

There are similarities and differences among the three Baltic states and Ukraine with respect to ethnic Russians and Russian-speakers as of July 2009 or, in the case of Ukraine, 1 January 2009. First, ethnic Russians are in a minority in all four countries. Their share of the total population, however, varies from only 6.3 per cent, or 224 thousand, in Lithuania, where they constitute the second-ranking minority after Poles (6.7 per cent, or 238 thousand), to 29.6 per cent (661 thousand) in Latvia. In Estonia the Russian minority is more substantial, amounting to 25.6 per cent (333 thousand) (CIA, 2009).[3] Ukraine, unlike the three Baltic states, is a medium-sized country, with an ethnic Russian minority of 17.3 per cent, or a little under 8 million compared with about 36 million ethnic Ukrainians.[4]

Secondly, especially as shown in map 5.1, the number of Russian-speakers in all four states is greater than the number of ethnic Russians. The main reason for this discrepancy in the three Baltic states is the presence of Russified Belarusians (Byelorussians) and Ukrainians. In Ukraine we find a drop of 14.8 percentage points, equivalent to 5.3 million people, between self-declared ethnic Ukrainians and ethnic Ukrainians who also gave Ukrainian as their native language. The two main reasons for this difference are the Russification policies of the Soviet regime from 1932 through 1991 and the inability of independent Ukrainian governments since 1991 to reverse the results of those policies by determined Ukrainization.

In their major article on the status of Russian, Vida Io. Mikhalchenko and Yulia V. Trushkova (2003, 260–1) acknowledge that Russian is not a world language, but that it "continues to be largely the ethnic language of Russians and the national language of the Russian Federation, the first or second language of the bulk of the population of the Russian Federation and the language of interethnic communication of the CIS." In essence, Russian is a regional language (ibid., 283). But it can also serve as a means of international scholarly communication. At a conference in Germany, I met a Soviet-trained Chinese expert on Ukraine. He spoke neither German nor English, and I did not speak Chinese. So we talked at length in Russian.

Mikhalchenko and Trushkova have admitted that in the USSR "the absolute predominance of Russian in all essential spheres of communication was really unwarranted. It existed at the expense of the national languages" (ibid., 265). Soviet linguistic policy provoked reactions in the Baltic states and Ukraine to limit the use of Russian. It is true, of course, that "in the USSR, Russian was a language that provided access to professional activity and success in the job market" (ibid., 267). But the most striking observation made by the two Russian scholars repeatedly is that ethnic Russians tend to be monolingual (ibid, 261, 262, 265). In a Quebec publication this fact has been confirmed by two Estonian analysts. Marju Toomsalu and Leeni Simm (1998, 40) summarized the results of various polls about why Russians in Estonia have not learned to speak Estonian: "those polled responded that the idea had never occurred to them and that they did not think that it would ever become a necessity."

In the following pages I will briefly comment on linguistic policies in Estonia, Latvia, and Lithuania, which have been relatively decisive and straightforward, and then examine the essentially postponed linguistic confrontation in Ukraine, relying especially on data from the first post-Soviet population census of 2001.

These linguistic policies are closely related to one another since the Baltic states and Ukraine were all part of the Soviet Union until its demise. Moreover, all these countries are in fairly close geographical proximity to one another, so that leaders in each country are aware of trends in – and impositions from – their neighbours. While the Baltic states and Ukraine all broke away from the Soviet Union, their subsequent domestic and international experiences with language policy have diverged significantly with regard to both their language policy objectives and the results. They have all shared resentment about the Soviet denial of their respective languages, but the expression of this resentment has varied greatly because of the different contexts of each case. A complete comparison would include all the now-independent former Soviet states, which extend as far as China, but a more manageable first cut is to focus on these four neighbouring countries.

There is some continuity in language policy from the Soviet Union to the successor rump state, Russia, in that the tradition of denial of other languages remains strong. However, the more limited ability of Russia to affect events in the now-independent former Soviet states in question has significantly altered the political calculus of influence. Moreover, as the quotation above from the two Russian scholars indicates, there is some recognition in the Russian Federation that the militant Soviet policy of denial of languages was ill-advised. The dividing line nonetheless remains blurred in the post–Cold War era of when Russian Federation assertion of the language rights of Russian-speaking minorities outside the federation is legitimate and when it reflects a long-standing bullying tradition. Ambiguities in the denial of language give added reason to focus on the specific contexts of all these states and their interaction.

What we have then is a comparison involving five related language policy cases over time: Estonia, Latvia, Lithuania, Ukraine, and the Soviet Union/ Russia. A sixth case, Canada, involves some interaction with these five, but by and large geographical distance has limited interaction. What is common to all these cases is that some actors were denying languages at different times and to different degrees, while others were asserting minority languages or at least at various times were wanting to assert them when they could. This relatively limited data set with significant variations positions us to add specificity about global and not just regional concern about denial of languages. What kinds of circumstances or contexts lead to confrontations about denial of languages? When and why has denial of languages been susceptible to compromise and accommodation?

In a concluding section, I will first present what I see as the possible lessons learned regarding language policy in Eastern Europe and Russia for their own benefit as well as their applicability to Canada and, secondly, lessons to be learned regarding language policies in Canada and their applicability to Eastern Europe and Russia.

LANGUAGE POLICIES IN THE BALTIC STATES

Lithuania, the largest Baltic state, played a leading role in political opposition, notably against Soviet efforts to suppress the Roman Catholic Church, and also was the first to declare independence. But because the Russian minority in Lithuania was so small (9.4 per cent in 1989, as low as 6.3 per cent in 2007), Lithuania gave these people automatic citizenship and did not restrict their use of Russian. It was the smallest Baltic state, Estonia, that first passed a law, while still under Soviet rule, to limit the inroads of the Russian language. As early as 7 December 1988, the Estonian SSR Supreme Soviet overwhelmingly (with 204 ayes, 49 nays, and 4 abstentions) passed a constitutional amendment making Estonian the state language of the republic. The Language Law of the Estonian SSR was approved on 18 January 1989, also with a large majority (204 ayes, 50 nays, 6 abstentions), despite growing objections by Communist politicians in Moscow (Raun, 1995, 517–18).

As best shown in its preamble, the purpose of the 1989 Estonian Language Law was straightforward: to restore Estonian to its pre-eminent position before the Soviet occupation of 1940. To this end, paragraphs one, two, and three spoke of Estonian as the state language of the republic, while paragraph four finally mentioned Russian as being useful for communication within the USSR. The fifth and last paragraph in the preamble promised not to infringe upon the rights of fellow citizens to develop their native languages (Raun, 1995, 527f).

The comparable law in the Latvian SSR was also passed in 1989, after Latvian had been designated the state language at the end of September 1988 (Hirša, 1998, 91).[5] But there was a significant difference, pointing perhaps to a weaker position of Latvian vis-à-vis Russian in the Soviet republic: the Latvian law was called "the law on *languages*" (Hirša, 1998, 96; emphasis added).

The language situation in Ukraine was more akin to that in Latvia than to the one in Estonia. The Ukrainian SSR language law was passed rather late, on 28 October 1989. Its title was similarly "On *Languages* in the Ukrainian SSR" (emphasis added). Its preamble only timidly mentioned Ukrainian as the state language in paragraph three. Similarly, the law recognized Ukrainian as the state language in article two, not article one, as did the Estonian law. The clear implication from the Ukrainian SSR law was that the predominant language in Ukraine was Russian.[6] Whereas in Estonia and even in Latvia, the republican Communist authorities tended to side with the advocates of the Estonian and Latvian languages in 1988, the Ukrainian nationalists had to wait a year. It was not until September 1989, when the fatally ill Volodymyr Shcherbytsky, who favoured Russian over his native Ukrainian, was dismissed from his key post as first secretary of the Communist Party of Ukraine by Gorbachev, that the Communist government in Kyiv (Kiev) became more receptive to claims for the Ukrainian language. In contrast, the pro-Russian Latvian first party secretary Boris Pugo already had been transferred to Moscow in September 1988.

It is important to bear in mind that during and after World War II, the titular nationalities in Estonia, Latvia, Lithuania, and Ukraine suffered heavy population losses, while new ethnic Russian immigrants arrived. The changing balance was seen as particularly threatening in the two smallest republics: Estonia, and Latvia. During World War II, Estonia's population decreased by one-fifth (or about 200,000 people), with about 10 per cent of the population, or more than 80,000, fleeing to the West. An anti-Soviet guerrilla movement during the years 1946–48 led in March 1949 to the punitive deportation of 20,722 people to Siberia. This amounted to the loss of 2.5 per cent of the total republican population. As a consequence of all those shocks, together with centrally directed industrialization, the number of ethnic Estonians in the republic decreased from 94 per cent in 1945 to 61 per cent in 1989. In that year, ethnic Russians accounted for as much as 30.3 per cent of the total population.[7]

The losses in Latvia were even worse: by the end of World War II, its population had dropped by about one-third. In one year of Soviet occupation, from June 1940 through June 1941, almost 33,000 Latvians were deported to Russia, including Siberia. On one day alone, 14 June 1941, 15,000 Latvians were deported. In addition, a large number of Latvian army officers were shot, the total of executions in 1940–41 being 1,350. Tens of thousands were then killed during the German occupation. The genocidal Soviet deportations continued after 1945: on 25 March 1949 Stalin deported another 42,000 Latvians. As a result, the proportion of ethnic Latvians in the republic dropped from 73 per cent in 1939 to 52 per cent in 1989. (In 1935 ethnic Latvians had made up as much as 77 per cent of the country's population.) More to the point is the increase of ethnic Russians in Latvia: they numbered 168 thousand, or 8.8 per cent of the total population, in 1935 and as many as 906 thousand, or 34.4 per cent, in 1989.[8]

Data on linguistic assimilation (because of the increasingly larger number of those who gave Russian as their "native language" in the Soviet censuses of 1959, 1970, 1979, and 1989) made the situation even worse. For that reason, after 1991 both Estonia and Latvia combined affirmative citizenship and language policies designed to limit the influence of the strong Russian minority. The re-nationalizing policies in Estonia and Latvia after independence, which at bottom were policies of ethnic and cultural survival, did improve the ethnic balance in the two countries. According to the 2000 census, Estonians accounted for 67.9 per cent and Russians 25.6 per cent of the total population of Estonia. According to US estimates, in 2002 ethnic Latvians constituted 57.7 per cent of the total population of Latvia, a gain of 5.7 per cent for the Latvians and a loss of 4.4 per cent for the Russians.[9] Similarly, in July 2009 there were 882 thousand ethnic Estonians and 333 thousand ethnic Russians in Estonia and 1,288 thousand ethnic Latvians and 661 thousand ethnic Russians in Latvia.

The 1993 and 1995 Estonian laws on citizenship did not give automatic citizenship to all permanent non-Estonian residents, except to those who had been born in Estonia before the Soviet occupation of 1940. Candidates who were not ethnic Estonians had to apply for naturalization, "demonstrate a knowledge of the Estonian Constitution and of the Law of Citizenship itself, in addition to the existing requirements of residency [a minimum of five years] and proficiency in Estonian."[10] In a related development, on 21 November 2001 the Estonian parliament passed the Laws on National and Local Elections, which eliminated the Estonian language requirement for candidates running for office. That requirement had provoked criticism among such international organizations as the Organization for Security and Cooperation in Europe (OSCE) and the Council of Europe. But in a countermove in the same month, November 2001, a law was passed making Estonian the official language in the national parliament.[11] Altogether, in the 1990s there were about 600,000 foreign residents in Estonia, of whom 355,252 had applied for permanent residency, which is the first step in the naturalization process. By 1997 about 90,000 had been naturalized, of whom 36,500 had to pass a proficiency examination in the Estonian language (Toomsalu and Simm, 1998, 52–3). After a drop in the pace of naturalization in the mid-1990s, "about 114,000 persons were naturalized altogether" in the period from 1992 to 2000.[12]

Defenders of the Russian minority's citizenship rights both inside and outside Estonia had hoped that the European Union would force the Estonian government to make major concessions for the remaining 300,000 non-citizens and also delay Estonia's entry into the EU (Pettai, 1998, 77, incl. note 1). But the historical baggage of Stalinist occupation and contemporary genocidal wars in Chechnya (the first Chechen War was started under Yeltsin in December 1994, the second under Putin as prime minister in September 1999) allowed Estonian diplomacy to score a triple victory. After persuading sympathetic Western states and NGOs to finance certain aspects of their language policy (Toomsalu and Simm, 1998, 50) in return for small Estonian concessions, Estonia, together with Latvia and Lithuania, was accepted into both NATO and the EU in the spring of 2004.

What are the most significant provisions of the Estonian language law of 1995, as amended through the year 2001? While minority languages (notably Russian) can still be used in primary schools, all secondary schools must use the Estonian language by the school year of 2007/08, and 60 per cent of the curriculum, even in private schools, must be in Estonian.[13] In practice, this requirement means that all university education in Estonia will be in the Estonian language. To obtain any worthwhile job, even in the private sector, the candidate must speak and write Estonian. At first, as many as six proficiency levels were established; in 1999 these were collapsed into three. Language proficiency tests and adherence to the spelling of geographical signs and announcements, notices, and advertisements in Estonian are all monitored by a National Language Inspectorate under the Ministry of Education.[14]

There have been complaints, some of which may be justified. For instance, "linguistic requirements are too often used as a mean [*sic*] of unfair competition."[15] The language certification process is very involved and expensive, and a number of fraudulent certificates have been issued. The switch from a six- to a three-level proficiency system in 1999 has invalidated many of those fraudulent certificates, but in practice many candidates had to pass a second comprehensive examination after the old certificates were scheduled to expire in July 2002, a deadline that was wisely extended to 1 January 2004. Preparation for the elaborate two-day tests for a middle-level certificate is expensive, for which the state pays only a nominal amount; the balance is usually shouldered by the employer or paid out of pocket.

In fairness to the Estonian government, it does take the preservation of the Estonian language and culture seriously. To some Western observers the following sounds like a horror story of ethnic intolerance, but I understand it as a measure of self-preservation. As reported by the US English Foundation Official Language Research: "In 2003, the [Language] Inspectorate tested teachers in nine municipal Russian schools in Tallinn, and Kohtla Järve. Language knowledge of hundreds of them has not reached the necessary standard. All municipal and state schoolteachers (including teachers of the Russian language in Russian schools) should have a 'middle level' proficiency certificate (an advanced level). According to the Baltic News Service, ten teachers were punished by the Inspectorate EEK 2,500 (160 euro) in December."[16] This figure amounted to more than one-half of the average teacher's monthly salary of 4,169 EEK, or 267 euros.

As matters stand, according to the 2000 census, 20 per cent of the population cannot speak Estonian. Minorities make up 46 per cent of the population in Tallinn, 67 per cent in Jõhvi, and 83 per cent in Kohtla Järve. Estonian is the mother tongue of 67 per cent of the population as a whole.

In April 2004 the Estonian Foreign Ministry opposed the demand of Russian residents of Estonia to make Russian a second state language. The ministry in fact liked the idea of signing the Charter on Regional and Minority Languages, since ipso facto it would obviate the possibility of Russian becoming the second state language.[17]

On 26 April 2007 the Estonian government moved a Soviet-era war memorial to a less conspicuous and, to Estonians, less objectionable place in a military cemetery near the centre of Tallinn. This action provoked riots in the Estonian capital and led to unofficial harsh economic sanctions by Russia and a secret "cyberattack" on Estonia, which was probably masterminded from the Kremlin. According to a Reuters article by Patrick Lannin (2008) on the first anniversary of the protest, roughly 147 thousand Russian-speakers had been naturalized. This figure would amount to about 44 per cent of the 337 thousand Russians in Estonia, or an increase of only 33 thousand from the 114 thousand in 2000 (see above, page 187, and note 12). What is dangerous about the slow pace of naturalization is that about 95 thousand, according to Estonian authorities, or about 147 thousand, according to Russia, have taken out Russian citizenship. Some of the Russian-speakers in Estonia have become disaffected. Lannin quotes Mikhail Stalnukhin, the head of the city council in Narva and a member of the opposition Centre Party: "After April [2007] there is a Cold War ... A year ago I thought we had different histories but a common future. Now I don't think that." This is not an ideal situation for a small democratic country.

As for Latvia, its citizenship law of 16 March 1995, as amended on 6 February 1997 and 22 June 1998, looks like a formidable instrument for the exclusion of non-Latvians.[18] On the surface, it has been very effective. In January 2003, according to the official Latvian Board of Citizenship Affairs, the government had registered 1,791,318 Latvian citizens and 514,298 former immigrants from the USSR, who had been granted permanent residence, "as well as full social and economic rights," but not citizenship as yet. Until 2002, "a little more than 50,000 persons," or only about 9 per cent of the potential total, had become naturalized (Pabriks, 2003, 134) Official statistics also show that in 2003, about three-quarters of the ethnic Latvians (75.6 per cent) were citizens and less than one-fifth of the ethnic Russians (17.9 per cent). In that year, ethnic Latvians numbered almost three-fifths of all permanent residents (59.3 per cent), while Russians numbered a little over one-quarter (28.6 per cent). The third most sizable minority was Poles (they numbered 2.2 per cent among Latvian citizens and 2.5 per cent among all permanent residents).[19]

Three comments explain the slow naturalization of ethnic Russians. First, for reasons of both state and national security, a slow and deliberate naturalization of non-Latvians was intended (Pabriks, 2003, 142; Jubulis, 2001, 212, 367n100). Second, research by Latvian scholars has shown that the accompanying language policy was not so effective (Hirša, 1998, 92–3, 100, 105–49). Third, international pressures have been countered, if with difficulty, as illustrated below.

The two-term Latvian president Dr Vaira Vike-Freiberga, who had taught at a French-language university in the province of Quebec, effectively articulated Latvian citizenship and language policies and also squelched inappropriate comparisons with Canadian language policies.[20] Paradoxically, as the following interview illustrates, after Latvia's major diplomatic triumph of simultaneous accession to both NATO and the EU, advocates of greater freedoms for the Russian minority have acquired a new political weapon because of Latvian membership.[21]

In May 2004, after Latvia joined the EU, President Vike-Freiberga gave an interview to Georgiy Zotov of Moscow's newsmagazine *Argumenty i Fakty* (Arguments and facts). Zotov repeatedly pressed the former Quebec university professor about Russian language rights:

ZOTOV Do you speak French?

VIKE-FREIBERGA Yes of course.

ZOTOV I was certain you do because you lived in Canada. There, 28 per cent of the population are French. Their language, however, is the country's second official language. Here, 30 per cent of the population are Russian, yet there are no plans to make (Russian) an official language.

VIKE-FREIBERGA There is one province in Canada, Quebec, where people only speak French, even though Canada is bilingual. This language needs protection, otherwise it will be supplanted by English. Our problem in Latvia is the influx of Russian speakers and their insufficient loyalty to the country, it is a completely different situation.

Later in the interview, Zotov erroneously asserted that "under EU laws," if a minority accounts for 20 per cent of the population, "its language automatically becomes an official language." Vike-Freiberga turned this comment aside by saying that the situation in Latvia was different because the large post-1940 Russian minority had been the result of "unlawful, brutal, totalitarian foreign occupation."

The heart of the Zotov–Vike-Freiberga exchange is the following:

ZOTOV You know, this is exactly what [Latvian] opposition leaders say: you can throw examples from all over the world at the Latvian authorities, and they will reply every time that these things are possible in other countries but here it is all completely different. What you have is a ready answer.

VIKE-FREIBERGA You see, there are many ideas how this situation can be resolved. There is just one principle, however: *you have to have respect for the heritage of the country you live in. I am sorry to say this, but even after 13 years of independence most Russian school-leavers have problems with Latvian at universities.*

ZOTOV Just as throughout that time they have had problems with Latvian citizenship.

VIKE-FREIBERGA That's because they don't apply for it. I'm surprised by this, but they don't want to be citizens of Latvia. Why not ask them why they behave like this? Why not get rid of passports with the hammer and sickle? Do they hope that Latvia will merge with Russia? It won't happen. *They need to understand that this is an independent country, and become Latvians. If they want to be Russians they can go to Russia, but if they want to be Latvians, we will only welcome that.*[22] (Emphasis added.)

At least in May 2004 the president of Latvia had the last word.

LANGUAGE POLICY IN UKRAINE

Language policy in Ukraine has consisted of the following elements, reflecting mixed results: "soft" Ukrainization of secondary schools; a more determined introduction of Ukrainian into higher educational institutions; a formal, but unsuccessful attempt to give equality to Ukrainian in television and radio programs but not in movie production; and a virtual collapse of Ukrainian-language book and journal publishing.[23]

Some of the effects of language policies in Ukraine can be inferred from the 2001 population census, which included one question on nationality and as many as three questions on language. That census was held on 5 December 2001, almost ten years to the day after voters in Ukraine had approved independence by 90.1 per cent (1 December 1991). Overall, compared with the 12 January 1989 census, Ukraine lost 3.2 million people.[24] There have also been major changes in ethnic composition. In 2001, as in 1989, there were two major nationalities, Russians and Ukrainians. In 2001 they together accounted for 95.1 per cent of the total, the third most numerous nationality being Belarusians (Byelorussians), who numbered only 276 thousand, or 0.6 per cent of the total.[25] For our purposes, we need be concerned only with the interplay between ethnic Ukrainians and ethnic Russians.

The exact wording of the nationality question, number 6, was as follows: "Your ethnic origin [*pokhodzhennya*] (give your nationality [*natsional'nist'*], ethnicity [*narodnist'*] or ethnic group)."[26] Altogether about 37.5 million people declared themselves Ukrainians in 2001, as opposed to around 37.2 million in 1989 (an increase of only 0.3 per cent). But the ethnic share of Ukrainians increased considerably: from 72.7 per cent in 1989 to 77.8 per cent in 2001, a jump of 5.1 per cent. This change was because of the decrease in the number of ethnic Russians, from 11.4 million in 1989 to only 8.3 million in 2001, or from 22.1 per cent of the population to 17.3 per cent.[27]

What about the language situation in Ukraine? The general question in the 2001 census, number 7, referred to "your linguistic characteristics," which was a relatively value-neutral formula. But the general question was broken down into three more emotionally charged sub-questions about (a) one's "mother tongue," or native language, the official Ukrainian website in English using the term "mother tongue"; (b) the respondent's command of Ukrainian; and (c) a "third language" known by the respondent. It is worth noting that the original forms to be filled in by the census-taker contained empty boxes without the names of the languages printed in a certain order; this approach solved the problem illustrated by the favoured placement of French in the French forms of the Canadian census of 2001.

Nonetheless, more was involved than concerns about the impartiality of language used in the census. The Ukrainian census was administered under Kuchma, who had changed his official nationality, was bilingual, and in 2001 was leaning toward Russia. This pro-Russian bias was evident in the census in encouraging language transfers toward Russian; note, for instance, the injunction in bold letters that "mother tongue" need not coincide with one's declared nationality. On the other hand, declared speakers of Ukrainian as their native language were given the psychological advantage of not having to prove that they spoke, wrote, and read it really well. This was Kuchma's concession to the pro-Ukrainian language camp. It is also in line with Soviet thinking that ethnicity controls one's "mother tongue."

If the real intention of the 2001 census was to show that there was a majority of Ukrainian citizens whose "mother tongue" – and, by implication, language of use – was Russian, it miscarried. Two-thirds (or 67.5 per cent) of the people opted for Ukrainian. Moreover, the number of citizens with Ukrainian as their native language increased by 2.8 per cent compared with 1989, whereas the number of citizens with Russian as their "mother tongue" dropped by 3.2 per cent. At least outside the south and the east, and definitely outside Crimea, language policy had worked. The census data on "mother tongue" are quickly summarized below, reflecting progress in promoting the Ukrainian language in some parts of the country and lack of progress in others.

Of the ethnic Ukrainians, 85.2 per cent gave Ukrainian as their "mother tongue," and 14.8 per cent gave Russian as their native language. Of the ethnic Russians, as many as 95.6 per cent gave Russian as their "mother tongue," 3.9 per cent gave Ukrainian as their native language, and 0.2 per cent listed a third alternative as their native language. But as with ethnic identifications, there are important regional differences. In the western and central regions, ethnic identity and native language largely coincide. The percentages are in the upper 90s, except for a low of 92.4 per cent in the Sumy region, in which the current Ukrainian president, Viktor Yushchenko, was born. In the solidly ethnic Ukrainian Ternopil' region, 99.9 per cent listed Ukrainian as their "mother tongue." But in the three southern regions outside Crimea, Ukrainian did not fare as well. In the Odesa region, only 71.6 per cent of ethnic Ukrainians chose Ukrainian as their "mother tongue," 28.2 per cent gave Russian, and 0.2 per cent cited some other language. In the same region, the ethnic Russians were practically monolingual, 97.0 per cent opting for Russian. In the southern Kherson region, however, as many as 87.0 per cent ethnic Ukrainians listed Ukrainian as their mother tongue, compared with 91.6 per cent of Russians who opted for the Russian language. Again, with the exception of Crimea, the Ukrainian language was weakest in the east. In the Donetsk region, only 41.2 per cent of ethnic Ukrainians opted for Ukrainian as their "mother tongue," compared with 58.7 per cent who chose Russian. (The ethnic Russians were practically monolingual, 98.6 per cent giving Russian as their native language.) In the neighbouring Luhans'k region, a bare majority, or 50.4 per cent, of ethnic Ukrainians opted for Ukrainian.

It is in Crimea that Ukrainian fared worst, with only 40.4 per cent of ethnic Ukrainians opting for the Ukrainian "mother tongue" and 59.5 per cent choosing Russian. Ethnic Russians in Crimea were solidly monolingual (99.7 per cent). The city of Sevastopol, with its ethnic Russian majority and predominantly Russophone Ukrainians, has remained a predominantly Russian naval base.[28]

In contrast, the city of Kyiv has changed to become more of a Ukrainian capital. While its total population decreased slightly compared with 1989 (by 0.2 per cent), the absolute number of ethnic Ukrainians increased by 13.3 per cent, and so did their relative share in the population, from 72.5 per cent in 1989 to 82.2 per cent in 2001. The absolute number of ethnic Russians in Kyiv fell by more than one-third (37.1 per cent), and their relative share in the city dropped from 20.9 per cent in 1989 to 13.1 per cent in 2001.

If language data are added, we find that in 2001, 1.8 million of the 2.1 million ethnic Ukrainians in Kyiv (or 85.7 per cent) listed Ukrainian as their "mother tongue," and 299 thousand (14.2 per cent) opted for Russian. Of the 377 thousand ethnic Russians in the capital, 309 thousand (91.7 per cent) gave Russian as their "mother tongue," and close to 27 thousand (7.9 per cent) opted for Ukrainian.[29]

Map 5.2 shows in great detail the geographic distribution of Ukrainian as "mother tongue" versus that of Russian. It should be borne in mind that ethnic Russians were in a 58.3 per cent majority in Crimea, or 1,145 thousand out of a total population of 1,967.3 thousand on 1 January 2009. Ethnic Ukrainians in Crimea numbered 478 thousand (24.3 per cent), and ethnic Crimean Tatars, 236 thousand (12.0 per cent). Ethnic Russians also strongly predominated in Sevastopol. The ethnic Russian majority in Crimea is the result of the genocidal deportation of the Tatars by Stalin in 1944 and their rehabilitation under Gorbachev as late as March 1991.

In all other areas, ethnic Ukrainians were in a majority. Nevertheless, we see from the map that in the east as many as 74.9 per cent of the population of the Donetsk region opted for Russian as their native language, and so did 68.8 per cent in the neighbouring Luhans'k oblast. In the main steel-producing region, Zaporizhzhia, the people split evenly (50.2 per cent Ukrainian, 48.2 per cent Russian). Somewhat more Ukrainian-speaking is the important industrial Kharkiv region (53.8 per cent versus 44.3 per cent). In the south, the Odesa region split 46.3 per cent Ukrainian versus 41.9 per cent Russian.

In the west, Ukrainian-speakers are in the 90 per cent range. A positive phenomenon, from the viewpoint of Ukrainian politics and culture, is that in the city of Kyiv itself 72.0 per cent opted for Ukrainian and 24.9 per cent for Russian. Furthermore, in the surrounding Kyiv region, in which some of the Kyiv elite may live, as many as 92.3 per cent chose Ukrainian and only 7.2 per cent Russian.

Recent events are troubling. The former Russian head of state and continuing strongman, Vladimir Putin, has manoeuvred effectively to promote Russian interests and the Russian language in Ukraine. These interests were promoted, for example, through the falsified second ballot of the presidential election in November 2004. In April 2008, at the NATO summit in Bucharest, Putin was able to enlist Chancellor Angela Merkel of Germany, among others, to bar Ukraine and Georgia from entering the organization via the Membership Action Plan. This manoeuvre came about after President George W. Bush, during his only state visit to Ukraine from 31 March to 1 April 2008, had voiced his and the United States' strong support for both Ukraine and Georgia being admitted to NATO. The United States and other countries were concerned that this negative outcome reflected Russian influence on European countries dependent on its gas and oil.

US vice-president Joe Biden, during his state visit to Ukraine, said on 21 July 2009, after meeting President Viktor Yushchenko:

We do not recognize – and I want to reiterate it – any sphere of influence. We do not recognize anyone else's right to dictate to you or any other country what alliances you will seek to belong to or what relationships you – bilateral relationships you have. I reaffirmed to the President what I said in Munich, as I said, in the earliest days of our administration, and it's worth repeating again in a brief statement, and that is – and President Obama, I might add, made it clear in his visit to Moscow this month – *the United States supports Ukraine's sovereignty, independence and freedom, and to make its own choices – its own choices – including what alliances they choose to belong.* We're working, as you know, Mr. President, to reset our relationship with Russia. But I assure you and all the Ukrainian people that it will not come at Ukraine's expense. To the contrary, I believe it can actually benefit Ukraine. *The more substantive relationship we have with Moscow, the more we can defuse the zero-sum thinking about our relations with Russia's neighbors.*[30] (Emphasis added.)

Map 5.2 Ukrainian versus Russian native languages in Ukraine (in percentages)

SOURCES: CIA map, "Ukraine Administrative Divisions," Base 802141 (R00339) 4-93, from the Map Division, Morris Library, University of Delaware. Language data from "All-Ukrainian population census 2001" website http://www.ukrcensus.gov.ua/results/general/language/... for the Ukrainian version and <http://www.ukrcensus.gov.ua/eng/results/general/language/...> for the English version; accessed 9 and 16 July 2009. The actual population of Ukraine, by administrative divisions, as of 1 January 2009, is available through the same website at http://ukrcensus.gov.ua/eng/news/article;891/; accessed 9 July 2009.
NOTE: The percentages of Ukrainian-speakers in the Autonomous Republic of Crimea, the city of Sevastopol', all oblasts, and the city of Kyiv have been presented first; the percentages of Russian-speakers come second. For ease of comparison, the same data presented in map 5.2 for speakers of Ukrainian versus Russian are also given in tabular form by area in the appendix to this chapter, as are comments, in the form of notes, on four particular cases.

With all due respect, given Putin's track record, the last sentence sounds like a counsel of perfection on the part of the United States, though American support of Ukraine's sovereignty is strongly welcomed in Kyiv.

Current Ukrainian domestic politics are best described as "multifactorial gridlock," to adapt a term from modern medicine. There is gridlock between the pro-Russian party of Viktor Yanukovych and the nationalist Ukraine "Orange" coalition headed by Yushchenko. Further blurring the political situation is the defection of Prime Minister Yulia Tymoshenko from the Orange coalition, while setting her own ambitious agenda, which includes running for the presidency of Ukraine in January 2010. This protracted, fluid political situation has impacted on language policy, with the status of Russian as well as Ukrainian remaining unsettled.

Yushchenko's two predecessors as president procrastinated about the task of building a Ukrainian nation with Ukrainian as the true state language. This inaction was in stark contrast to the approach taken by the presidents of Estonia, Latvia, and Lithuania, all three of whom concentrated on establishing the primacy of their respective languages and cultures. As a result, reliance on Ukrainian has been delayed in publishing, the mass media, and secondary schooling. There also has been a long-term effort to keep Russian as the primary language of communication through recurrent campaigns to have it recognized as "a secondary state language." This restoration of Russian would place Ukrainians and Ukraine at a disadvantage vis-à-vis its European neighbours, because Ukrainians would be deprived of the opportunity to study English as a second language – a true global language, while Russian is only a regional one (Velychenko, 2006).

COMPARISONS WITH CANADA

Quebec's language policy often has been characterized in English-speaking Canada and the United States as radical and destabilizing in both feeding separatism and undermining rights of English-speakers in the province (see, for example, a synthesis of these allegations in the chapter by Jacques Maurais in this volume). Since the 1960s, Quebec's language policy has been quite consistent and successful in promoting French and subordinating the hitherto dominant position of English in the province. This considerable progress in promoting these language policy goals has been achieved through moderate, democratic methods, including respect for rights of English-speakers.

The contrast with Eastern Europe is instructive. The prominence of Russia and the Russian language has been daunting for the relatively tiny

Baltic states both before and after the demise of the Soviet Union. The isolated position of French-speaking Quebec in English-speaking North America also is challenging, but the threat has been less direct and is receding. For example, Canada, including Quebec, freely joined the United States and Mexico in the North American Free Trade Agreement. Pressures and counter-pressures have been more complex in Eastern Europe. The hard-line posture of the Baltic states toward their Russian-language minorities did not prevent them from joining the European Union and NATO, thereby gaining Western allies. At the same time, their pro-Western policy tilt, in addition to their hard line toward Russian-language minorities, has tended to aggravate long-standing tension with these minorities and Russia. Both the Russian-speaking minorities and the Russian Federation are embedded geographically in and around the Baltic states, so this is a high and continuing price to pay for having pursued hard-line language policies and a pro-Western tilt.

While both Quebec and the Baltic states have suffered from denial of language, the latter experienced draconian oppression, as documented above. For the Baltic states, compromise has been especially difficult since, because of the historical legacy, national survival has been regarded as imminently threatened. Quebec has been equally committed to preserving the province's distinctive culture and language, but its language policy has been moderate in being careful to respect rights of the English-speaking minority in the province. Elements of this minority were intransigent and ended up leaving the province, but the remaining minority by and large has been democratically oriented and moderate as well. In addition, the denial of language imposed on Quebec by English-speaking Canada over the centuries was less rigid than its Soviet counterpart, and a subsequent federal policy of bilingualism has in fact encouraged use of French in the country. These distinctive Canadian circumstances encouraged a spirit of compromise to emerge gradually on all sides, while in the Baltic states positions and antagonisms have remained rigid. There is another major difference between the two continents: to Canada, the United States has generally been a good neighbour, while Russia frequently has not acted in a good neighbourly fashion toward the three Baltic states and Ukraine.

A related contrast therefore involves the dominant power and language group in each case: English-speakers in North America (Canada with the United States in the background) and Russian-speakers in Eastern Europe (with the Russian Federation in the background). The chapter by Jurgen Erfurt in this volume shows that the federal government of Canada has moved away from confrontation after initially wanting to deny Quebec's representation in the international Francophonie. And Pierre Anctil's analysis in this volume shows that both sides in the Canadian language debate have adopted a more conciliatory approach over time while continuing to promote their distinctive interests. If the Baltic states can be faulted for an unnecessarily confrontational approach in denying the rights of a linguistic minority, the Soviet Union and its successor state, the Russian Federation, have tended to be intolerant in language matters as well. While a mutually beneficial federal-provincial dialogue developed in Canada over time, there has been no such counterpart dialogue in Eastern Europe. The deep concern of Russia with Russian-speaking minorities outside the Federation has been accompanied by an assertion of the rights of these groups that threatens to take an overbearing, non-democratic form. The resentment and resulting formidable determination of the very small Baltic states to reverse Soviet and later Russian denial of language should constitute an important lesson for any dominant power contemplating the imposition of its language.

It follows that the unleashing of dangerous forces which results from the denial of languages applies not just to minority languages that are suppressed by a dominant power but also to speakers of a dominant language in a minority situation, such as English-speakers in Quebec and Russian-speakers in Eastern Europe. The case of Quebec has not been without considerable tension, since the gradual change in status of English-speakers in the province from dominant to minority group resulted in an exodus, especially in the early period of Quebec's language policy. However, Quebec has recognized and respected the language rights of the English-speakers who have remained in the province. In Eastern Europe the contemporary relationship between locally dominant titular language groups and minority Russian-language groups tied to the outside great-power patron has tended to be confrontational. Since the demise of the Soviet state, all the successor states selected for study here have become democratic in form, but democratic methods have still not pervaded all domains of the body politic, including language policy. The Western notion of civil society involving compromise and give-and-take between all social groups on all major issues is not deeply embedded.

Ukraine's situation poses additional problems. The Baltic states and Canada (both the federal and provincial governments) share language policies that have been quite persistent in pursuing goals supported by resources. Ukrainian governments have often been ineffective on both fronts, although this chapter has shown that there have been some results in promoting the Ukrainian language. While supporters of Orange Ukraine have their share of the blame for an all-too-often dysfunctional situation, the Russian-speaking minority and the Russian Federation share blame as well. We return to the lack on all sides of an effective civil society that can articulate and mediate interests in a democratic way.

While the Canadian experience is relatively successful in some important ways, Canada also reflects the limits of language policy, even when supported by relatively consistent goals and resources. The federal policy of bilingualism promotes the equal status of English and French throughout the country, but the status of French is endangered outside New Brunswick and Quebec. Other chapters in this book indicate that Quebec's language policy has not been concerned with reversing this ominous trend until recently. One lesson to be learned is apparently that in some cases the goals and resources supporting language policy must be yoked to a territoriality peopled by a critical mass of language speakers. The main reason why French has remained as a true living official language of Canada is that it has remained predominant in a fairly autonomous Quebec peopled by a French-speaking majority. Quebec authorities have wisely placed prominence on the territorial principle to save their native French from being overwhelmed by English. Yet this policy has tended to separate Quebec from other French-speaking areas in Canada and to accentuate their decline, which has not been prevented by the personality principle of the federal government. Another lesson to be learned is therefore that any language approach has limitations and must be adapted to the specific political realities in place to be successful.

The very same territorial principle, together with some implementing institutions, has successfully and properly been applied in the three Baltic states. In spite of large Russian-speaking minorities, local language groups have remained in the majority in all the Baltic states. Only in the province of Quebec in Canada are French-speakers in a majority, with New Brunswick having a sizable French-speaking minority (about a third). It may be argued that Quebec should have pursued a more all-inclusive policy of promoting French outside as well as within the province, but it is uncertain that this would have worked. What the pages of this volume do attest is that given the right conditions, as in the Baltic states and Quebec, the territorial principle for promoting a language can work. Yet a substantial price has been paid for this approach in each case.

Paradoxes therefore abound. The solution of territoriality has been applied in the Baltic states but at the very high cost of recurring confrontation with the Russian minorities and the Russian Federation. And it is not at all clear how territoriality could be applied in the case of Ukraine, since two separate

and probably autonomous language areas could lead to dismemberment of
the country. On the other hand, the personality principle of leaving language
choice to the individual has been demonstrated in the case of Ukraine to be
open to political manipulation. A mutually satisfactory language solution for
Ukraine requires compromise on all sides, while in fact the different language groups and their representative politicians have at important junctures been either rigid or unimaginative or both. Compromise is alive and
well in Canada, and it offers a useful lesson for Ukraine.

	Ukrainian	*Russian*
Autonomous Republic of Crimea	10.1	77.0
Sevastopol' city (city council)	6.8	90.6
Cherkasy region	92.5	6.7
Chernihiv region	89.0	10.3
Chernivtsi region	75.6	5.3
Dnipropetrovsk region	67.0	32.0
Donetsk region	24.1	74.9
Ivano-Frankivsk region	97.8	1.8
Kharkiv region	53.8	44.3
Kherson region	73.2	24.9
Khmel'nyts'kyi region	95.2	4.1
Kirovohrad region	88.9	3.5
Kyiv region	92.3	7.2
Kyiv city	72.0	24.9
Luhans'k region	30.0	68.8
L'viv region	95.3	3.8
Mykolaiv region	69.2	29.3
Odesa region	46.3	41.9
Poltava region	90.0	9.5
Rivne region	97.0	2.7
Sumy region	84.0	15.6
Ternopil' region	98.3	1.2
Vinnytsia region	94.8	4.7
Volyn' region	97.3	2.5
Zakarpattia (Trans-Carpathian) region	81.0	2.9
Zaporizhzhia region	50.2	48.2
Zhytomyr region	93.0	6.6

NOTE: The percentage of Ukrainian-speakers and Russian-speakers in Kyiv has been calculated by the author from still-incomplete Ukrainian 2001 census data. The exact method is available on request. In Crimea, 11.4 per cent of the population indicated Crimean Tatar as their native language. In the Zakarpattia (Trans-Carpathian) region, 12.7 per cent of the population speak Hungarian and 2.6 per cent Romanian, factors that may explain the low percentage for Russian (2.9 per cent). In the Kirovohrad regon, however, the Russian language figure of 3.5 per cent appears too low. I triple-checked the 2001 census website on 16 July 2009.

NOTES

I would like to thank the following persons, in alphabetical order: Dennis Donahue, statistician with the International Programs Center of the US Census Bureau, for help with 2001 Ukrainian linguistic data, especially on Crimea and the city of Kyiv; Dr Eugene Fedorenko, Learned Secretary of the Ukrainian Academy of Arts and Sciences in the US, Inc., for facilitating my meeting with Academician Professor Petro P. Kononenko, in New York City in June 2006; Academician Professor Dr Petro P. Kononenko, director, Research Institute of Ukrainian Studies, Ministry of Education and Science of Ukraine, for his consultation on educational policies in Ukraine, 11 June 2006; Professor Michael A. Morris for faithfully abbreviating my manuscript after my car accident and for a superb job of linking my piece to Canadian language policies; the reference librarians at the Morris Library, University of Delaware, for assistance with databases on the politics of the Baltic states and the staff of its Map Division for scanning two maps; Professor Joseph A. Pika, Department of Political Science and International Relations, University of Delaware, for advice on presidential politics; and Dr Stephen Rapawy, a former employee of the US Census Bureau, for providing me with samples of the 2001 Ukrainian population census forms and official instructions how to fill them out and for sending me key excerpts from the 2007 Statistical Yearbook of Ukraine.

1 The classic survivors' book is Hryshko, 1983, vii, 1–2. Best known is Conquest, 1986, especially chapter 13.

2 Public lecture, in Ukrainian, by Professor Dr Petro P. Kononenko, "Problemy osvity i movy v protsesi derzhavotvorennya [Problems of education and language in the process of state-building]," Ukrainian Academy of Arts and Sciences in the US, New York, 11 June 2006. I attended his lecture and consulted with him privately afterwards. Kononenko pointed out that in 2005–06, only 19 out of a total of 527 secondary schools in Kyiv taught in Russian and that in the same year as many as 1,810,328 (or 82.1 per cent) of the university students studied in Ukrainian.

3 As in map 5.1 above. The estimated July 2009 population total for Estonia was 1,299,371; for Latvia, 2,231,503; and for Lithuania, 3,555,179.

4 For Ukraine, I have used the actual population total as of 1 January 2009, that is, 46,143.7 thousand. It is easily available as a link on the "All-Ukrainian population census 2001" website <http:ukrcensus.gov.ua/eng/news/article;891>; accessed 9 July 2009.

5 See also "Latvia: Introductory Survey," in *The Europa World Yearbook 2005*, 2: 2635b.

6 "Zakon Ukrainskoi Sovetskoi Sotsialisticheskoi Respubliky O yazykakh v Ukrainskoi SSR [Law of the Ukrainian SSR on the languages in the Ukrainian SSR]," in Fierman, 1995. The original law is in Russian.

7 *US Fed. News* (Washington, DC), 1 July 2005, 12:00 AM EST: "State Department Issues Background Note on Estonia." Lexis-Nexis search. Term: "Capitalism in Estonia."

8 *US Fed. News*, 1 May 2005, 7:25 AM EST: "State Department Issues Background Note on Latvia." Lexis-Nexis search. Term: "Capitalism in Latvia." See also "Latvia: Introductory Survey," in *The Europa World Yearbook 2005*, 2: 2635a. Also table 3.1, "Population of Latvia by ethnic origin: 1934–89 (thousands)," in Melvin, 1995, 32.

9 See chapters on Estonia and Latvia in CIA, 2005.

10 US English Foundation Official Language Research – Estonia, "1. Legislation: Legislation dealing with the use of languages," 3; http://www.us-english.org/foundation/research/olp; accessed 7 June 2006.

11 Ibid., 1. See, however, "Estonia: Introductory Survey," in *The Europa World Yearbook 2005*, 2: 1626a.

12 US English Foundation Official Language Research – Estonia, 3.

13 Ibid., 1.

14 Ibid., 4.

15 Ibid., 2.

16 Ibid., 7–8.

17 Aleksandr Shegedin, *Eurolang News* (Tallinn), 5 April 2004, in US English Foundation Official Language Research – Estonia, 10–11.

18 "Citizenship Law," as translated in 1999 by Ilona Ceica and Ligita Vasennene, of the Riga Graduate School of Law, for the Talkošanas un terminologijas centrs (Translation and terminology centre), *Latvian Law Guide*. Yahoo search for "Current language laws in Latvia," 24 June 2006.

19 "Table 12.1: Latvia's Permanent Residents and Citizens by Ethnic Origin," Pabriks, 2003, 134.

20 She was born on 1 December 1937 in Riga, Latvia. Her parents left Latvia in 1945 and lived as "displaced persons," or World War II refugees, in Germany and then in Morocco and Canada. She studied at the University of Toronto and McGill University in Montreal. Her approval ratings in Latvia have been between 70 and 85 per cent. See http://en.wikipedia.org/wiki/Vaira_Vike-Freiberga.

21 Francesca Mereu, "EU Party Defends Russian Speakers," *Moscow Times*, 18 June 2004; BBC Monitoring/…/BBC Monitoring International Reports, 11 August 2004, "Leftist Latvian MEP [member of European Parliament] Defends Actions on Behalf of Russian Speakers," <politika.lv> web site, Riga, in Latvian, 10 August 2004. Lexis-Nexis search. Term: "Russians in Latvia."

22 Georgiy Zotov, interview with Latvian president Vaira Vike-Freiberga, "Latvian President Vaira Vike-Freiberga: 'We want to turn Russians into Latvians,'" *Argumenty i Fakty* [Arguments and facts] (Moscow), no. 19 (11 May 2004),

via BBC Monitoring //.../BBC Monitoring International Reports, 14 May 2004,.
"Latvian President Defends Her Country's Treatment of its Russian Community."
Lexis-Nexis search. Term: "Russians in Latvia."

23 Larysa Masenko, "Movna sytuatsiya Ukraïny [Linguistic situation in Ukraine]"
and Volodymyr Pas'ko, "Dolya movy – dolya natsiyi (Do problem derzhavnoyi
movy v Ukraïni [Fate of language is the fate of our nation (Concerning the problem of the state language in Ukraine)]," *Yi*, no. 35 (2004): "Mova nimoyi krayiny"
(Language of a dumb country). http://www.ji.lviv.ua/n.35 texts/. Masenko is a
professional linguist and Pas'ko a medical educator and author of two novels. See,
however, the more optimistic evaluation of Petro P. Kononenko, above, page 202,
and note 2.

24 Derzhavnyi komitet statystyky Ukraïny (State Statistics Committee of Ukraine),
"Vseukrains'kyi perepys naselennya 2001 r. [All-Ukrainian population census
of 2001]," 1. Website of State Statistics Committee of Ukraine. For 1989 cen-
sus, see table "Chislennost' naseleniya [Population count]," in Gosudarstvennyi
komitet Ukrainskoi SSR po statistike (Ukrainian SSR State Statistical Committee),
Narodnoe khozaystvo Ukrainskoi SSR v 1989 godu: Statisticheskii ezhegodnik
(National economy of the Ukrainian SSR in 1989; Statistical Yearbook) (Kiev:
"Tekhnika" [Technology], 1990), 26.

25 State Statistics Committee of Ukraine, All-Ukrainian population census of 2001,"
English version, General results of the census, National [ethnic] composition of
population, 1 of 7.

26 Derzhavnyi komitet statystyky Ukraïny (State Statistics Committee of Ukraine),
Vseukrains'kyi perepys naselennya 2001 roku (All-Ukrainian population census
of 2001), *Instruktsiya shchodo provedennya vseukrains'koho perepysu naselennya 2001 roku i zapovnennya perepysnoyi dokumentatsiyi* (Instruction concerning
the carrying out of the All-Ukrainian population census of 2001 and the filling
out of the census documents) (Kyiv, 2001), 25. Source supplied by Dr Stephen
Rapawy. The full instructions for handling the sensitive ethnic origin question are,
as translated by me, as follows: "Recorded is the nationality (ethnicity), or ethnic
background, which is indicated by the respondent himself or herself. The childrens'
nationality is determined by their parents. If complications arise with respect to the
nationality of children, predominance is given to the nationality of the mother."

27 State Statistics Committee of Ukraine, "All-Ukrainian population census 2001,"
1–2; absolute population figures for 1989 from Arel, 1995, 598.

28 State Statistics Committee of Ukraine, "All-Ukrainian population census of 2001,"
Linguistic composition of the population. The English version does not have language data for the cities of Sevastopol' and Kyiv.

29 The most complete source is Osaulenko, 2003, 209. Source supplied by Dennis
Donahue.

30 "Statement by Vice President Biden after meeting with President of Ukraine Viktor
    Yushchenko" (White House, Office of the Vice President, Washington, DC); "House
    with Chimaeras," Kyiv, Ukraine, 21 July 2001, in *Action Ukraine Report (AUR)*,
    no. 938 (23 July 2009, Kyiv, Ukraine), morganw@patriot.net. See Danilova, 2009,
    A13.

6

Canada's Domestic French-Speaking Groups and the International Francophonie Compared

JÜRGEN ERFURT

The aim of this chapter is to identify the discursive dynamics in francophone areas in Canada, including the interests and conflicts of the actors and institutions in Canada. A further purpose is to portray the Francophonie (the international French-speaking organization) in its role as global actor in political, economic, and cultural relations. How do these domestic and international trends interact and impact on one another? It is of significance for an analysis of language policy to show how processes of globalization are articulated in a multitude of tension and conflict zones and what role a cultural phenomenon such as language plays in the social organization of communities, countries, and country coalitions.

METHODOLOGICAL ISSUES

The problem of *tertium comparationis* (third comparative reference point) is posed when we compare the francophonie in Canada to the international Francophonie. Being aware of the complexity of the phenomenon, I propose to focus the comparison on an analysis of institutions and the process of institutionalization that characterizes each francophonie. The aim of a comparison of the process of institutionalization is to recognize the glotto-political dimensions of the francophonie by showing how the communities define themselves largely through their relation to the French language domestically as well as internationally, how they are structured, and what interests they represent. If we have found the *tertium compartionis* for the comparative analysis of francophonies, it remains to be determined how the latter should be carried out for each of them. By relying on the approaches of cultural anthropology and ethnography of communication (Geertz, 1987;

Hymes, 1996), the narration of history allows us to understand social phenomena not only in their historicity but also by observing them through the angle of the comparison. For this reason, this chapter presents numerous case studies about the institutions of the francophonie which allow us, through induction, to prepare the way for the comparison.

The structure of this chapter is based on application of these methodological issues. The third part of the chapter addresses the topic of diversity and heterogeneity in the francophonie, in which the Canadian and Québécois francophonies are used as reference points to shed light later on the meaning of the concept. The fourth part reconstructs the axes of the institutionalization processes in the context of the international Francophonie from the early 1960s until today. It offers two theses regarding the politicization of cultural relations and bureaucratization in the francophonie. Against the backdrop of these two theses, in the fifth part of the chapter I will discuss the transformation and institutionalization processes in the francophonies of Canada and Quebec in the context of language policy from the early 1960s.[1] With the help of case studies, I will demonstrate how the communities of Canadiens français are organized, how francophone matters are integrated into government affairs at the federal and provincial levels, and how their nationalization progresses. It is important to draw attention here to the dialectic of national and international interests of glotto-political actors (see note 1 for a definition). The chapter as a whole will show how the politicization and bureaucratization of the francophonie led to its transformation into a platform for competing forms of nationalism, as well as for global engagement and the enforcement of specific social norms and values. The sixth part outlines the glotto-political discourses that constitute the Canadian francophonie. Finally, in the last part I synthesize the results of the comparison between the Canadian and Quebec francophonies and the international Francophonie.

The data presented in this paper were collected through extensive research projects conducted among the francophone minorities in Ontario and Acadia,[2] through studies of ethnocultural communities and language politics in Quebec and Ontario (see Erfurt 2000 and 2007), and through investigations of transculturalism and hybridity in francophone areas (see Erfurt 2005b). In addition and complementing this body of research, a study of transformational processes in the international Francophonie is included (Erfurt, 2005a). The third part of the chapter further discusses the arguments of M. Tétu (1996) and D. Ager (1996) regarding the French language in Canada and the international Francophonie.

HETEROGENEITY AND DIVERSITY IN
THE INTERNATIONAL FRANCOPHONIE

To analyze the relationship between Canada and the international Franco-phonie, it is necessary first and foremost to examine heterogeneity and divers-ity in the realm of social development, economy, history, cultural geography, demography, and language and to relate these to the global context. Like other international communities or groupings, the francophonie is far from representing a socially and linguistically homogeneous entity. Rather, it has to be understood as a tension-laden discursive construction, created in the Bourdieu sense as a field of social identification, cultural resource, market-place, and cultural capital.

The phenomenon of the francophonie is also complex in another way. During the decolonization process and the reshuffling of international rela-tions, especially since the early 1960s, speaking French became the founda-tion of an intricate web of transnational and intergovernmental relations in the areas of education, science, and culture among the elites of Africa, North America, and Asia as well as in Europe. After the first significant process of institutionalizing these relationships by founding the Agence de coopération culturelle et technique (1970), France then pushed for the nationalization of the Francophonie in the mid-1980s. This process was followed by the Francophonie's transformation into a global political actor and its represen-tation today as the Organisation internationale de la Francophonie (OIF).

For the analysis of the relationships between Canada and the Francophonie, certain issues will be presumed as established and undisputed. Cataloguing them here will be a way of using them as points of reference for the subse-quent discussion.

a. In the global context today, the OIF is seen as the most significant political actor and representative of French-speaking culture. Currently, seventy states and governments constitute its membership. Canada is represented three ways at the OIF – through the memberships of Canada, Quebec, and New Brunswick. This approach is similar to that of Belgium, which is represented by its federal state as well as by the government of the Communauté française de Belgique. Canada is one of twenty-nine coun-tries in the world in which French is an official language; those states are all members of the OIF. There are, however, also a number of member states – forty-one out of the seventy – where French is not one of the of-ficial languages. Further, there are areas in which French is spoken that are not part of the OIF – such as the American state of Louisiana, Algeria, and the Italian autonomous region of Val d'Aoste – where French in fact plays a very significant role. With the exception of Switzerland, it is important to note that none of the twenty-nine countries that joined the OIF since 1990 are officially French-speaking. Until 1989 the opposite had been true. Since the early 1990s the status and level of dissemination of French in a given country became noticeably secondary as a criterion for membership in the OIF. This fact indicates that a process of transformation has been taking place, which will be discussed in detail at a later point in this chapter.

b. Canada, as the second largest state in the world, is the largest country in the Francophonie. It has always considered itself to be an immigrant country because of the pressures created by the relationship between gigantic spatial dimensions and a small population. For some time, however, Canada has been pursuing a selective immigration policy in which humanitarian, especially economic, and – upon the request of Quebec – linguistic criteria play a strong role. One of the declared goals of the shift in Canada's immigration policy is the demographic support of the francophonie in Canada and Quebec through francophone or francophile immigrants.

c. Globally, Canada is one of the richest countries as well as a country with a high quality of life. Besides containing a small number of highly developed countries, the Francophonie includes a large number of extremely poor and underdeveloped ones.

d. Historically, from 1534 to 1763, Canada (as a component of New France) was a colony of France; later, until 1982, it was part of the British Empire, even after the founding of the country in 1867. Canada itself has never been a colonial power; this is one of the reasons that, unlike either France or Belgium, it has rarely been suspected of following colonial interests.[3] Because of this and other factors, Canada has a high level of credibility in the development of international relations in Africa and Asia.

e. Like Switzerland and Belgium, Canada is a federal, democratically governed state. It thus functions differently from centrally governed France, monarchies such as Morocco, or numerous other OIF member states, whose current heads of state have come to power through military coups or in which public life has been shaped for decades by wars, marauding youth gangs, and lawlessness. Within the Francophonie, Canada represents a type of state whose values and principles were defined by the OIF Charter (1997) as the common good and also as reference points, even while the current political reality, especially in Africa, remains the opposite.

f. The language debate in Canada is politically and emotionally charged, and thus it is similar to that in many other countries. Language conflicts between anglophone and francophone communities, on the one hand, and between the two languages of the former colonial powers and those of the Native peoples, on the other, have been intense and long-lasting. Moreover, new conflict situations originating in the immigration context are continually being added. Canada became a bilingual state in 1969, and the federal level of government as well as all public bodies work in both English and French. An officially bilingual Canada does not, however, mean that its citizens are also bilingual. On the contrary, Canada is dominated by monolingualism in either English or French, although a sizable portion of the French-speaking population is fluent in both languages. Canada's official bilingualism therefore represents an initiative by the state to modify the double monolingualism of its population. The French language is, besides its function as an official language, the largest minority language in Canada. In the province of Quebec it is the majority language, with 85.7 per cent of the population, or 6.4 million, being francophone in 2006. The percentage of francophones in other Canadian provinces ranges from 32.7 per cent in New Brunswick (0.2 million) to 4.5 per cent in Ontario (0.5 million) and 0.4 to 3.9 per cent in the remaining provinces.

g. Even beyond the OIF member states, the French language is globally one of the widest spread languages.

In order to better distinguish between diverse cultural and political realities of the francophonie, we must also distinguish between at least two meanings of the word. The term "la Francophonie" with a capital *F* is used when speaking, in political and institutional terms, of the current agreement between seventy countries, including eleven observers and three associate members, that constitute the OIF. "La francophonie" with a lower-case *f* represents the cultural spaces in the world within which French is prominent or has an influence on linguistic relations, as is the case for the francophone cultures of North America, the Caribbean, and the Maghreb and the Maschrik of sub-Saharan Africa. In terms of geographical distribution, notions of "Francophonie" (capital *F*) and "francophonie" (lower case *f*) are not identical. A number of states that share specific values with France yet are not francophone belong to the OIF – Bulgaria, Romania, Lithuania, Moldavia, Poland, Laos, Vietnam, Cape Verde, and Guinea-Bissau as well as new members such as Cyprus, Greece, Austria, Hungary, Macedonia, Serbia, Ukraine, and Armenia. In other countries, such as Lebanon or Algeria, French has no official status but plays an important social role. For historical reasons, Algeria is not part of the OIF. Many African countries are officially francophone, even though their populations – with the exception of the social elite – contain a very small percentage of French-speakers.

PROCESSES OF INSTITUTIONALIZATION AND TRANSFORMATION IN THE FRANCOPHONIE

The early 1960s are significant as well as contradictory for the constitution of the discourse surrounding the Francophonie and the transformation of the founding idea into a process of institutionalization. Soon after France gave up its role as colonial world power and several African states reached independence from France and Belgium, a number of African politicians arose as initiators of a new solidarity between the French-speaking countries and the previous colonial powers. These were, incidentally, politicians who were well-established in the French political class. L.S. Senghor attributes this fact to the societal circumstances of many African states that were not culturally, economically, or politically prepared for independence (see Senghor, 1980, 242). Pro-Francophonie events gained momentum during and in the wake of decolonization: in 1960 the education ministers of several African states and France conferred for the first time and created the still operating Conférence des ministres de l'éducation nationale (CONFEMEN). In September 1961 several African heads of state founded the Union africaine et malgache (UAM), the first institutionalized association of French-speaking states, which was transformed in 1965 into the Organisation commune africaine et malgache (OCAM). Senghor also repeatedly recommended the creation of a "Commonwealth à la française" at the first summit of the UAM in 1962 in Bangui, Central Africa. French president Charles de Gaulle, on the other hand, was concerned for a long time about a Francophonie falling into the trap of neo-colonialism, as has been repeatedly reported (see Baggioni, 1996, 798).

The first decade of the institutionalization process of the Francophonie was marked by important events, in which Canadian actors played a part. The previously mentioned conference of francophone education ministers (CONFEMEN) in 1960 initially took place without Canadian participation. In September 1961, however, representatives of 150 universities founded the Association des universités partiellement ou entièrement de langue française (AUPELF) in Montreal, a university network for multilateral cooperation. Solidarity between educational institutes of the north – Canada, France, and Belgium – with the newer universities of the Southern Hemisphere stood at the core of the AUPELF. The body was founded as an international non-governmental organization based on Quebec law and has in its four-decades-long existence experienced significant transformations. At several points, AUPELF has acted as an arena for the diverging ambitions of France, Canada, and Quebec. In 1994 the organization merged with the Universités des réseaux d'expression française (UREF), which was founded in 1987, to form the AUPELF-UREF; the latter was finally transformed into the Agence universitaire de la Francophonie (AUF) in 1997. Today 685 universities and research institutes from a total of eighty-one countries belong.

At the end of the 1960s a number of interest groups related to the Francophonie already existed, one of which was the Assemblée internationale des parlementaires de langue française (1967). As a result, the call for coordination and institutionalization grew stronger. At that point France played only a marginal role in the politics of the new Francophonie, as it focused on Africa predominantly via a bilateral relationship. Francophone Africans and Québécois, on the other hand, emphasized the importance of employing the Francophonie not only as a new access point for international cooperation but also as a means to further national interests. In 1969, representatives of twenty-eight francophone governments came together for the first conference in Niamey, Niger. In March 1970, at the second Niamey conference, twenty-one governments signed the Charter founding the Agence de coopération culturelle et technique (ACCT). To anticipate potential neo-colonial sensitivities, explicit reference to the term "Francophonie" was avoided in its title. Yet this decision did not prevent its development into the most important intergovernmental agency of the Francophonie for technical, cultural, economic, and political cooperation between francophone and partially francophone countries at the ministerial level under the leadership of the Québécois Jean-Marc Léger. The founding of the agency in 1970 coincided with the confrontation between Canada and Quebec about Quebec having a seat of its own next to Canada at the ACCT (see Le Scouarnec, 1997. 72, 79f.).

In 1975 the Senegalese president L.S. Senghor suggested to the French president, Valéry Giscard d'Estaing, the initiation of a meeting between the heads of state of French-speaking countries. In France, however, this proposal was only accepted a decade later (see Le Scouarnec, 1997, 71), as too many difficulties with and within the ACCT shaped the political attitude of the French administration. During his election campaign at the end of 1985, François Mitterrand envisaged a foreign policy success by initiating a meeting of heads of ACCT member states, to which he invited the representatives of forty-one governments to Versailles in February 1986. Algeria and Cameroon were not present; Cambodia had at that point not been internationally recognized; Vietnam, Laos, and, after hesitation, Switzerland participated as observers. Louisiana received guest status. The federal states of Belgium and Canada were confronted with the by then familiar problem of international representation. In the end, Belgium was represented by its federal government as well as by the Communauté française, and Canada by representatives of the federal government and the provinces of Quebec and New-Brunswick.[4] Mitterrand's initiative in holding the first meeting indicates that a high-level international political forum took its place alongside the ACCT. In the long term this meant that the Francophonie ceased to be a political taboo in international relations since Mitterrand introduced it as an official dimension of French foreign policy and institutionally anchored it in the administration.

We refer to the nationalization of the Francophonie in the following part of this chapter – that is, the process in which the Francophonie was transformed into a field of official national politics. At the same time, it was integrated into the administrative structures of the state, and this process occurred not only in France but also in the administrations of all the member states.

Up to 1993 the summit was commonly referred to as the "Conférence des chefs d'État et de gouvernement des pays ayant en commun l'usage du français." For the summit in Mauritius the title was modified to "Conférence des chefs d'État et de gouvernement des pays ayant le français en partage." The change in terminology is partly an indicator of the international political transformations that would lead in the early 1990s to important changes in the political unions and networks as well as a change in the identity of the Francophonie. The end of the Cold War, the collapse of the Soviet Union, the failure of the socialist countries of Central and Eastern Europe, and the resulting consequences for numerous Asian and African states created a global political vacuum that forced powerful competitors such as France and the United States to act. At the summit in Paris in November 1991, Romania, Bulgaria, and Cambodia become new member states of the Francophonie, which introduced the process of integrating non-francophone states into the organization. The meeting of 1991 is also relevant on another level since the member states voted on resolutions pertaining to the Israel-Palestinian conflict, Haiti, military coups, and wars in several African states, thus rendering the 1970 ACCT position of "strict neutrality in political and ideological matters" obsolete.

Between the summits of Cotonou (1995) and Hanoi (1997), the Francophonie undertook a reorganization of its structures and core components to adapt to the new state of international affairs. What was the best stance to take to cope with shifting global spheres of influence, the effects of globalization, and neo-liberalism? At Cotonou the heads of states signed the "Projet francophone pour le temps présent et le siècle à venir" with the aim of granting the Francophonie *sa pleine dimension politique* ("its full political dimension") (Agence, 1995). The concept is loosely defined via key words such as rationalization, effective leadership structures, subsidiarity, and operationality; it comes down to the idea of reconstructing the Francophonie as a global player that can actively and proactively shape the face of international relations. It was further decided in Cotonou to elect a general secretary of the Francophonie at the next summit, held in Hanoi. The concept of "expansion of the political dimension" also meant that the 1970 Charter of the ACCT required a fundamental rewrite, because it was especially in the interest of France to introduce a pyramidal structure with a general secretary at its head. The ACCT, up to this point a predominantly supranational coordination and governing centre, had its power diluted by being transformed into the Agence de la Francophonie, a largely operational body, and becoming subordinate to and controlled by the general secretary.

The conference of ministers of the Francophonie adopted a new "Charte de la Francophonie" in 1996. The new institutional reorganization became official at the seventh summit in Hanoi in 1997. After much lobbying by French president Jacques Chirac, former UN secretary general Boutros Boutros-Ghali was elected as general secretary of the Francophonie (see Kolboom 2002a, 465). He went on to represent the unity of all commissions and institutions that have operated since that point under the umbrella of the OIF.

The reorganization process meanwhile has not been concluded. The key conflict consists of the two opposing positions of more supranational or more international politics, which in turn have quite distinct consequences. The supranational position is primarily anchored in the old ACCT, with its key points of reference in the linguistic-cultural domain. The ACCT's last general secretary, Jean-Louis Roy from Quebec, who was highly regarded, especially in Africa, embodied a supranational Francophonie. The international position, on the other hand, found its platform in the summit, whose heads of states, especially the competing donor countries of France and Canada, saw in it the possibility of creating an intergovernmental Francophonie as an "equal actor in international politics" (B. Boutros-Ghali, *Lettre de la Francophonie* 106 [1997]: 5). The victory of the latter position and the associated disempowerment of the Agence de la Francophonie is above all expressed in the renaming of the former ACCT as the Agence intergouvernementale de la Francophonie (ibid., 465ff.).

Since the Hanoi summit in 1997, the AIF has launched several new programs, as the economic dimension of cooperation and the introduction of new information and communication technologies became increasingly more prominent. The new OIF emphasizes its claim to be an actor in international politics by centralizing all functions on Francophonie-related issues and representing them at the international level. This is especially the case as globalization has increasingly overcome all barriers between politics, the economy, technology, culture, and language and catapulted English into the position of the world's lingua franca. The French demand for an *exception culturelle* and "cultural pluralism" as part of global trade carries a strong political significance, especially because it has become part of the French and francophone criticism of the globalization of communication under American hegemony (see Kolboom, 2002a, 466).

By the time of the eighth summit in Moncton in 1999, the new face of the Francophonie had taken shape; it consisted in the launching of the organization's identity as a political actor that internally discusses questions of democracy, human rights, and rule of law. Even though officially the Moncton conference was dedicated to the rather uncontroversial theme of "global francophone youth," the parallel alternative conference by francophone human rights groups focused especially on issues such as democracy and human rights in the Francophonie member states. Discussion was, for instance, sparked about the participation of the Congolese president and dictator Laurent Désiré Kabila (1939–2001). The recently formulated aim to recognize and enforce democracy and human rights in all member states introduced tensions that reflected a fundamental problem for the new course of the Francophonie. For nearly half the member states, the realization of this aim was not only challenging but also difficult, as they did not want to be singled out or abide by political norms and values that at this point in time were predominantly northern. Thus the situation presented another example of the heterogeneity of interests between north and south.

Under the shadow of the unrest in the Ivory Coast, French military intervention, and the exodus of about eight thousand French citizens from the formerly best model of French-African cooperation, the tenth OIF summit took place in the neighbouring capital of Burkina Faso in November 2004. The theme "La Francophonie, espace solidaire pour un développement durable" highlighted more strongly than ever the importance of issues such as peace, the economy, and democracy. The economic debate addressed questions such as debt reduction for poor countries, the development of a distribution system for micro-credits, improved access for southern countries to international markets, and the expansion of trade relations between countries in the south. The conference also specifically dealt with the importance of peace and security as a condition for sustainable and ongoing development. The Francophonie has faced immense challenges with regard to fostering peace and democracy within its member states, especially in light of the political crises in the Middle East, Haiti, and the Ivory Coast, the tensions between Ivory Coast and Burkina Faso, and the military threats of Rwanda vis-à-vis the Democratic Republic of Congo and the Darfur crisis in Sudan.

The applications for OIF membership of seven states were discussed at the summit in Ouagadougou. Greece and Andorra joined as associate members, and Armenia, Georgia, Croatia, Austria, and Hungary as members with observer status. After the twelfth summit of the OIF, which took place in Quebec in October 2008, the organization now comprises seventy states and governments.

Meanwhile, the reorganization of administrative structures continued under Abdou Diouf, who was elected general secretary in 2002. A recent example of this process was the new Charter of the Francophonie, adopted by the conference of ministers of the Francophonie in November 2005 in Madagascar, which enforced the principle of subsidiarity and hierarchy through the creation of a post of an *administrateur* as well as a Conseil de coopération (see article 8). This change also diminished the influence of the AIF and lent more power to the pyramid-like structure. The general secretary, Diouf, nominated the Quebec diplomat Clément Duhaime for the role of *administrateur de l'OIF*, and he took up the position in January 2006. The eleventh summit in Bucharest in September 2006 further deliberated about the charter.

The argument in the following section can be summarized with two theses (for more detail, see Erfurt 2005, 119ff.). The first is the politicization thesis. The history of the Francophonie since the early 1960s has been shaped by a growing politicization of the cultural discourse and the replacement of its actors by a professional and bureaucratic elite. The politicization is three-fold. The first aspect has been the transformation of the intellectual monopoly in the early phases of the Francophonie, which was located outside France and especially among the intellectual elites of Africa and Quebec, into prominence of the bureaucratic elite in France in the 1980s. Secondly, politicization is expressed through the transformation of cultural relations on the basis of a common language into transnational political relations that partially neglect or subordinate language. The goal of this transformation is to promote the reorganization of international spheres of influences. And thirdly, politicization is revealed in the extent to which multilateral political relations play a role in the founding of institutions, which are an expression of political will and in turn are subject to political transformations. The latter can be witnessed in the numerous reorganizations of institutions and projects of the Francophonie during the last decade.

The second thesis is that of professionalization and bureaucratization. This thesis implies that the Francophonie is subject to considerations of specialization and efficiency, because it actively follows processes of institutionalization, nationalization, and globalization. The created institutional structure requires, on the one hand, a high level of administration and creates, on the other hand, steadiness and continuance. To the extent to which the institutions of the Francophonie benefit from diversity, the recruitment of professionals increases significantly for a growing number of activities. At the same time, processes of analysis and strategy building have been launched that are linked to efficiency considerations since they require a considerable amount of resources from the French government. The Francophonie therefore represents not only a field for professional careers and for the application of educational resources but, under neo-liberal influences, also for the implementation of improved administrative structures, more efficient administrative processes, and control. The restructuring of the Francophonie into the OIF and the introduction of a pyramidal structure of hierarchies provide a fitting example of this process.

Later in this chapter I will show how the nature of the two trends has expressed processes of politicization, on the one hand, and bureaucratization and professionalization, on the other, thereby shaping relations between Canada and the Francophonie. Special focus will be placed on how the francophonie is organized in Canada and which structures and institutions it creates.

THE INSTITUTIONS AND ACTORS OF THE CANADIAN FRANCOPHONIE BETWEEN POLITICIZATION AND BUREAUCRATIZATION

At the Government Level

The election of Liberal Jean Lesage as premier of Quebec in 1960 under the slogan of "C'est le temps que ça change" marked the beginning of the Quiet Revolution, which ushered in the modernization of Quebec. Signs of social change had already been discernible in the postwar period. The painter Paul-Emile Borduas and a group of fifteen young artists protested against the clerical-conservative policy of Maurice Duplessis by publishing a manifesto entitled *Refus global* in 1948. The following year saw workers, particularly in the asbestos industry, go on strike to demand the introduction of social welfare measures and the recognition of the trade union movement. In 1952 Radio Canada introduced a French-language channel featuring shows that were specifically designed for Quebec, thus fostering a feeling of solidarity among the Québécois. Sharp criticism of Duplessis's autocratic policies was to be found in the columns of the magazine *Cité Libre* – a title sounding like an echo of the *Refus global* manifesto – founded by Gérard Pelletier and

Pierre Elliot Trudeau in 1950. When Jean Lesage came to power, the stage was set for a reform policy whose political and psychological dimensions boiled down to the fact that Quebec no longer saw itself as a social minority in the otherwise anglophone Canadian state but "as a self-sufficient entity" (Weinmann, 2002, 443). More than any other project, the nationalization of Hydro-Québec – and thus the entire hydroelectric power supply – in 1962 symbolized the electoral slogan "Maître chez nous" of the political program aimed at sovereignty. The creation of a strong and secular state that would take care of energy and social welfare policies as much as it would of culture, higher education, and foreign policy was probably the most significant innovation of the Quiet Revolution. In this spirit Quebec opened general missions abroad – in New York and Paris in 1961, in London in 1962 – and economic offices, such as those in Milan (1965); in Boston, Dallas, Chicago, and Los Angeles (1969); and in Düsseldorf (1970). It also made a special effort to achieve a political rapprochement with France.

The first fruit borne of this policy was the founding in 1964 of the Commission permanente franco-québécoise, which coordinated cooperation in the fields of education and culture. As nationalism took shape in Quebec and demands were voiced for independence for the province, especially under Daniel Johnson and above all under René Lévesque, who had founded the Parti Québécois in 1968, a struggle broke out between the Canadian federal government and the provincial government in Quebec over which was to control the foreign policy of the state. In July 1967 anglophone-dominated Canada, at this time the only part of the country to be active in the Commonwealth, heard French President Charles de Gaulle proclaim his (in)famous "Vive le Québec libre!" in Montreal.[5] Alarmed by the approval of Quebec's population, the federal government admitted to shortcomings in its foreign policy contacts with francophone countries and reacted by setting up a Francophone Affairs Division.

In February 1968 tensions between Ottawa and Quebec came to a head when the provincial government received an invitation to the conference of education ministers of the francophone states (CONFEMEN) in Libreville, and Quebec, being responsible for its own educational policy, wanted to be represented there with or without the permission of the federal government. The lines of conflict followed a similar course over the next two years when preparations were made to found the Agence de coopération culturelle et technique (ACCT) in Niamey. This conflict between the federal and provincial governments also revolved around the question of whether Quebec was to be allowed to operate in the international arena as an independent political actor or whether the right to represent Canada and its provinces to the outside world was solely reserved for the federal government. The fact that Quebec finally was able to join, together with Canada, as founding members of the ACCT was the result of a compromise on the definition of membership according to which both states and governments could be members (see Le Scouarnec, 1997, 63).

During the 1960s two processes were observable. One was the development of international relations between Quebec and France as well as between Quebec and the new francophone states of Africa. The other, taking place within Canada, was a shift in the balance of power between Canada, Quebec, and the francophone minorities in the other provinces. Various groups, ranging from the Quebec independence movement to the Front de libération du Québec (FLQ), which were inspired by the anticolonial writings of Frantz Fanon, Albert Memmi, Ernesto Che Guevara, and the American Black Power movement (see Vallières, 1994. 108ff.) and the ideologies of the African liberation movements, vigorously demanded the end of the inequality between the anglophone majority and the francophone minority. Their arguments were highlighted in the 1965 preliminary report of the Royal Commission on Bilingualism and Biculturalism (B and B Commission), which had been set up by the federal government two years earlier. The report drew attention to the glaring differences in social welfare and income between English- and French-speaking Canadians. As a result of the commission's work, the Canadian Official Languages Act, which declared both English and French to be official languages at the federal level, was passed into law in 1969.

The Official Languages Act and the setting up of the Francophone Affairs Division in the Canadian Department of Foreign Affairs were two events that were to have lasting effects on both the French-speaking communities in Canada and the French-speaking world as a whole. These two events represented in both symbolic and concrete terms the process of recognizing Canada's *dualité linguistique* (linguistic duality) and the institutionalization of francophone affairs at the federal and provincial levels of the state apparatus. Outside this new political framework, the francophone communities had long had a well-organized civil society. Francophone communities in the provinces have had a large number of institutions since the nineteenth century: ecclesiastical-religious, charitable, professional, artistic, social, and so on. These represent the interests of their members, and they show solidarity with one another, providing social facilities and networks to enable the francophones to communicate in French. In addition to these established institutions within francophone communities, the state has created its own institutions to act as contact points for matters regarding Quebec and the

French-speaking minorities, on the one hand, and the implementation of government policies in the provinces, on the other. How this process has worked in practice may be seen from four sample institutions that function at the level of francophone communities.

Non-governmental Organizations

An institution such as the Association canadienne-française de l'Ontario (ACFO), a successor organization to the Association canadienne-française d'éducation de l'Ontario (ACFEO), initially founded in 1910, for decades regarded itself as a mouthpiece for the French-speaking communities of Ontario and also as an umbrella organization for a large number of local and regional francophone associations in that province. The ACFEO saw its paramount role in organizing opposition to Regulation 17 of 1912, which made it illegal to use French as a language of instruction in Ontario's schools. It was able to expand its area of operations considerably after it was renamed the ACFO in 1969. As a result of the Official Languages Act, the ACFO, now recognized by the state as a negotiating partner and institutional recipient of subsidies from the federal government, was able to extend its activities beyond the schooling sector to all aspects of life in French-speaking communities: promotion of work with children and youth; the founding of schools, publishing houses, and galleries; and support for local radio stations, theatre groups, and music festivals. To these areas were later added support for francophone economic structures, health and social welfare, and the integration of French-speaking immigrants in Ontario (see Augerot-Arend, 1996). As the traditionally powerful representative of the francophonie in Ontario's minority milieu, the ACFO had to face attacks from not only the ranks of anglophones. In recent years, anti-francophone organizations such as the Association for the Preservation of English in Canada (APEC) and Canadians Against Bilingualism Injustice (CABI) have repeatedly hit the headlines in both Ontario and New Brunswick in their fight against the use of French as an official language in Canada and against the Canadian policy of bilingualism.

Since the 1990s there have been signs of conflict and a questioning of the organization's policy and leadership within the ACFO itself. The cutting of state subsidies exacerbated the conflict between the organizations and groups belonging to the ACFO. At the same time, Ontario's francophones were founding new societies and associations, such as feminist groups, artists' associations, and lesbian and gay organizations, which questioned not only the hegemony of the ACFO but also its values and structures; many saw a conflict in being represented by the ACFO and demanded separate subsidy structures directly from the state. Just as the fabric of society as a whole has changed since the early 1990s, the francophone community in Ontario too is undergoing a transformation.

One aspect of this change originates with the French-speaking immigrants that are settling in large numbers in the Greater Toronto Area, Ottawa, and the Niagara Peninsula, in the south of the province. Their cultural experiences and interests in emerging issues are frequently at odds with the experience that Canadian-born francophones have accumulated over decades of conflict with the anglophone majority. As ethnocultural and racial communites (*communautés ethnoculturelles et raciales*), the newcomers also claim access to resources and distribution mechanisms of the francophonie in the minority milieu. Finally, francophone institutions inside and outside the ACFO are subject to considerable pressure by the federal government, which has the final say over administrative regulations and subsidy priorities.[6] This was the case in 2003 when the Department of Canadian Heritage (DCH) again cut, this time drastically, its subsidies for the ACFO, while at the same time demanding a radical review of its mandate and a rethinking of its strategy. The background to this state intervention in the affairs of a civil institution was the conflict of interests between the ACFO and other francophone groups and organizations that did not feel represented by it (see Thériault, 2005). The federal government started intervening in the conflict in 1995 when the DCH drafted an agreement with the province of Ontario – parallel agreements were made the other provinces, except Quebec – known as "Entente Canada – communauté Ontario." According to the department, government subsidies should be administered and distributed through an institution that represented the interests of all organizations. Within the framework, the Entente Canada – communauté Ontario in 2000 saw the founding of the Direction entente Canada – communauté Ontario (DECCO), a type of counterpart to the ACFO. After the financial debacle of 2003, the renaming of the ACFO as the Assemblée des communautés franco-ontariennes in 2004, the replacement of the old leadership, and a tense transformation process, the ACFO and the DECCO finally merged on 31 March 2006 to form the Assemblée de la francophonie de l'Ontario (AFO).[7]

A second example is provided by the ACFO, which in 1975 merged with the umbrella organizations of other Canadian provinces under the auspices of the newly founded Fédération des francophones hors Québec (FFHQ) and in 1991 changed its name to the Fédération des communautés francophones et acadiennes (FCFA). The new umbrella organization was a reaction of francophones to alarming changes regarding their situation in Canada. The reasons for the merger were, first, to present a united front vis-à-vis the federal government, from which they expected a higher degree of commitment regarding the francophone minority, which saw itself threatened by assimilation into the dominant anglophone society, and, second, to respond to the aspirations of Quebec nationalism, especially after the electoral victory in 1976 of the Parti Québécois, whose political agenda envisaged the founding of an independent nation-state. In the view of Quebec nationalists, francophones outside Quebec were "dead ducks," since a francophonie could not survive in North America without its own state. At the same time, the Québécois claimed to represent the Canadian francophonie on the principle of *dualité linguistique*, with the result that the bridges between Quebec and the francophone minorities in the other provinces were, if not completely destroyed, at least seriously damaged. The fragmentation of the "francophonie canadienne" into Acadiens/Acadiennes, Franco-Ontariens, Franco-Manitobains, Fransaskois, Franco-Albertans, and other groups was accompanied by an institutional restructuring, from which the FFHQ/FCFA emerged as the mouthpiece of francophones vis-à-vis the federal government. The third reason for the merger was the looming discussions on the Canadian constitution, in which the FCFA aspired to represent the interests of francophones by acting as negotiating partner with the federal government.

For a third example we go back to the year 1834, which saw the founding of the Société Saint-Jean-Baptiste de Montréal (SSJBM), an association of French-speaking elites devoted to the protection of French and the *peuple canadien français*. Initially politically cautious, the society engaged in charitable activities before taking on – under the suspicious eyes of the Catholic Church and the anglophone elites – activities in the field of commercial and technical training (see Augerot-Arend, 1996, 272ff.). In the second half of the nineteenth century the SSJBM played a major role in the founding of the Chambre de commerce, the *Écoles des Hautes études commerciales*, and the *École des* beaux-arts in Montreal, which served as a counterweight to the anglophone predominance in business and trade. With its clerical-conservative and nationalist orientation, the Société Saint-Jean-Baptiste saw itself as a linchpin of Quebec patriotism, promoting its heroes and myths and giving support to national monuments (such as La Croix de Montréal), national anniversaries, and mass rallies; 24 June has been a national holiday since 1977, the occasion of the annual *défilés* (marches) of the SSJBM. Since 1968 the organization has actively supported the cause of Quebec's sovereignty and pursued an ultranationalist course of French monolingualism. The SSJBM can act independently of government grants. It is a major presence in public life, and the population of Quebec supports the organization with generous donations, which in turn have enabled it to confer its own grants, prizes, and awards and even to set up a chair in Quebec history at the Université du Québec à Montréal in 2003. As a non-governmental francophone actor, the Société Saint-Jean-Baptiste is represented throughout the whole province of Quebec and is an active member of the Mouvement national des Québécoises et Québécois, which was founded in 1947 and has a current membership of about 200,000, organized in nineteen sections representing all regions of Quebec.

A fourth and last example is provided by the Maison d'Haïti and the ethnocultural Centre N a Rive, which were founded by Haitian migrants in Montreal in 1973. These institutions were initially set up to provide social and legal assistance to members of the Haitian community in Quebec. Later on, literacy courses were sponsored in response to an urgent need, especially for those whose schooling in Haiti had been sporadic or non-existent. In 1978 the first regular literacy course was organized in Montreal, in which the emphasis was placed from the start on the ideas of the Brazilian Paolo Freire concerning *concientisation* (consciousness-building). From this approach followed the decision of the Haitian educational activists to begin by teaching the migrants to read and write in their native language, Creole, before proceeding to the second stage of teaching them French. As long as the Haitians regarded themselves as refugees or exiles from the Duvalier dictatorship, literacy in Creole meant a preparation for a return to their country. This situation changed in February 1986 when Haiti freed itself of the Duvalier dictatorship. Some of the refugees returned to Haiti, but many others remained in Montreal. The institutions of the Haitian community in the city since then have had a different mandate, namely, helping their fellow citizens integrate into Quebec society. After the Centre N a Rive had been recognized as an autonomous community centre in 1986, the discussion resumed as to how the work of imparting literacy, on the one hand, and of integration into Quebec society, on the other, was to be continued. While Creole continued to be the starting point and point of reference for acquiring literacy, efforts also were made to provide social and vocational training. Since the early 1990s, courses in sewing, cooking, and baking have been offered as a preparation for paid employment. Later a computer course was added. Throughout the 1990s the primary emphasis on literacy in Creole proved a successful model, especially as Creole continued to be supported in its function as stepping stone toward the acquisition of French and is thus seen as a resource for the acquisition of French.

With the establishment of neo-liberal ground rules in Quebec society, the basic framework for bringing literacy and the French language to migrants has fundamentally changed. In the years between 2000 and 2003 the state remodelled both the infrastructure and the concept of language acquisition and literacy. The French term for the new concept is *alpha-francisation* (rather than *alphabétisation*), a term used in the institutions and language courses of the Immigration Ministry which is now part of the vocabulary of the Centre N a Rive as well. While *alphabétisation* and *francisation* had been treated separately in the 1990s, the concept of *alpha-francisation* has been pursued for the past three years with the aim of developing direct access to French. Thus *alpha-francisation* means that proficiency in the native tongue has to be suppressed or even perhaps eliminated in the process of making migrants literate. The current management of the centre is obliged to uphold the new language policy of its partner, the state. To justify this policy, the administration relies on the argument that the clientele of the centre is linguistically heterogenous since Creole is no longer the common language of all the participants. The current new orientation for the community/ethnic Alpha centres in Quebec is increasingly on access to the labour market.

These four institutions exemplify a very large number and dense network of francophone associations and institutions that have represented the professional, religious, cultural, linguistic, charitable, economic, ethnic, and other interests of Canadiens français and Néo-Québécois since the nineteenth century. They also stand for processes of differentiation within the francophonie, and especially for the role of francophone elites. The examples shed light on the expansion of the economic and educational resources of the francophones in the nineteenth and twentieth centuries and on the debates about cultural identity, which were long dominated by the tripartite formula *langue, religion, race*. The above-mentioned institutions make it possible to trace the lines of conflict and ethno-linguistic boundaries in the second half of the twentieth century, which appear, on the one hand, in the context of monoglot areas – in Quebec and in the francophone minority milieu – and, on the other, in the discussion as to who is Québécois and who is not, and how Quebec society is defined in the context of migration processes.

Federal Francophonie Policies

The Official Languages Act, the setting up of a division for francophonie affairs in the Canadian Department of Foreign Affairs, and above all Quebec's ambitions to become a nation-state marked the beginning in the late 1960s of a dynamic within and between the institutions of the federal and provincial governments in which the francophonie – sooner and on a larger scale and in a more differentiated way than in any other country – emerged as a field of activity for official state policy and became integrated into its administrative structures. In the course of the nationalization of francophone affairs, the state consequently responded to the aspirations of the long-established institutions of francophone communities by setting up its own authorities, thus intervening in the relations existing between as well as within the ethnic communities.

Who are the agents of the state and how do they operate in the context of the francophonie? At the level of the federal government there are now – since the cautious beginnings in the late 1960s – a large number of ministries, authorities, departments, and institutions concerned with francophone affairs, although individual dossiers, spheres of competence of ministerial authorities, and their institutional assignment have in many cases changed from government to government. Francophone affairs have been dealt with by the ministries of Justice, Environment, Industry, and Immigration, the Privy Council Office, and especially the Department of Canadian Heritage, the Department of Foreign Affairs, and the new Department of International Cooperation, Francophonie and Official Languages, created by the Conservative government in January 2006. It is not yet clear in what way individual dossiers that were located in various ministries under the Liberal governments of the last ten years are to be coordinated and/or consolidated. This process chiefly concerns the *cadre stratégique* immigration policy of 2003 for francophone or francophile persons;[8] the Privy Council's coordination of measures in the field of official languages; the Industry Canada projects for the development and expansion of information technologies and data highways in the French-speaking world and the virtual francophonie; the Department of Justice's measures to implement the Official Languages Act; and legal cooperation with francophone countries to promote democracy. It seems clear, however, that the Conservative government will also assign key responsibilities to the Departments of Canadian Heritage and International Cooperation, Francophonie and Official Languages.

A major role regarding the international Francophonie is played by the Canadian International Development Agency (CIDA), formerly part of Foreign Affairs but now part of International Cooperation, Francophonie and Official Languages. CIDA's budget, "Aide publique au développement" (APD), consists of considerable funds that Canada invests in the international Francophonie. It also brings its extensive logistical and technical experience to the organization and administration of cooperation projects in the field of education (e.g., Can$35 million in grants in the period 2000–05); peace and security (Can$5 million on peacekeeping missions in Africa, 2001–05); promotion of young entrepreneurs (Can$5 million for north-south and south-south corporate cooperation); technological and pedagogical training in francophone Africa (Can$15 million in the period 2000–05); and combating corruption in

Africa (Can$1.3 million for Transparency International, 2003–05), to name but a few current projects.[9]

A large number of other political actors in the Francophonie are or have so far been reporting to the Department of Canadian Heritage, which is primarily responsible for national programs promoting Canadian identity and civil society. It supports, among others, cultural programs of francophone communities, sports, communications, and communications technologies. Within the framework of a comprehensive program known as "Développement des communautés de langue officielle," the department underwrites a wide range of francophone community activities[10] in schools of the provinces and territories[11] and in connection with the sport and cultural festival Jeux de la Francophonie. According to a government website, "Day-to-day responsibility for managing Canada's participation in la Francophonie has been assigned to the Francophonie Affairs Division of the Department of Foreign Affairs and International Trade, which coordinates all aspects of this participation at the departmental and interdepartmental levels. The Division also manages the bulk of budget resources that Canada devotes to the Organisation internationale de la Francophonie and to Francophonie institutions."[12] One of the focal areas of international cooperation, especially with African countries, is that of information technology, the creation of data highways (inforoutes), and the training of personnel, which is largely the domain of the former Institut francophone des nouvelles technologies de l'information et de la formation, now the Institut de la Francophonie numérique.

One of the principles of the Canadian federal government's Francophonie policy is that of multilateralism and networking within the Francophonie. In so doing, it pursues a different strategy of international cooperation from France, for instance, whose Francophonie policy is directed entirely towards bilateral relations, that is, agreements between France and a given francophone country, thus pursuing its hegemonic ambitions toward other francophone countries. These rival views of the principle of international cooperation have repeatedly led to conflicts and tensions between the representatives of Canada, France, and Quebec in the institutions of the international Francophonie.

Relations between Quebec and the Federal Government

As explained above, the other members of the OIF besides Canada are the governments of Quebec and New Brunswick. Quebec, which sees itself as a French-speaking nation state and the "foyer de la francophonie en Amérique du Nord," is held to be a principal actor in the Canadian francophonie and a pillar of the international equivalent. This latter status is expressed in the facts that Quebec hosted the second summit in 1987; that since the 1980s it has repeatedly hosted important political conferences of the Francophonie; that representatives of Quebec, such as J.-M. Leger, J.-L. Roy, and C. Duhaime, were nominated for top functions in the Francophonie; and that the 2008 OIF summit meeting was held in Quebec City in honour of the 400th anniversary of the founding of the city.

Meanwhile, the conflicts between the federal and Quebec governments concerning the province's foreign-policy commitments have been resolved. At first glance, both sides seem committed to the same principles in their work together in the international Francophonie, principles expressed in Quebec government parlance by the key concepts of multilateralism, partnership, and cooperative networking.[13] Yet it is obvious that the interests of Canada and Quebec are not identical and that inside Quebec other principles are discussed from those mentioned above. To take one example: in the "Rapport Larose" (Commission des États généraux, 2001),[14] which is a key document in the formulation of a strategy for Quebec's linguistic policy, the emphasis is different. First, the report suggests that cooperation be geared more toward bilateralism.[15] At the same time, it expects from the OIF "un soutien concret à sa politique d'affirmation du français sur le double plan national et international" ("concrete support for its policy of affirmation of French both on the national and international scenes") (ibid., 164). Second, it is critical of the policy of the OIF that admitted as members many non-francophone countries since the early 1990s. The international Francophonie thus runs the risk of compromising its fundamental aims: "promotion du français et relation de complémentarité entre le français et les langues nationales des pays en voie de développement ... le moment est venu de préciser le statut du français dans la francophonie" ("the promotion of French and the complementary relationship between French and the national languages of developing countries ... the time has arrived to specify the status of French in the Francophonie) (ibid., 165).

From an institutional perspective, the Department of Foreign Affairs is responsible for Quebec's relations with the international Francophonie. On the other hand, the administration of francophone affairs inside Canada has a much more complex structure. If the key text for the work of government institutions at the federal level is the Official Languages Act, which plays an important role in all the federal ministries, the key text in Quebec is Bill 101, or the Charter of the French Language (1977), which is binding on all ministries as well as their subordinate institutions, such as the Conseil supérieur de la langue française and the Office québécois de la langue française. Thus, institutionally speaking, a large number of governmental, para-governmental, and non-governmental institutions are involved in linguistic matters and the francization of Quebec society.

It is a well-known fact that both the practice of French in Quebec and the province's language policy are full of tensions and conflicts. To illustrate this fact, I would like to select two areas to support the thesis of the politicization and bureaucratization of the francophonie, on the one hand, and to outline the discourse of the linguistic-political actors, on the other. The first area is immigration, the second the relations between Quebec and the francophone communities in the minority milieu.

IMMIGRATION AND QUEBEC IDENTITY

The phenomenon of migration to Canada or Quebec has already been mentioned above. In the current discussion about Quebec's civil society, its identity, and the status of French, immigration represents a key challenge to the nation-state project.[16] For years, actors of various factions in language policy, demo-linguistics, and civil society have engaged in vigorous debates about how Quebec society is changing as a result of immigration. Views differ about the implications of immigration for French as the *langue commune* (common language) of Quebec society. The discussion centres on potential discourses and concepts with which Quebec's intellectual elites and political class assess demographic and cultural change. Not least of all, the question to be resolved is who, in fact, is francophone? The evolution of the debate can be traced with reference to the key terms used in each of its stages: from biculturalism in the 1960s to multiculturalism in the 1980s,[17] followed by the rival Quebec notion of interculturalism in the 1990s[18] and the more recent concept of transculturalism.[19]

French in Quebec in the 1950s and even up to the 1970s was described by F. Dumont in ethnic terms: as the language of an ethnic group that was indissolubly linked to French culture. According to this discourse, anglophones, Natives, and immigrants did not belong to the Quebec nation unless they assimilated to the French-language culture. Since the 1980s an integrationist concept has been gaining ground in Quebec (see Pagé, 2006, 32ff.), according to which French is postulated as the basis of Quebec identity in that it is the language which is learned and used in public places, regardless of what the speaker's primary language may be. The important point is that French is seen as the *langue commune* and as an expression of the collective identity of Quebec society. With increasing recognition for the plurality of Quebec society, French is perceived in the geopolitical area of the francophonie as the incarnation of a North American French-speaking society (ibid., 36). The question is: how do these discourses – as applied in the institutions of the state – translate into a practical language policy toward immigrants?

In 1977, a few months after the Parti Québécois came to power and in the middle of the hot phase of the conflict between the advocates and opponents of French as the official language of Quebec, the government surprised many by launching a program, "Programme d'enseignement des langues d'origine" (PELO), to promote the languages of origin at all levels of the school system. The opponents of Bill 101 saw this as a tactical manoeuvre on the part of the government to distract attention from its linguistic nationalism, while many Quebec nationalists saw it as a program directed against the francization of their society. On the other hand, the allophone ethnic communities, such as the Greeks, Portuguese, and Italians, perceived PELO as a government effort to compete with their own language courses as well as a blow against their own silent attempts to move closer to the anglophone minority in Quebec (see McAndrew, 2001, 49ff.). I mention this example in order to sketch the discursive dynamics of the period in broad outline. PELO had been preceded since the year 1969 by the so-called *classes d'accueil*, which were designed for the children of immigrants to facilitate their integration in the French-language school system. Adult immigrants in turn were served by the French courses of the Centres d'orientation et de formation des immigrants, also founded in 1969. These two instruments of the state's integration policy for immigrants clarify two issues: first, they were mainly intended to provide linguistic support and integration in the context of the school, where their beneficiaries were children and young people; and, secondly, they were aimed at a literate clientele. The corollary to this policy, however, was that adult immigrants could not profit from government programs to promote their languages of origin, and that for adult illiterates, there were no educational programs at all – neither in French nor in their languages of origin.

How did Quebec's immigration and language policy respond to this state of affairs? For the first decade and more, there was no response at all. Then, in the mid-1990s came the first program. Finally, the return of the Liberals to power in 2003 launched a flurry of reform activity. What happened was as follows.

It was only in 1994 that the government of Quebec had inaugurated its first program for the linguistic integration of adult immigrants. The "Programme générale d'intégration linguistique," as it is officially known, was directed at two categories of people: first, immigrants who had attended school and were literate but did not speak French and, second, those who were either illiterate or had only minimum schooling. In 1994–98 the Ministère des Relations avec les citoyens et de l'immigration presented a program (Gouvernement du Québec, 1998) for the latter group comprising full- or part-time language courses amounting to 600 to a maximum of 800 hours of instruction conducted entirely in French. The course's main aim is the mastery of the *spoken* language and cultural codes of Quebec society, while learning the *written* language is dependent on the initial degree of illiteracy. It was stressed that "le programme conçu pour les populations peu alphabétisées ou peu scolarisées n'est pas un programme d'alphabétisation et qu'il vise d'abord l'apprentissage du français langue seconde dans des situations de la vie quotidienne" ("the program, devised for populations with low literacy levels or little schooling, is not a literacy program and was chiefly aimed at teaching French as a second language for everyday use"). In addition to initial aptitude tests to determine the language level of a speaker, the program involves performance assessments during and at the end of the course, so as to document the level of competence achieved (ibid., 23).

At this point, we can see in broad outline that a fundamental change in the social narrative was taking place. The discourse of "Alpha populaire"[20] now has to compete with that of government agencies, while the administration – and the administration of illiteracy – is being reorganized at the same time. The new philosophy of measuring efficiency, evaluation, and best practice in the field of francization requires two further measures. One is that the ministry is to define proficiency levels for the acquisition of French as a second language (Gouvernement du Québec, 2000). In the year 2000, using the standards of the American Council on the Teaching of Foreign Languages, the ministry introduced the "Niveaux de compétence en français langue seconde pour les immigrants adultes," which were binding on all educational institutions. By setting a total of twelve levels of second-language acquisition, the ministry intended to provide a frame of reference that facilitates language diagnosis (the first measure) as well as an increase in language proficiency (the second measure). The logic behind this intervention is clear: in keeping with the neo-liberal, market-oriented spirit of the times, all those involved in the process – whether *enseignants*, *conseillers pédagogiques*, *directeurs*, or *décideurs* – are given standards of assessment to measure efficiency and guarantee state control, especially in view of the fact that subcontractors and service centres, including all the universities in the Greater Montreal Area, are contractually involved. From now on, the new catchword for the linguistic training of immigrants is to be *employabilité*, that is, imparting language skills as a work qualification.

What followed next as a third step was the institutional reorganization of the authorities and service centres, during which time the pendulum swung back and forth between centralization and decentralization. In the year 2000, during the restructuring of the ministries, the Centres d'orientation et de formation des immigrants, which had been in existence since 1969, were transformed into the Carrefours d'intégration as part of the Services d'immigration. A bare three years later, following the political change of course in Quebec and the realignment of the ministries in 2003, the initially centralized Carrefours d'intégration were again restructured and this time decentralized, so that the provision of language courses for immigrants in Montreal is currently organized into four regional service centres in the north, south, east, and west of the metropolis. The length of the language courses was increased from about 700 to 1,000 hours. A full-time course now runs for 33 weeks, with 30 hours of language instruction each week. Another new feature is that students sign a contract with the ministry, granting them various "allocations" such as child care and reimbursement of tuition fees and transport costs, while obliging them to complete all assigned work.

The imposition of neo-liberal ground rules in Quebec society marks a basic change in the mode of promoting literacy and francization. Since the end of the 1990s, we can discern in both Quebec and Ontario the emergence of a *discours bureaucratique* (bureaucratic discourse; see Budach, 2003) in competition with *alphabétisation culturelle* (cultural literacy). The prime agent of bureaucratic discourse is the state, whose administrative structures organize the program of francization, evaluate and classify those attending the courses, assess linguistic skills, standardize levels of performance, and, finally, control the implementation and efficiency of courses – just as today's service philosophy requires. This bureaucratic discourse represents an alliance between the technocratic elite and the administrators, with the state equally redefining the framework for other actors in the literacy field. Certificates granted upon completion of courses in the ethnocultural centres – to give but one example – are only recognized if they correspond to the proficiency levels introduced in the year 2000. The scope for alternative educational concepts in the Centres communautaires is thus significantly restricted.

RELATIONS WITH OTHER PROVINCES

A separate, albeit cursory, treatment must be provided for the relationship between the francophone province of Quebec and Canada's other provinces, especially with regard to the language policy pursued toward the francophone minorities. According to J. Woehrling (2005, 313ff.), the language policy of the anglophone provinces can be divided into two categories: that of New Brunswick and Ontario, whose legislation broadly follows that of the official federal policy of bilingualism, and that of the seven other provinces,[21] where the official policy of bilingualism is met with deep reservations and the rights granted to francophones are clearly restricted. In both cases, demographic factors are cited as the reason for granting more or fewer rights. An exception to this rule is Manitoba, the former Métis province. Although the number of francophones currently resident there cannot exceed 31,000, or 3 per cent, the official policy of bilingualism has been applied to the legislature and justice affairs since 1979.

In the current Quebec government, responsibility for internal Canadian francophone affairs rests with the Secrétariat aux affaires intergouvernementales canadiennes. Comparable institutions also exist in the governments of the other provinces. Quebec's government, like the federal government,[22] maintains agreements with the other provincial governments to support the francophone communities in such fields as education, communications, culture, health, economics, and immigration.

The fact that the current relationship between Quebec and the francophone minorities is not always free of tensions is the result of a process that began in the 1960s with the aspiration of Quebec nationalists for autonomy and eventually led to the fragmentation of the Canadian francophonie. The brief reference made above to the history of the Fédération des communautés francophones et acadiennes (FCFA) shows us that the founding of this institution in 1975 was a response on the part of those francophone institutions in minority milieux, who felt themselves isolated and forced to fight for a new identity (see Cardinal, 1993; Juteau, 1994; Thériault,1999). For several years now, the idea of a Conseil de la francophonie has been growing in Quebec government circles. The task of such a council would be to merge the francophone communities in North America or Canada, thus overcoming the schism between the francophonie of Quebec and that of the rest of Canada.[23] So far, however, this concept has not progressed beyond the planning stage.

GLOTTO-POLITICAL DISCOURSES OF THE FRANCOPHONIES IN CANADA

This chapter sheds light on the complexity of the relationship between Canada and the francophonie. This complexity goes beyond the facts that I analyzed of the interpretations and meaning of heterogeneity and diversity in the francophonies. What is of significance here is to understand how these facts are constructed and reproduced in the discourses of the glotto-political actors, what meaning is attributed to them, and what their function is for the realization of specific social interests. Further, it is important to understand how these facts are positioned in the transformation processes of social relations, identity, and power in the francophone realm. Which types of discourses can be identified from the discussion in this chapter?

The Traditionalist Discourse

This discourse developed under the economic and social conditions of Canada as a British colony from the middle of the eighteenth century until the years after World War II, when the francophones defined themselves as a *nation canadienne-française*. The discourse was shaped by the francophone elite, who used it to legitimate their position of power vis-à-vis the majority of workers, farmers, fishermen, and others, and finally also led to an implicit acceptance by the British-dominated power structures. Elements of the traditionalist discourse include the construction of homogeneity (*langue, religion et race*) and the belonging to a marginalized and oppressed group (see Erfurt, Heller, and Labrie, 2001; Heller and Labrie, 2003, 16ff.). This discourse is based on the fear of assimilation – in other words, the loss of identity, tradition, and values, which the British adopted as a political strategy with regard to the Canadiens français (outlined in the infamous Durham Report) and which at the same time led to the dependence of the francophones on their own elite.

The Dominance and Control Discourse

This discourse developed during the years after World War II and especially during the clashes between rival factions of Quebec society in the 1960s regarding cultural hegemony and political power over nationalism. Initiated by artists and intellectuals opposed to the dominance of the traditional elite and their clerical-conservative values, this discourse transformed itself quickly into one backed by a large part of the francophone population and elites, who supported the nationalist project of Quebec and also, beyond that, of the Parti Québécois. Its symbolic power consisted in the implementation of monolingual spaces that received legal legitimacy through Bill 101 in 1977; its real power, on the other hand, consisted in the securing of economic and political interests and the autonomy of the Quebec elite vis-à-vis an anglophone Canada and North America. As a correlate to the "state nationalism" of Quebec and the principle of monolinguism, an "institutional nationalism" was created within the francophone minorities that also supported the creation of and control over monolingual spaces in schools, churches, the healthcare system, administrative structures, and associations of the francophonie.

The Discourse of Social Diversification in the Context of Competing Nationalisms and Immigration

This discourse developed also during the years after World War II and especially since the 1960s. Significant for its evolution was the antagonism between Quebec and federal nationalism regarding the role of francophone culture and the social situation of the francophonie. If the previously mentioned dominance and control discourse marks the linguistic and political actions of Quebec, this discourse shapes the conflict, first, concerning the recognition and, later, concerning the interpretation of the principle of biculturalism and bilingualism in Canada. The legal framework for a Canada with two official languages came into effect in 1969 but was already questioned or weakened in the 1980s by the federal state. Besides the principle of biculturalism, which provides francophones with a relatively high degree of recognition, a principle of multiculturalism was adopted in 1971 at the federal level. This concept was greeted with skepticism in Quebec, although the fact that immigration had transformed Canada into a multicultural society was recognized. To oppose the concept of multiculturalism, Quebec supported the discourse of interculturalism, which entails the notion of a convergence of cultures and the implementation of a common French-speaking culture, independent of what other language(s) the members of society may speak. The *francophones de souche* are thus confronted with an ethnoculturally influenced *nouvelle francophonie* or, in other words, a large number of Néo-Québécois or Néo-Canadiens. At the same time, this discourse neglected the francophone communities outside Quebec and provoked a deep rupture in the Franco-Canadian identity: on the one side are the Québécois, and on the other are the Acadiens, Franco-Ontariens, Franco-Manitobains, and others, who feel a sense of betrayal by Quebec.

The Discourse of the Nationalization of the Francophonie and Its International Networking

The beginning of this discourse was linked to the conflict between Canada and France over the role of Quebec on the international stage, as well as the conflict between Quebec and Canada about the recognition of French-speaking culture. For this discourse as well, the official languages law (1969) marked an important legal framework, which allowed francophones to establish administration of their affairs at the federal and provincial levels. Parallel to the long established institutions in the francophone milieu, the state now created structures for the administration of francophone affairs and started formulating rules and conditions for the distribution of federal subsidies. What signified bureaucratization from a domestic perspective took the shape of international cooperation, solidarity, and multilateral networking, as well as the support of cultural diversity within the structure of the OIF. The supporters of this discourse are bureaucratic elites and actors in governmental and non-governmental organizations that deliver development aid, especially to the francophone countries of Africa, the Maghreb, and the Antilles, and in this way support the guidelines of immigration politics.

COMPARISONS

These four types of discourse emphasize once again the dynamics that have transformed the Francophonie since the 1960s and the heterogeneity of different actors' interests in Canada as well as at the international level. Finally, it is possible to draw multiple comparisons using the types of discourse as reference points to describe each constellation.

The francophone communities have created numerous institutions in the course of their history that have served as much for internal organization as for the preservation of their interests vis-à-vis the supremacy of the anglophones. The Catholic religion and the French language constituted the two main factors for the identification of French Canadians. As is evident in the case study of the Société Saint-Jean-Baptiste, from the second half of the nineteenth century they extended their activities to commerce, economics, and higher education, thereby beginning to develop and spread a francophone nationalism in these areas. From the 1960s, in the context of the Quiet Revolution and Quebec nationalism, the law on official languages, the engagement of Quebec in international relations, and strains within the Canadian francophonie, the institutionalization process gained dynamism on all levels and in all provinces. Language policy henceforth constitutes a bridge between anglophone and francophone Canada (see Fraser, 2007). At the same time, language policy is oriented toward the often complex relations between the francophone communities of Canada and the international Francophonie.

As indicated in the second part of this chapter, institutions and the institutionalization process represent the *tertium comparationis* of this study. Institutions exert considerable influence on social relations and the process of identification of communities. The comparison that follows contrasts the institutionalization process in the Canadian francophonie with that in the international Francophonie.

Domestic Comparisons

In the context of traditionalist discourse, the comparison extends to the social structure and the socio-cultural framework of the francophonie. Among French Canadians who see themselves as expressing the myth of homogeneity, a social elite appears composed of members of the church, the middle class, the liberal professions, and bureaucrats, who, because of their relatively high level of education, were often bilingual and, as defenders of francophone interests, played the role of mediators in dealing with relations with the dominant anglophone society. In contrast, at that time, the majority of the francophone population was composed of salaried workers in agriculture or forestry, mines, industry, or fishing. They were predominantly unilingual. The powerful Catholic Church faction shaped the orientation within this elite. Members of this same elite also formed non-public networks such as the secret society of the Order of Jacques Cartier and founded their own institutions – the Caisses populaires, for example – which led to a modernization of social relationships between francophones (see Heller and Labrie, 2003).

In the context of dominance and control discourse, the comparison refers to relationships of power. From the 1960s, the majority of the francophone population of Quebec adopted a state nationalism based on unilingualism of institutions and altered the economy so that francophones could work in French. In reaction to Quebec separatism, francophones in the other provinces in a minority position supported an institutional nationalism that would be applied through the intermediary of unilingual institutions in the areas of education, religion, health, and associations. As we have seen in the case of ACFO/AFO, state subsidies have been allocated to that association as an institution of a official-language minority in order to promote francophone culture, while that support also enabled state intervention in community life. This example of a transformation process shows an institution that must adjust to a diglossic situation in society as well as to cultural change affecting persons who are considered francophones.

Concerning the social diversification discourse, the comparison relates to the institutionalization process in a multi-ethnic society. By relying on an example of a cultural centre for Haitian immigrants, we identified a process through which the ethnocultural minorities created their own institutions throughout Canada. Besides the traditional institutions, other francophone ones thus appear which represent the change in Canada toward a multicultural society and are henceforth organized in a national network. Thus the Haitian literacy centre in Montreal has played an active role in the organization of the first Haitian cooperative network (États généraux de la communauté haïtienne), which took place in 2007. In contrast, there are institutions that defend the interests of traditional francophone society and have long been hostile to immigration, such as the Société Saint-Jean-Baptiste.

International Comparisons

International comparisons can be drawn between the positions of the federal government and the provincial governments of Quebec and New Brunswick relating to principles and the structure and institutions of the international Francophonie. Similarly, comparisons can be drawn between the interests of the bureaucratic elites of the institutions of the OIF and the interests of the francophone communities. And our analysis has shown that multiple actors in the international setting interact dynamically as each promotes its distinctive interests, which likewise evolve over time.

NATIONALIZATION OF THE FRANCOPHONIE

Nationalization of francophone affairs occurred in Canada well before the process came about at the international level. In addition to the traditional actors of the francophonie in each province, by the 1970s, at the federal and provincial levels, numerous new institutions appeared and were given responsibility for the administration of the francophonie. These were in addition to the institutions already subordinate to federal and provincial authorities. Accordingly, they came to function by the rules of the bureaucracy, implying a permanent political engagement which generated a bureaucratic elite. At the international level, the process of nationalization of francophone affairs soared in the second half of the 1980s, after the first summit of the Francophonie in Versailles in 1986, and especially in the 1990s. The founding of the Organisation internationale de la Francophonie (OIF) in 1997 can from this perspective be considered a culminating point. That the spread of French language and culture in the world was far from being the main aim of member states became clear. The OIF was defined as an actor in international relations in the areas of peace, democracy, the state of law, development policy, and economic and technological cooperation. Not forgotten but not primordial was language and culture, and besides, since 2000 cultural diversity has become an explicit part of the OIF program.

MULTILATERAL COOPERATION

An international network that includes more than 685 universities and schools of higher education in eighty-one countries was the responsibility of the Association des universités entièrement ou partiellement de langue française (AUPELF), founded in 1961 in Montreal. In 1997 the AUPELF became the AUF (Agence universitaire francophone) and was integrated into the OIF structure as an active coordinator. This institution illustrates the principle of engagement by Canada, Quebec, and New Brunswick in the international Francophonie through multilateral cooperation. Here the position of Canadian institutions differs clearly from that of France or French institutions; the latter emphasize the principle of bilateral cooperation, including agreements between France and a country or an institution of the OIF.

It is therefore clear from our analysis that domestic and international comparisons or constellations overlap, interact, and change over time. Amidst these shifting constellations, different actors exhibit varying degrees of change and continuity as well as cooperation and tension in their behaviour. These dimensions provide a differentiated picture about the role of culture affecting the domestic and international francophonie in the ongoing process of globalization.

NOTES

1 In this text, the term "glotto-political" will be used as the adjective for "language policy." Moreover, "language policy" is used according to the definition in Guespin and Marcellesi, 1986.

2 See Erfurt, 1998, 1999, 2000a, and 2000b; Erfurt, Heller, and Labrie, 2001; as well as "Prise de parole: La construction discursive de l'espace francophone en Amérique du Nord, " in Heller and Labrie, 2003.

3 What is valuable for Canada is not necessarily so for the two founding nations that have been imposed as colonial powers vis-à-vis the Native population of North America. Tensions resulting from the colonial heritage still weigh on relations between the federal and provincial governments and the First Nations.

4 For the initiation of the first meeting of heads of state, the change in the political climate of Canada was significant. After the Liberal prime minister Pierre Elliott Trudeau was succeeded by the Conservative Brian Mulroney at the national level and the Liberal Robert Bourassa took over power from René Lévesque of Parti Québécois at the provincial level in Quebec, a constellation was created that allowed for the participation of the province of Quebec at the meeting. Earlier, the Canadian government under Trudeau had blocked Quebec membership; French

interest, however, was to include Quebec in the Francophonie (see Le Scouarnec, 1997, 72, 79ff.)

5 See J.-M. Adam's analytical study of the speech (2004), which traces the various interests at work in France, Canada, and Quebec.

6 See also Labrie, Grimard, Lozon, and Quell, 2003, on the forum of francophone organizations in Ontario.

7 See http://afo.franco.ca/documents/2005-2006_rapportannuel.pdf; accessed 24 November 2007.

8 See http://www.cic.gc.ca/francais/ressources/publications/etablissement/cadre-minoritaire.asp and the ministry's survey of the initiatives taken to promote immigration and immigrants in the francophone minority milieu at: http://www.cic.gc.ca/francais/ressources/publicatons/etaslissement/plan-minoritaires.asp; accessed 24 November 2007.

9 See http://www.acdi-cida.gc.ca/INET/IMAGES.NSF/vLUImages/stats/$file/RappStat_04-05.pdf; accessed 24 November 2007.

10 See http://www.canadianheritage.gc.ca/progs/lo-ol/pubs/2003-2004/ra-ar/2_f.cfm; accessed 24 November 2007.

11 See http://www.patrimoinecanadien.gc.ca/progs/lo-ol/pubs/2005-2006/ra-ar/index_f.cfm; accessed 24 November 2007.

12 See http://www.international.gc.ca/foreign_policy/francophonie/menu-en.asp; accessed 25 November 2007.

13 See http://www.mri.gouv.qc/fr/francophonie/quebec_francophonie/contributions/contributions.asp; accessed 28 February 2006.

14 The chairman of the commission was Gérald Larose.

15 In terms of political strategy, this approach is expressed in Gouvernement du Québec, 2005, 10–11.

16 The list of relevant publications is long. Those most recent ones include Georgeault and Pagé, 2006; Stefanescu and Georgeault, 2005; Maclure and Gagnon, 2001; Kymlicka, 2001; and Venne, 2000.

17 The principle of multiculturalism is defined in article 27 of the Canadian Charter of Rights and Freedoms. Also, in 1988 the Canadian Parliament passed the Multiculturalism Act.

18 The federal policy of multiculturalism is encountering open resistance in Quebec because it is seen as a weapon against the principle of duality – against the policy of biculturalism and bilingualism. Quebec is countering this principle with a strategy based on the concept of interculturalism, which is also interpreted as a concept of "convergence of cultures" or of a "common culture" *(culture commune)*. Common culture is defined as francophone, democratic, and pluralistic (see Woehrling, 2005, 311ff).

19 For more details, see Erfurt, 2009.

20 See the remarks above on the Haitian literacy centre Centre N a Rive.

21 The three territories of Yukon, Northwest, and Nunavut, where francophones represent a small population percentage of otherwise already thinly populated regions, have been omitted here.

22 See the Entente de collaboration Canada–Colombie Britannique or the Entente Canada-Nouveau Brunswick relative à la presentation de services en français 2005–2009, to name but two examples.

23 See "Allocution du ministre responsable des Affaires intergouvernementales canadiennes et de la Francophonie canadienne du Gouvernement du Québec, B. Pelletier, à l'occasion du Brunch des élus de l'ACFO régionale d'Ottawa," 28 May 2005, and the articles in *Le Droit*, 30 May 2005, 3, and 31 May 2005, 12.

Introduction to Part Three

MICHAEL A. MORRIS

A SURVEY OF THE LITERATURE

Language policy issues are the major concern here, but these are usually entangled with other issues, such as immigration, multiculturalism, and population. These factors, especially as they interact, constitute an important perspective on language policy.

Not only do linguistic and non-linguistic issues tend to overlap with one another (Part Three), but important groups in the population (Part Four) interact constantly over both sets of issues. Issues and groups are both present in the literature; particular sources are discussed here or in Part Four, depending on their relative emphasis. The main orientation of each publication determines where it is considered. With language policy as the point of reference, we shall here review how population, immigration, and multiculturalism have been related to one another in the literature.

Duchesne (1980) represents a fairly early, if brief, comparative assessment of population trends as they relate to language in Canada, as does a more lengthy study by Lachapelle and Henripin (1982). A later book (*Demolinguistic Trends*, 1989) examines the impact of related demographical and linguistic trends on Canadian institutions. Its introductory chapter, though laden with statistics, does not make systematic comparisons, however.

A chapter in a book by Wardhaugh (1987, chap. 10, 230–64) compares the impact of migration on language issues in five developed countries: Australia, Britain, Canada, France, and the United States. There is a short profile of each country, but only the first two pages of the chapter briefly compare them. Relations between immigration and language in Canada and the United States are compared in a book edited by Barry Chiswick (1992).

Some important differences in the approach of each country are identified, and implications for the job market are derived.

Canadian federal governmental policies towards official languages, multiculturalism, and feminism are compared in Pal (1993). This study is generally critical of federal government support of private groups in each of these areas.

AN OVERVIEW OF THE CHAPTERS IN PART THREE

Chapter 7, "Linguistic Issues and Immigration in Quebec: Relating the 'Cultural Communities' to the 'Quebec Nation' and the French Language," by Louise Fontaine, approaches issues of language, culture, and immigration in Quebec through an analysis of the evolution of official discourse and its representations of what it means to be a Quebecer, who exactly are Quebecers, and how immigrants and the descendants of immigrants fit into the overall picture (as members of the so-called "cultural communities"). There is an unresolved tension between competing definitions of identity based on place of residence, language, and culture respectively. All factors considered, the unilingual territorial approach defined by Quebec does not resolve a number of questions. To be a Quebecer, is it necessary merely to live within the borders of Quebec and speak French, or must one also be a speaker of French whose culture is in the French tradition? Who exactly is a Quebecer? What role does language play in this determination? How do immigrants relate to Quebec's identity? The originality of the chapter lies in discussing several of these unresolved questions.

In chapter 8, "Canadian Federal Policies on Language, Multiculturalism, and Immigrant Language Training: Comparisons and Interaction," Eve Haque compares three issues at the federal level and also places these issues in historical context. The relationship between language and multicultural policies is examined, including the implications for immigrant language training. Tensions and synergies between these policies are clarified and contrasted with provincial language policies. Just as Fontaine's chapter suggests fruitful future lines of comparative inquiry from a provincial perspective, Haque makes a similar contribution from a federal point of view.

Chapter 9, "Canada's Official Languages in the Provinces of Quebec and Ontario: A Demographic Comparison," by Michel Paillé, compares Canada's two central provinces: Quebec, the only one whose majority is French-speaking, and Ontario, the most populous province and the one with the most immigrants, who adopt English as their everyday working language. Immigrants have also tended to assimilate into the Anglo-Canadian population of the neighbouring French-speaking province, with its rapidly decreasing birth rate of native French-speakers. Consequently, Quebec has had to enact laws that could save French from becoming a minority language in the province.

7

Linguistic Issues and Immigration in Quebec: Relating the "Cultural Communities" to the "Quebec Nation" and the French Language

LOUISE FONTAINE

KEY ISSUES AND QUESTIONS

This chapter addresses issues of language, culture, ethnic groups, and the "national community" relative to the situation as it has evolved in Quebec, with some sidelong glances at how the same issues are dealt with elsewhere in Canada, more particularly in Nova Scotia, and also in Belgium. Some reference is made to the influence of Canadian federal policies in the areas of language, immigration, and multiculturalism on the development of provincial immigration, linguistic, and cultural policies in Quebec, but the main analysis of the federal dimension is left to the following chapter, by Eve Haque. Our study focuses on the evolving criteria used by authoritative actors[1] in Quebec to define "who is a Quebecer," the meaning of the term "immigrant" in the Quebec context, and the basic characteristics of what is termed the "national community" in Quebec. Our concern will be to examine the processes of social differentiation and stratification that have been instituted by the public authorities of the province, as reflected in official discourse, especially in the period since 1960.[2]

As we shall see, a recurring concern of the major actors within the state apparatus in Quebec has been to define the basic characteristics of the "Quebec nation." This concern is both political and administrative and has led to the construction of a number of indicators of identity, such as the possession of a common language, a common territory, a common heritage, a history with a "heroic" past, and so on. These efforts, while understandable and inevitable in their way, nonetheless have the unfortunate potential of stigmatizing some individuals (Goffman, 1975, 14) while serving the interests of others. In order to better understand how the definition of the "national community" in Quebec has been a problematical phenomenon, we will be taking a look mainly at the period from 1960 until the present. It was in 2000 that the Quebec government created new francization[3] programs and instituted the so-called Carrefours d'intégration (Fontaine, 2004, 35). In the present study, we will be giving an overview of how the definition of "we Quebecers" (*nous Québécois*) has evolved with reference to a series of definitions proposed by governmental actors to describe "non-Quebecers," in other words, the "others" who live in Quebec.

The defeat of the independence referendum on 30 October 1995 may be considered to constitute a turning point in the quest for national independence and to have had a profound effect on the demarcation of the "national community." We shall therefore be asking the following questions. During the 1990s, did the Quebec government modify to a considerable extent its official policies concerning immigration and citizenship? If so, how and for what reasons? What were the issues that underlay this change of perspective concerning the "integration of immigrants" who had lived in Quebec for a number of years? What was proposed for the purpose of integrating so-called "immigrants" in the "national project"? These are questions that we will endeavour to answer in the following pages. In this context, we will be looking in particular at a category of actors whom I describe as "authoritative actors" and who in this case are primarily public servants in the employ of the Ministry of Immigration and Cultural Communities (Ministère de l'immigration et des communautés culturelles, or MICC). We will be interested, in particular, in the role of these actors in the demarcation of the "national community" in Quebec.

THEORETICAL AND METHODOLOGICAL CONSIDERATIONS

The contemporary state features, among other characteristics, mechanisms for classifying the population over which it has legal jurisdiction. In this way, it institutes differences among individuals through the creation and demarcation of categories. The construction of frontiers between states is accompanied by the development of "cultural" frontiers within. This distinction between a collective "we" and the "others" – that is, between "fellow nationals" and "foreigners" – gives rise to a proliferation of debates concerning immigration and citizenship. In such a context, the contemporary state intervenes in the area of culture by producing a legitimizing rhetoric whose purpose, it would seem, is to "preserve national identity."

In general, it would seem that the phenomenon of immigration can be characterized in three ways. First of all, it has to do with the determination of certain immigration quotas in order to fill specified economic, demographic, humanitarian, and other needs in a given country. Under immigration policy in Quebec, in Canada, and in other industrialized countries, the "determination of the annual level ... depends on three variables: 'demographic considerations,' 'economic imperatives,' and 'international obligations of a humanitarian nature'" (Crépeau, 1986, 146). In other words, this first axis of analysis corresponds to migration flows, that is, to the examination of temporary or permanent movements of population from the territory of one state to the territory of another. Recently, this axis of analysis seems to have been abandoned in favour of a second one having to do with how states deal with "ethnic groups" established on a particular territory for a certain period of time. The management of this question has given rise to a number of rather virulent political and ideological debates. In this context, we see that the contemporary state produces a dynamic between a so-called majority of "nationals," who are contrasted with minorities often described as "ethnic" or "non-national" (Crête and Zylberberg, 1991, 421–33). Finally, the development of action programs targeting individuals "originating in another country" (Lochak, 1985) corresponds to the third way of defining the phenomenon of immigration. This last approach participates in the definition of legal and administrative rules for access to the territory of a state and settlement therein.

Immigration policy in Quebec and in Canada as a whole has followed much the same pattern as in other countries, especially during the period following the Second World War (Babie, 1993; Hollifield, 1993), in which an increasing emphasis has been placed on the questions of human rights and the status of refugees. These changes have become even more evident in the period since 1960.

In this study, we will be mainly interested in various actions taken within the Quebec Ministry of Immigration and Cultural Communities. As I argue in my book *Un labyrinthe carré comme un cercle*, this ministry "constitutes an important social space (*lieu social de première importance*) for the definition of the place of newcomers in present-day Quebec and in the Quebec of the future" (Fontaine, 1993b: 16).

My argument is similar to that of Bernard Lacroix (1985, 473) when he proposes to think of the state as "the organized form of the nation." This political form reflects power relationships existing within society while "reflect[ing] a space where the representation of a certain 'desirable' social order is defined" (Burdeau, 1980, 30) for a particular society as a whole, as for example for Quebec society.

The Ministry of Immigration and Cultural Communities can be seen as a microcosm that is constantly changing in response to various political factors.[4]

For example, in 1968, a Ministry of Immigration was formed in Quebec. In 1981, about one year after the defeat of the independence referendum of 20 May 1980, this ministry became the Ministry of Cultural Communities and Immigration. On 12 January 1994, a date that saw the amalgamation of a number of other administrative units, it became the Ministry of International Affairs, Immigration and Cultural Communities. On 21 June 1996, less than a year after the defeat of the referendum of 30 October 1995, this same ministry became the Ministry of Relations with Citizens and Immigration. On 17 June 2004 it took on its present name of Ministry of Immigration and Cultural Communities. Table 7.1 offers a chronology relating these successive ministerial changes to key events about how the "we" and the "other" have been conceived at different times.

The administrative instability of the ministry is confirmed by Josée Boileau, who notes that in the period from 1968 to 2005 the ministers changed twenty-four times – an average of one minister every eighteen months. Under the Parti Québécois and Liberal governments over the last eleven years, there have been eight different ministers (Boileau, 2005). A Montreal daily newspaper reports that the succession of each new minister gives rise to speculation among the ministry's employees as to whether the new minister will be there long enough to have his or her photograph on the wall (Lévesque, 2007).

In February 2007 the Quebec government created the Consultation Commission on Accommodation Practices Related to Cultural Differences, commonly referred to as the Bouchard-Taylor Commission. Under the terms of its mandate, the commission has chosen "to perceive the debate on reasonable accommodation as the symptom of a more basic problem concerning the sociocultural integration model established in Québec since the 1970s. This perspective calls for a review of interculturalism, immigration, secularism and the theme of Québec identity ... with a view to grasping the problem at its sources and examining it from every angle" (Gouvernement du Québec, 2007a). The first stage of the commission's work plan involved the drafting of documents and establishing focus groups. The second stage, from September to December 2007, consisted of "public hearings in 17 cities in regions of Quebec (submission of briefs, personal testimony and regional and national forums)" (Gouvernement du Québec, 2007b). In the words of William Mackey, "these hearings opened a valve to unexpected explosions of pent-up frustration of the traditional French majority (children of the Quiet Revolution and *les familles souches*) as they witnessed the erosion of their cherished patrimony by an avalanche of foreigners of distant races, exotic faiths and uncivic customs with whom they were now expected to identify."[5]

Table 7.1
How the "we" and the "other" are categorized in official discourse, in relation to the name changes of the government ministry: a chronology

Year	How the "we" and the "other" are categorized	The ministry changes its name to:
1968		Ministry of Immigration
1972	A Quebecer is any resident of Quebec who speaks French.	
1978	A Quebecer is a speaker of French whose culture is in the French tradition.	
1977–80	The "non-Quebecer" is defined.	
1981	The "cultural communities" appear.	Ministry of Cultural Communities and Immigration
1990	The term "Quebecer of the cultural communities" is introduced.	
1994		Ministry of International Affairs, Immigration, and Cultural Communities
1995	The term "Quebecer of the cultural communities" is equated to "citizen of Quebec."	
1996		Ministry of Relations with Citizens and Immigration
2004	The "other" is simultaneously a citizen of Quebec and a member of the cultural communities.	Ministry of Immigration and Cultural Communities

In order to demarcate the "national community" in Quebec and define its main components, we will examine how the questions of immigration and ethnicity have been managed by the Quebec state since 1960. The chronology of our narrative is indicated in table 7.1.

"QUÉBÉCOIS": DEFINED AS ANY RESIDENT OF QUEBEC WHO SPEAKS FRENCH

We begin with the reminder that after defining itself as a bilingual and bicultural country from 1963 until 1971, Canada in 1971 officially became

a bilingual and multicultural country. As Eve Haque argues in the following chapter, "it is through the B and B Commission [Royal Commission on
Bilingualism and Biculturalism] that a hierarchy of belonging was articulated which established modern Canada as a white settler nation with only
two founding groups (the English and the French) while all 'other ethnic
groups' were homogenized as 'multicultural,' and through a differential accommodation of their language and culture in the Multiculturalism Policy
(1971), they were positioned peripherally of the two founding nations."

The policy of multiculturalism, which was announced in the House of
Commons on 8 October 1971, proposed a conception of Canada as a society
characterized by ethnic and cultural heterogeneity. By fostering the preservation of the cultural characteristics of "minority" groups in Canada and by
favouring an ideal of equality and mutual respect among these ethnic groups,
this new policy placed on an equal footing the members of all ethnic groups
that were of neither British nor French origin (Canada, House of Commons,
Debates, 1971, 8546). In the period subsequent to 1971, this policy became
increasingly interested in "immigrants" who had been in Canada for a number
of years already and who, in many cases, had already obtained their Canadian
citizenship (Burnet, 1987, 1289; Kallen, 1982, 51–63) with the objective of
maintaining and promoting their "cultures of origin."

Since the policy of multiculturalism also represents a countermeasure to
Quebec nationalism, which had been growing in strength during the 1960s,
it sparked a number of ideological debates around the new conception of
Canada as a mosaic. There was a "lack of agreement on nomenclature, with
'multicultural' conflicting with 'mosaic,' and 'New Canadians' rejecting
'third force.' [In 1965] the term multicultural emerges as a way to define
'other ethnic groups'" (see chap. 8 below). Henceforward, immigration
would be managed by the federal government in Ottawa not only between
the time of official admission to Canadian territory and the granting of citizenship but also, and even more importantly, during the years that follow
the settlement of new arrivals in the country. In this context, various governmental actors engage in the glorification of a mystified past for the benefit
of these newly arrived persons. As François Rocher (1993) has emphasized,
"the debates revolving around multiculturalism and pluralism ... reflect political and social projects which are mutually exclusive."

The "political affirmation of French-speaking Quebec" that was taking
place in this political and social context gave rise to a new form of nationalism in Quebec. In its widest sense, the change defined by the term "Quiet
Revolution" was characteristic of the 1960s and the 1970s. During these
years we find "a continuity in the orientations of the various governments

which came successively to power in Quebec" (Linteau, Durocher, Robert, and Ricard, 1986, 393). The term also describes the beginning of a period of political, institutional, and social reforms in Quebec (Ambroise, 1987, 181).

As has been emphasized by Kenneth McRoberts and Dale Postgate (1983, 292), the Quebec provincial government has by stages come to represent the state of Quebec (*État du Québec*). This "state," which was in the process of constructing itself, becomes "democratic," "administrative," and "interventionist" (Pelletier, 1992, 615), and it increasingly demands a "special status" with regard to the other Canadian provinces. This desire to obtain political sovereignty for Quebec opened the way for a questioning of Canadian federalism. In this context, the "national question" – or what Louis Balthazar (1986, 127) has called "state nationalism" (*nationalisme étatique*) in Quebec – increasingly became the theme of debates that took place in Quebec during the 1970s. These debates turned mainly on the status of the French language in the province.

As early as 1965, Pierre Laporte, who was then Quebec minister of cultural affairs, had recommended that the government give the French language the status of "priority language" (*langue prioritaire*) (L'Allier, 1976, 30). Such status was in fact given to French by Bill 63 (1969). It was reinforced during the 1970s with Bill 22 and Bill 101, by which French became the sole official language in Quebec. The debates over the development of the policy of multiculturalism, to replace that of biculturalism, were echoed in Quebec by the report of the Commission of Inquiry on the Position of the French Language and on Language Rights in Quebec, often called the Gendron Commission.

This commission, which was created in 1968 and submitted its report on 31 December 1972, defined a "Québécois" as "any resident of Quebec (Franco-Québécois, Anglo-Québécois, Québécois of other origins or an immigrant)" (Gouvernement du Québec, 1972, 4). Here belonging to Quebec society is defined in terms of territory. During this period, however, the majority of Quebecers defined themselves by reference to the French language. But these criteria were destined to evolve during this period as the result of legislation. Bill 101, passed in 1977 – that is, shortly after the arrival to power of the Parti Québécois on 15 November 1976 – introduced a new concept: *nous Québécois* ("we Quebecers"). The new government reaffirmed its political will to bring about the francization of Quebec. Turning once again to the Charter of the French Language, we discover that the French language represents "the distinctive language of a people which in its majority is francophone" (Loi 101, 1977, 1). The French language, it was announced, "provides the opportunity for the Quebec people to express its identity. The [Quebec] National Assembly ... is therefore resolved to make French the language of government and law as well as the language of work, education, communication, trade, and business" (ibid.). This law marks the beginning of a systematic dichotomy between the majority and the minorities as well as of a certain stratification among the categories used to designate the minorities.

It is perhaps relevant to recall at this point that in earlier draft legislation (Bill 1) from which Bill 101 was derived, the term "Quebecers" (in French, *Québécois*) had been defined as constituting the "francophone Quebec nation" and the term "minorities" as including all "non-Quebecers." In Bill 101 the term "minorities" was replaced by "ethnic minorities." In 1983 the category "community of English-speaking Quebecers" (*communauté québécoise d'expression anglaise*) was added in the preamble to Bill 101.

The passage of Bill 101 marks the beginning of a process of systematic francization throughout the province. French increasingly became the official language in all areas of social life. The territory of Quebec and the French language represented indicators of identity in terms of which the "Quebec nation" might be defined. However, this process of redefinition of who could be considered one of "us Quebecers" (*nous Québécois*") – and implicitly of who could be considered as excluded from this category – was to be pushed yet further with the adoption by the Quebec government of a policy of "cultural convergence."

THE QUEBECER: DEFINED AS A SPEAKER OF FRENCH WHOSE CULTURE IS IN THE FRENCH TRADITION

The new definition of "Quebecer" was now "any resident of Quebec who speaks French and whose culture is in the French tradition." The Quebec Policy of Cultural Development, which was officially announced in 1978, defined three types of "minorities" and aimed to bring about a rapprochement between the "francophone majority of Quebec" – which was synonymous with the "Quebec nation" – and the "others," associated with the following "minorities": the "aboriginal minorities" (*minorités autochtones*); the "colonial minority" (the descendants or "heirs" of the conquerors); and "those who in the course of history join an already constituted nation" (Gouvernement du Québec, 1978, 61–93).

This (di)vision of social reality was founded on the idea that language "is not merely a series of words or a syntax. It expresses the life of a group of men and women in its meaningful aspect [*la vie d'un ensemble d'hommes et de femmes en ce qu'elle a de significatif*]" (Gouvernement du Québec, 1978,

45). Language was thus viewed as the vehicle of a particular culture viewed as having "unique characteristics [*traits originaux*]."

Gérard Bergeron (1984) notes that the question of language is here associated with the concept of "identité québécoise." He writes:

> This was especially obvious in the white paper, which, in many passages, seemed to play on the ambiguity[6] of the adjective as referring both to the territorial unit where the future legislation would apply and, by a form of equivalence, to the Franco-Québécois as the true and perhaps the only "Québécois." It was possible to read this presentation as suggesting an implicit exclusivity, and this in any case was how some Anglo-Quebecers and New Quebecers, whose sensitivity in the matter was understandable, did in fact read it, feeling themselves more or less relegated to a citizenship which, culturally, was second-class. (140; in translation)

The "majority" in Quebec thus had, as the "basis of its unity," its "culture in the French tradition." According to this conception of social reality in Quebec, the "francophone majority" and "Quebec society" were one and the same. In order to be a part of the *peuple québécois*, it was no longer sufficient, according to Bill 101, to be a resident of Quebec and to speak French. It would now be necessary to satisfy additional criteria associated with the notion of identity. The latter referred to mythical entities of an essentialist nature, such as the "people" or the "nation" (Shiose and Fontaine, 1995, 99).

Kjersti Bergheim (1997) comes to much the same conclusions in a thesis defended at the University of Oslo in which she analyzed the question: "What does it mean to be Québécois?" In order to answer this question, Bergheim studied public occasions such as the *fête nationale des Québécois*, celebrated on 24 June, and Canada Day (*la fête du Canada*), celebrated on 1 July (10), and she interviewed individuals from various groups within Quebec society (ibid., 9–13). Among her conclusions, Bergheim advances the following:

> In my view, this apparent confusion and ambiguity has to do with the fact that such categorization is a question of politics and there is a complicated relationship between popular categories and "bureaucratic" categories. Politicians (and other ideology-deliverers) must on the one hand take into consideration people's self-definitions and sense of attachment, while on the other hand they may try to change these, to give "new directions," as when the term Québécois was introduced as part of a reformulated nationalist project. (ibid., 178–9)

"NON-QUEBECERS": WHO ARE THEY?

In this politico-ideological context, in which language and "culture" had become inextricably associated, authoritative actors of the ministry of the Quebec government responsible for immigration attempted to define who were to be considered "Québécois" and who were to be considered "non-Québécois." In government documents such as *La philosophie de la politique québécoise d'immigration* (Larue, 1977), *L'État et les communautés culturelles: pour une action concertée* (Gouvernement du Québec, 1979), and *Les communautés culturelles et la fonction publique québécoise* (Lapointe, 1980), an extensive reflection was undertaken with a view to determining who formed a part of the *communauté québécoise* and, by implication, who did not. These discussions, which took place within several ministries of the Quebec government and other government agencies, were part of a process that delineated the contours of the "national community" in Quebec.

The upshot of these developments came in 1981 with the official announcement, by the Quebec government, of an action plan for the "cultural communities" (as they were then termed). The document *Autant de façons d'être québécois* (Gouvernement du Québec, 1981) outlined the societal project (*projet de société*) that the Quebec government intended to promote (Fontaine, 1993b, 40–7). This official policy defined a "hierarchical structure," distinguishing two categories: the "Quebec nation" and the "cultural communities" (Fontaine, 1999a, 153). The model that was announced was thus different from both the American melting pot, which aims at complete integration of the newcomer, and the Canadian mosaic, which favours a supposedly egalitarian juxtaposition of groups.

It should be noted that the proposed renewal of the dichotomy between the "francophone majority of Quebec," also referred to as the "national community," on the one hand, and the "cultural communities,"[7] on the other, implied an almost systematic exclusion of certain individuals and groups considered "non-national" from the Quebec government's societal project and the nationalist ideology that served as its basis.

HOW THE "NON-QUEBECERS" BECAME
THE "CULTURAL COMMUNITIES"

The political and administrative category of the "cultural communities" came increasingly to be used by "political actors, public servants, journalists, leaders of various associations and many academics ... to describe a part of the population which they consider to be somewhat hybrid in comparison with the 'Quebec nation'" (Fontaine, 1999a, 149). In this sense, as is argued by Tajfel (1981,46), by so categorizing a part of the Quebec population, certain social actors consolidated their action aimed at the establishment of a sovereign or even an independent Quebec. Bruno Ramirez (1991), in his analysis of the Canadian policy of multiculturalism, described this principle of action as falling under an "electoralist logic." The author has argued elsewhere that "both the 'minorities' and the bureaucratic and political elites centered around Ottawa and Quebec are thus seen as acting in their own narrow interests, rather than working toward the abstract ideal of cultural diversity (contrary to what their rhetoric would have us believe)" (Fontaine, 1995b, 1046).

According to Pierre Bourdieu (1982, 31), actions such as these correspond to the special interests of various social groups who have recently experienced upward mobility. This ideological rhetoric aims at securing recognition for a new authoritative discourse, with its new political vocabulary, its terms of address and reference, and its representations of the social universe.

In a number of interviews[8] conducted with various authoritative actors, who were asked the question "What is a 'cultural community?'" the answer that was forthcoming was to the effect that this political category of "cultural communities" had been "parachuted in from above," meaning from the office of the premier, in 1981. Furthermore, it appeared that this term had been adopted because it represented an ideological compromise which included under one and the same label "anglophones" and "visible minorities," the latter being a term introduced by the federal government in 1984.[9]

The ideological tension inherent in the term "cultural communities" is reflected in two of the main criteria used to define it: mother tongue and birthplace (Pelletier, 1985, 33). But these criteria are the only ones used to define inclusion in a "cultural community." As we have argued elsewhere (Fontaine, 1990, 60–74), a number of different, and largely indefinable, criteria are used to reinforce the dichotomy between the "cultural communities" and the *communauté québécoise francophone* – roughly, the "community of French-speaking Quebecers," although there is no really perfect translation into English, since the adjective *québécois* has to be rendered either by the adjectival noun "Quebec," by a reference to "Quebecers," or by the adjectival phrase "of Quebec."[10] The result is a legitimation of the existence of a "Québécois nation" by defining who does not form part of it.

Bureaucratic tinkering of this sort has, over the years, instituted an official distinction between "Quebecers," on the one hand, and "members of the cultural communities," on the other. As Serge-Henri Vicière (1994, 27) has pointed out, "there is no expiration date on one's belonging to a cultural community. The 'we' represented by the authoritative actors has rendered its final decision. This is thus a perpetuation of otherness. Symbolically, and perhaps also in practice, the possibility is ruled out that any assimilation, hybridization [*métissage*], or integration will take place."

During the 1980s, the use of the category "cultural communities" spread "like wildfire" (Fontaine, 1999a, 153)[11] throughout various spheres of social life. It was only at the beginning of the 1990s that it was fully realized that this concept was a cause of exclusion and that it was contrary to the principle of equality of individuals living in Quebec, and it was at this time that the Quebec government attempted to come up with a "solution" to the problem (Shiose and Fontaine, 1995, 103).

THE MEMBERS OF THE "CULTURAL COMMUNITIES" BECOME "QUEBECERS OF THE CULTURAL COMMUNITIES"

In 1990 the Quebec government announced a policy that modified its approach to the "others," that is, towards those who were not associated with the *majorité québécoise francophone*. The expression *Québécois des communautés culturelles*, or "Quebecers of the cultural communities," was at this time officially enshrined in *L'énoncé de politique en matière d'immigration et d'intégration* (Gouvernement du Québec, 1990), a "Statement of Policy with Regard to Immigration and Integration." This new category had, as its "ultimate" purpose that of breaking the previous dichotomy between the *majorité québécoise francophone* and the "cultural communities" within Quebec. The category, it was hoped, would be more inclusive and render more permeable the invisible frontier between "Quebecers" and the "others." This official policy favoured what was termed an "intercultural rapprochement," in order to bring together the various groups that made up Quebec society. It can be mentioned here that according to the definition put forward, "Quebecers of the cultural communities" was an expression designating "Quebecers whose origin is other than French, British, or First Nation [*autochtone*]" (Gouvernement du Québec, 1990, 4).

Even though the intention was that this latter characterization would be more inclusive, eliminating the opposition between "Quebecers" and members of the "cultural communities," there remained an element of ambiguity. Joseph H. Carens (1995, 69–70) comes to this conclusion in his analysis of the phenomenon of immigration, identity, and "political community" in Quebec.

THE CATEGORY "QUEBECER OF THE CULTURAL COMMUNITIES" COMES TO CORRESPOND WITH "CITIZEN OF QUEBEC"

In the wake of the referendum of 30 October 1995, the Ministry of Relations with Citizens and Immigration was officially constituted on 21 June 1996. It is significant to note that the term "cultural communities," present in the title of the two preceding ministries[12] responsible for immigration, had disappeared and been replaced by "Relations with Citizens." It would reappear in June 2004 with the name Ministry of Immigration and Cultural Communities (Ministère de l'Immigration et des Communautés culturelles, or MICC). One cannot help but wonder what the motivation for this political decision might have been, and one is immediately reminded of the controversy surrounding those memorable words pronounced by Quebec premier Jacques Parizeau when he officially announced the results of the 1995 referendum, attributing the defeat to "money and ethnic votes" (*Globe and Mail*, 31 October 1995; quoted in Fontaine, 1999a, 157).

A number of other factors may also have contributed to the elimination of the category "Quebecer of the cultural communities" and its replacement by that of "citizen of Quebec." In 1997 the assistant deputy minister for civic relations of the newly created Ministry of Relations with Citizens and Immigration stated that "this name change came about because it was realized that the term 'cultural communities' carried with it the suggestion of exclusion,[13] because it was too closely associated with ethnic origin and culture and because it did not take into account the dynamic character of cultures and the multiplicity of influences which immigration has on cultural identity" (Molinaro, 1999, 117).

In 1997 the deputy minister gave the following description of the four main priorities of her ministry: "The drafting of a government action plan for youth, the francization[14] of immigrants, the establishment of a network of services for citizens, and the promotion of civic participation" (Gouvernement du Québec, 1997a, 2). Concerning this last priority, she stated: "In this area, the government's way of thinking can be summed up in the concept of 'zero exclusion' based on the equality of all citizens, whatever may be their personal, social, or economic circumstances" (ibid., 3). In order to reach this objective, in July 1997 the Ministry of Relations with Citizens and Immigration, in collaboration with the so-called Ministère de la Métropole, created a "Fund for Visible Minority Youth." This $700,000 fund "provides for the financing over a period of three years of community organizations working with visible minority youth who wish to develop tools and services adapted to their needs" (Gouvernement du Québec, 1997b, 6).

But is there not some kind of a contradiction here? On the one hand, a group – namely, youth – is targeted with a view to facilitating its access to the labour market, while, on the other, the same young people for whom this government program was intended are designated "visible minority youth" (*jeunes des minorités visibles*), which is a category adopted by the federal government in 1984. There seems to be some kind of a double standard at work here. Can we really speak, in this context, of "zero exclusion"?

If we consult the official website, we learn that this ministry is responsible for action in three areas: "civic relations," "relations between the State [*l'État*] and its citizens," and "immigration and the settlement of newcomers." Pursuing our exploration of the ministry's website, we discover, under "civic relations," that the concept of "intercultural rapprochement" is still present, structured around the idea that "cultural diversity is first and foremost a collective challenge" (*la diversité culturelle est d'abord un défi collectif*) (Gouvernement du Québec, 2000). We read further that the challenge in question is to "ensure harmony by favouring the maintenance and the development of values and guiding principles [*principes d'action*] which unite citizens of both genders [*les citoyens et les citoyennes*] above and beyond their personal, linguistic, cultural and religious differences" (Gouvernement du Québec, 2000).

With regard to this last sentence, we make two comments. First of all, the very strength of the affirmation of a will to promote harmony and unity can be seen as an admission that the rhetoric of the previous ministries had (perhaps involuntarily) been a factor of exclusion. Secondly, we observe a tension between, on the one hand, the political will expressed by this sentence to become more inclusive with regard to the population actually living in Quebec and, on the other, a nation-building project in which the government actors do not seem to know quite what to make of these so-called "ethnic minorities," whose members seem, in a certain proportion, to prefer the federalist option – when they have any particular political allegiance at all! The preference of this part of the Quebec population, the majority of whom use French in their everyday life, seems in fact to be that the government of Quebec should use public funds to solve problems of a concrete nature, in the areas of health, education, employment, and so on.

WIDENING THE PERSPECTIVE: WHAT DO MEMBERS OF THE ETHNIC ORGANIZATIONS MAKE OF ALL THIS?

For the purposes of this study, we have chosen to analyze certain actions undertaken by government actors in Quebec that result in a categorization of individuals living within the borders of the province. One of the political purposes that underlies these processes of social differentiation and hierarchization seems to be that of defining the outlines of the "national community" in Quebec, in order to demarcate themselves from government actors associated with the central government in Ottawa. These actions tend to reinforce the political rhetoric describing Quebec as "a distinct society" relative to the other Canadian provinces. This manner of speaking is shared by all three political parties that have formed provincial governments in Quebec since 1960. It can be further remarked that the compatibility of these developments with the project of attaining national sovereignty for Quebec can hardly be considered entirely coincidental.

Our investigations led us to haunt the corridors of a Quebec government ministry in order to observe and, it is hoped, better understand the interventions of various governmental actors. In addition, in the context of this and other studies, we have met and interviewed various members of ethnic organizations in order to determine their respective points of view on various matters and, in particular, concerning the concept of "cultural communities" and their use of the French language in everyday life. Among the difficult and enigmatic questions which, over the years, we have been asking and for which we have been documenting the answers given, are the following: "Who is a Quebecer?" "Is it possible to *become* a Quebecer?" and "If so, how?" or "If not, why not?"

At various stages, our empirical work has been with the Fraternité multiculturelle de Québec, the Maison internationale du Québec, the Confédération des associations latino-américaines (CASA), the Corporation de développement économique communautaire Côte-des-Neiges/Notre-Dame-de-Grâce (CDEC), and the Association latino-américaine de Côte-des-Neiges (ALAC) (Fontaine, 1993b, 1996, 2004). Initially, though, our empirical studies of ethnic organizations were directed towards the two major Irish groups in Montreal, the St Patrick's Society (SPS) and the United Irish Societies (UIS). This choice was motivated by the consideration that the Irish represent a group situated in the indeterminate zone between the "French-speaking Quebec majority" and the "other" ethnic groups in Quebec (Fontaine, 1993a, 121). We discovered that, although members of the UIS tended to define themselves, first and foremost, as Quebecers and frequently reminded us of how they had been living in Quebec for three or four generations, they nonetheless consider this form of ethnic identity to be interchangeable and negotiable and that, on the day of the St Patrick's Parade, they are, one and all, "Irish." Our observations of the other main Irish organization in Montreal, the St Patrick's Society, were somewhat different. Leaders of this organization described to us the strategies they had adopted in order to obtain grant money from the Quebec government, and they seemed to have understood that it was in their interest to adopt as their own the official government rhetoric concerning "ethnic minorities" (Fontaine, 1993a).

According to the official classification of the Quebec government, the "Irish community" (*communauté irlandaise*) is categorized as "anglophone" and "mono-ethnic," while our interviews show that these groups are characterized by considerable heterogeneity and that many individuals who define themselves as "Irish" speak French. This practice is particularly to be observed in families where the ancestry of the mother is French Canadian (Fontaine, 1993a, 131). It is perhaps worth mentioning here that, in addition to "mono-ethnic communities," the Quebec government grant program also recognizes the existence of "multi-ethnic communities" and "pluri-ethnic communities." The "community of Anglo-Quebecers" (*communauté anglo-québécoise*) would be an example of the latter (Fontaine, 1993b, 62).

The tendency among the leadership of ethnic organizations has been to adopt the governmental classifications. We have observed that they are not particularly inclined to give up the rhetorical exaltation of difference, presumably because of the advantages they derive from it, including both government grants and visibility in a number of social spheres. Other social actors, such as public servants and academics, also derive considerable advantages from the production, continual modification, legitimation, and (in my own case, for example) analysis of systems used to classify the "others" who live in Quebec. This paradoxical situation can also be observed in the federal sphere. "The bilingual framework, as articulated through the Official Languages Act, ... [means that] a bilingual in the Canadian context is someone who speaks English and French. Speakers of an official language and a non-official minority language are not recognized as bilinguals, and minority languages are granted neither recognition nor rights at the federal level" (see chap. 8 below).

QUEBEC IN COMPARATIVE PERSPECTIVE

Before concluding, we will add some remarks concerning the extension and application of our analysis to policies concerning language and immigration in Atlantic Canada and Belgium, which we have also studied. In Nova Scotia, first of all, where we have been conducting investigations since 2003, the leaders of ethnic organizations, like those of associations in Quebec, devote considerable energy to advocating for the maintenance and promotion of their "culture of origin." They undertake various initiatives and attempt to obtain grants, in particular from the federal government in Ottawa.[15] However, the equation "language equals culture" does not seem to apply with the same force as in Quebec, for various reasons, including the obvious absence of a debate over future independence from the rest of Canada. In Nova Scotia, for example, English is taught to new arrivals with the utilitarian purpose of preparing them to enter the labour market as quickly as possible, and with no particular emphasis on culture and nationhood. The teaching of French to new arrivals, on the other hand, in New Brunswick, Nova Scotia, and other areas of Canada where francophones are in a minority situation (Quell, 2000) has given rise to a number of debates (Dyer, 1998) that go beyond what can be dealt with in the present chapter (except perhaps by doubling its length). This cautionary note having been sounded, we may say that the French language in Quebec is an ever-present and integral part of political discourse because since 1977 it has been continually cited as one of the most important criteria (but not a sufficient one, it would seem) defining who is a Quebecer and who is not (Fontaine, 2004). The teaching of English to immigrants does not have a similar ideological resonance in the rest of Canada.

The Belgian case is somewhat different both from that of Quebec and from what we have observed elsewhere in Canada, since Belgium, unlike Canada, is not a country where immigration has contributed in a major way to its population. Up until 1974 Belgium's official immigration policy was oriented towards migrant workers who resided temporarily in the country without any intention of taking up permanent residence. But even before 1974 this tendency had begun to change, as a result of the tumultuous events of the 1960s, during which the role of the unitary state came to be questioned in a number of areas of social life. Beginning in 1970, we see the progressive establishment of a federalized state through a number of institutional reforms (in 1970, 1980, 1988–89, and 1993). In the general context of these reforms, and with a view to solving what was termed the *contentieux communautaire*, immigration policy was complemented by an "intercultural policy" (Fontaine, 1992). This policy of "cohabitation" concentrates on problems of employment, housing, and access to education, and the actions of the various levels of government were oriented towards these issues. But the members of ethnic organizations in Brussels began to become increasingly concerned with linguistic issues, since the adoption of French or Flemish can play a key role in determining the electoral representation of various groups, especially in the context of municipal elections. A Royal Commission for Immigrant Policy was created in 1989 and became, four years later, the Centre for Equality of Opportunity and the Campaign against Racism (Fontaine, 1999b).

In 1998 Serge Govaert (1998, 1) observed that "Brussels is ... a thirtyyear-old bone of contention between Flemish and Frenchspeaking politicians." A decade later the same pattern still prevails. One of the key factors behind the perpetual political instability in Belgium described by Vincent De Coorebyter (2007, 2) is the Flemish demand that "the bilingual electoral district and the bilingual judicial arrondissement covering both Brussels and part of the surrounding Flemish areas (Hal-Vilvorde) be split in two. Since this double division would cancel certain electoral and legal rights of the French-speaking residents of Hal-Vilvorde, the francophone parties demand, in exchange, the enlargement of the Brussels Capital Region – which is bilingual – a measure that is completely unacceptable [*inconcevable*] for the Flemish-speaking parties." Another factor making for political instability in Belgium has to do with how, since the 1970s, the political parties have developed in two parallel French-speaking and Flemish-speaking worlds. As Richard Werly (2008, 1) notes, "the much apprehended signs of disintegration of the federal State have become more and more numerous" and "a distinct deterioration of the communitarian climate has occurred." A recent collection of essays, *Bruxelles, ville ouverte*, edited by Pascal Delwit, Andrea Rea, and Marc Swyngedouw (2007), the subtitle of which translates as "Immigration and Cultural Diversity in the Heart of Europe," sheds helpful light on the multicultural dimensions of Brussels as the capital of Europe in the context of the Belgian conundrum.

With regard in particular to the situation of "immigrant newcomers," Jacobs and Rea (2007, 265) note that nine European Union countries have "introduced integration courses, citizenship tests and/or citizenship trajectories as instruments in their civic integration policies for immigrants." The case of Flanders is part of the discussion. The authors argue that geographical proximity is one of the main reasons for similarities between the approaches adopted in Belgian Flanders and in the Netherlands. But, they add, "the Flemish preoccupation with mastery of the Dutch language has [also] to be understood in the light of the ongoing linguistic struggle in federal Belgium between Flemish and francophones" (ibid., 268). The multicultural model developed in the north of Belgium has some similarities with the Canadian policy of multiculturalism, in that it promotes integration to some extent but not assimilation.

CONCLUSIONS

Our analysis of government documents, in counterpoint with our fieldwork among the administrative and political staff of the Quebec Ministry of

Immigration and Cultural Communities, suggests that we are dealing with an administrative reality which is continually changing and which we have elsewhere termed as a "fragmented rationality, to the extent we can speak of rationality," (*une "rationalité éclatée, si rationalité il y a"*; Fontaine, 1993b, 127) that varies according to the most recent interpretation of the national project, as conceived by various government actors in Quebec. Our conclusion is that the societal project of transforming Quebec into a sovereign country is closely connected with the perpetual definition and redefinition of the Quebec government's policy concerning immigration.

In this context, we have observed a certain alternation between the political will to be inclusive of all persons living within the borders of Quebec, regardless of their "mother tongue" and their birthplace, and the will to achieve integration, but only on the condition that "intercultural rapprochement" maintains an invisible but real boundary between those who, culturally and linguistically, are fully Quebecers and those who somehow do not quite correspond to this model. A number of government actors have proclaimed that the category of "immigrant" can and does correspond with that of "Quebecer" and that the former is a temporary and transitory status, a step on the way towards becoming a "Québécois." Our analysis shows, however, that the status of immigrant is considered by a number of government actors to be a permanent one (Simard, 2001), not transitory. These public authorities favour what they call "intercultural rapprochement," but only on the condition that there is a preservation and a glorification of the so-called "culture of origin," distinct from that of "Quebecers whose culture is in the French tradition."

This paradoxical situation that characterizes the case of Quebec is different from what we observe in the rest of Canada, where the immigration policy of the central government is predominant. Under the latter policy, it is true, linguistic skills are indeed taken into account when evaluating applications to immigrate, but greater weight is given to other factors, such as "economic integration," associated with being part of the labour market, and paying taxes, in preference to more "cultural" criteria. Legally speaking, after having obtained permanent resident status, it is possible, through various administrative procedures, to become a Canadian citizen.

Socio-politically, however, the situation has become somewhat more complicated since the 1960s, with the gradual formation of an "ethnic elite." The passage of the Official Languages Act in 1969 and of the Canadian Multiculturalism Act in 1971 introduced a number of "cultural" considerations into the definition of what it is to be a Canadian. Eve Haque concludes in the following chapter that "language policies become the vehicle for the management of racialized others, in this case newcomers, through the rubrics of cultural and linguistic traits." All things considered, Quebec policies in the areas of language, culture, immigration, and "national identity" are seen to be related in many ways to the corresponding federal policies.

The crossing of an international boundary in order to enter a particular "country" with the intention of permanently settling there has become a problem that is of increasing concern for present-day governments. In this perspective, the comparison of Belgian and Canadian policies (including those of Quebec) concerning immigration and citizenship becomes particularly interesting (Fontaine, 1995a) because of the shared characteristics of the two countries, the most notable of which are linguistic duality and a federal constitution.

NOTES

This text was translated and adapted for presentation in English with the precious help and clear-sighted advice of James Crombie, Université Sainte-Anne.

1 An actor is defined as an individual who plays a role in a social context with a particular kind of behaviour in order to fulfill the expectations of other individuals. "Authoritative actors" are those who by their social position are endowed with power considered legitimate (Etzioni, 1971, 97). In this chapter the terms "authoritative actor," "public actor," and "governmental actor" will be used more or less interchangeably.

2 For a discussion of the long evolution of the identity question previous to 1960 – for example, on how "les Canadiens" became "Canadiens-français" and then "Québécois" – the reader is referred to Rioux (1974, 5–24) and Balthazar (1986). See also Ailsa Henderson's recent chapter, "The Political Use of National Identity" (Henderson, 2007, 80–114).

3 This term is given as the English translation for the French *francisation* and is defined as follows (and in French) by the *Grand dictionnaire terminologique*: "Process aiming at the generalized use of French as the language of work in both government and private enterprise" (entry for *francisation*, translated at www. granddictionnaire.com; accessed 22 February 2005). The *Grand dictionnaire terminologique* is published by the Office québécois de la langue française, an agency of the Quebec government.

4 The original study, involving in-depth interviews with the political and administrative personnel of this ministry, was presented as a doctoral thesis. Since then, we have conducted a number of additional interviews in order to bring the empirical data up to date (Fontaine, 1993b, 16n).

5 From manuscript comments on an earlier version of the present chapter. The author wishes to thank Professor Mackey for his particularly attentive and constructive comments and suggestions. Since the hearings were underway as this chapter was in the process of revision - and the final report of more than 300 pages was made public only on 22 May 2008 - it is impossible here to provide a more detailed analysis of how the issues of language and immigration have been affected by the work of this Commission.

6 The "ambiguity" referred to here is the fact that the word *québécois* is only sometimes an adjective meaning "pertaining to Quebec" and sometimes (when capitalized) a noun meaning a person living in or originating from Quebec.

7 It is perhaps worth mentioning that the term "ethnic minorities" had been previously used in section 43 of La Charte des droits et libertés de la personne (Gouvernement du Québec, 1976, 12).

8 Transcription of interviews conducted 15 May 1987, 3 March 1988, 7–8 March 1988, 9 May 1988, 29 July 1988, and 2 August 1988.

9 The notion of "visible minority" was introduced by the federal government in 1984. It corresponds to those "non-whites who do not fully participate in Canadian society" (Canada, House of Commons, 1984, 2).

10 See note 4 above.

11 In the original: *comme une traînée de poudre.*

12 Ministère des communautés culturelles et de l'immigration (1981); Ministère des affaires internationales, de l'immigration et des communautés culturelles (1994). The original Ministère de l'immigration was created in 1968 (Fontaine, 2004, 10n). See table 7.1.

13 *Était considéré comme porteur d'exclusion.*

14 This term is explained in note 3.

15 We were able to make observations to this effect on the occasion of two important events: *Communities Uniting: An Atlantic Multicultural Conference*, Multicultural Association of Nova Scotia, Dartmouth, 7–9 November 2003, and *Immigration and Outmigration: Altantic Canada at a Crossroads*, Economics Domain Conference, Atlantic Metropolis Atlantique, Halifax, 18–19 November 2004.

8

Canadian Federal Policies on Bilingualism, Multiculturalism, and Immigrant Language Training: Comparisons and Interaction

EVE HAQUE

This analysis has two related dimensions, a historical perspective and comparison of three issues. The historical focus concentrates on the origins of three interlocking Canadian policy issues – language, multiculturalism, and immigration, with a focus on immigrant language training – and their subsequent interaction with one another.

BACKGROUND

The Royal Commission on Bilingualism and Biculturalism (B and B Commission; 1963–70) arose out of the socio-historical imperative to reconsider the positioning of francophone Canadians in the national narratives of the era, as so aptly outlined earlier by William Mackey in chapter 3. The commission produced six volumes in its final report, and two of the most significant of these were the first volume, *Book I, The Official Languages*, which gave rise to the Official Languages Act (1969), and the fourth volume, *Book IV, The Cultural Contribution of the Other Ethnic Groups*, which became the impetus for Prime Minister Pierre Trudeau's declaration of his government's Multiculturalism Policy (1971). It was through these two steps that Trudeau was able to declare that Canada would be a nation defined by "Multiculturalism within a Bilingual Framework" (Canada, House of Commons, 1971b, 8546). This new national formulation for Canada in the post-commission era meant the rearticulation of belonging for different groups in the nation as compared to the pre-commission era, which was characterized by its overt Anglo-Celtic hegemony.

In the preceding chapter, Louise Fontaine has outlined the emergence of a hierarchy of belonging between those whom the Quebec government understands to be fully Quebecers and those, such as immigrants, who do not quite correspond to this model. In this chapter I want to outline how, at the federal level, a similar hierarchy between "founding races"[1] and "other ethnic groups" came to be established and articulated through the B and B Commission. The terms of reference for the commission, as they were laid out by the government of Lester Pearson, were outlined as follows:

> To inquire into and report upon the existing state of bilingualism and bi-culturalism in Canada and to recommend what steps should be taken to develop the Canadian confederation on the basis of an equal partnership between the two founding races, taking into account the contribution made by the other ethnic groups to the cultural enrichment of Canada and the measures that should be taken to safeguard that contribution (Royal Commission, 1963, App. 1).

Although the commission was, in the terms of reference, to address the un-equal situation of both the francophone and "other ethnic groups" (as all non-anglophone and non-francophone groups were referred to throughout the commission's work) in relation to anglophone groups, in this chapter I will argue, first, that in fact it is through the B and B Commission that a hierarchy of belonging was articulated which established modern Canada as a white settler nation with only two founding groups (the English and the French) while all "other ethnic groups" were homogenized as "multi-cultural," and that through a differential accommodation of their language and culture in the Multiculturalism Policy, they were positioned peripherally to the two founding nations. Second, with the concomitant changes that were taking place in federal immigration policy, immigration levels and pat-terns were also changing, which meant a growing concern with issues of integration and, as a result of the B and B Commission, the government's increasing emphasis on language as central to the process of integration. Thus English-as-a-second-language (ESL) training programs in anglophone Canada increasingly became the vehicle for integration. However, as I will discuss, these ESL programs, which continue to grow at present, in fact serve to reproduce the same hierarchies of citizenship and national belonging that were originally set in place by the B and B Commission.

THE PRELIMINARY PHASE OF
THE B AND B COMMISSION

One of the first tasks of the commission was to hold preliminary hearings late in 1963, followed by regional meetings throughout the country in the spring and summer of 1964. The hearings had to be extended as a result of the enormous interest they generated. In this initial stage of the inquiry, the hearings were primarily a consolidation of the terms of reference for the commission (see Royal Commission, 1963, App. 1), since they were to set the parameters and terms for the rest of the inquiry, as well as the delineation of the specific nature of the crisis that was to be the central concern of the commissioners. For the "other ethnic groups," the preliminary hearings were a contestation around the specific terms of reference, with particular concern about the positioning these terms seemed to imply.

During the two days and evenings of the preliminary hearings that were held on 7 and 8 November 1963 in Ottawa, seventy-six different organizations and individuals were heard by the commissioners (Royal Commission, 1965a, 25). All through these hearings, contestation of the terms of "the problem" surfaced repeatedly, particularly from members of the "other ethnic groups." Dr J.A. Wojciehowski, representing the Canadian Polish Congress, began by questioning the very name of the commission:

> Now as a member of an ethnic group which is neither French nor English-speaking, I would like to mention that for us the question of the very name of the Commission causes a certain problem. Although it is stated that the Commission is to study other ethnic groups and cultures, the very name of the Commission suggests that Canadian culture is or should be bicultural ... Moreover, it seems to me that as far as culture is concerned, we cannot limit a culture in a mechanical way to one or two or three or four elements. Culture is not something which you can govern. Culture is not a regiment which you can command. Culture is something which results from the co-operation, from the fullest co-operation of various principles and to the country where no ethnic group has a majority. Uni-culture is impossible and multi-culture is a necessity. (Royal Commission, 1963, 183–4)

Dr Wojciejowski's attempt to point to the futility of dividing culture into discrete components led him to suggest the necessity for multiculture, foreshadowing Trudeau's eventual formulation of a policy of multiculturalism. Numerous other opinions also challenged various items of the terms of reference during these preliminary hearings. A common concern was with the contrast between the terms "other ethnic groups" and "founding races," which seemed to imply, as Dr I. Hlynka, representing the Ukrainian Canadian Committee, observed, "a division of Canadian citizens into two categories ... first and second class citizens" (Royal Commission, 1963, 84). He went on the state that his organization "emphatically reject[s] any principle which would tend to recognize or to imply the superiority of one group of Canadians over another, whether it be on the basis of their ethnic origin, their culture, or the so-called prior historic right, because this means a return to a colonial status from which it has taken so long to emerge" (ibid., 1963, 83). This so-called "prior historic right" manifested itself as a particular problem of naming and identification for the "other ethnic groups." The hierarchical disjuncture between "race" and "ethnicity" was a central contestation around the terms of reference. It signalled one of the most contentious issues that would plague the hearings of the commission, and although it would be minimized in the *Preliminary Report*, the commission, after many of the submitted briefs and discussions during the public hearings of 1965 continued to focus on this concern, would devote an entire first section of *Book I* of the final report to explicating its position on each of the terms of reference, with particular attention given to race and ethnicity.

The *Preliminary Report* (Royal Commission, 1965b), which was based on the preliminary hearings (November 1963) and the regional meetings (March–June 1964), was published on 1 February 1965. It was a surprise bestseller; five thousand copies were sold within twenty-four hours of its release. As commission co-chair André Laurendeau recalled in his diary, "the event caused a stir from sea to sea" (Laurendeau, 1991, 130), indicating a profound national interest in the initial findings of the royal commission. Despite the contestations by "other ethnic groups" during the preliminary hearings and regional meetings over the hierarchy implied in the terms of reference, the commissioners had to organize the various submissions in order to persuade the public of the existence and particular nature of a national crisis; that is, a crisis between the French and the English "races." Even in the inaugural speeches at the preliminary hearings, Laurendeau anticipated this crisis: "The Canadian government, in setting up the Royal Commission on Bilingualism and Biculturalism clearly indicated its belief that we are in a state of emergency – an emergency that can jeopardize the very existence of Canada" (Royal Commission, 1965b, 179).[2] In the explication of the terms of reference in the preliminary report, the weight of the inquiry was clearly placed on issues pertaining to bilingualism, and the only mention of other cultures is as an addendum, a "subsequent contribution," to the "basically bicultural character of our country" (ibid., 1965b, 152).

Among the discursive strategies used by the commission in the preliminary report to reinforce the hierarchy between "other ethnic groups" and "founding races" was presenting the opinions of other ethnic groups as fragmented because of ethnic, linguistic, and geographical diversity. Specifically, ethnic groups were atomized by their ethnicity and language in order to demonstrate their lack of collectivity in speech and opinion: "It is difficult to describe the character of a segment of the population that is so diverse: each ethnic group has its own original language and culture. And even within one group, because of factors of geography or individual characteristics, many divergences are to be found. These people's experiences of 'Canada' differ in both time and space" (Royal Commission, 1965b, 126).

Although the range of geography and individual characteristics were in fact proof of Canadian collectivity in the case of founding races, for the other ethnic groups, diversity atomized and hence negated their opinions. Also, the uniformity of the collective "other ethnic groups" opinion was seen to be undermined by the diversity of their ethnicities, languages, and relative participation: "Moreover, some of these groups did not present themselves to us at the regional meetings. We met very few Canadians of German or Dutch origin, relatively few Poles, Italians or Finns, but many Ukrainians. Finally, among those who participated in the discussions, reaction differed greatly from one minority to another" (Royal Commission, 1965b, 126–7). Here, not only are absences from the collectivity indicated, but also the disproportionate representation of Ukrainian opinion[3] is specified in order to underscore the fragmentation of other ethnic groups. One of only two brief sections of the report that dealt directly with the other ethnic groups concluded with a summary statement about the lack of cohesion and consistency in this "other ethnic group" collectivity: "An attempt was made at some regional meetings to discover what unifying values are held in common by Canadians of German, Italian, Chinese, Ukrainian and other ethnic extraction, but a full discussion didn't seem to follow, and this variant on the multicultural theme tended to blend with the mosaic idea. Indeed the notion of a 'third force' had few supporters even among the 'New Canadians'" (ibid., 1965b, 51–2).

This lack of unifying values as a stated barrier to collectivity was never specified in the report, whereas the lack of unifying values in each of the founding race groups, insofar as the report tracked the wide range of opinions from English and French communities, seemed to present no barrier to their respective collective representation in the report. Also, the lack of unifying values was paralleled with lack of agreement on nomenclature, "multicultural" conflicting with "mosaic" and "New Canadians" rejecting "third force." The latter comment was paradoxical, given the strong aversion of most ethnic groups to the term "New Canadians" (Haque, 2005). However, here the term "multicultural" emerges as a way to define "other ethnic groups," even though at this point its primacy over other terms such as "third force" and "mosaic" had not yet been established. The centrality of "multiculturalism" as a defining term for "other ethnic groups" would begin to emerge with the commission's public hearings.

THE PUBLIC HEARINGS OF THE B AND B COMMISSION

Immediately after the publication of the *Preliminary Report* in February 1965, the commission began the regular public hearings that were to inform the writing of its final report. There were fourteen sessions of public hearings across the country, lasting between one and four days, from March to June and November to December of 1965. These differed significantly from the preliminary hearings in that briefs were prepared according to set guidelines. During the public hearings, groups and individuals submitted 404 public briefs and 4 confidential briefs to the commission (Royal Commission, 1967, 177). An overview of the briefs submitted reveals the wide array of groups and individuals represented. Of the briefs that could be considered to be from "other ethnic groups," roughly half, or about 25, were submissions from Ukrainian community groups. Nevertheless, smaller groups that had been less active in the commission activities to date, such as the Japanese community, also submitted briefs. For most other racialized (that is non-white, non-European) groups, such as the Chinese and Black communities, commissioned research reports, studies, or essays such as *The Chinese in Canada* and *Negro Settlement in Canada* were the only source of information for the inquiry, and there were no South Asian community briefs, research reports, or essays. Calls for briefs were apparently publicly distributed, but the resultant imbalances in representation reflected the built-in partialities already identified in the terms of reference.

Patterns for making claims and contesting the terms of reference set during the preliminary phase of the commission became blueprints and starting points for subsequent petitions for more central inclusion in the inquiry by other ethnic groups during the public hearings. For example, the variety of monikers used for other ethnic groups during the preliminary hearings – "third force," "third element," "New Canadians," among others – although still in circulation throughout the inquiry, began to coalesce around the term "multiculturalism," and this term began to represent many of the patterns of claims that emerged out of the preliminary phase of the inquiry. Thus multiculturalism started to signify such strategies for inclusion as the prior claims of history by other ethnic groups, the present and increasing future numbers of other ethnic groups, and claims based on demographic and territorial numbers of other ethnic groups (Haque, 2005). Multiculturalism, although deployed in various ways by different groups, began to acquire a range of meanings across which the location and inclusion of other ethnic groups could be discussed.

Building on the soon-to-be-familiar claim that Canada was a land populated through immigration sources, the brief from the Social Study Club of Edmonton, a group self-described as "nearly all old-timers in the Province of Alberta," commented on the goals of the inquiry: "Now, it seems, a campaign is to be attempted to compensate for alleged economic injustices with an artificial form of bi-culturalism which will try, through an artificial bilingualism, to overcome an economic problem with a cultural remedy. We say artificial because bi-lingualism has not been adopted spontaneously. This effort is following an unnatural course rather than recognizing the actual fact that a multi-culturalism has already been adopted spontaneously by the people themselves" (Social Study Club, 1964, 4). Here, spontaneous adoption naturalized an emerging conception of "multi-culturalism" against bilingualism and biculturalism. Although relatively short, this brief signalled the emergence of new, important discourses around multiculturalism, among which were the naturalization of multiculturalism and its identification as a distinctive Canadian culture. Also, here the emerging link between multiculturalism and language was established.

The link between multiculturalism and language was also considered by the Mutual Co-operation League of Toronto, which described itself as a "multicultural and multilingual body." Beginning with reference to the 1961 census data, the league argued that "there is neither one race nor language in this country forming a clear majority" (Mutual Co-operation League of Canada, 1964), and it continued, "For these reasons, we consider the advancement of bilingualism as insufficient in scope, and that of biculturalism as limited in vision" (ibid., 1). Claiming a distinct "lack of enthusiasm for 'bilingualism,'" the league proposed a demographic basis for language education: "With respect to the inherent right of a human being to preserve his identity and heritage, we propose that children from any community of our member group, with at least 500 souls in a compact area, should be able to receive instruction in their own language of at least 2 weekly periods from first grade of public school, and treated as regular subject of the school curriculum" (ibid., 2). However vague the delineation of "compact area," in all other aspects, the brief was quite clear about the specificities of multilingual schooling, and similarly, in many of the other briefs submitted for the public hearings, petitions for multilingual schooling would be linked with multiculturalism.

The Canadian Mennonite Association also took up multiculturalism and multilingual schooling. In its brief the association warned that English-French biculturalism would push other minority cultures into third place; in particular, "they [minority groups other than the English or French] would not be opposed to having French or English taught as an additional language in the public school, but they would resent it crowding out their language now placing second" (Canadian Mennonite Association, 1965). For the association, a policy of bilingualism and biculturalism was useful only insofar as "it moves society from a monocultural status to multilingualism and multiculturalism" (ibid., 3). Thus the concluding suggestion to the commission was that "it is our hope, that, while the Royal Commission must address itself to a specific problem indicated by its name (Bilingualism and Biculturalism), the larger frame of reference will be multilingualism and multiculturalism" (ibid., 4). In this brief the example of multilingual schooling was used to point to the dangers of bilingualism and biculturalism on their own, and instead it was suggested that they were just stepping stones to the ideal of multilingualism and multiculturalism. The notion of multiculturalism as the teleological endpoint of a model society would resurface often during the course of the public hearings. The concept of multiculturalism in relation to bilingualism and biculturalism was broached and developed through these and other briefs from ethnic groups or organizations representing their interests (Haque, 2005). In many of these briefs, multiculturalism was naturalized as being Canadian, both in the past and into an increasingly cosmopolitan future. Bilingualism and biculturalism were seen as stages on the path to this ideal, and the substantive vision of multiculturalism proposed was one that was linked to multilingualism and multilingual schooling.

As the idea of multiculturalism began to emerge in the preliminary hearings, another set of briefs also engaged with multiculturalism, but from the position of challenging the idea that Canada was a multicultural country. One of many examples was the brief presented by the Imperial Order Daughters of the Empire (IODE), founded in Canada in 1900 and one of the largest Canadian national voluntary women's organizations, which at the time of the commission was, on average, raising and spending over a million dollars annually on education, emergency welfare, and other community services (IODE, 1964). The IODE was supportive of bilingualism and biculturalism, particularly as it saw this foundational duality as something that differentiated Canada from "the one melting pot" system of the United States: "The I.O.D.E. appreciates that for nearly one hundred years this duality of culture has been, and is still, one of the strong factors which has helped to develop and preserve a distinctive Canadian nationality – one that makes it fundamentally different from that of our next-door neighbour, the United States" (ibid.,10). Having recognized biculturalism and bilingualism as a bulwark against the United States, the brief went on to describe the danger of what might happen if this Canadian duality failed: "Should our 'two melting pots' system disintegrate or fail, it is our belief that Canada would probably be unable to resist eventual 'Americanization'" (ibid.). Thus the Americans had a "one melting pot" system, but the duality of Canada constituted a "two melting pot" system. However, this formulation had particular implications for the other ethnic groups in Canada.

The position of the IODE on multilingualism and multiculturalism was quite clear: "Canada is not a multilingual or multiculturalism society" (IODE, 1964,10). Arguing against the "hyphenated Canadian" form, "the I.O.D.E. believes that all native-born and naturalized Canadians should be dignified by being referred to simply as 'Canadians'" (ibid., 8). The IODE said that all immigrants must learn one of Canada's two official languages, as it was a requirement of citizenship, and to this end, "many I.O.D.E. chapters conduct their own basic English classes for immigrants" (ibid., 17). Acknowledging that immigrants may initially wish to speak their own languages, the IODE warned that this practice could lead to divisions:

> It is only natural that, initially, immigrants should wish to speak in their own language and should endeavour to preserve their own culture. However, these contributions are only beneficial and contribute to enrichment so long as old prejudices and animosities are not transplanted and perpetuated or nourished in Canada. This would only serve to split or divide us into the same old discordant pattern of Old Europe. This, Canada does not want. It is our experience that immigrants are usually eager and anxious to integrate into English or French-speaking communities, because it is to their social and economic advantage to do so. In fact, it is a necessity. (IODE, 1964, 9)

Although the IODE did recognize that immigrants wanted to and needed to learn the majority languages, by invoking the fears of balkanization, the organization understood any desire by immigrants to preserve their languages of origin as a threat to Canadian unity; hence the IODE advocated the model of Canada as a nation of two melting pots. Thus, recognizing a fundamental duality in being "Canadian," the IODE still advocated assimilation for other ethnic groups into either of the two melting pots in order to prevent the divisiveness of cultural retention by other ethnic groups. Specifically, it was the preservation of ethnic languages that was seen as potentially divisive to being "Canadian." This fear of "balkanization" and fragmentation of Canadian unity, even if it was characterized as two melting pots, was a common counter-strategy to any kind of "multicultural" notion.

During the course of the public hearings, multiculturalism emerged as a way to break with the hierarchy established through the terms of reference for the other ethnic groups. The claims made for a multicultural, instead of bicultural, mode of inclusion were based on a variety of strategies, many of which had already been advanced during the course of the preliminary hearings, including historical, demographic, and territorial claims (Haque, 2005). Nevertheless, multiculturalism remained unspecified as a wide range of definitions were advanced on all sides of the debate. It was posited as a naturalized Canadian trait, as an expansion beyond the two founding-races conception of "unity in diversity," and bilingualism and biculturalism were seen as just stepping stones to the ideal of multiculturalism. However, multiculturalism was also understood to be a threat to social cohesion and pan-Canadian identity, be that a single Anglo-centric identity or a bicultural Canadian one, and also as a compromise to the Canadian dualism perceived as a bulwark against the United States. In many of these discussions, language emerged as the substantive element for advancing and demarcating the boundaries of other ethnic group rights and inclusion, through such issues as multilingualism, formal versus private multilingual schooling, the level at which multilingual schooling would begin if at all, and the positioning of majority (English/French) language learning as incompatible with the preservation of the language of origin (Haque, 2005). Thus, during the course of the public hearings, multiculturalism acquired a salience, albeit across a range of meanings, in relation to other ethnic groups, and language emerged as the terrain upon which other ethnic groups' inclusion was to be negotiated. Related ideas that grew out of these discussions were the assumptions around immigration -- that immigrants chose to come, that they knew the socio-cultural and political context before arriving, and that, in so choosing, they forfeited the right to ask for any formal recognition of their cultures and languages. This notion of choice would also become an important element in the locating of other ethnic groups by the commission in its final report.

BOOK I, THE OFFICIAL LANGUAGES

As the investigative phase of the inquiry came to a close, there was a discernible shift from the explicit articulation of national belonging through race and ethnicity, as outlined in the terms of reference, towards language and culture as the new terrain upon which inclusion would be organized. The first volume, *The Official Languages*, of the commission's final report stood apart from the rest of the volumes not only because it was the first but also because it contained what are now known as "the famous blue pages" (Laurendeau, 1991, 4). These pages emerged out of the commission's desire to clarify its terms of reference before embarking on the full report. Given the strong objections that had been mounted and maintained throughout the investigative phase of the inquiry to key terms in the terms of reference, chief among these the use of the word "race" and the implied hierarchy between race and ethnicity, the commission had to clarify its key terms before it could even begin to report its findings.

One of the first contentious terms defined in the blue pages of *Book* 1 was "race," which was discussed in tandem with the term "people." Although "people" was not used consistently in the English version of the terms of reference, in the French version, instead of "the two founding races," the text read, "les deux peuples qui ont fondé la Confédération" (Royal Commission, 1967, xxii). This wording may have provided the rationale behind discussing the definitions for both "people and "race" together, but even though there were two terms, this was still the shortest discussion of any of the key terms, consisting of only two paragraphs in the blue pages. The authors began by admitting, "This wording, particularly the use in the English text of the word 'race,' has been a source of misunderstanding" (ibid.). Referring to the submissions made by groups during the preliminary and public hearings, the misunderstanding was outlined as follows: "Should it be taken to mean that two 'races' or two 'peoples' will receive special treatment at the expense of the 'other ethnic groups'?" The authors were clear on this point; in no way did they understand the terms of reference to indicate a "special birthright of the two founding peoples ... perpetuating itself from father to son," or any suggestion of a "lower order of other ethnic groups, forever excluded from spheres of influence" (ibid.). Rather, the report explained, "In our view, the reference to the two 'founding races' or 'peoples who founded Confederation' was an allusion to the undisputed role played by Canadians of French and British origin in 1867, and long before Confederation" (ibid., xxii). More important here was the further explanation, "The word 'race' is used in an older meaning as referring to a national group, and carries no biological significance" (ibid.). The report found additional proof of this position in the fact that in subsequent paragraphs of the terms of reference (see ibid., App. A) there was "no mention of race, people, or ethnic group" but, rather, just the "bicultural character" of the country and the issues of teaching English and French (ibid.).

The authors of the report were in a difficult position here; they had at all costs to divorce the notion of race from any biological significance, not only because the idea of biological races had become anathema in the aftermath of World War II but also because division of the French and English people into two races would not survive scrutiny under any scientific definitions of "race." However, by invoking the older meaning of race as nation, the problem of conceptualizing the country as composed of two nations was posed, a problem that finds resonance into the present. The final paragraph in this section on "race" and "people" in the blue pages concludes: "Consequently, we feel that language and culture are truly central concepts in the terms of reference. For this reason, we shall give them more emphasis than the notions 'race,' 'people,' or even 'ethnic groups'" (Royal Commission, 1967, xxii). Therefore, in the definitional blue pages of the final report, language and culture have been catapulted into prominence over race, people, and ethnicity, even before a discussion of the key term "ethnic group" has taken place.

Now with race and its outmoded biological connotations being redefined in the inquiry as really a question of language and culture, the next phrase to be considered, "other ethnic groups," posed its own challenges and therefore required a different strategy. Understanding that the objections for "other ethnic groups" lay mainly in their being "other" to the "two founding races," the authors, having removed "race" as a key term, also made the strong statement that "'ethnic' seemed to be given a sense something like 'foreigner' ... We object in the strongest terms to this practice" (Royal Commission, 1967, xxiv). However, the commission was clear in reasserting that even as ethnicity was a "natural but often complex phenomenon," it was "on the whole unrelated to its [the commission's] objectives" (ibid., xxv). In this way, "ethnic groups" as a key term was also discounted from the original terms of reference. As a result of the intangible qualities of ethnicity outlined in the final report (Haque, 2005), the commission reprised its earlier conclusion: "since it [the commission] must make recommendations based on easily discernable realities, ... it must give much more importance to language than to ethnic origin" (Royal Commission, 1967, xxiv).

Expanding on the issue of language, the report drew on census data to indicate that although ethnic groups and mother tongues often coincided, 26 per cent of non-British Canadians identified English as their mother tongue. It went on to say that even the French-speaking group, which "has assimilated others to a much lesser extent," also included about 3 per cent of non-French with French as their mother tongue. The implications were clear to the authors of the report: "In Canada, membership in linguistic group is a matter of personal choice, provided that the conditions and consequences are accepted. There is nothing, at least in law, to bind Canadians to the prevailing language of their ethnic group. Since their choice is free, it would be grossly unfair not to accept the results of this freedom, and to make two classes of citizens, one consisting of Anglophones of British origin and Francophones of French origin and the other of Anglophones and Francophones of other origins" (Royal Commission, 1967, xxiv).

This statement was paradigmatic and laid the foundation for future understanding of how non-French and non-English groups could fit into the nation, as well as inaugurating the use of the terms "anglophone" and "francophone" (Jenson, 1994, 316). Here, by outlining language as a personal choice, the report implied that language shift was also a matter of personal choosing, discounting the larger structural constraints that channel language choices in society and across generations. Even more important, the question of personal choice suggested to the authors that such "free choice" resulted in "two classes of citizens"– those that replicated the divisions in the original terms of reference into the "two founding races." On one hand, the founding races were now termed the "Anglophones of British origin and Francophones of French origin," and, on the other, "other ethnic groups" were now called "Anglophones and Francophones of other origins." Therefore, although the commission had so far in the blue pages handily discounted the key terms of "race" and "ethnicity" by featuring language, it had duplicated the original divisions of the groups, albeit now in linguistic terms. In fact, by retaining the division into two groups in this way, the hierarchy of race and ethnicity had not been eliminated but, rather, had been shifted into a linguistic hierarchy.

This bifurcation into two groups, originally based on race and ethnicity and now defined through language, was echoed in the description of how the inquiry would consider "other ethnic groups": "Canadian who are of neither British nor French origin are covered by our inquiry in two ways: a) to the extent that they are integrated into English-or French-speaking society, all that is said of Anglophones or Francophones applies to them; and b) to the extent that they remain attached to their original language and culture, they belong to other ethnic groups, whose existence is definitely beneficial to the country" (Royal Commission, 1967, xxv). First, there was an implication that the integration of other ethnic groups was linguistic, as these two "founding" societies were now no longer defined as "races" but, rather, through the language they spoke. Second, the elements of "ethnic" difference were clearly delineated as linguistic or cultural differences. Therefore, although ostensibly not defined through race and/or ethnicity anymore, the elements of "ethnic" difference remained; they were now specified as simply a difference of language and culture. Again, although race and ethnic groups had been relegated to the background as language moved to the fore, it was clear that this repositioning had still not shifted the distinction between founding groups and non-founding-group others.

Another important distinction made in this report was the one between individual and institutional bilingualism. The report stated that individual bilingualism, where people "know, *more or less*, two languages" – in Canada at this time only about 2,230,000 people did so – was not as important for the inquiry as the idea of institutional bilingualism (Royal Commission, 1967, xxviii). In this case, institutional bilingualism could be expanded to include the bilingual nature of "the province, or a country" (ibid.). Such bilingualism, the report clarified, was quite different from the individual form: "A bilingual country is not one where all the inhabitants necessarily have to speak two languages; rather it is a country where the principal public and private institutions must provide services in two languages to citizens, the vast majority of whom may very well be unilingual . Consequently, 'the existing state of bilingualism' in Canada is not so much a question of the number of bilingual people as of the position of each of the two languages in everyday life" (ibid., xxviii). By highlighting the importance of institutional bilingualism over individual bilingualism, the commission made its priorities clear: "and that is the question of the life and vigour of each language must have priority" (ibid.), by which it meant the life and vigour of either the French or the English language (Haque, 2005).

The report also emphasized the strong link between language and culture in maintaining the viability of official-language communities: "language is the most evident expression of culture"; however, this conclusion was in direct contrast to the report's discussion of ethnic groups, where it asserted that, "quite apart from heredity, much of the culture of one's forbears could be preserved even when one no longer spoke their language" (Royal Commission, 1967, xxiii). This contradiction regarding the importance of language for cultural maintenance between English and French language groups and "other ethnic groups" introduced a differentiation in the definition of culture between both groups, again reproducing the hierarchy between founding races and other ethnic groups – only now in terms of language and culture.

Therefore in *Book* I of the final report the decisive shift of race and ethnicity into the terrain of language and culture was clearly made. As well, the terms "anglophone" and "francophone" were introduced to signal that the boundaries of language were open, that the borders of English and French were porous to any ethnic group who chose to speak the respective language, and that language was a "personal" and "free" choice, thereby countering any structural and institutional pressure that facilitated language shift. However, even as the purported openness of these linguistic groupings was immediately foreclosed through the report's explication that these groups contained "two classes of citizens" (Royal Commission, 1967, xxiv), it was in the discussion of bilingualism and the link between language and culture that the contradictory mechanism through which the commission deployed language and culture was made concrete. Despite the myriad alternatives submitted throughout the hearings, bilingualism in the report was defined as an "equal partnership" of the two main languages, English and French (Haque, 2005). The commission's focus on the institutional bilingualism of English and French, together with recognition of the importance of language in the expression and preservation of official-language culture and therefore a guarantee of language as a collective right, was what separated the "founding" groups from the "other ethnic" groups. Whereas, in the discussion on cultural contribution of other ethnic groups, language was seen as unnecessary for the maintenance of ethnic culture, here in the case of English and French bilingualism, a living and vigorous language could exist only within the collective right to a viable cultural community. This contradictory understanding of the link between language and culture laid the foundation for *Book IV, The Cultural Contribution of Other Ethnic Groups*, and the ensuing Multiculturalism Policy.

BOOK IV, THE CULTURAL CONTRIBUTION OF OTHER ETHNIC GROUPS

Approximately two years after the publication of Book I of the B and B Commission's final report, *Book IV*, entitled *The Cultural Contribution of the Other Ethnic Groups,* was published on 23 October 1969. By this time, the Official Languages Act had been adopted by Parliament, and *Books II* (on education) and III (on the work world) had already appeared. In *Book IV* the discourses of multiculturalism that had emerged from the public hearings and the weak link between language and culture of other ethnic groups, which was defined in contradiction to the strong link between language and culture for what were now the official-language groups, all came together. In *Book I* the ascendancy of language and culture over race and ethnicity in the terms of reference was established. Therefore, in its fourth volume the report specified the contribution of other ethnic groups as linguistic and cultural: "We will look at the contribution to Canadian life, and especially to the enrichment that results from the meeting of a number of languages and cultures. This contribution is seen, within the Canadian reality, in the active participation of those whose mother tongue is neither French nor English in various facets of community life" (Royal Commission, 1969, 3–4). Here, in the wake of the linguistic redefinitions of race and ethnicity of *Book* 1 and the redefinition of "core" groups as "official linguistic groups," other ethnic groups were also now being defined as linguistic groups – "those whose mother tongue is neither French nor English" – albeit still in contradistinction to English and French. And here the groundwork is also being laid for defining cultural contribution as substantively about language, as other ethnic groups' enrichment to Canadian life is said to result from "the meeting of a number of languages and cultures," as opposed to a clash between other ethnic groups and founding races (ibid.).

The report also considered the "semantic problems" associated with the term "other ethnic groups." The argument from the blue pages of *Book* 1 for moving away from notions of race and ethnicity were featured again: "We have already stressed in our General Introduction the danger of using ethnic origin as the basis for a simplistic distinction between the two 'founding peoples' and the members of 'other ethnic groups' … We repeat that we accept the words 'race' and 'people' only in their traditional sense – meaning a national group, with no biological significance – and we prefer to emphasize the fact of language and culture rather than the concepts of 'race,' 'people' or even 'ethnic group'" (Royal Commission, 1969, 7).

This was an important point to emphasize because to date in the report there had been only a qualified semantic shift from "founding races" to "Anglophones and Francophones" as a result of the rationale outlined above. This approach had still left the awkward collocations "other ethnic groups" and "non-British and non-French communities" to refer to all "immigrant" groups. If the prioritizing of language and culture over "race," "people," and "ethnic group" was to apply to the French and the English, then the next step in *Book* iv was to apply this logic to other ethnic groups as well. Therefore the report concluded as the only possible way to address other ethnic groups, "Consequently, we would rather regard the 'other ethnic groups' as *cultural groups*" (Royal Commission, 1969, 11; italics mine). In the case of "other ethnic groups," the closed idea of "ethnicity" became a more amorphous "cultural groups," but here the critical difference was that, although culture was highlighted, language was not. Therefore the transformation of "other ethnic groups" to "cultural groups" was a critical, but similar, step in the reconceptualization and rearticulation of the place of "other ethnic groups." Hence, even with the shift in terminology onto the terrain of language and culture, the secondary positioning of "other ethnic groups" to "founding races" in the terms of reference remained consistent in the hierarchical differentiation between the "Anglophones and Francophones" and "cultural groups."

In *Book* IV, details of the existing and recommended legislation and support for non-official languages clearly relegated their preservation to the private sphere, despite the celebration of "linguistic variety" as the substantive and unidirectional cultural contribution of other ethnic groups to the two dominant linguistic communities. For example, a host of reasons were given for not providing public financial support to private schools, and the conclusion was drawn that these schools should rely instead on local arrangements, relegating support for these schools back in the private realm and putting support for private ethnic schools on a par with other private schools and thereby negating the special role played by these schools in maintaining "the languages and cultures" of other ethnic groups (Royal Commission, 1969).

Earlier volumes of the final report had already provided a comprehensive and "systematic" overview of how official-language education, as well as the teaching of official second languages in official-language minority communities and "where numbers warrant," should proceed. It was made clear that this same level of support or "development" for non-official languages could not be recommended, but some opportunities would be provided, thereby establishing a hierarchy between support for official languages and that for non-official languages, based on the established dominance of the British and French cultures. As the report stated, at all times the bilingual and bicultural context had to be considered: "where public support is concerned, the question of language and cultural maintenance must be seen within the broader context of the question of bilingualism and biculturalism in Canada as a whole; for example, the learning of third languages should not be carried on at the expense of public support for learning the second official language" (ibid., 138–9).

Here it was specified that the learning of "third languages" should not compromise public support for learning the second official language; a logic which implied that the first goal of schooling would be official-language bilingualism and then, as a third, additional language, a non-official language. Given the extremely low rates of official-language bilingualism at this time, particularly among other ethnic groups, such a policy would mean that the possibility of acquiring a third, non-official language would be very remote. This statement reiterated the central point that support for non-official languages must not compromise the bilingual and bicultural hegemony. Despite the repeated emphasis on locating non-official language support within a bilingual and bicultural framework, some recommendations were made, among these that "it is not feasible for Canada's public education systems to employ languages other than English and French extensively as languages of instruction. While our recommendations below will propose substantial educational opportunities for languages other than English or French where sufficient demand exists, the aim of improving educational opportunities in the official languages must be maintained as the primary objective" (Royal Commission, 1969, 139).

It became evident that almost everywhere that the topic of support for non-official languages was raised, the report also had to reiterate the need for language and cultural dominance of the "founding groups" in schooling. Thus the authors of the report had to make sure that their suggested support for non-official languages did not in any way detract from their previous three volumes of recommendations about the official languages and cultures. The few recommendations that were made regarding the safeguarding of other ethnic languages were addressed largely through institutional education, which was mainly a provincial concern. At all levels of education, non-official language preservation was marginalized through the paucity of recommended legislative support as a result of the stated concern that maintenance of non-official languages must not compromise the hegemony of bilingualism and biculturalism. The commission had to balance support for non-official languages against weakening the federal government's material and symbolic support for both official languages and cultures. Therefore the disparity in support between official and non-official languages thrust the main task of non-official language preservation back into the private realm of other ethnic groups and reasserted the dominance of official bilingualism.

With integration identified both as the key element in cultural contribution and a way to locate other ethnic groups in relation to official linguistic communities, official-language competency became the concrete measure of integration and therefore a significant focus of the commission's recommendations (Haque, 2005). As well, integration gave rise to the rhetoric of diversity or "unity in diversity," through which cultural groups were at "liberty" to integrate into anglophone and francophone societies, as first articulated in *Book* 1, which they had to do in order to enjoy full citizenship rights, while paradoxically they remained the heterogeneous "diverse" and centrifugal elements within these "fundamental dualities." Therefore the report also highlighted the importance of official-language competency for participation in Canadian life:

> Lack of fluency in at least one of the official languages of Canada is obviously a barrier to participation in Canadian life, and one which is first felt in the economic sphere. Since Canada receives immigrants from many

countries where neither English nor French is the language of daily life, they are inevitably handicapped by this lack and it is essential that we attempt to minimize this handicap by making available facilities for learning the official languages of the country. Such facilities should be available both to young people in conjunction with their education and to adults in conjunction with their work. (Royal Commission, 1969, 65)

The concern with facilitating official-language learning for adult immigrants for the purposes of occupational integration and the learning of official languages for their children was clearly delineated in the final report. Also, official-language competency was required for "full participation" and "citizenship" in Canadian life, the report thus echoing earlier statements that full citizenship rights had be exercised as integrated members of official-language communities (Royal Commission, 1969). The role of provincial, municipal, and private agencies in providing official-language training to immigrants was also described, and the federal contribution was detailed: "The federal government enters into agreements with the provinces to reimburse them for the expense of language textbooks used by adult immigrants in programmes of language instruction, and for half the teaching costs of citizenship instruction (including English and French) for adult immigrants" (ibid., 65).

Thus, in the case of official-language instruction for adult immigrants, the federal government provided concrete support. As well, recommendations were made in volume 2 (*Education*) of the final report for the establishment of a Language Research Council, whose activities would relate to second-language teaching in Canada and serve as a resource for adult immigrant official-language instruction. Although such a council was never ultimately established, the federal government did encourage the creation of privately funded bodies to take on this work, with intermittent project support from the Secretary of State (Mackey, personal communication, 2007). Therefore there was a marked difference between the support provided for official-language instruction, both for children and immigrants who did not speak the official languages, and that provided for non-official "ethnic" languages, particularly for adults. In the case of the former, financial help was made available, and structural help was recommended, but for the latter, nothing was provided or even recommended.

RESPONSE TO THE FINAL REPORT
OF THE B AND B COMMISSION

Following the publication of the final report of the B and B Commission on 23 October 1969, responses from other ethnic groups emerged. Those that had presented heterogeneous responses and recommendations for *Book* IV were fairly uniform in their aversion to the bicultural hegemony of the report and their desire for some form of substantive multiculturalism, variants of which had emerged during the public hearings (Haque, 2005). Although *Book* IV was tabled in the House of Commons on 15 April 1970, an official federal government response was not made until almost a year and half later in the House of Commons. Though the commission had came into existence under the auspices of Lester Pearson, it would be Pierre Trudeau, prime minister since August 1968, who would be associated with the outcome of the commission's work, first by overseeing the introduction of the Official Languages Act and then by responding to the final report. On the morning of 8 October 1971 Trudeau made his famous and often-cited speech announcing the implementation of a policy of multiculturalism within a bilingual framework (Canada, House of Commons, 1971b, 8545).

Trudeau began his announcement in the House by stating that the government had accepted all the recommendations contained in *Book* IV that were "directed to federal departments and agencies" (Canada, House of Commons, 1971b, 8545). The rationale for this acceptance laid the groundwork for multiculturalism:

> It was the view of the royal commission, shared by the government and, I am sure, by all Canadians, that there cannot be one cultural policy for Canadians of British and French origin, another for the original peoples and yet a third for all others. For although there are two official languages, there is no official culture, nor does any ethnic group take precedence over any other. No citizen or group of citizens is other than Canadian, and all should be treated fairly. The royal commission was guided by the belief that adherence to one's ethnic group is influenced not so much by one's origin or mother tongue as by one's sense of belonging to the group, and by what the commission calls the group's "collective will to exist." The government shares this belief. (Canada, House of Commons, 1971b, 8545)

Trudeau's comments reprised the contradiction between language and culture developed in *Book* I of the final report, which maintained the hierarchy of founding races on the terrain of language and culture. In the final report, the commissioners declared that they advocated a position which supported the hegemony of French and English bilingualism and biculturalism. In the passage quoted above, Trudeau countered the commission's position on biculturalism and used a strategy through which all groups were homogenized as "Canadian"; in his words, "No citizen or group of citizens is other than Canadian." Trudeau drew upon arguments made in the final report that culture was not so much about origin or mother tongue as it was about "one's sense of belonging to the group" or the "collective will to exist" (Royal Commission, 1969, 7). However, in the final report this formulation was contradictorily applied only to the other ethnic groups and not to the two official linguistic communities, for whom the report stated, "the life of two cultures implies in principle the life of the two languages" (ibid., xxxviii). This concept was the foundation of the bilingual and bicultural formula of the commission's final report. Thus, although Trudeau seemed to overturn the implicit hierarchy of biculturalism by stating that ethnicity or "mother tongue" was not a central feature of cultural identity since we were all "Canadians," by maintaining that there were "two official languages," he was recalling the same cultural contradiction of *Book* 1 in order to sustain the dominance of the two founding groups. Thus, even as he disavowed the hierarchy of biculturalism, he smuggled it back in by maintaining that there were two official languages. Trudeau identified the various groups using the same divisions of the population as in the inquiry – the British and the French, the Aboriginal or "original peoples," and "all others." The homogenization of "other ethnic groups" as "all others" resurrected the "third element" or "third force" categorization the commission had worked so hard to disavow.

In the next part of his speech, Trudeau outlined his formulation of the most suitable framework for national unity:

The individual's freedom would be hampered if he were locked for life within a particular cultural compartment by the accident of birth or language. It is vital, therefore, that every Canadian, whatever his ethnic origin, be given a chance to learn at least one of the two languages in which his country conducts its official business and its politics. A policy of multiculturalism within a bilingual framework commends itself to the government as the most suitable means of assuring the cultural freedom of Canadians. Such a policy should help to break down discriminatory attitudes and cultural jealousies. National unity if it is to mean anything in the deeply personal sense, must be founded on the confidence in one's own individual identity; out of this can grow respect for that of others and a willingness to share ideas, attitudes and assumptions. A vigorous policy of multiculturalism will help create this initial confidence. It can form the base of a society which is based on fair play for all. (Canada, House of Commons, 1971b, 8545).

In this passage, Trudeau placed an emphasis on the individual's freedom to learn one of the two official languages. This statement putatively encompassed "every Canadian, whatever his ethnic origin," that is, official-language minorities and other ethnic groups. However, substantively it addressed the other ethnic groups because, although Trudeau did not mention the word "integration" in his speech, the "cultural freedom" he was espousing was the "individual freedom" for members of other ethnic groups to integrate into one of the two official language communities. This position echoed the final report's assertion that other ethnic groups were at "liberty" to integrate, particularly if they wanted to enjoy and exercise full political citizenship rights. For Trudeau, it was a policy of multiculturalism within a bilingual framework that could ensure this design of "cultural freedom" and, ultimately, national unity.

Where he seemed to depart significantly from the final report was in his insistence that national unity could be founded on "individual identity." If the final report highlighted collective rights of the two official-language communities as essential for national unity, here Trudeau foregrounded individual rights as the basis of national unity. Although the idea of collective rights was new to Canada at this time, and there was some debate about whether these rights were considered pre-emptive or complementary, this emphasis on individual rights and freedoms would come to be associated with Trudeau as part of his political legacy, particularly as exemplified through the Canadian Charter of Rights and Freedoms. As well, he was very much in support of the collective notion of two official-language communities, something that would also be prominently entrenched and safeguarded as collective rights in the Charter. In effect, the individualization of identity and rights, couched as freedoms, were specific here only to the other ethnic groups, in contrast to the collective claims of bilingualism. Thus the individualization of other ethnic identity, in contrast to the official-language collectivities, effectively dispersed any collectively based "third force" or "third element" claims once and for all. Therefore the formulation of multiculturalism that emerged from Trudeau's speech and was detailed in the policy paper that followed was a restricted and limited notion of multiculturalism which in the main reprised the exclusions of biculturalism by largely adopting the recommendations of *Book* iv. Trudeau's version of multiculturalism submerged the competing visions of multiculturalism that had surfaced during the public hearings in order to endorse a hegemonic interpretation of the terms of reference and allow the report to authoritatively advocate a dominant position for bilingualism and biculturalism. The universal appeal of his policy was underpinned by the vast disparity between the policies, legislation, and funding levels recommended for official-language communities and those for other ethnic groups.

Trudeau's announcement of a policy of multiculturalism within a bilingual framework had to balance myriad forces and tensions in the government's overriding interest in national unity. These included facilitating the social integration of other ethnic groups and acknowledging their wishes, while also not being seen as undercutting Quebec's demands and official-language minorities' concerns, all against the backdrop of a historically assumed British dominance. The need to balance these concerns was specific to this era, which witnessed the Quiet Revolution, an escalation in demands for civil rights, and increasing awareness of Aboriginal claims. The resulting formulation for national unity was a white-settler bilingual and bicultural hegemony that entrenched a hierarchical framework of difference and belonging articulated on the terrain of language and culture as multiculturalism within a bilingual framework. This formulation for nation-building, established through the work of the royal commission, has come to define the parameters of the contemporary Canadian nation-state. Official state multiculturalism in Canada remains deeply embedded within a bilingual framework that has entrenched substantively different collective rights between official-language groups and what are now known as "multicultural" groups.

MULTICULTURALISM AND IMMIGRATION

Jean Brunet, who played a significant role in the preparation of *Book* IV, has stated that multiculturalism was "framed under pressure from and in regard to the aims of Canadians who had come, or whose ancestors had come, from Europe," these being the "cultural groups" of the inquiry (Brunet, 1978, 109). However, during the course of the inquiry there was a crucial shift in the category "cultural groups" that would have lasting implications for the organization and management of racial difference in Canada and link cultural groups with immigration into the present. At the beginning of 1962, the same year as Laurendeau's pivotal editorial in *Le Devoir* and just a year before the B and B Commission was announced, critical changes were occurring in Canadian immigration policy. These changes, announced in the House of Commons on 19 January 1962 by then minister of citizenship and immigration Ellen Fairclough, focused on "education, training and skills as the main condition of admissibility regardless of the country of origin of the applicant" (Canada, House of Commons, 1962, 9). This announcement marked a pivotal shift away from Prime Minister Mackenzie

King's post–World War II formulation of immigration policy based on racial and geographical exclusions. As Taylor (1991, 2) states, Canadian immigration law "from 1885 until 1962, was explicitly racist in wording and intent: non-white, non-European immigration was openly discouraged and/or prohibited." This history of racial exclusion was built on such policies as the "single continuous journey" provision, the Chinese Immigration Act and its subsequent revisions, and a variety of "all-purpose exclusion provisions" outlined in the 1906 act, and when these exclusions failed, the government could make a proclamation to "prohibit the landing in Canada of any specified class of immigrants" (quoted ibid., 2).

In 1947 the Chinese immigration Act was repealed, the "single continuous journey" clause was removed from the Immigration Act, and amendments were made to the immigration policy which focused on the advantageous economic absorption of carefully selected immigrants. This concern with "absorption" would later be couched in the language of "integration" and pointed to the government's awareness of the economic importance of immigration to nation-building. It led to the tabling of a white paper on immigration in the House of Commons on 14 October 1966. The white paper was a long-awaited document intended to assist in public discussion within and outside Parliament on the principles and policies that the government believed should be embodied in new immigration legislation (Canada, Department of Manpower and Immigration, 1966, 5). It was significant in that it articulated in general terms the new framework for immigration now that the policy had moved away from explicitly racial criteria. This discernible shift was the result of an emphasis on the economic importance of immigration, as opposed to the pre-1962 focus on racial and geographical exclusion.

By 1 October 1967 the new immigration regulations had come into effect; according to the minister, they would be universally applied, increase recognition of family relationships, and be more closely attuned to Canada's economic needs. Thus a set of immigration regulations that for the first time were not couched in overtly discriminatory regulations was in place, and a whole new mode of modern nation-building was underway. These changes to the immigration regulations, which were significant, began to result in changes in the numbers of immigrants from various countries. Specifically, from 1962 to 1970 there was a steady increase in immigration from Asian, African, and South and Central American countries, while, after a peak in immigration in 1967, European immigration began to decline significantly (Hawkins, 1988, 57). Perhaps most telling was the shift in the top source countries from 1967 on. In that year Britain and Italy were the top two sources of immigration, at 62,420 and 30,055 respectively, but by 1970 their numbers had dropped dramatically to 26,497 and 8,533 respectively, while Asian immigration numbers had increased approximately sevenfold, from 3,912 in 1963 to 23,319 in 1969 (ibid., 56–7).

These changes to Canadian immigration, all of which were taking place during the course of the B and B Commission's work, began to result in a change in source countries and the distribution of immigration numbers. Thus the category of "cultural group" that had emerged out of the commission's work underwent a fundamental shift in who came to inhabit this category in the "multiculturalism within a bilingual framework" formulation. Multiculturalism emerged within the framework of pressures from other ethnic groups, which, as Brunet (1978) suggests, were mainly those who had come or whose ancestors had come from Europe. She makes the important point that, by the 1960s and 1970s, language had became the most salient marker of ethnic identity for this group, while during this period a more visibly marked, or racialized, group of immigrants were beginning to arrive in increasing numbers to Canada. Lupul (1983) divides these two groups into the "white ethnics" and the "real minorities." He describes the "white ethnics" as "undistinguished in external appearance and therefore socially invisible," whose main concerns were therefore "language and cultural retention and development," whereas the "real minorities" were the "visible peoples" who could not be readily assimilated (ibid., 1983, 104). The strategy to gain recognition for the other ethnic groups or the "white ethnics" had been to argue for inclusion into the white-settler category alongside the "founding" groups. However, this strategy was forever out of reach for the "real minorities" as the visibility of their racialization thwarted any such possibility. Thus "cultural groups" came increasingly to signify a racialized category, or what the federal government termed "visible minority," as the "white ethnics," who were the original other ethnic groups around which multiculturalism was initially framed, slowly assimilated, particularly linguistically, into the "white settler" category and became "socially invisible" (ibid.). This genealogical link between multiculturalism within a bilingual framework and immigration policy has meant that the concern of multiculturalism has come to be a concern with the integration of this "visible minority" cultural group.

ENGLISH-LANGUAGE TRAINING

At present, the problem of the integration of this visible minority cultural group has revolved around a concern with linguistic integration, specifically, the integration of newcomers into at least one of the official languages.

However, given the marginalization of these programs and the paucity of their funding, the substantively different rights to collective claims between official-language groups and "cultural groups" can now be traced in the English-language training programs, which were developed to address the ongoing – and at present, increasing – concerns with the integration of immigrants. Federal English-language training programs can be traced back to 1947, when a policy called the Citizenship and Language Instruction and Language Textbook Agreements (CILT) to fund adult ESL under school boards and NGOs through provincial education departments was created (Burnaby, 2002, 69). Although not all provinces accepted or implemented this program fully, it did pay the costs of textbooks and one-half the costs of instruction, and the goal of the program was to prepare immigrants with language and knowledge to pass the citizenship test (ibid.).

In 1967 Canada's booming economy meant an emphasis on the federal government's part on the selection of the most suitable workers and the creation of the Manpower program, which provided funding for a range of full-time occupational and pre-occupational training, with ESL for immigrants comprising a considerable portion of the training offered (Burnaby, 2002). Between this time and the 1980s a confusing assortment of ESL programs and responsibility for such programs evolved and devolved at both at the federal and provincial levels. By 1986–87 the federal Canada Employment and Immigration Commission (CEIC) had launched the Settlement Language Training Program for newly arrived immigrants and eliminated the CILT program. With the new immigration plan of 1990, a revised adult language training program was introduced to replace the Manpower program with the current Language Instruction for Newcomers to Canada (LINC) program, which is available to all immigrants in their first three years in Canada, as well as a restricted Labour Market Language Training (LMLT) program, which has now virtually ceased to exist.

The strong emphasis in the new LINC policy announcement on the importance of language training as part of settlement services and the increased availability of programs masked an important change in the new policy – there would be a marked reduction in the level of instruction to be provided[4] (Haque and Cray, 2006). Currently, the federal government directly spends only about $350 million dollars annually in settlement services for the integration of newcomers (Frith, 2003), with the bulk of this money going to support official-language instruction programs (Citizenship and Immigration Canada, 2001). As the policy announcement made clear, when formulating the LINC policy, the Canadian government made a decision to restrict the level of instruction to survival-level language. Immigrants and refugees were now seen as requiring no more than "the basic ability to communicate" and "a first level of language competency" (Immigrant Policy and Program Development Branch, 1991, 3). The policy announcement continued with the requirements that language instruction must "normally be offered during an immigrant's first year in Canada," a provision which reflects the assumption that language classes would be structured within settlement services, rather than as part of the process of integrating newcomers into the labour market (ibid.).

With the establishment of the LINC policy, language instruction was no longer viewed as a part of the strategy to integrate new Canadians into the labour market, nor was there any acknowledgment that it was desirable to encourage newcomers to further their education. Inherent in the policy is the assumption that the state does not have a responsibility to provide instruction to levels that would facilitate economic or social mobility. The policy mandates a provision that offers very limited language instruction with severely restricted objectives. The association of language learning with access to employment and education has been replaced by an association of language learning with access to basic settlement services and an understanding that the state posits this as an adequate provision for newcomers (Haque and Cray, 2006). As stated in the policy announcement, learning an official language is "often the essential first step towards successful integration," and the state's responsibility ends at this first step.

The language policies that govern the language learning of newcomers have a clear marginalizing effect. Given the shift in recent decades to the increased racialization of immigration to Canada, as described above, this effect has meant the emergence of a distinct racial stratification in the social and economic marginalization of newcomers to Canada (Bannerji, 2000). The LINC policy ensures that only low levels of language are made available for newcomers in LINC classes, so that these newcomers will have access to only low-level jobs – these are jobs that most often provide the least protection and job security for employees and almost no upward employment mobility. As well, low levels of language proficiency mean that newcomers will have access to only basic settlement services, ensuring further restrictions to social mobility and personal advocacy. The LINC policy is also embedded in the framework of national belonging that is articulated through the two main federal language documents: the Official Languages Act and the Multiculturalism Policy (since 1988 the Canadian Multiculturalism Act). These effectively outline a cultural and linguistic hierarchy which, through the mechanism of multiculturalism, renders the language resources that newcomers bring with them simply a cultural trait. Therefore newcomers at present have restricted access to official languages and no recognition of their own first languages. The uncoupling of language and culture is an important part of managing difference, particularly racial difference, since, as Rassool (1998, 91) argues, linguistic diversity can come to represent linguistic difference, which then becomes the "primary variable in the structuring of cultural and social 'Otherness.'" In this way, language policies become the vehicle for the management of racialized "others," in this case newcomers, through the rubrics of cultural and linguistic traits.

CONCLUSION

In this chapter, I have argued that although the Royal Commission on Bilingualism and Biculturalism was created out of the need to establish the "Canadian confederation on the basis of an equal partnership between the two founding races," the accounting of the "contribution made by other ethnic groups" resulted in a formulation of "multiculturalism within a bilingual framework" that set into place a hierarchy of belonging within the nation. Furthermore, a differential accommodation of "multicultural" language and culture in tandem with the changes in immigration policies has meant, in the present, an increasing concern with newcomer "integration" for non-official-language minority groups (elided now into immigrant minority groups), with language as the central locus of this process.

The bilingual framework, as articulated through the Official Languages Act, does not allow for the recognition of non-official minority languages (the languages of both established and newly arrived immigrant groups), since the definition of bilingualism is restricted to the two official languages. This understanding of bilingualism is both official and pervasive – a bilingual in the Canadian context is someone who speaks English and French. Speakers of an official language and a non-official minority language are not recognized as bilinguals, and these minority languages are granted neither recognition nor rights at the federal level. Although the Multiculturalism Act recognizes non-official cultural identities, this is a notion of culture that is essentially uncoupled from language. When combined with the LINC policy, which in practice provides only low levels of English-language training for newcomers, the hierarchy of national belonging that was set into place with the B and B Commission remains firmly established at present through this differential recognition of linguistic rights.

Federal and provincial language policies differ in goals and methods, yet the Ottawa-Quebec contrast is telling. Language policies at the federal and provincial levels have attended to the interests of the respective majority group, but each has had problems in responding effectively and uniformly to non-official-language minority group needs and interests. Recurring efforts have been made to reach such an accommodation at both levels, although a viable solution remains elusive.

The United States–Canadian contrast is instructive as well. Canada has taken a more activist approach in the three policy areas of language, multiculturalism, and immigration, while the United States has been more inclined to a free-market, laissez-faire approach. Neither approach has worked very well in practice in dealing with minority groups. In the case of Canada, LINC resembles a US free-market approach in providing minimal levels of language support to newcomers. Both countries, although in different ways, emphasize that newcomers must assimilate, or "integrate," into dominant groups.

Inasmuch as all of the comparisons are interrelated, a multidimensional perspective helps clarify that, although Canadian language policies have attempted some forms of accommodation, they remain minimal for non-official minority languages and minority groups. Concepts and approaches which emerged from the origins of policy have continued, thereby giving momentum to established policy goals, but generally without substantive accommodation of minority needs.

The attempts of the Canadian government to address the interrelated challenges of these three policy areas is to be applauded, although ambitious intentions and high expectations have remained unfulfilled. Continuity of policy across administrations can demonstrate consensus and dedication to fundamental objectives, but in the case of non-official-language minority groups in Canada such continuity in the three policy areas under consideration usually does not foreground their interests.

Ultimately, as this study demonstrates, policy is a crude mechanism to promote complex social needs, and although Canada has introduced some innovative policy initiatives in all three areas across time, minority groups in particular have not benefited substantively from these initiatives.

NOTES

1 Although "races" was used in the English version of commission publications, the term used in French was *peuples*. Thus this use of "races" can be seen as the contemporary equivalent of people, group, or community.

2 It is predominantly this statement that was taken as proof, particularly in the media, in arguments that the commission from the very start had set out to manufacture a crisis. Wardaugh (1983, 40) enunciates a common concern in the wake

of the *Preliminary Report*: "To what extent the work of the Royal Commission
helped create or validate a 'crisis' one can only surmise."

3 The various Ukrainian communities were very active in the discussions about the
  "other ethnic groups" during the B and B Commission. This involvement was
  reflected in the fact that one of the commissioners, J.B. Rudnykyj, was a prominent
  member of the community.

4 The Canadian Language Benchmarks 2000 framework provides guiding and exit
  criteria for LINC classes. Although there are twelve levels in CLB 2000, most programs in Canada offer courses up to benchmarks 3–4, the highest level in the first
  stage, which is labelled "Basic Proficiency"; Ontario alone offers classes with exit
  criteria referenced to benchmarks 6–7. Thus while CLB 2000 describes language from
  basic to advanced levels of proficiency, the upper level benchmarks describe levels
  of language that are never taught to newcomers in federally funded programs.

9

Canada's Official Languages in the Provinces of Quebec and Ontario: A Demographic Comparison

MICHEL PAILLÉ

Comparisons are often made between Canada's two most populous provinces, Quebec and Ontario (Dupré, 1993; Polèse, 1996; Guilbault, 1999), home to more than six out of ten Canadians. These provinces – the cradles of Canadian civilization – developed in parallel, making it easier to note their similarities and differences.

In this country, where English and French are the official languages, Quebec recognizes only French, while Ontario, unlike New Brunswick, refuses to declare itself bilingual (Castonguay, 2003, 208). It is only natural to compare Quebec and Ontario linguistically, especially given the size of their populations (see Mackey in chap. 3 above). In the debate surrounding its 1977 language law, the Quebec government clearly stated its objective: to make Quebec a province as deeply marked by French as Ontario was by English (Laurin, 1977, 36, 137).

Canada has long categorized its inhabitants according to their "ability to carry on a conversation in French or English (knowledge of the official languages)," the "*first language learned* at home *in childhood* and *still understood* at the time of the census ('mother tongue')," the "language *most often* spoken at home at the time of the census (commonly called the 'home language')," and "ethnic origin." These data have been highly useful for a long time.

Note that these variables cannot be used to "define" Quebec francophones, anglophones, or allophones. Louise Fontaine in chapter 7 asks, "Who is a Quebecer?" and Normand Labrie in chapter 10 inquires as to "how francophone identities are currently structured," but current data "can only be used to measure ... French usage ...; it has nothing to do with the sense of belonging to a language group" (Paillé and Comeau, 2005).

Taking inspiration from Max Weber's approach (Paillé, 2003b, 178–83), our language categories do not reflect "mythical entities of an essentialist nature" (Fontaine in chap. 7) and are not clear-cut. Nor do the categories form homogenous groups, even the francophone majority, wrongly perceived as totally "old stock" (Paillé, 1998). Like the francophone minority in Ontario (see Labrie in chap. 10), it is not homogenous. Furthermore, as William Mackey underlines, "different allegiances may sometimes be merged into a hierarchy of belonging ... [which] may be ascendant (e.g., first a Montrealer, second a Quebecer, and thirdly a Canadian) or inversely, top-down (a Canadian first, etc.)" (see chap. 2).

In discussions of Bill 101, which led to the adoption of the Charter of the French Language[1] in 1977, these four variables were mentioned frequently (Amyot,1980), particularly by Louis Duchesne (1977). Based on 1971 census data, his comparison between Quebec and Ontario helped anchor our previous comparative studies (Paillé, 2003a; 1988), which we have updated here. For reasons explained at length by Castonguay (1999a; 2003, 185–9) and acknowledged by Yaroslav Bilinsky in chapter 5, we will not consider ethnic origin. In short, mother tongue is our independent variable, while knowledge of French and English and home language are our dependent variables.

This is not my first such comparative initiative. I have made a number of comparisons (Paillé, 1991a; 2003c) in studies of minority-language education in each province (English in Quebec, French elsewhere in Canada),[2] guaranteed under the Canadian Charter of Rights and Freedoms (1982). I have also looked at migration between Quebec and the other Canadian provinces (Paillé, 1997), as well as the language choices of international immigrants (Paillé, 1991b). This chapter synthesizes and extends my previous research, while benefiting from the synergy of being an integrated part of a comprehensive, comparative study.

OVERVIEW OF CANADA

Tables 9.1 and 9.2 show the population of Quebec and Ontario by mother tongue in 1971 and 2001 (the far right column indicates the net relative change observed for the period). Table 9.3 gives the same type of information for the country as a whole.

Between 1971 and 2001, Quebec's population increased by just over 18 per cent (1.1 million people), compared to over 39 per cent for Canada as a whole. Quebec's share in the Canadian population has therefore dwindled from 27.9 per cent to 23.7 per cent in thirty years. Population growth has been much greater in Ontario. Nearly 3.6 million additional residents

Table 9.1
Population by mother tongue, Quebec, 1971 and 2001

Mother tongue	1971		2001		1971–2001
	N	%	N	%	%
French	4 866 405	80.7	5 802 033	81.4	19.2
English	788 830	13.1	591 393	8.3	−25.0
Other	372 530	6.2	732 175	10.3	96.5
Total	6 027 765	100.0	7 125 600	100.0	18.2

SOURCES: Duchesne, 1977, 44; Marmen and Corbeil, 2004, table A.1.

Table 9.2
Population by mother tongue, Ontario, 1971 and 2001

Mother tongue	1971		2001		1971–2001
	N	%	N	%	%
French	482 355	6.3	509 267	4.5	5.6
English	5 967 725	77.5	8 041 992	71.3	34.8
Other	1 253 030	16.3	2 734 297	24.2	118.2
Total	7 703 110	100.0	11 285 555	100.0	46.5

SOURCES: See table 9.1.

Table 9.3
Population by mother tongue, Canada, 1971 and 2001

Mother tongue	1971		2001		1971–2001
	N	%	N	%	%
French	5 793 650	26.9	6 782 289	22.9	17.1
English	12 973 810	60.2	17 521 897	59.1	35.1
Other	2 800 850	13.0	5 334 844	18.0	90.5
Total	21 568 310	100.0	29 639 030	100.0	37.4

SOURCES: Lachapelle and Henripin, 1980, 336; Marmen and Corbeil, 2004, table A.1.

increased the population of Canada's most densely inhabited province by more than 46 per cent. While 35.7 per cent of the Canadian population lived in Ontario in 1971, 37.6 per cent lived there in 2001. Thus, during the period in question, Ontario was gaining ground, while Quebec was dwindling.[3]

The exact opposite occurred with regard to the relative weight of the linguistic majorities. While Quebec francophones and Ontario anglophones grew in number, the percentage of the former increased slightly (from 80.7 per cent to 81.4 per cent), while that of the latter dropped over 6 percentage points (from 77.5 per cent to 71.3 per cent). Still, it is important to note that Quebec's French mother-tongue population grew only 19 per cent, while Ontario's English mother-tongue population rose nearly 35 per cent: Quebec francophones increased from almost 4.9 million to 5.8 million; Ontario anglophones increased from almost 6 million in 1971 to 8 million in 2001.

Only anglophone Quebecers show absolute and relative losses. Quebec's English mother-tongue population, which made up 13 per cent of the province's population in 1971 (789 thousand), dropped by one-fourth over the thirty years in question to 8.3 per cent of the population in 2001 (591 thousand). During that time, francophone Ontarians increased 5.6 per cent, reaching more than 509 thousand in 2001. However, their relative weight declined from 6.3 per cent to 4.5 per cent of the Ontario population, despite recognition of their rights between 1968 and 1988 (see Labrie in chap. 10). "Emerging individual strategies" based on bilingualism as part of the "global economy" (ibid.) probably have something to do with this decline.

Comparing the data in tables 9.1 and 9.3 confirms the long-term trend of Canadian francophone concentration in the province of Quebec. In 1971, 84 per cent of Canada's French mother-tongue population resided in Quebec. In 1996 and 2001 the figure was 85.5 per cent. Consequently, as a result of a net migration deficit compared to the rest of Canada (Termote, 1994, 84; 1999, 132), the relative weight of anglophone Quebecers in Canada's English mother-tongue population declined from 6.1 per cent in 1971 to 3.4 per cent in 2001. In a nutshell, Quebec continues to attract more Canadian francophones (Henripin, 1974, 3) as it becomes less and less appealing for Canada's anglophone majority.

As the preferred destination of international immigrants (Statistique Canada, 2001;[4] Castonguay, 2003, 210), Ontario is increasingly becoming a centre for third-language speakers. From tables 9.2 and 9.3, we can calculate that the percentage of people with a mother tongue other than French or English ("allophones") who resided in Ontario increased from 44.7 per cent in 1971 to 51.3 per cent in 2001 (2.7 million out of 5.3 million in Canada).

KNOWLEDGE OF FRENCH AND ENGLISH

The Quebec government's objective was not "to make English disappear" (see Maurais in chap. 4) or even to make the francophone majority as "unilingual" as Ontario's anglophone majority. On the contrary, the minister shepherding the bill through the assembly stressed the importance of individual

Table 9.4
Distribution (percentage) of knowledge of French and English by mother tongue, Quebec, 1971

Mother tongue	Knowledge of French and English				
	French only	English only	French and English	None	Total
French	74.3		25.7		100.0
English		63.3	36.7		100.0
Other	14.0	35.8	33.1	17.0	100.0
Total	60.9	10.5	27.6	1.1	100.0

SOURCE: Duchesne, 1977, 46.

Table 9.5
Distribution (percentage) of knowledge of French and English by mother tongue, Ontario, 1971

Mother tongue	Knowledge of French and English				
	French only	English only	French and English	None	Total
French	18.3		81.7		100.0
English		95.7	4.3		100.0
Other	0.4	81.1	5.0	13.6	100.0
Total	1.2	87.3	9.3	2.2	100.0

SOURCE: Duchesne, 1977, 47.

acquisition of English language skills (Laurin, 1977, 15, 17, 21, 48, 55, 151). Ontario thus served as a foil, rather than a model to be emulated. Keeping in mind that Canada's censuses are limited to a basic self-evaluation of the ability to carry on a conversation in French or English (Castonguay, 2003, 177), let us look at 1971 and 2001 census data on this topic.

WHAT DO THE CENSUS DATA REVEAL?

Tables 9.4 and 9.5 show for 1971, for the population as a whole and for each language group in Quebec and Ontario, the relative distribution (in percentages) of respondents according to their self-perceived ability to carry on a conversation (1) in French only, (2) in English only, (3) in both languages, or (4) in neither language.

According to the 1971 Census

First, we note that 27.6 per cent of Quebecers, regardless of mother tongue, considered themselves able to carry on a conversation in French or English, compared to only 9.3 per cent of Ontarians. At that time, there were over two bilingual Quebecers for every bilingual Ontarian (almost 1.7 million versus 716 thousand). Far more unilingual English-speakers resided in Ontario (87.3 per cent) than unilingual French-speakers resided in Quebec (61 per cent). While the vast majority of Quebecers were francophone, unilingual English-speakers still made up 10.5 per cent of the province's population in 1971. In contrast, Ontario had only 1.2 per cent unilingual French-speakers. Lastly, it is worth pointing out that 96.6 per cent of Ontarians in the 1971 census could speak English, while only 88.5 per cent of Quebecers could speak French.

A breakdown of census data by mother tongue shows that more than one-fourth of Quebec's francophone majority was bilingual (25.7 per cent), compared to 4.3 per cent of Ontario's anglophone majority. The former numbered more than 1.2 million, while the latter numbered only 259 thousand – nearly five times fewer. Regarding the official-language minorities, far more francophone Ontarians (nearly 82 per cent) than anglophone Quebecers (nearly 37 per cent) reported they were bilingual. While Ontario's francophone minority was smaller than Quebec's anglophone minority, there were still 394 thousand bilingual francophones in Ontario versus 290 thousand bilingual anglophones in Quebec (a difference of slightly more than 104 thousand). Lastly, nearly 36 per cent of Quebec allophones knew only English in addition to their mother tongue, while over 81 per cent of Ontarian allophones fit this category. Only 47 per cent of Quebec allophones could speak at least French, compared with 86 per cent of Ontario allophones who considered themselves able to speak at least English.

In short, while Ontario's francophone minority was not able to spread French to allophones in the province (0.4 per cent + 5 per cent), Quebec's anglophone minority, benefiting from the definite predominance of English in North America, had been largely successful in spreading its own language (35.8 per cent + 33.1 per cent) in the very heart of the only francophone majority stronghold on the continent. We may even go so far as to say that Quebec's proximity is of no avail to francophone Ontarians, while English makes its way to Quebec even without a sizable anglophone community.

According to the 2001 Census

Using 2001 census data, we can make the same comparison one generation later. Data of interest, adapted slightly in 2001 for comparison with 1971 (Paillé, 2003a, 118n33), appear in tables 9.6 and 9.7.

In thirty years, bilingualism has grown in Canada's two main provinces. In Quebec it has increased more than 13 percentage points to almost 41 per cent of the population. In Ontario it has increased only 3.7 percentage

Table 9.6
Distribution (percentage) of knowledge of French and English by mother tongue,
Quebec, 2001

Mother tongue	Knowledge of French and English				
	French only	English only	French and English	None	Total
French	63.1		36.9		100.0
English		32.0	68.0		100.0
Other	23.0	18.6	50.5	7.9	100.0
Total	53.7	4.6	40.9	0.8	100.0

NOTE: Data shown as in 1971.
SOURCE: Statistics Canada, 2002.

Table 9.7
Distribution (percentage) of knowledge of French and English by mother tongue,
Ontario, 2001

Mother tongue	Knowledge of French and English				
	French only	English only	French and English	None	Total
French	7.1		92.9		100.0
English		91.6	8.4		100.0
Other	0.2	84.5	6.9	8.3	100.0
Total	0.4	85.7	11.9	2.0	100.0

NOTE AND SOURCE: See table 9.6.

points (from 8.3 per cent to 12 per cent). Therefore Quebec far outpaced its neighbour at a time when it nevertheless initiated and upheld a language-management policy to promote French. In 2001 and 1971, 2.2 times more bilinguals were recorded in Quebec (2.9 million) than in Ontario (1.3 million). In Quebec the general rise in bilingualism caused French unilingualism to drop 7 percentage points to less than 54 per cent, and English unilingualism to drop 6 percentage points to 4.6 per cent of the total population. In Ontario, English unilingualism has dropped a few percentage points (85.7 per cent of the population). In short, English unilingualism continues to clearly prevail in Ontario, unlike French unilingualism in Quebec.

While 97.6 per cent of Ontario's population could at least speak English,[5] 94.6 per cent of Quebecers considered themselves able to carry on a conversation at least in French. In this regard, Quebec filled much of the gap separating it from neighbouring Ontario.

Between 1971 and 2001, the percentage of francophones speaking English increased in Quebec: nearly 37 per cent of French mother-tongue

speakers indicated they were able to carry on a conversation in English, up
71 per cent.[6] In Ontario, thanks in particular to French immersion classes[7]
(Grenier, 1989, 42–4; Churchill, 1998, 39), anglophone majority French-
English bilingualism increased 4 percentage points (from 4.3 per cent to 8.4
per cent). However, the actual number of unilingual anglophone Ontarians
rose from 5.7 million to 7.4 million.

We note a significant increase in Quebec anglophone knowledge of the official languages. In the 2001 census, 68 per cent indicated they could carry on
a conversation in French, up more than 31 percentage points in 30 years; likewise for francophone Ontarians, whose bilingualism reached nearly 93 per
cent in 2001.

ONTARIO, THE REFERENCE PROVINCE

Duchesne (1977) compared language behaviours in Quebec and Ontario
in the 1971 census using the "standard population" method (Pressat, 1969,
140–3). This method consists of applying the distribution of French and
English knowledge observed in Ontario to the Quebec population by mother tongue.[8] It is applied to the language issue with any necessary modifications: "e.g., the percentage of allophones speaking only English in Ontario
[becomes] the percentage of allophones speaking only French in Quebec"
(Duchesne, 1977, 47). As Mackey (chapter 2 above) has said, "French in
Ontario should be treated as is English in Quebec and vice versa." Taking
Quebec's anglophone minority as an example, figure 9.1 shows that the
abilities of Ontario's francophone minority (bottom of section A) can be
applied to Quebec's English mother-tongue population (top of section A).
The results (section B) give the number of unilingual English-speakers and
the number of bilingual French-English speakers within Quebec's English
mother-tongue population (bottom of section B).

According to the 1971 Census

The top half of table 9.8 shows absolute numbers based on the 1971 census.
In the bottom half, we have added the differences between data observed
in the 1971 census and those obtained using the comparative method. First,
note that in 1971 Quebec would have had nearly 5 million people with
knowledge of only French instead of 3.7 million, for a positive difference
of more than 1 million. Had this been the case, the three other categories would subsequently have declined: 789,500 fewer bilingual people and
486,500 fewer unilingual English-speakers. Quebecers unable to converse in

Figure 9.1
Numbers of persons in Quebec knowing English only and knowing English and French
among those with English as the mother tongue (based on the knowledge of French only and
English and French among persons with French mother tongue in Ontario)

A: As observed by censuses

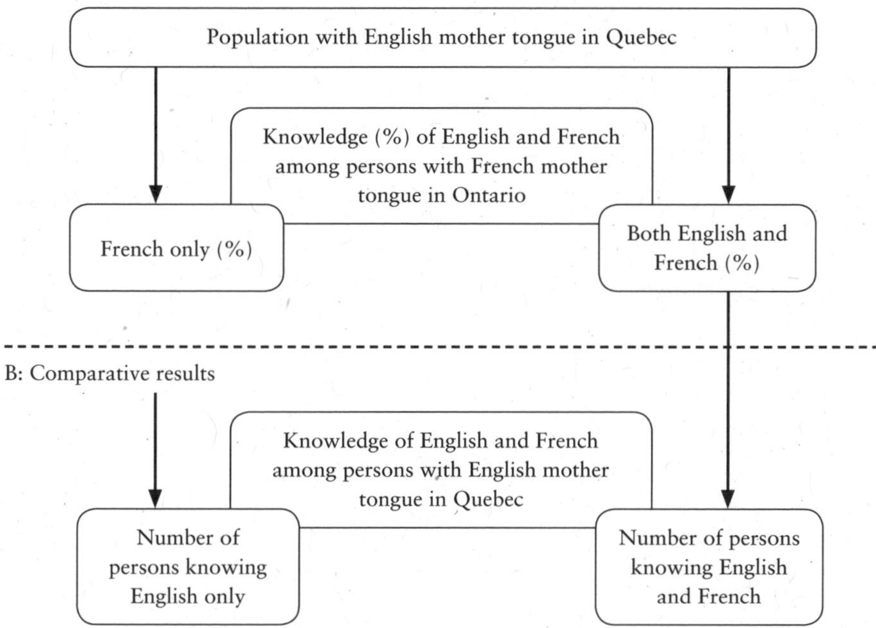

B: Comparative results

either French or English would have declined by nearly 13 thousand. In all,
applying Ontario rates to the Quebec population would have affected more
than 1.6 million people, or 27.3 per cent of the population in 1971.

Duchesne pointed out that applying Ontario rates to the Quebec population in 1971 would have yielded six times fewer bilingual francophones, or
under a quarter-million instead of 1,250,600! Conversely, bilingual anglophones would have more than doubled, exceeding 350 thousand. Lastly, trilingual allophones would have been "the most relieved of what is sometimes
called the burden of bilingualism" (Duchesne, 1977, 48). With Ontario rates,
less than 19 thousand people in this group would have considered themselves
able to converse in French or English instead of more than 123 thousand
(6.6 times fewer). Assuming an identical distribution as in Ontario at the time,
the status of Quebec allophones would have changed the most, as applying
Ontario rates would have affected 67 per cent of this group, compared to
nearly 45 per cent anglophones and only 21.4 per cent francophones.

Table 9.8
Knowledge of French and English by mother tongue should the Ontarian distribution be
applied to Quebec: absolute differences with census, Quebec, 1971

| | Knowledge of French and English | | | | |
Mother tongue	French only	English only	French and English	None	Total
French	4 655 023		211 382		4 866 405
English		144 660	644 170		788 830
Other	301 930	1 305	18 716	50 568	372 520
Total	4 956 953	145 965	874 268	50 568	6 027 755

	Absolute differences with 1971 census				Relative (%) differences
French	1 039 253		–1 039 253		21.4
English		–354 420	354 420		44.9
Other	249 685	–132 125	–104 689	–12 872	67.0
Total	1 288 938	–486 545	–789 522	–12 872	27.3
Sum of positive values					1 643 359

SOURCES: Duchesne, 1977, 48; according to tables 9.1 and 9.4.

According to the 2001 Census

Table 9.9 shows results using 2001 census data. Applying 2001 Ontario bilingualism rates to Quebec's population would alter the responses of nearly 2.3 million people[9] (31.6 per cent of the population; 4.4 percentage points more than in 1971). Emulating the distribution of bilingualism in Ontario would cause this category in Quebec to increase by more than 37 per cent (25 per cent in 1996; Paillé, 2003a, 122), while Quebec's population grew only 18.2 per cent. Quebec and Ontario therefore diverged during this period, as tables 9.4 to 9.7 indicate.

The number of people able to converse only in French in Quebec in 2001 would have exceeded 2.1 million, subtracting more than 1.8 million people from the bilingual group. Nearly 281,400 fewer unilingual anglophones would have been counted in, compared to over 486,500 in 1971 (table 9.8). This considerable difference shows the decline of English unilingualism over this thirty-year period.

The French unilingualism of the francophone majority would have increased more than in 1971, as applying the distribution of anglophone Ontarians to the Quebec population would have altered the responses of

Table 9.9

Knowledge of French and English by mother tongue should the Ontarian distribution be applied to Quebec: absolute differences with census, Quebec, 2001

| | Knowledge of French and English | | | | |
Mother tongue	French only	English only	French and English	None	Total
French	5 312 917		489 110		5 802 028
English		42 232	549 153		591 385
Other	618 784	1 500	50 790	61 099	732 173
Total	5 931 701	43 732	1 089 054	61 099	7 125 585

	Absolute differences with 2001 census				Relative (%) differences
French	1 653 558		–1 653 558		28.5
English		–146 850	146 850		24.8
Other	450 439	–134 514	–319 065	3 140	61.9
Total	2 103 997	–281 364	–1 825 772	3 140	31.6
Sum of positive values					2 253 987

SOURCE: According to tables 9.1, 9.6, and 9.7.

28.5 per cent of francophones, or an additional 7 percentage points. In contrast, minority English-speakers in Quebec improved their knowledge of French to such an extent that a little less than one-fourth of this group in 2001 would have been affected. The number of changes in favour of English unilingualism would have dropped by 25 per cent, compared to calculations made according to the 1971 census. Lastly, almost 454 thousand allophones would have been affected, a lower percentage than in 1971 (62 per cent instead of 67 per cent). Figure 9.2 illustrates what we can observe about the allophones (from tables 9.4, 9.6, and 9.9).

On the whole, despite the language policy to promote French, updating the comparison with Ontario clearly shows that Quebecers learned English more and more throughout the three decades of the study.

Fixing the Reference Point

The results in tables 9.8 and 9.9 show only "net" changes that occurred in Quebec in thirty years – net changes because Ontario also changed during this time. To carry the comparison further, we need only apply the situation observed in Ontario in 1971 to the 2001 Quebec census population. Since knowledge of the official languages spread in Ontario, we assume that

Figure 9.2

Distribution (percentage) of knowledge of French and English among population whose mother tongue is neither French nor English, Quebec, 1971 and 2001

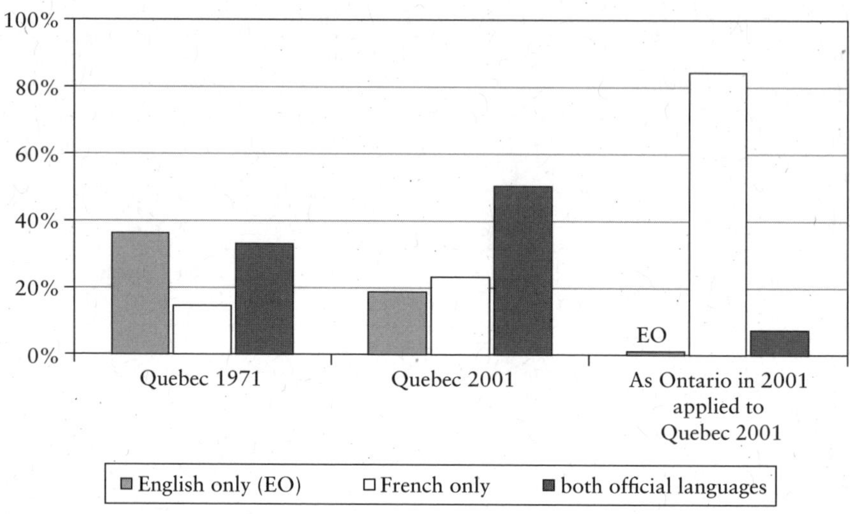

SOURCES: Tables 9.4, 9.6, and 9.9.

Table 9.10

Knowledge of French and English by mother tongue should the Ontarian distribution of 1971 be applied to Quebec in 2001: absolute differences with census, Quebec, 2001

	Knowledge of French and English				
Mother tongue	French only	English only	French and English	None	Total
French	5 550 005		252 023		5 802 028
English		108 451	482 934		591 385
Other	593 432	2 565	36 786	99 390	732 173
Total	6 143 437	111 016	771 742	99 390	7 125 585

	Absolute differences with 2001 census				Relative (%) differences
French	1 890 646		−1 890 646		32.6
English		−80 631	80 631		13.6
Other	425 087	−133 448	−333 069	41 431	63.7
Total	2 315 732	−214 079	−2 143 084	41 431	34.2
Sum of positive values					2 437 794

SOURCE: According to tables 9.1, 9.5, and 9.6.

comparing table 9.10 to table 9.8 will yield more divergent results. Basically, increasing knowledge of English in Quebec should be more apparent if we fix the reference point at its 1971 level.

Our assumption is confirmed in table 9.10, as the results show significant progress in Quebec between 1971 and 2001. When we apply the 1971 Ontario model to the Quebec population in 2001, more than 2.4 million people are affected (34.2 per cent of the 2001 census population).

The bilingualism of Quebec's francophone majority was such in 2001 that applying the rates of Ontario's anglophone majority in 1971 would subtract nearly 1.9 million bilingual francophones (32.6 per cent of French-speakers). The opposite is true for Quebec's anglophone minority. Among tables 9.8, 9.9, and 9.10, the last shows the smallest number of people added to the French-English bilingual group, or only 13.6 per cent of Quebec's anglophone population (11 percentage points lower than in table 9.9). Because more francophone Ontarians learned English over these thirty years, a comparison that returns them to their former status sets the bar lower for anglophone Quebecers in the 2001 census.

Lastly, the relative numbers of allophones affected in tables 9.9 and 9.10 are very close (61.9 per cent and 63.7 per cent respectively). This outcome is no surprise, since the distribution of this population relative to the knowledge of French and English is almost identical in both censuses. In addition, the number of allophones unable to speak either French or English would jump by over 41,400 (table 9.10) instead of only 3,140 (table 9.9).

LANGUAGES MOST OFTEN SPOKEN AT HOME

Considering oneself able to converse in a language does not mean one speaks it regularly. In order to compare certain language behaviours in Quebec to those in Ontario, we will look at languages used at home. In the 2001 census, people were asked to give "the language *most often* spoken at home at the time of the census"[10] (Marmen and Corbeil, 2004, 11).

Democratic countries cannot dictate the language used in private conversations, particularly in households. No Canadian or Quebec language laws do so (Paillé, 2003a; 2004). However, lawmakers have been aware of "language shift," whereby people choose to use a language at home other than the one they learned in childhood. Taking as an example the adoption of English by francophones in other Canadian provinces (Laurin, 1977, 133), and fully aware that people with different languages marry (ibid., 102), Quebec legislators hoped their language policy would lead more and more people to freely choose French over English as their home language (Groupe de travail ministériel, 2000, 6–9). The pull of English in Ontario can be used as a point of comparison for measuring the pull of French in Quebec in 1971 and 2001.

FROM MOTHER TONGUE TO HOME LANGUAGE: A DYNAMIC PHENOMENON

By comparing responses to the question on home language to that on mother tongue, we can measure the net gains or losses in language groups (Paillé, 2003b, 174–6). Responses to the first question establish language use at the time of the census, while responses to the second go back to respondents' childhood. This distinction means that the average distance between the two events is equal to the average age of the census population, that is, thirty in 1971 and thirty-nine in 2001 (Statistique Canada, 2005). Changes in home-language behaviour are infrequent (Termote, 1999, 49–59), almost always permanent, and generally occur before age forty-five (Castonguay, 1994, 27–31).

Canada's requirement that respondents still understand their mother tongue in order to declare it as such leads to an underestimation of reality (Castonguay, 2003, 189–93), as it forces people who no longer understand the first language they learned to give the same answer to both questions. Consequently, these people are not taken into account when it comes to changes in language behaviour.

While Castonguay (2003, passim) often uses the word "assimilation" to describe this phenomenon, we prefer the expressions "language shift" (the phenomenon) and "language transfer" (the event)[11] because subtracting the number of people who speak a given language at home from the number for whom it is the mother tongue yields a highly mixed group. The results make it impossible to distinguish people who are perceived as or consider themselves "assimilated" from those still immersed in their mother tongue and the related culture (Paillé, 2003b, 190–3). Furthermore, Quebec's language policy is not aimed at assimilation (see Maurais in chap. 4).

THE 1971 CENSUS: THE FIRST PORTRAIT OF ITS KIND

Tables 9.11 and 9.12 show the relative distribution (percentage) of languages most often spoken at home in 1971 by each language group in Quebec and Ontario, according to mother tongue. The two variables distinguish the French, English, and other groups.

Table 9.11
Distribution (percentage) of language used most often at home
by mother tongue, Quebec, 1971

Mother tongue	Language used most often at home			
	French	English	Other	Total
French	98.4	1.5	0.1	100.0
English	6.2	92.5	1.2	100.0
Other	9.3	22.7	68.1	100.0
Total	80.8	14.7	4.5	100.0

SOURCE: Duchesne, 1977, 45.

Table 9.12
Distribution (percentage) of language used most often at home
by mother tongue, Ontario, 1971

Mother tongue	Language used most often at home			
	French	English	Other	Total
French	69.7	29.9	0.4	100.0
English	0.2	99.0	0.8	100.0
Other	0.3	40.3	59.4	100.0
Total	4.6	85.1	10.3	100.0

SOURCE: Duchesne, 1977, 46.

First, note that in 1971 Ontario was a bit more anglophone than Quebec was francophone. More than 85 per cent of Ontario's population spoke English at home, while less than 81 per cent of Quebec residents spoke French at home. However, tables 9.1 and 9.2 show the opposite situation according to mother tongue: when we reach into the past of linguistic majorities, Quebec appears more francophone (80.7 per cent) than Ontario appears anglophone (77.5 per cent). Thus, as Duchesne (1977, 44) indicates, until the 1971 census French was at a standstill in Quebec (net gain of only 3,700 francophones), while English had clearly spread in Ontario (net gain of over 590 thousand people).

According to home language, Quebec's anglophone minority made up 14.7 per cent of the population in 1971, or three times more than Ontario's francophone minority with only 4.6 per cent. But a comparison of official-language minorities in these two provinces according to mother tongue (tables 9.1 and 9.2) yields a ratio of almost 2 to 1 (13.1 per cent anglophones in Quebec versus 6.3 per cent francophones in Ontario).

If we consider the data according to home language and mother tongue, a comparison of official-language minorities in Quebec and Ontario thus results in net gains for anglophone Quebecers versus net losses for francophone Ontarians. In absolute numbers, Quebec's anglophone minority gained more than 99 thousand (Castonguay, 1974a), while Ontario's francophone minority lost nearly 130 thousand (Castonguay, 1974b). As Bilinsky writes in chapter 5, "anglophones are not always aware of the harm they have caused francophones"; such is the case of Ontario's anglophone majority with regard to its francophone minority.

Ontario welcomed 53 per cent of international immigrants to Canada between 1951 and 1971. In the latter year 10.3 per cent of the province's population spoke a language other than English or French at home. In contrast, Quebec welcomed only 20.4 per cent, or less than its quota (ISQ, 2004), and only 4.5 per cent of its residents spoke a third language at home. But the nearly 6 percentage points spread between the two provinces in this regard is much smaller than that calculated according to mother tongue: tables 9.1 and 9.2 show a difference of more than 10 percentage points, illustrating that more allophones were being anglicized in Ontario than were being francized in Quebec.

Almost all French mother-tongue Quebecers and English mother-tongue Ontarians spoke mostly their language at home in 1971. In Quebec 98.4 per cent did so; Ontario fared a bit better with 99 per cent. Such was the situation of the francophone and anglophone majorities.

Tables 9.11 and 9.12 reveal very different behaviours for the official-language minorities. While only 6.2 per cent of anglophone Quebecers chose to speak French, nearly 30 per cent of francophone Ontarians spoke English. The absolute numbers back this pattern up: 49 thousand Quebec anglophones spoke French at home, compared with more than 144 thousand Ontario francophones who spoke English.

Lastly, we note a considerable difference in home language distribution among third mother-tongue populations. As we saw above, in 1971 a larger percentage of Quebec allophones than Ontario allophones continued to use their mother tongues. While 68.1 per cent of Quebec allophones spoke their heritage language, only 59.4 per cent of Ontario allophones did so.

But what language did allophones in these two provinces use when their mother tongue was not their first choice? In Ontario almost all used English, while in Quebec they spoke French or English, with a pronounced preference for the latter. Only 9.3 per cent freely chose French, while 22.7 per cent chose English. Because of the strong power of English in North America and its official status in Canada, this language spread extensively throughout

Table 9.13
Distribution (percentage) of language used most often at home
by mother tongue, Quebec, 2001

	Language used most often at home			
Mother tongue	*French*	*English*	*Other*	*Total*
French	98.2	1.4	0.4	100.0
English	12.5	85.7	1.8	100.0
Other	19.7	21.6	58.6	100.0
Total	83.1	10.5	6.5	100.0

SOURCE: Statistique Canada, 2003.

Table 9.14
Distribution (percentage) of language used most often at home
by mother tongue, Ontario, 2001

	Language used most often at home			
Mother tongue	*French*	*English*	*Other*	*Total*
French	55.7	43.4	0.8	100.0
English	0.2	98.9	0.9	100.0
Other	0.3	42.5	57.2	100.0
Total	2.7	82.7	14.5	100.0

SOURCE: See table 9.13.

the population as the common language of public activities, as well as the usual language in immigrants' home, the principal place where parents raised their children.

According to the 2001 Census

Tables 9.13 and 9.14 show the distribution of home languages in 2001 for each of the three language groups in Quebec and Ontario. The population of these provinces as a whole shows an overall increase in the use of French in Quebec homes compared to English in the Ontarian model (last row of percentages in tables 9.13 and 9.14). Quebec's francophone majority increased to 83.1 per cent of the population, compared to Ontario's anglophone majority, which dropped 2.4 percentage points (from 85.1 per cent to 82.7 per cent).

The data in these tables are not fully comparable to those in tables 9.11 and 9.12. Major changes regarding language made by Statistics Canada, starting in 1991, launched a new statistical series. The impact of these changes suddenly strengthened the official-language majorities to the detriment of minorities. Assuming the same bias in the majorities of both provinces, we could say that progress in the use of French in Quebec is real, compared to the use of English in Ontario. Other changes were made to the French version of the 2001 census, further complicating data comparability.

We have already observed that Quebec's anglophone minority underwent a demographic decline. According to the percentages calculated based on home language, anglophone Quebecers dwindled from 14.7 per cent to 10.5 per cent of the 2001 census population, for an absolute loss of 141 thousand people in one generation. This is due primarily to greater anglophone migratory deficit between Quebec and the rest of Canada (Termote, 1991, 308; 1999, 132). The relative weight of francophone Ontarians dropped to 2.7 per cent in thirty years. Ontario had 45 thousand fewer francophones in the 2001 census than in 1971. Anglicization was the main cause of this erosion.

Lastly, Ontario far outpaced Quebec with regard to the number of third home-language speakers. In 2001, allophones made up 14.5 per cent of Ontario's population, compared with only 6.5 per cent of Quebec's. In absolute numbers, Ontario had nearly 1.2 million allophones more than Quebec (1.6 million versus 460 thousand).

There are no significant changes between the 1971 and 2001 censuses with regard to the home language of the two majorities. Almost all French mother-tongue Quebecers and English mother-tongue Ontarians usually spoke their respective mother tongues in 2001. This trend even intensified slightly between 1996 and 2001 (Paillé, 2003a, 150–1).

A comparison of the language minorities of these two provinces shows the disruptive effects of changes made by Statistics Canada in data collection and processing in the 1991 and 2001 censuses. It is hardly surprising that more francophone Ontarians used English at home in 2001 than in 1971. However, the scope of this anglicization may raise doubts, as it took fifteen years to go from 29.9 per cent in 1971 to 30.9 per cent in 1986 (Statistique Canada, 1989), compared with only five years (1986–91) to jump to 38.4 per cent (Statistique Canada, 1993)![12] The anglicization rate increased to 43.4 per cent over the subsequent ten years (1991–2001).

The same is true of the percentage of anglophone Quebecers using French at home. After increasing slightly from 6.2 per cent in 1971 to 6.6 per cent in 1986 (Statistique Canada, 1989), it appears to have jumped to 9.3 per cent in 1991 (Statistique Canada, 1993) and then 12.5 per cent in 2001. Francized anglophones in Quebec have supposedly increased from 49 thousand to 74 thousand in thirty years, or 51 per cent. The number of francophone Ontarians using English at home appears to have risen from more than 144 thousand in 1971 to more than 221 thousand in 2001 (an anglicization rate increase of 53.3 per cent in one generation). But given the significant changes in data collection for the 1991 and 2001 censuses, it is possible that these increases are largely artificial, especially in the five-year period from 1986 to 1991.

In both provinces we observe a lower percentage of allophones using their mother tongue at home. Ontario shows a slight difference from the 1971 census: 57.2 per cent versus 59.4 per cent thirty years earlier. But the difference is significant in Quebec, where the percentage of allophones still speaking their mother tongue at home dropped nearly 10 percentage points (from 68.1 per cent to 58.6 per cent). Again, these changes are due in part to modifications in data collection.

All language choices made by allophone households in Ontario were to the benefit of English. In the 2001 census 42.5 per cent of Ontario allophones usually spoke English, up 2.2 percentage points in one generation, while the use of French remained unchanged at only 0.3 per cent. As we already noted (Paillé, 1991b), Ontario remained a very anglicizing destination for international immigrant language groups.

In Quebec a significant change occurred over the period. While English was still the language choice of most allophones, with 21.6 per cent (down only 1 percentage point), French made significant headway. From only 9.3 per cent in 1971, it rose to 19.7 per cent in 2001. While in 1971 only 29 per cent of allophones had made a language transfer toward French,[13] nearly 48 per cent had done so in 2001.[14] Although this growth is partially artificial, as a result of the unlikely jump from 28.6 per cent to 36.7 per cent observed between 1986 and 1991 (Statistique Canada, 1989; 1993), it may still be considered a sign that language policies had an indirect effect on the use of French at home (Castonguay, 1999b, 46–8). Quebec thus moved closer to the Ontario model.

BACK TO THE ONTARIO REFERENCE

As in our earlier evaluation (Paillé, 2003a, 132–6), we will use the "standard population" method discussed above. As illustrated in figure 9.3, we calculate how many people may have spoken a given language in Quebec households in 1971 and 2001 (bottom of section B), assuming that the three language groups behaved in a similar way to those in Ontario. Here again, the behaviours of Ontario's language majority are applied to the Quebec majority. We do the same for the official-language minorities. With regard to the allophone language choices given as an example in figure 9.3, anglicization rates in

Figure 9.3
Language most often spoken at home in Quebec among persons with a mother tongue other than English or French (based on the language most often spoken at home among Ontarians with a mother tongue other than English of French).

A: As observed by censuses

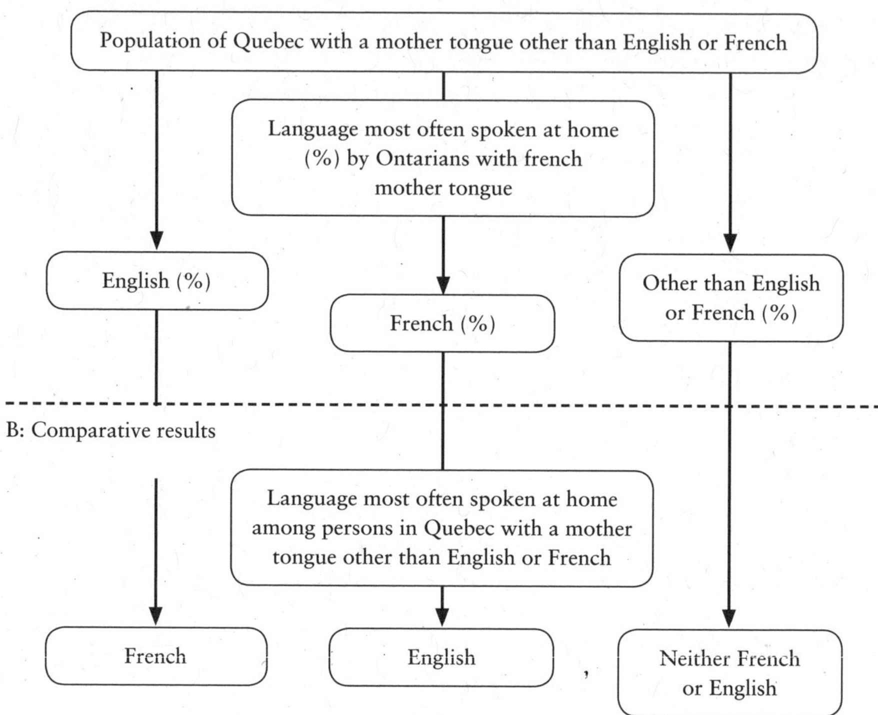

Ontario become francization rates in Quebec. Conversely, the very low francization rates in Ontario are used to calculate the number of allophones who would have chosen to speak English in Quebec, according to our assumption.

1971 Quebec Modelled on Ontario

Table 9.15 lists the absolute numbers we would have obtained in the 1971 census. They show that Quebec's French home-language population would have exceeded 5.2 million, or an additional 334,400 people. The province's francophone majority would have made up 86.3 per cent of the population, reducing the number of English home-language speakers by slightly over 561 thousand. The anglophone minority would then have made up 9.3 per cent

Table 9.15
Language used most often at home by mother tongue should the Ontarian distribution be applied to Quebec: absolute differences with census, Quebec, 1971

| Mother tongue | Language used most often at home | | | |
	French	English	Other	Total
French	4 818 477	9 920	38 008	4 866 405
English	235 878	550 188	2 764	788 830
Other	150 103	1 151	221 277	372 530
Total	5 204 457	561 259	262 049	6 027 765

	Absolute differences with 1971 census			Relative (%) differences
French	32 012	–63 595	31 583	1.3
English	186 818	–179 732	–7 086	23.7
Other	115 523	–83 289	–32 233	31.0
Total	334 352	–326 616	–7 736	6.1
Sum of positive values				365 935

SOURCE: Duchesne, 1977, 48; according to tables 9.1 and 9.11.

of the population instead of 14.7 per cent. In all, 6.1 per cent of Quebec's total population, or 366 thousand people, would have changed their home-language behaviour in favour of French, regardless of mother tongue.

A close look at the results in table 9.15 shows that the three language groups contributed to the virtual increase of French use at home. Applying Ontario rates to Quebec would have led 32 thousand more francophones to continue using their mother tongue. Had Quebec's anglophone minority behaved in 1971 like francophone Ontarians with regard to English, nearly 24 per cent of them would have changed their language behaviour in favour of French. As Duchesne (1977, 47) writes, "through language transfers with anglophones, francophones would have achieved net gains instead of net losses." Thirty-one per cent of Quebec allophones would have joined home-language French-speakers, mostly at the expense of the group that had already chosen English (83,300) instead of mother-tongue speakers (32,200).

Ontario Rates Applied to 2001 Quebec

As we see in table 9.16, modelling the language behaviours of Quebec households in 2001 on those of Ontario would force almost 421 thousand people to change their home language (5.9 per cent of the census population that year). But this would be only 0.2 per cent fewer than according to the 1971

Table 9.16
Language used most often at home by mother tongue should the Ontarian distribution be applied to Quebec: absolute differences with census, Quebec, 2001

| | Language used most often at home | | | |
Mother tongue	French	English	Other	Total
French	2 739 264	10 317	52 451	5 802 033
English	256 821	329 610	4 961	591 393
Other	311 011	2 454	418 710	732 175
Total	6 307 097	342 381	476 122	7 125 600
	Absolute differences with 2001 census			Relative (%) differences
French	39 636	–71 691	32 054	1.2
English	182 633	–176 929	–5 704	30.9
Other	166 448	–155 907	–10 541	22.7
Total	388 717	–404 526	15 809	5.9
Sum of positive values				420 772

SOURCE: According to tables 9.1, 9.13, and 9.14.

census (table 9.15). Must we conclude that Quebec simply stood still between 1971 and 1996 (Paillé, 2003a, 134) and then made weak progress between 1996 and 2001? A close look at table 9.16 leads to a more measured answer.

While there was no significant change among francophones (only 1.3 per cent in 1971 and 1.2 per cent in 2001), we observe major differences among anglophones and allophones: 30.9 per cent of anglophones would have to change their home-language behaviour, compared to 23.7 per cent thirty years earlier – an increase in their case. In contrast, as figure 9.4 clearly illustrates, allophones show a decrease: 22.7 per cent of those surveyed in 2001 would not speak the same home language if their language behaviours matched those in Ontario (a decline in thirty years, given the 31 per cent indicated in table 9.15). Anglophones and allophones balanced each other out to produce overall results that are almost identical to those in 1971. Quebec anglophones would have strayed from the francophone Ontarian model, while allophones would have approximated the behaviour of their Ontario counterparts.

In a quarter-century, progress was made in the adoption of French by Quebec allophones, compared to the adoption of English by Ontarians whose mother tongue was neither French nor English. We can calculate this progress at nearly 27 per cent of the 1977 objective.[15] This figure is significant, as home-language behaviours change slowly.

Figure 9.4
Distribution (percentage) of language used most often at home among population whose
mother tongue is neither French nor English, Quebec, 1971 and 2001

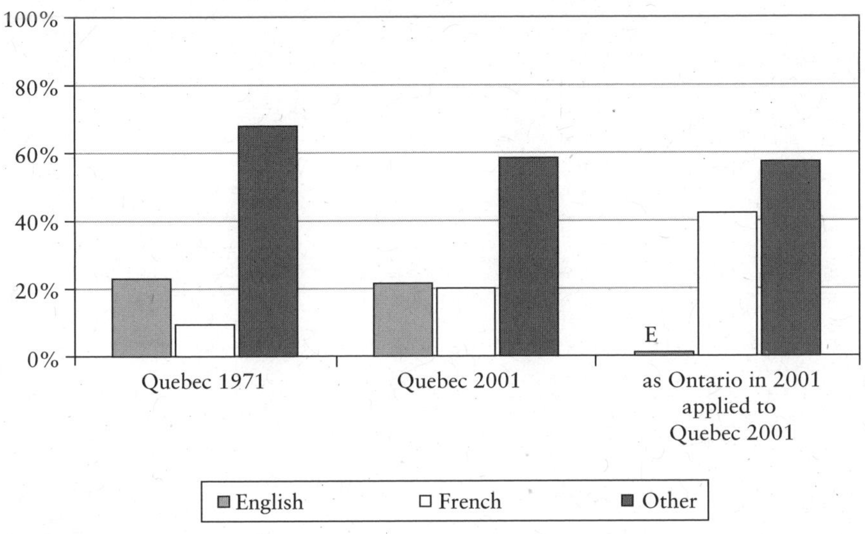

SOURCES: Tables 9.11, 9.13, and 9.16.

2001 Quebec Modelled on 1971 Ontario

This last observation is somewhat substantiated in table 9.17. When we apply
the home-language behaviours observed in Ontario in 1971 (table 9.12) to
the three language groups surveyed in Quebec in 2001 (table 9.1), we arrive
at 9 thousand fewer allophones, or 21.3 per cent of those surveyed. Regarding
the relative number of people affected in 1971 (table 9.15), 31 per cent of the
established objective would have been achieved.[16]

Lastly, we note that the results in table 9.17, compared to those in table
9.16, reduce the number of Quebec anglophones speaking French at home
by nearly 80 thousand. Instead of 31 per cent of Quebec anglophones (2001
rates), we obtain 17.4 per cent by applying Ontario rates for 1971 with any
necessary modifications. This type of comparative exercise shows, in turn,
how the status of francophone Ontarians has declined over a quarter-century!

CONCLUSION

From the very beginning, the Ontarian model gave rise to studies comparing Quebec and Ontario. Initial analysis based on 1971 census data looked

Table 9.17
Language used most often at home by mother tongue should the Ontarian distribution of 1971 be applied to Quebec in 2001: absolute differences with census, Quebec, 2001

Mother tongue	Language used most often at home			
	French	*English*	*Other*	*Total*
French	5 744 889	11 827	45 316	5 802 033
English	176 840	412 481	2 072	591 393
Other	295 013	2 261	434 900	732 175
Total	6 216 742	426 569	482 288	7 125 600

	Absolute differences with 2001 census			Relative (%) differences
French	45 261	–70 181	24 919	1.2
English	102 651	–94 058	–8 594	17.4
Other	150 450	–156 100	5 650	21.3
Total	298 362	–320 338	21 976	4.6
Sum of positive values				328 932

SOURCE: Aaccording to tables 9.1, 9.12, and 9.13.

at the knowledge of Canada's official languages and their use in the home, where children learn their mother tongue. Using 1996 census data, we updated these studies for the first time (Paillé, 2003a) a quarter-century later. Using 2001 census data, this report assesses the entire journey one generation later.

Knowledge of French and English

In 1971 Quebec considerably outranked Ontario with regard to bilingual knowledge of French and English. The Charter of the French Language was not aimed at making Quebec as "unilingually French" as Ontario was "unilingually English." One generation later, we note that bilingualism has progressed further in Quebec than in Ontario.

While French immersion courses have helped promote bilingualism in Ontario, Quebec's language policy has had a far greater impact, particularly among anglophones, 68 per cent of whom consider themselves able to speak French. Although the language policy strengthened the status of French in Quebec, it did not have the adverse effect of leading Quebecers toward personal French unilingualism. On the contrary, Quebec has made greater strides than Ontario with regard to individual bilingualism. Is it not ironic that bilingualism in Canada, although called a "symbol of Canadian identity" (Churchill, 1998, 13), is more highly concentrated in Quebec than in English-speaking Canada?

Home Language

Seeing as the knowledge of English in Ontario is much more widespread than the knowledge of French in Quebec, it is highly likely that English is spoken much more often in Ontario households than French in Quebec. Relevant data from the 1971 and 2001 censuses confirm this supposition.

In the 1971 census, 85 per cent of Ontario's population spoke English at home, while 81 per cent of Quebecers spoke French at home. A comparison of home-language and mother-tongue data shows that French made only a slight net gain in Quebec (fewer than 4 thousand), while English in Ontario enjoyed a net gain of nearly 600 thousand additional speakers.

Both in Ontario and in Quebec the percentage of allophones speaking a third language at home decreased between 1971 and 2001. Despite the non-comparability of data, we were able to conclude that Ontario is still a place where international immigrants are anglicized, while in Quebec the percentage of allophones using French at home increased (9.3 per cent for 1971 versus 19.7 per cent for 2001). French, then, has made some significant progress.

Lastly, applying the language shift rates observed in Ontario to the Quebec population allows us to measure the positive effects of Quebec's language policy thirty years after its adoption. Though the data from different censuses are not fully comparable, we can say with Pierre Anctil that "a new trend on the language front … will probably continue to grow in the coming decades" (see chap. 11 below). But will this expected growth be jeopardized by both the lack of political will and the general demographical context?

A Lack of Political Will

Although one cannot say that the current decade (2000–10) has been characterized by a "linguistic crisis" of the same nature as before, some particular situations require an attentive examination. A recent poll revealed that "three Montrealers out of five find that the state of the French language in their city continues to deteriorate" (*Journal de Montréal*, 2009). So numerous are those that rely on the backing, or even the extension, of the language policies in force.

In the first place, one suggestion to better implement the Charter of the French Language (Bill 101) is mainly about the language used at work, in signs, and in relationships between both citizens and enterprises (MMF, 2008). Often, the media note a slackening in these domains that should be, after three decades, entirely Frenchified.

Others suggest the need to further extend the intervention of Bill 101, especially concerning language in the workplace. The law, which currently imposes French where workers are numerous enough, it is alleged, also should apply to small and mid-sized firms. The Mouvement Montréal français, among others, "considers it essential that enterprises of less than 50 employees be subject to a certification process" (MMF, 2007). Such groups believe the same for the language used in teaching immigrants' children, inasmuch as they would like to extend the obligation of schooling in French up to CEGEP students, who are at a level just before university (Beaulieu, 2005), which proved to be an unequivocal success in elementary and high schools.

Parts of language policy fall outside the Charter of the French Language, escaping the minister responsible for its application. This is the case with the teaching of French to adult immigrants, which falls under the responsibility of the Ministère de l'immigration et des communautés culturelles" (Paillé, 2008c). Thus many immigrants who know only English upon their arrival in Quebec evolve comfortably in this language in Montreal, where they can find a job.

The Quebec government is committed to ensuring adequate services in French training to adult immigrants "as early as their arrival" (Paillé, 2007, 94). However, as "the calendar of French formation only includes four cycles per year" (MICC, 2008, 12), the delay is averaging more than two months. To fulfill its commitments, the government should establish a sufficient number of new French classes every week to match the steady stream of recently arrived immigrants. An agency in charge of this vital mission is therefore imperative (Paillé, 2008c). Considering the 55,000 immigrants whom Quebec hopes to welcome by 2010, seventeen new classes would have to start every week and should last as many weeks as necessary.

But beyond relying on, or even widening, Quebec's language policy, one observes over a decade a change in the attitude of the government. Some contend that the Quebec government "doesn't behave with immigrants, allophones, or enterprises as if French were the official language of Quebec" (Courtois, 2009, 27). On the contrary, "the logic that prevails in our public utilities is bilingualism" (ibid., 25–6). Besides, "the Quebec government pays for English courses for immigrants who suffer the handicap of knowing only French" (Dutrisac, 2008).

Finally, the attitude of French-speakers themselves toward their own language is often not constructive (Dufour, 2008). Too numerous are French-speakers who take advantage of the least opportunity to express themselves in English. Proud of their capability and their openness – a euphemism to hide their servitude – they heighten the prestige of English, losing as many opportunities to give build reliance on French.

Prominent Demographical Trends

The Quebec-Ontario comparison for 1971 and 2001 that we have made in this chapter, relative to the knowledge of Canada's two official languages and language shifts, provides a global profile resulting from many factors. The method we have used does not measure the relative importance of these factors. Let us describe those major factors briefly in the following paragraphs.

First, Quebec's language policy must be considered in the demographical context of recent decades. For forty years the province's fertility level has stagnated below the replacement level, which is 2.1 children per woman (ISQ, 2008). With an average total fertility rate (TFR) of 1.55 children per woman from 1976 to 2007, the deficit of births compared to a TFR of 2.1 children is about 25 per cent. Despite some sudden rises in each decade, the TFR never increased above 1.67 children in any single year. The fertility contribution of allophone women who have adopted French as their language most spoken at home is steadily rising (Paillé, 2008a). However, the newborns they add to the French-speaking group – assuming that those children will be raised in French – remains quite insufficient to increase the language majority to a sustainable TFR (ibid.).

In spite of a 68 per cent rise in international migration to Quebec in less than ten years (from 26,600 in 1998 to 44,700 in 2006), no one can yet see a compensatory factor to offset the weak fertility level. Besides, migrants stay very strongly concentrated in Montreal: three out of four of them settle in this major city, where only 16 per cent of Quebec's French-speaking population live. The Montreal metropolitan area attracts up to nine immigrants out of ten, as compared in 2006 to both 48 per cent of Quebec's population and 40 per cent of French-speakers.

Immigrants' concentration in Montreal contributes to the relative bending of the French-speaking majority, no matter its definition (mother tongue or language most spoken at home). By 2006, French mother-tongue Montrealers accounted for less than half the population (Statistique Canada, 2007), a loss of more than 10 points within 20 years (Paillé, 1989, 23). As for the Montrealers expressing themselves mostly in French at home – relatively bending as well (OQLF, 2005, 15) – the most recent demographical projections confirm their erosion: around 2016–21, an absolute majority of 50 per cent will have been eroded (Termote, 2008).

"Making Quebec a province as deeply marked by French as Ontario is by English" (quotation from the minister appointed to manage Bill 101) does not seem to be any more on the Quebec government's agenda. More than thirty years after the linguistic laws of the 1970s, French is not yet as entrenched in Montreal as English is in Toronto. Reliance on and widening of the language policies therefore appear urgently necessary. However, in the present demographical context, they could still prove to be insufficient.

NOTES

This study was funded by the Hector-Fabre Chair. A first draft of this chapter has been summarized in French in *L'Action nationale* 97, no. 7 (2007): 2–33.

1 In Canada and Quebec, laws are often referred to by the number of the original bill. Thus "Bill 101" is the same as the Charter of the French Language.

2 Contrary to the United Nations Human Rights Commission, which believes that "anglophone Canadian citizens may not be considered a linguistic minority" (see Maurais in chap. 4 above), Canada defines its linguistic minorities on a provincial or territorial basis.

3 A peak of 29.7 per cent was attained in the 1951 census (Lachapelle and Henripin, 1980, 36).

4 Between 1986 and 2003 Ontario welcomed 54.6 per cent of international immigrants to Canada.

5 Jacques Maurais indicates that 97 per cent of the United States population speaks English (see chap. 4). On the whole, Ontario is part of the same trend.

6 Changes to the French version of the 2001 census questionnaire may explain the considerable difference between this result and that in our earlier study based on the 1996 census, when we obtained only 56 per cent in twenty-five years (Paillé, 2003a, 119).

7 In the mid-1990s Ontario had over 150,000 French-immersion students, or almost half the total in Canada.

8 In the French version of this text, we also referred to certain urban ecology studies (Paillé, 2003a, 120).

9 See the "sum of positive values" in table 9.9.

10 Boldface type was used in the 2001 census question. In the 1971 census the question read as follows: "What language do you MOST OFTEN speak at home now?" (boldface capitals) (Dominion Bureau of Statistics, 1971, Question 17).

11 Transfers are to shift what births are to fertility.

12 Calculated based on single statements (a single mother tongue and a single home language) in the 1991 and 1996 censuses respectively.

13 According to table 9.11: 9.3 ÷ (100 − 68.1) × 100.
14 According to table 9.13: 19.7 ÷ (100 − 58.6) × 100.
15 Using the formula (1 − (22.7/31)) × 100, we obtain 26.7 per cent.
16 The same formula, (1 − (21.3/31)) × 100, gives 31.2 per cent.

PART FOUR

Group Perspectives

Introduction to Part Four

MICHAEL A. MORRIS

A SURVEY OF THE LITERATURE

Group perspectives on language policy are especially important, since language policy generally aspires to influence the behaviour of groups while also being influenced by them. The comparative group literature relates Canadian groups to one another as well as to international counterpart groups.

McRae (1978) compares bilingual language districts in Finland and Canada, including a list of factors explaining why this aspect of Canadian federal language policy failed. McRae (1983–98) also compares groups in various democratic multilingual societies while giving attention to language policies (see Part One above). This series of books includes separate volumes on the language policies and approaches of Switzerland, Belgium, and Finland in which occasional brief comparisons are made with Canada. McRae's contrast of these same four countries in 2007 was reviewed in chapter 1. Also see McRae's excellent chapter on Canadian language policy in Edwards (1998), likewise cited in my general introduction.

McRae updated his assessment of Switzerland, including brief comparisons with Canada in a section on "Multilingual Societies" of a book edited by Schneiderman (1991, 167–72). In the same section, another short article by Jean Laponce compared Canadian language policy with that of other multilingual societies (ibid., 173–9). Laponce, like McRae, is critical of Canadian federal language policy in relying excessively on the principle of personality rather the principle of territoriality, a criticism he made earlier in a well-known book (Laponce, 1984, 1987). Territoriality, it is argued, best protects the cultural and linguistic diversity of minority groups.

Laponce (2006) returned to his theme of territoriality in a recent book with particular emphasis on laws or patterns governing relations between dominant and minority languages. Of particular interest for us, he includes short profiles of how five countries deal with the teaching of dominant and minority languages in schools (France, Quebec/Canada, Switzerland, Belgium, and Catalonia/Spain). Laponce generally views in a positive light the contrasting ways the latter four have promoted minority languages in schools.

A book edited by Wardhaugh (1983) assesses competing Canadian language groups and their relationship to language legislation (see Part One), but his purpose is to interpret Canadian nationhood rather than to develop sustained comparisons. A volume edited by Edwards (1984) is broader in scope in assessing linguistic minority groups in Australia, Britain, Canada, and the United States in separate chapters. However, there is no sustained comparison between the policies of these countries.

Current thinking of the Quebec government about groups within the province as related to language policy is reflected in the final summary chapter by Pierre Georgeault, at the time director of research and administration of the Higher Council of the French Language, in an edited volume sponsored by the same governmental body (Georgeault, 2006). While language policy makes French the dominant language for all inhabitants of Quebec in the public sphere, the rights of ethno-linguistic groups, including anglophones, allophones, and the indigenous nations, are recognized and encouraged.

A journal issue on "official language minorities in Canada" (anglophones in Quebec and francophones in Canada outside Quebec) acknowledges in the introduction that the "aim of this issue is not directly comparative in its approach" (Landry and Forgues 2007, 4). A final article in the issue (Thériault, 2007) does compare the identity process in these Canadian minority groups with the United States, although little attention is given to language policy.

Parts Three (non-linguistic issues) and Four (groups) of this study overlap, since assessment of issues usually includes relations between groups and, conversely, analysis of groups tends to delve deeply into issues. The relative emphasis of different publications on issues or groups determines in which part they have been placed. A case in point is *Demolinguistic Trends and the Evolution of Canadian Institutions* (1989), which was reviewed above in the introduction to Part Three but also gives sustained attention to relationships between the anglophone and francophone communities.

Similarly, there is overlap between Parts Two (international comparisons) and Four (group comparisons), as in the case of Maurais's important collection of articles cited above on indigenous languages and groups in Quebec (Maurais, 1992). A sizable work edited by John Edwards (1998) does give considerable attention to Canadian language policies (Part One), although the basic orientation of the book is on groups (Part Four). Current language questions are assessed in the first fifteen chapters, which are followed by eleven chapters dealing with the language situation in every Canadian province and territory; many of these assess groups from different perspectives. Substantial materials are thus assembled by Edwards for making group as well as other kinds of comparisons. However, the introduction to the book does not make comparisons, and there is no final chapter formulating overall conclusions and comparisons.

AN OVERVIEW OF THE CHAPTERS IN PART FOUR

In chapter 10, "Language Policy in Ontario: From the Recognition of Linguistic Rights to the Free-Market Policy," Normand Labrie discusses how the phenomenon of globalization currently affects the totality of linguistic minorities, at least in the Western world, such as in Canada or the European Union. Migration and the prominence of economic factors, both typical of globalization, force linguistic minorities to avail themselves of new strategies, as much toward the state of which they are a part as toward the rest of the world, and to redefine themselves inwardly, to reinvent themselves to some degree. From this perspective, Franco-Ontarian communities are not an exception; they can in fact serve as an illustration of a larger phenomenon that affects various linguistic communities. The Franco-Ontarian minority of about half a million people is the largest francophone group in Canada outside Quebec and hence holds particular importance for the future of the two official- language communities.

In this chapter Labrie examines the evolution of language policy in Ontario through discourse analysis, focusing particularly on Franco-Ontarian communities. For him, language policy is defined as the exercise of social control over pluralism and linguistic variation. Three types of predominant discourses over the course of recent decades are identified – traditionalist, modernizing, and globalizing – each corresponding to successive historical periods and to the dominant ideologies of their respective time.

In chapter 11, "The End of the Language Crisis in Quebec: Comparative Implications," Pierre Anctil carefully tracks population and linguistic characteristics of the anglophone, francophone, and allophone groups in Quebec over time. While the main focus of his chapter is on these evolving group traits in relation to one another (Part Four), his concern with history (Part One) and non-linguistic issue comparisons (Part Three) complements other parts of the book.

While he focuses on key groups in Quebec over time, Anctil, in reaching well beyond this subject into other comparisons, reinforces his conclusion that the long-standing language crisis in Quebec is ending. Broader comparative implications are drawn in the conclusion of the chapter.

10

Language Policy in Ontario:
From the Recognition of Linguistic Rights
to the Free-Market Policy

NORMAND LABRIE

Francophones' position in Ontario regarding language politics evolved during the twentieth century as a result of political struggles led by French Canadians across Canada and of social, political, and economic transformations in Canadian society. In this chapter we examine the evolution of language politics in Ontario. Language politics is defined as the exercise of social control over linguistic diversity and linguistic variation. Three types of discourse were dominant in the past decades – traditionalist, modernizing, and globalizing – which correspond to three distinct periods and to the dominant ideologies of their respective eras (Heller and Budach, 1999; Heller and Labrie, 2003). Nowadays, elements of each of these discourses coexist in francophones' position on language politics, while one can observe a transition of discourse based on the recognition of linguistic rights within a juridical framework towards one based on the application of free-market rules in an economic framework. Here the comparative approach consists mainly in situating language politics within a federated state, Ontario, in relation to its links to a federal state, Canada, and in nuancing the meaning attributed to current discourse formations on language politics according to their emergence on a diachronic level.

Starting with a brief presentation of a conceptual framework for the study of language politics that draws on discourse analysis, this chapter will focus on the changing positions of Franco-Ontarians regarding linguistic diversity and language policy in the twentieth century. It will conclude with an analysis of the current coexistence of discourse formations typical of the diverse eras and of the new balance in their articulation.

A DISCOURSE ANALYSIS OF LANGUAGE POLITICS

Many definitions of language policy and language planning have been proposed in the last fifty years from different perspectives (Cooper, 1989; Calvet, 1996). A sociolinguistic study of language politics implies that one considers more than just written policies such as legislation, and that any form of social control on language use needs to be taken into consideration. Therefore I opt for the larger notion of "language politics," a notion that entails language policy. Language politics corresponds to the exercise of social control on linguistic diversity and linguistic variation through political channels, which include, on one hand, the expression of power relationships within the civil society and, on the other, the codification of language practices by agents who hold institutional power. This sociolinguistic definition of language politics allows one to study the politics of language through the analysis of discourse about linguistic diversity and linguistic variation elaborated at different sites: institutions, civil society, media, and academia (Labrie, 1999).

A discourse analysis approach to language politics has already been proposed by Blommaert (1996a; 1996b; 1999), who demonstrates that specialists in language planning are creating a discourse that is part of language policy. He argues that it is therefore important to analyze their implicit ideological positions. Fairclough's (1992) critical discourse analysis can be useful in this matter, although it has been based essentially on the analysis of political texts. Such an analysis has also been undertaken by van Dyjk (1993), who has studied the political discourse of politicians on linguistic diversity. Finally, Bokhorst (1998) has provided a discourse analysis of media production on language policy in Singapore. Guespin and Marcellesi (1986) made an important distinction between the practice of language politics (which they call glotto-politics) and its analysis. In terms of practice, discourse on linguistic diversity and linguistic variation can be considered a manifestation of social control of these phenomena. Such discourse might be aimed at the definition of new linguistic regulations that are intended to increase or decrease linguistic diversity and linguistic variation, as well as at the modification or abolishment of existing linguistic policies. When it is produced by institutions, it can coincide with the formulation of language policies. In terms of analysis, the discourse on linguistic diversity and linguistic variation produced and reproduced in the media, as well as by social scientists, may also be considered part of language politics.

Basing my analysis on the literature (Bourhis, 1994; Breton, 1968; Coulombe, 1995; Foucher, 1993; Labrie, 1995; Mougeon, 1994), I first examine in this chapter how Franco-Ontarians' positions on language politics changed during the twentieth century and what the new dimensions of the political struggles resulting from linguistic diversity and variation are. As a result of these new realities and perceptions, I further examine the coexisting positions of Franco-Ontarians today on language politics, which were expressed through various types of discourse related to three important historical periods, described as traditionalist, modernizing, and globalizing discourses. Data for this last section originate from participant observation conducted during a two-day provincial meeting at which leaders from approximately two hundred provincial francophone organizations participated, in order to establish an umbrella organization that would be responsible for negotiating financial support from the federal government and the distribution of monetary resources granted to the francophone community.[1]

FRANCOPHONES IN ONTARIO

A small part of the French-speaking population of Ontario originates from the original French population established there as long as three hundred years ago. But most descend from Quebecers who moved to Ontario during the nineteenth century to work in the farming, mining, or lumber industries or in the twentieth century to work in industries such as automobile manufacturing. During the past several decades, French-speaking people started to migrate to larger cities such as Toronto and Ottawa from the Middle East, the Maghreb, and Europe. More recently, an important influx of French-speaking immigrants from Africa and the Caribbean Islands has also contributed to francophone diversity in Ontario. At the same time, highly educated French-speaking Canadians moved to Ontario to work either as bilingual civil servants or as bilingual white-collar employees.

As indicated by the 2001 census, the number of persons who have French as their mother tongue is 509,265, or 4.5 per cent of the total population, and the number of people who speak mostly French at home is 307,295, or 2.7 per cent of the total population of the province (Statistique Canada, 2002). In comparison, in the 1911 census the population of French origin in Ontario was 202,442, representing 8 per cent of the province's total population (Joy, 1992). There has been an increase in the total French-speaking population, although its relative proportion compared to the total population has decreased. However, comparison of data from censuses that are based on different questions, as well as different respondents, should be approached with caution. For example, recent data on the speakers of French as mother tongue do not include francophones originating from Haiti who

have Creole as their mother tongue or from the Maghreb for whom Arabic
is the mother tongue, while French is their usual language of public use.

A BRIEF RETROSPECTIVE OF LANGUAGE POLICY IN THE TWENTIETH CENTURY

Three distinct periods characterize the evolution of language policy regarding the French-speaking minority in Ontario: a first period of assimilation policy (1912–68), a second period of recognition of minority rights of
francophones as one of the two founding nations of Canada (1968–88),
and a third period (from 1988) that I refer to as the period of free-market
policy. Corresponding with these three periods are the different strategies
among the francophone communities regarding the social control of linguistic diversity and linguistic variation. Simultaneous with the change in social
context has been a shift in strategies to cope with language politics.

Assimilation Policies, 1912–1968

In the first period, which followed Confederation in 1867, the Ontario
Department of Education adopted regulations in 1890 making English the
language of instruction, while allowing French in the early grades of bilingual schools if students did not understand English. Later, in 1912, the provincial government enacted Regulation 17, declaring English to be the sole
language of instruction after grade 3 and limiting the study of French to one
hour a day. Regulation 17, which was abrogated in 1927, coincided with the
general belief in the Western world that bilingualism was detrimental to the
cognitive development of students (Tabouret-Keller, 1988). This language
policy, adopted by a government controlled by the anglophone majority
and aimed at the assimilation of the French-speaking minority (as well as
of other linguistic minorities, such as German-speakers), is what Skutnabb-
Kangas and Phillipson (1995) now call "linguicide."

The policy was clearly a traumatic experience for Franco-Ontarians, as
it was aimed at restricting linguistic diversity via the assimilation of the
francophone minority. This kind of language policy resulted in the mobilization of members of the minority in a long-term struggle for the survival of
the linguistic community. The francophone elite in Ontario faced, on the one
hand, the abolition of French schools and, on the other, unequal representation and little chance of professional advancement in the federal public
service, which was operating mainly in English. One of their strategies was
to create a lobby organization that would be responsible for representing

publicly the interests of the minority, especially in the field of education. This organization later extended its mandate to political lobbying in all socio-political matters. At the same time, while they were victims of racist secret organizations such as the Orange order, francophones also created their own secret organization, the Ordre de Jacques Cartier, whose aim was to make sure that francophones would be represented at the highest levels of the most important governmental institutions and public organizations. This secret order led to the creation of many francophone institutions and associations (Heller, 2003).

At that time, the social and economic life of francophone communities was organized around the parish, with the Catholic Church as the main institution to which social organizations (Erfurt, 2003), such as men's and women's Catholic volunteer support clubs, would gravitate, as well as around neighbourhood retail businesses that operated in French. Francophones were employed mostly in the primary and secondary sectors of the economy.

The survival of the francophone community was based essentially on deterring assimilation by means of grouping according to a common language and a common religion. Discourse stressed the importance of unity within the minority. The culmination of these strategies was reached in the 1960s, when the independence movement in Quebec challenged the very existence of a homogenous "Catholic French Canadian minority," and when the patterns of migration from rural to urban areas and from city centres to suburbs started to change the spatial organization of the francophone communities. The time had come to prepare their institutional capacities for social, cultural, and linguistic reproduction.

The Recognition of Rights, 1968–1988

Language policy affecting the French-speaking population in Ontario took a positive turn in the sixties, which I refer to as the second period, in the context of the rise of the sovereignty movement in Quebec, which lead the Canadian federal government, first, to establish the Royal Commission on Bilingualism and Biculturalism, which lasted from 1963 until 1969, and consequently to adopt the Official Languages Act (1969), which recognized the official character of both languages, French and English, in the institutions of the federal government. Simultaneously, the Ontario provincial government in 1968 adopted a more positive approach towards its French-speaking minority in adopting new legislation related to the Education Act that authorized the establishment of public elementary and secondary schools in which French was the language of instruction. This change resulted in a partial separation of language, education, and religion. The recognition of rights took a further important step in 1982 with section 23 of the Canadian Charter of Rights and Freedoms, which stipulated that citizens of Canada had the right to have their children educated in the official minority language. Following the adoption of the Charter, a decision of the Court of Appeal of Ontario considered that certain provisions of the province's Education Act were unconstitutional, thus recognizing the right of all Franco-Ontarians to an education in French. This decision, as well as another decision rendered by the Supreme Court of Canada, interpreted section 23 as granting francophones the right to manage and control minority official-language schools. However, autonomous school boards administered by the French-speaking population were not introduced by the Ontario government until January 1998, which saw the creation of twelve separate francophone district school boards to be administered by francophone trustees. Prior to these developments, the provincial government had adopted the French Language Services Act in 1986, guaranteeing certain provincial government services in French. Finally, in 1988 the federal government adopted a new version of the Official Languages Act which recognized the linguistic duality of Canada and re-established the commitment of the Canadian government to enhancing the vitality of the English and French linguistic minority communities in co-operation with the provincial and municipal governments and the private sector. These measures completed the constitutional, legislative, and regulatory framework that established the rights of the francophone linguistic minorities in Ontario and allowed francophones from then on to challenge public institutions which failed to comply with this framework in their various public policy initiatives.

From the sixties until the end of the eighties, francophones created new social spaces for their own communities in various institutions, which were made possible by the new language policies implemented by the federal and Ontario governments. French schools were among the first institutions to be developed, followed by government services and media. The establishment of French-language institutions attracted educated francophones, mainly from Quebec but also from European francophone countries, to fill positions requiring competence in French (for the school system) or bilingual ability (for government services).

The strategy adopted by francophones during this period was organized around the official recognition of their rights as one of the two founding nations of Canada. If the Catholic religion still remained more important in Ontario than in Quebec during this period, the social life of the community was reinforced by a large number of associations with various interests, which relied mainly on government support. Living patterns changed from parochial to suburban lifestyles, while small businesses owned by francophones spread in various locations, usually serving bilingual customers. Following the modernizing discourse, francophones needed to develop autonomous institutions, organizations, and associations that could function parallel to their anglophone counterparts (for example, Farmer, 1996, documents the establishment of francophone cultural centres in Ontario as vehicles of modernity).

The strategy developed during this period towards the official recognition of rights reached its limits at the beginning of the nineties, when governments started to face rising budget deficits and opted to no longer provide the same financial support to francophone minorities.

Free-Market Policies, 1988 to the Present

The third period began in the nineties as supranational entities emerged, such as the European Union and the North American Free Trade Agreement, and at the same time the collapse of Communism occurred, all contributing to the globalization of the world economy and the rising popularity of neo-liberalism. State governments started to lose some of their quasi-monopolistic control of economic exchanges. A recession developed, and budget deficits were scrutinized by the World Bank and the International Monetary Fund. The solution seemed to reside in downsizing the public administration, reducing budgets, devolving powers to local administrations, and privatizing services. Globalization also meant an intensification of migration from abroad, with new immigrants from non-European francophone countries. In addition, it caused a transformation in the economy, with a decrease in the primary and secondary sectors and the development of the tertiary sector, including services, information, and communication, as well as tourism.

Such phenomena, together with the failure of the federal and provincial governments to amend the constitution, contributed to francophones giving up the collective struggle for the recognition of fundamental rights of linguistic minorities, in favour of individual strategies to integrate into a globalized economy and collective strategies to redefine the boundaries of the community (i.e., who is really Franco-Ontarian, according to language practices and geographical origins).

Committed to a neo-liberal approach to economic development, the Conservative government of Ontario did not dare to revisit existing language policies regarding the French-speaking population, but it nevertheless withdrew financial support, thereby allowing these policies to become unviable. The federal government also introduced budget cutbacks, and its strategy was aimed at sponsoring the creation of umbrella organizations representing francophone minorities in order to rationalize the negotiation and distribution of financial resources. This policy, in turn, impacted on the intensification of internal struggles among the various organizations that represented the interests of different sectors of the civil society (Labrie et al., 2003).

In this context, the strategy that had been aimed at the recognition of rights was no longer easily applicable. New approaches emerged at the individual level aimed at exploiting bilingual resources to integrate into a globalized economy and at the collective level at redefining the "francophonie," that is, who belonged to the community and who did not.

Each of these three historical periods we have examined gave rise to various types of discourses, which still coexist today and have been described elsewhere (Heller and Budach, 1999; Heller and Labrie, 2003) respectively as traditionalist, modernizing, and globalizing discourses. Traditionalist discourses are linked to the importance of maintaining the traditional close-knit francophone networks, the unity being necessary to fight assimilation. Modernizing discourses are associated with the continuous pursuit of the recognition of rights and the creation of autonomous francophone institutions, organizations, and associations, while globalizing discourses are characterized by cultural heterogeneity and the exploitation of individual linguistic resources as a means of taking advantage of a globalized economy. As an illustration, we will briefly examine the coexisting positions of Franco-Ontarians today on language politics, based on these various types of discourses.

COEXISTING OR CONFLICTING DISCOURSES ON LANGUAGE POLITICS TODAY

In 1998 a two-day provincial meeting with leaders from approximately two hundred provincial francophone associations was organized in order to establish an umbrella organization that would be responsible for negotiating financial support from the federal government and redistributing the resources made available to the francophone community. The need for such an umbrella organization resulted from the implementation of the new Official Languages Act of 1988 and from the federal government's goal to rationalize its services, given the context of budget reductions and the downsizing of the government apparatus (Patrimoine canadien, 1995). This event was important because it revealed the concurrent, and sometimes conflicting, discourses, which originated in the past but still coexist today, and because it brought to light the challenges faced by the Franco-Ontarian communities in the era of globalization.

The formation of an umbrella organization presupposes that the francophone minority is homogenous. But in fact, as a result of modernity and globalization, it has become extremely diverse, and finding a consensus among the main actors has become almost impossible (Quell, 2000). On the one hand, the traditional lobby groups have positioned themselves to act as the most representative entities of the entire francophone community. On the other, feminist organizations and artists' associations have contested the legitimacy of the traditional lobby groups to speak on their behalf and to negotiate and distribute the financial resources offered by the federal government. These apparent opposing forces united temporarily, however, when associations representing new immigrants insisted on being part of the umbrella organization and being treated on an equal basis with the mainstream francophone minority. This two-day meeting finally resulted in the expression of deep tensions between the various interest groups in the francophone minority, which revealed internal struggles linked to opposing views of language politics. Interestingly enough, the arguments used by the various speakers reflected, in different combinations, the three types of discourses that developed during the three historical periods mentioned earlier. Some people were advocating the need to create an umbrella organization in order to enter into negotiations with the federal government. They insisted that since the Franco-Ontarian society was becoming more and more diversified, in order for the linguistic community to survive, Franco-Ontarians must stand united and speak with one voice. People associated with the traditional lobby organizations offered this first type of argument.

Another type of argument was that Franco-Ontarians must preserve the rights they had achieved as one of the two founding nations of Canada. This kind of argument was expressed by people who opposed the traditional lobby groups; they identified with the mainstream Franco-Ontarian minority and claimed that the federal government should maintain high levels of funding but should not favour the traditional lobby groups. This same group also claimed that Franco-Ontarians form a diverse community and must therefore find alternative ways to share power, an argument that was also expressed very clearly by people who sympathized with the organizations representing new immigrants. Representatives of new immigrant groups, however, felt that the former groups had united to reach a consensus among themselves regarding their collective position towards the government, so that, although claiming to be inclusive of newcomers, they actually excluded them. Here is how a vocal representative put it (my translation, using transcription conventions to convert spoken into written language whereby a short pause is represented by a / and a longer pause by //):[2]

Amadou Ngala: we have in front of us / a complete deletion of convictions // this allows us to get back to the reading we already made, i.e. the problem was not addressed within the Franco-Ontarian community / one was ready to consider adjustments or accommodations only / the fundamental problems were rather / to know in which type of modern (and future) relationship / of the millennium we want to live together // I think that there are opportunities in history and some have already referred to this / where one has to take a turn / and I regret that this opportunity has been missed I still believe however / that this opportunity will come back some day / probably not with the same agents with others and this is maybe (better) we are leaving from this meeting highly disappointed and I call upon the Ministry of Canadian Heritage and I was right to identify the ministry in my speech they are the only interlocutors with whom we should refer to to ask them the question about which future which policies what is the meaning that you want to give to our existence within the francophonie and to our community relationships with you

This excerpt is a powerful expression of the power struggles among French-speaking collectivities regarding their coexisting, shifting, and conflicting positions towards the state as a privileged way to access and control the redistribution of resources in a globalized society and economy.

CONCLUSION

This short analysis of the discourses surrounding Franco-Ontarians' positions on language politics – that is, on the social control of linguistic diversity – shows that the various discourses that developed during the twentieth century as a consequence of political struggle and the social, political, and economic transformation of Canadian society still coexist today. According to the new orientations developed in the era of globalization, less emphasis is given to fighting assimilation by maintaining close-knit networks based on traditional institutions such as the parish or the church, although the idea of unity remains present. Less emphasis is also given to developing new language policies, the focus being more on maintaining the rights that have been acquired in the past thirty years. New positions tend to locate language politics in an economic framework, where communities are more diversified and where individuals can exploit their linguistic resources to capitalize on globalization. At present, it is difficult to predict when this kind of reasoning will reach its limits and how Franco-Ontarians' positions on language politics will eventually evolve. Only time will tell.

NOTES

1 The participant-observation data from this two-day provincial meeting were col-
lected as part of the project "Prise de parole," funded from 1997 to 2001 by the
Social Sciences and Humanities Research Council of Canada (principal investiga-
tors: Normand Labrie, Monica Heller, University of Toronto, and Jürgen Erfurt,
Johann-Wolfgang-Goethe Universität, Frankfurt am Main; collaborators: Annette
Boudreau and Lise Dubois, Université de Moncton). It was also funded by the
Transcoop Program of the German-American Academic Council Foundation (principal investigators: Jürgen Erfurt, Monica Heller, and Normand Labrie) and the
Agence universitaire de la Francophonie (principal investigators: Patrice Brasseur
and Claudine Moïse, Université d'Avignon et des Pays de Vaucluse) (Heller and
Labrie, 2003). Our team collected some 550 tape recordings of interviews, public
meetings, and social gatherings among members of many francophone communities, from which we wanted to find out how the identity of francophones was
currently being constructed through discourse. What types of discourses were developed, and what types were disseminated? What types of discourses were domin-
ating, and which ones were marginalized? Finally, what were the consequences for
the people who initiate, reproduce, or reject them? The data for the analysis were
collected from a variety of participants, ranging from people who play an active
role in the francophone community to those who can be considered as francophones but who prefer not to participate in any form of community life in French.
They were recruited from age groups from sixteen years and upward.

2 Amadou Ngala: nous avons vu devant nous / un effacement complètement des
convictions // ça permet de rejoindre la lecture que nous avions depuis le problème
ne se posait pas dans la communauté franco-ontarienne c'était juste des ajuste-
ments et des accommodements / les problèmes de fond étaient plutôt / de savoir
dans quel type de rapport moderne / (et d'avenir) du millénaire est-ce qu'on peut
vivre ensemble // je pense qu'il y a des moments dans l'histoire et on en a fait état /
où il faut savoir prendre le cours des événements / et je regrette que ce moment ait
été manqué je continue néanmoins à croire / que ce moment sera retrouvé un jour /
sans doute pas avec les mêmes les acteurs avec d'autres et c'est ça peut-être la (foi)
nous partons d'ici fortement déçus et j'interpelle Patrimoine canadien et j'avais
raison de les identifier dans mon discours ce sont les seuls interlocuteurs auxquels
il faut nous référer pour leur poser la question quel avenir quelle politique quel
est le sens que vous voulez donner à notre existence dans la francophonie et à nos
rapports de communautés avec vous

11

The End of the Language Crisis in Quebec: Comparative Implications

PIERRE ANCTIL

IMMIGRATION TO CANADA AND QUEBEC

Immigration has been a major social and economic phenomenon in recent Canadian history, especially from the very end of the nineteenth century, when new waves of immigrants were admitted to Canada on an unprecedented scale (Knowles, 1992). From 1911 on, these new populations of neither French nor British origin accounted for more than half of inhabitants of the provinces located in the middle of the continent – Manitoba, Saskatchewan, and Alberta. In Canada's big cities, particularly Montreal and Toronto, the arrival of tens of thousands of immigrants recruited from southern and eastern Europe also had far-reaching consequences for the structure of the labour market, the ethnic makeup of neighbourhoods, and the development of a sense of identity. In Canada the greatest influx of immigrants occurred between 1896 and 1914, when more than three million people came to Canada – a figure that has never been reached since. Basically, these immigrants were let in by the federal authorities to make up for the shortage of workers in specific economic sectors, especially the manufacturing industry, which was expanding rapidly in Canada's large cities.

Furthermore, another segment of this new population would fulfill a strategic function in the political context of that time: to settle the farmlands in the Canadian West at a time when Ottawa was trying to limit American territorial ambitions in that region. Immigration to the new Prairie provinces met with little resistance as newcomers settled in relatively unpopulated areas where communities had only recently been established. However, it was the complete opposite in the cities of Montreal and Toronto, both of which embodied in their own way the political, civil, and moral values of the new Canadian Confederation of 1867 and had developed a vision of the country that was modelled in large measure on the values of the British Empire. The same tendency to racial and religious purity was apparent, albeit to a lesser degree, in the coastal regions of Canada – the Maritimes and British Columbia – both of which represented major gateways for newcomers from Europe to the east and China and India to the west. However, during this period and until the outbreak of the Second World War, the federal government alone looked after the management of migration flows, and its decisions were influenced above all by the economic interests of big business and the needs of the major employers in the country.

Before 1945, Ottawa did not take into account the binational reality of Canada in its management of migration flows. Particularly in Montreal, where the majority of the inhabitants were of French descent, very little effort was made to direct immigrants toward French-speaking communities, with the result that the majority of newcomers to Montreal gravitated toward the English-speaking community. The economic appeal of the English language on the North American continent, the higher social standing of English Canadian business circles and banks, and the promise of greater geographic mobility prompted most immigrants to simply avoid learning French in this city. Many newcomers came to the conclusion that it would be pointless to do so. The problem of a lack of ongoing contacts between the new communities and the francophone majority was compounded in Montreal by the fact that French Canadians withdrew behind their religious and cultural identity. Their attitude did not easily allow for contact with other ethnic groups or structured exchanges with other communities (Linteau, 2000, chap. 7). In face of the arrival of so many immigrants with unfamiliar customs and traditions, many leading francophone spokespersons and media outlets adopted a discourse that was hostile toward immigration or often xenophobic (Anctil, 1988). Many French Canadian nationalist circles decided that Ottawa's ultimate goal was to isolate francophones and to push them even further toward a minority position in relation to the rest of Canada, with its allegiance to Great Britain (Morin, 1966).

After the First World War, and particularly during the second half of the 1920s, immigration to Canada significantly declined from the peaks reached a decade earlier. The triggering of the Great Depression in the thirties and the outbreak of the Second World War marked an even steeper decline in international migration, with the result that, for almost a full generation, from 1929 to 1948, Canada welcomed relatively few newcomers. During this time, as in previous decades, it was with great reluctance that federal authorities let in immigrants from the Middle East, Africa, and Asia – not to mention their refusal to help the German and Austrian Jews who were victims of Nazi persecutions from 1933 on (Abella and Troper, 1983). For years, the question of taking in and integrating immigrants from faraway countries and those with visibly different religious and cultural practices was, for all practical purposes, no longer discussed in English or French Canada. In 1941, when battles were raging in many European countries and just before the Japanese attacked Peal Harbor, only 16.7 per cent of the population of Montreal proper was of an ethnic origin other than French or British, that is, had recently immigrated. Twenty years later the number had climbed to 19 per cent, and by 1971 it had risen to 21.1 per cent (Linteau, 1982). Following the 1945 Armistice, a new wave of migration took shape and would result in the highest number of immigrants settling in Montreal in the history of the city.

VARIOUS ATTEMPTS AT FACING THE ISSUE

The French Canada that was developing just after the war carried the seeds of major socio-economic changes, the most striking being the affirmation of the Quebec state as the primary political and ideological reference point for francophones living in Quebec. In the early twentieth century French Canadians perceived their influence as a kind of geographic and human continuum stretching from Acadia to the Prairies, with a central zone of high concentration in the St Lawrence valley (Morrisset and Waddell, 2000; Louder, Morrisset, and Waddell, 2001; Anctil, 1999). After 1945 and following important identity changes, francophones in Quebec decided to set out alone within the Canadian francophonie, using the powerful legislative and administrative levers of a provincial legislature under their own control. This major turning point in the affirmation of a separate Quebec identity redefined the nationalist strategy advocated since 1867 by the political heavyweights of French Canada, such as Henri Bourassa and Lionel Groulx, according to whom French-speaking Quebecers were a component of a minority people within the broader Canadian federation. As francophones in Quebec formed a new image of themselves during the Cold War, they came to realize that the British North America Act gave extensive powers to the provinces, especially for the management of cultural and linguistic issues. The discovery of areas of Canadian constitutional jurisdiction never before occupied by Quebec governments would have major effects during the sixties and seventies, triggering among other things a new affirmation of the French fact.

The great watershed of the fifties, even under the conservative and ruralist government of Maurice Duplessis, also signalled the transformation of a defensive French Canadian nationalism into a new "Quebec" wave of affirmation based largely on the majority status of francophones in Quebec and the rapid modernization of social structures. At the same time a tool rarely used by politicians also came to the fore – the Quebec state, which had adopted a secular ideology and had considerable financial resources at its disposal. Redefined as territorial and no longer ethnic, in that it represented all inhabitants of Quebec, not just those who were of French Canadian and Catholic background, the Quebec state was the launching pad for a set of political changes known as the Quiet Revolution (McRoberts and Postgate, 1988). The affirmation of the French fact was seen from the sixties on as a priority for the new Quebec state. Yet in spite of the rapid pace of change during those years, one question remained unanswered: What attitude would Quebec francophones, as a demographic majority, take toward the anglophone minority and toward the immigrant communities who had settled permanently in the province before the Second World War. Above all, how would the Quebec government welcome the newcomers who had been encouraged to settle in huge numbers under the federal government's open door policy in order to fill major labour shortages in specific sectors of the economy?

Since 1867, consecutive Quebec governments had largely ignored the management of immigration, preferring to let Ottawa act alone. Until 1960, for the structural reasons outlined earlier, immigrants to the province had generally chosen to integrate through the network of anglophone institutions, thereby increasing the number of parents sending their children to English-speaking Catholic and Protestant schools (Corcos, 1997). As long as newcomers were let into Quebec in small numbers, it was assumed that the rapid anglicization of allophones would not have long-term effects and that the cultural identity of the French Canadian school systems in Montreal would thus be preserved. The dramatic increase in immigration and the significant drop in the birth rate of francophones during the immediate postwar period raised fears toward the end of the fifties that francophones would become a minority on Montreal Island. In fact, the linguistic transfers in Montreal that were already working very much to the benefit of English in the early forties, because newcomers with no knowledge of either official language adopted English rather than French, were now affecting communities that had historically adopted French, such as the Italian community. In 1941, 74.4 per cent of about 28,000 cases of linguistic transfer within the immigrant population of Montreal were toward English; by 1961 the proportion had risen to 89.8 per cent, or 114,885 linguistic transfers toward English (Charbonneau and Maheu, 1973, 71–3). Even within the population whose origin was francophone and had been identified as such for many generations, a new trend emerged on Montreal Island: many children whose mother tongue was French were enrolled in anglophone schools by their parents (Levine, 1990, 213).

Most, if not all, tools for measuring a language's force of attraction in a region cover relatively long periods of time or several generations of speakers. In the case of the language situation of immigrants in Montreal during the fifties and sixties, at least one set of data drew a clear picture of what the future would be like for the French language in the city over the short term: it would be contingent on the language of education that immigrants whose children were born in the country chose for their children. In Quebec two separate public school systems were provided for under section 93 of the British North America Act of 1867: a Protestant one and a Catholic one. In fact, the first was basically for anglophones and the second for francophones. With respect to Catholic institutions, however, following the growth of a large Irish minority during the nineteenth century in Montreal, an anglophone Catholic sector developed too and welcomed students who were not French Canadian, and subsequently, during the 1950s and 1960s the anglophone Catholic schools served a large number of young allophones from the new immigrant communities, who followed a curriculum that prepared them for life as part of Montreal's English-speaking minority.

During the 1930–31 school year, 46.8 per cent of allophone students (mother tongue neither French nor English) in the Montreal Catholic School Commission (CECM) were studying in the anglophone sector. Forty years later the proportion had risen to 89.2 per cent (Taddeo and Tarras, 1987). In the early thirties, in a context where parents could choose the language of education for their children, this figure translated into about 3,500 young allophones adopting English instead of French; by 1971 the number had risen to 25,000. The Italian community, in particular, made a significant shift toward English during the postwar period, following a major influx of immigrants (Boissevain, 1971). In 1943 the Italian-speaking community accounted for 11.9 per cent of anglophones in the CECM, or 1,691 students. Almost two generations later, in 1977, they formed a contingent of 18,135 students, or 45.3 per cent of the CECM anglophone student population. The same year, the Italian-speaking community in the francophone sector represented 1.2 per cent of the CECM, or only 1,532 students. Note also that similar trends affected the other allophone Catholic communities – the Germans, Poles, Ukrainians, and Portuguese. In 1971, for example, 88.3 per cent of students from the Polish community and 85 per cent from the Portuguese community were in anglophone Catholic schools (Taddeo and Tarras, 1987, 47, 108). During this same period, even students with French as their mother tongue and a French Canadian culture started to succumb to the attraction of the English language in Montreal: around 3 per cent of this group preferred going to anglophone Catholic schools rather than francophone Catholic schools.

The trend among recent immigrants toward an ever-stronger identification with Montreal's anglophone community developed during the 1960s and 1970s, in a broad context of social upheaval and a sense among the French majority that their position was being threatened. In the years following the Second World War, the spokespersons for French Canadian nationalism and francophone academics often denounced the structural economic inferiority of French Canadians in Montreal's economy and the fact that this group was lagging far behind in terms of acquiring the skills needed to manage large businesses. In 1970, for example, unilingual French males in Montreal had an average annual income of $5,636, compared with $9,123 for unilingual English males. Even bilingual francophones at the time did not match unilingual anglophones, achieving an average annual income of only $7,686. Another important fact to note is that bilingual anglophones, with an average annual income of $9,367, did not really derive any benefit from knowing both official languages[1] (Levine, 1990, 196). Aware of the fact that they were historically disadvantaged in the economic sphere, francophones now realized that they might soon also lose their precarious status as the demographic majority on Montreal Island as a result of the high levels of immigration after the Second World War.

Today it is easy to underestimate the intensity of the language debate that raged in Montreal in the sixties and seventies, particularly with respect to the language used by newcomers. Along with a number of social issues of primary importance to francophones, such as the creation of a modern Quebec state, the nationalization of hydroelectric resources, and the secularization of the health and education systems, the francization of immigrants was a matter the urgency of which has not been matched since. The desire of a growing number of francophone Montrealers to force allophones to learn French through the education system came up against strong resistance from cultural communities as a result partly of the anglicization process they were undergoing and partly because of hostility from the wealthier segment of Quebec society of British origin. However, the conflict struck closer to home in 1967, when the Saint-Léonard Catholic School Commission in the eastern part of Montreal Island, which was controlled by francophones, decided to remove the bilingual courses that had been offered for a number of years to newcomers, primarily Italian-speakers. In the minds of many postwar immigrants, the bilingualization of French schools pushed the door wide open to the adoption of English as the primary language of use. The commission's decision to take away parental choice of the language of education for their children, one of a number of events connected to francophones' new rally behind this overall objective, would tear the delicate social fabric that had remained untouched for years, even decades:

> The 1960s ended in Montreal with a year of unprecedented linguistic unrest. By 1969, with the festering Saint-Léonard Crisis and the conflict over Bill 63, Francophone discontent had spawned a veritable wave of street demonstrations, fiery speech, terrorist violence and riots. However, few Montrealers were prepared for the linguistic turbulence with which the city began the 1970s ... The city's French- and English-speaking communities were now polarized in ways that seriously threatened social peace. For the remainder of the decade, life in Montreal would be dominated by linguistic discord, with the possibility of violence always lurking in the background. (Levine, 1990, 87)

Against this backdrop of political unrest, two fundamental language issues that had lain dormant for years finally emerged at the heart of Montreal society and would haunt politicians for the next twenty years. Francophones wanted to determine which measures they could legitimately take to ensure their language maintained a leading role in Quebec and what they could do to convince new immigrants to join them in working toward this overall objective. Emerging just after the onset of the Quiet Revolution and clearly fed by the new francophone nationalism of the sixties, the crisis of language relations in Montreal was handled very differently by the Union nationale, which was in power until 1970, by Robert Bourassa's Liberal Party, and by the Parti Québécois, elected in 1976. No fewer than two major pieces of language legislation were enacted from 1969 (Bill 63) to 1974 (Bill 22) by two different Quebec governments, and they both failed to straighten out the situation in schools and to calm down public opinion until the Parti Québécois, founded in 1968 by René Lévesque, took power unexpectedly in November 1976 on the strength of an agenda focused on achieving political independence for Quebec. As the vehicle for a new form of francophone nationalism open to the modern world and North American trends and values, the Parti Québécois in its first few months in power implemented a proposal to solve the language tensions that had been plaguing Montreal society for about fifteen years. For this political party, the defence and illustration of the French language assumed a highly symbolic importance because of its blueprint for Quebec society and because party members had clearly indicated for many years their willingness to settle the issue of what schools children of immigrants should attend.

The solution to the Montreal language dilemma presented by the Parti Québécois in 1977 via the Charter of the French Language would be the most successful and longest-lasting: it would be applied until 1985, when the Liberals regained power with Robert Bourassa as leader. Even though minor adjustments were made to the Charter, notably following the Ford judgment of 1988, when the Supreme Court of Canada struck down certain provisions regarding the obligation to post signs in French only, all the major language management principles established by the Parti Québécois have remained untouched to this day. In March 1977 the PQ published a white paper on language policy clearly stating, among other things, its intention to deal with the language situation among immigrant populations: "If the current demographic trend in Quebec continues, the number of Quebec francophones will keep on declining. In this context, what would people expect us to do if not circumscribe the language options for immigrants in order to ensure Quebec's language future?" (Gouvernement du Québec, 1978, 6). The PQ proposed that any parents who had not studied in an English-language institution in Canada should enrol their children in francophone schools, whether private or public.[2] This policy meant that all people born outside the country and arriving in Quebec after 1977 would have to enrol their children in French schools. At the same time, the Lévesque government undertook to make a special effort to bridge the gap between the two solitudes:

> While the [Quebec] government is committed to respecting minorities and contributing to their development, it is also committed to taking all possible measures to foster relations between minorities and the culture of the French majority. Between slowly implemented or rapidly imposed assimilation and the preservation of cultures behind walls of segregation, there exists a third, practicable option: communicating with one another within a common Quebec culture. In the course of daily life in a city like Montreal, for example, two-way exchange and communication have been taking place for a long time. It is not always smooth and it is not always simple, but working openly toward this goal is of utmost importance. (Gouvernement du Québec, 1978, 79)

Many other avenues had already been devised by the Quebec government at the time to help newcomers adopt the French language, including the creation of a Quebec Department of Immigration in 1968 and, in the same year, the establishment of the Centres d'orientation et de formation des immigrants (COFI), which were given the responsibility of teaching French to adult immigrants. Francization programs were set up in various workplaces with high concentrations of allophones undergoing the integration process. The purpose of this measure was to enhance the profile of the French language in the Quebec labour force as a whole. The province's firm commitment to the francization of immigrants was facilitated in no small measure by the Gagnon-Tremblay-McDougall Agreement of 1991, under which Ottawa transferred to Quebec total responsibility for selecting and integrating new citizens, in exchange for a fixed annual amount of financial compensation to cover increasing levels of immigration (Gouvernement du Québec, 1991). The agreement also included a clause stipulating that French would be the only second language taught to immigrant adults and that this would be exclusively Quebec's responsibility. This transfer of power to the constitutional jurisdiction of Quebec turned the province into a truly distinct society in Canada with regard to the language rights of immigrants (Anctil, 1996). It was preceded in 1990 by an important policy statement on immigration and integration entitled *Au Québec pour bâtir ensemble*, which stressed the importance of harnessing the province's resources to francize new immigrants. The document lists four major challenges. The first two are reversing the population decline and achieving economic prosperity. The third is ensuring the long-term survival of French:[3]

> The knowledge and use of the common language [French] in everyday life plays a key role in the process of integrating immigrants and their descendants. Language is a tool that breaks down the walls of isolation and makes communication and participation possible ... Because of its unique language situation, Quebec must make more significant and fundamental efforts in this area ... To achieve this objective, it will have to significantly increase the accessibility and the quality of French language learning services, not only for newly arrived adults and school children but for established immigrant communities as well. (Gouvernement du Québec, 1990, 50)

TOWARD A LASTING CONSENSUS ON LANGUAGE

More than thirty years after the enactment of the Charter of the French Language, it is now possible to gauge, to a degree, the impact of the major pieces of language legislation on the learning of French by immigrants and their descendants. Selected data from the Quebec education sector already reflected the magnitude of the changes that had taken place over the course of just one generation. During the 1971–72 school year, only 10 per cent of allophone students in Montreal went to schools where French was the primary language of instruction. By 2000–1, this figure had climbed to 78 per cent. What still had to be examined was the impact of Bill 101 on the workplace and on language use at home and in public. The opportunity to conduct such an assessment arose in 2003, with the publication of the main language data from the 2001 Canadian census, particularly with regard to the language behaviour of newcomers. Regardless of the exact quantitative census statistics, it already seemed obvious to most observers that the shift by immigrant students to the French-language school sector had profoundly altered the nature of cross-cultural relationships within francophone Quebec (Joly, 1996). In fact, there was no longer any denying the fact that the Charter of the French Language was a powerful tool for cultural transformation of the demographic majority, injecting a diversity into the francophone social fabric that had been largely absent until the end of the twentieth century. With the great language shift of 1977, the francophone population, faced with a wave of immigrants settling in Quebec, finally undertook to define itself as a "host society" for all immigrants to the province and to take responsibility for the integration of immigrants. Subsequently, for the first time in Quebec history and at least in theory, French became the "common language" of all Quebecers, regardless of their background, beliefs, or date of arrival. For all intents and purposes, though, such a goal could be realized only over a long period of time.

In Quebec, data on routine language practices, particularly on Montreal Island, is of highly significant political import and has been the subject of intense ideological debates in academic milieus. In all likelihood, Canada is one of the few countries in the world where the publication of official statistics regarding the mother tongue and language of use receives extensive media coverage. This phenomenon is particularly apparent in reports on the growth of French and adoption of French by allophones. Montrealers often feel as if they are under a microscope when they read their newspapers. The smallest change on the spectrum from one end toward the other can have widespread repercussions for the whole country and be perceived as a harbinger of upcoming trends in other regions. Over the years, this emotional and highly symbolic dimension of the language issue has helped make certain kinds of data highly sensitive, especially those released at regular intervals by agencies responsible for updating official statistics.

We have already noted that, in the late sixties and throughout the seventies, the issue of regulating language behaviour through the federal Official Languages Act of 1969 and legislation enacted by the Quebec legislature provoked considerable tension in Quebec and Canadian society. In contrast, the Charter of the French Language of 1977 created a climate of moderation and dialogue between the language communities, something that no other legislation had achieved. The simplicity and clarity of the measures laid out in the Charter, the consensus it generated among francophones, and the acceptance of French as the predominant language of all Quebecers by recent immigrants would help to lower tensions considerably. At the end of the nineties and the beginning of the new millennium, the general impression was that the winds had changed on the language issue, and the language groups decided that the measures adopted twenty-five years earlier had established a truce, if not a lasting peace. In this period, the anglophone community, with its increasingly diverse ethnic makeup, finally accepted that French would be the dominant language used in public in Quebec, the only resistance to such acceptance perhaps coming from an increasingly marginalized group embodied by a lobby organization called Alliance-Quebec. The same was true for the Jewish community, which was very sensitive to issues regarding fundamental rights and which, through its representatives in the Canadian Jewish Congress, has on several occasions over the past few years upheld the underlying principle of the Charter of the French Language (Anctil, 1997).

The publication of the 2001 census data undoubtedly reinforced the impression that Quebec society as a whole had reached a new stage in its quest for a linguistic balance satisfying all of its major components. Essentially, the crisis of the sixties and seventies in Montreal was due to the fact that francophones, although they were the province's demographic majority, could not convince themselves that the future of French was safe within the Quebec and Canadian political and legislative framework of the time. It seemed that adoption of English by allophones living in Quebec, together with the very low rate of bilingualism among anglophones, would condemn the French language to minority status. As a result, the guarantees in the Charter of the French Language took a long time to succeed in concrete terms and even longer to change the perceptions that francophones had inherited from previous generations. According to a joint study carried out by the Association for Canadian Studies and a private research group in 2003, 55 per cent of Quebecers of all origins thought that the future of the French language and culture was very or fairly secure in Quebec in 2003, compared with 74 per cent of Canadians who shared that opinion as a whole. In Quebec, only 53 per cent of francophones shared that opinion, compared with 81 per cent of anglophones (Jedwab and Baker, 2003). These figures clearly show that many Quebec francophones, despite the progress made by the French language in their society over the last thirty years, are not convinced that a point of no return has been reached on the language issue.

The data collected in the 2001 census must be studied from a twofold perspective: first, by keeping in mind that the Quebec linguistic majority has still not achieved a reasonable level of comfort on the issue and, second, by taking into account the fact that attitude toward languages and resulting behaviours change very slowly in a given society. The reversal in perspective at the start of the twenty-first century, however small it may seem in strictly statistical terms, represents a major shift in the short history of the Quebec government's efforts to integrate and francize immigrants. The fact is that the changes brought out by the 2001 census followed several decades of laissez-faire against a background of strong attraction to English and were the leading edge of a new trend on the language front that will probably continue to grow in the coming decades. These conclusions, which today can be drawn from both sociological and demographic standpoints, have yet to exert an impact on the collective imaginations of francophones or the dominant political discourse, including that of supporters of sovereignty or of a strong autonomous structure for Quebec in relation to the rest of Canada. Yet it is no doubt fair to say that, on the strength of the 2001 census data, the acute language crisis in Montreal during the late sixties and early seventies is now dissipating and is no longer likely to take centre stage as it has in previous years.

The data from the 2001 census reveal that three significant demolinguistic trends are developing in Montreal and in Quebec and are directly influencing the integration of allophones. First, there is a very slow decrease in the number of people stating that French is their first language, but this trend is offset by a significant increase in the number of immigrants with a knowledge of French (second trend) in a broader context where Montrealers and Quebecers are becoming increasingly bilingual (third trend) within the meaning of the federal Official Languages Act. The first trend (see tables 11.1 and 11.2) was expected because of the declining fertility rate of the majority French population and the steady influx of immigrants into Montreal over the last twenty years or so. Based on a total Quebec population of 7.1 million in 2001, the percentage of native French-speakers fell slightly from 81.5 to 81.4 over a five-year period.[4] In Montreal, where the question is more sensitive because of the political environment, the percentage of French-speakers dropped from 55.9 to 53.2 over a ten-year period from 1991 to 2001. This trend, which had become apparent many years earlier and had been referred to in the 1977 white paper on language policy, points to potential minority status for the next generation of native French-speakers on Montreal Island

Table 11.1
Mother tongues, province of Quebec (percentages)

	1996	2001
French	81.5	81.4
English	8.8	8.3
Non-official languages	9.7	10.3

SOURCE: Census of Canada, 2001, 1996; see also
Marmen and Corbeil, 2004, 145 table A.1.

Table 11.2
Mother tongues, Montreal (merged city) (percentages)

	1991	1996	2001
English	19.4	18.9	17.7
French	55.9	53.4	53.2
Non-official languages	24.7	27.7	29.1

SOURCE: Census of Canada, 2002; see also Office québécois de la
langue française, 2005, 11, table 1.1.

(Gouvernement du Québec, 1977). Allophones are the only group gaining ground in the city, increasing from 24.7 to 29.1 per cent between 1991 and 2001. A number of experts have ventured to conclude from this pattern that the behaviour of recent immigrants will be a major determining factor in the future survival of the French language in Montreal.

Before going further along this road, we must ask how much knowledge of Canada's official languages new Quebec citizens admitted between 2001 and 2005 had (see table 11.3). This is an important question to answer because we can then measure the linguistic distance immigrants must cover in order to adjust to Quebec requirements. The evaluation of the costs involved in francization and the quantity of human resources needed are both contingent upon our findings. In the period between 2001 and 2005, according to the Quebec Ministère de l'immigration et des communautés culturelles, 47 per cent of new citizens had a reasonable and functional knowledge of French, compared with 37.5 per cent who had the same level of proficiency in English. Because a part of this immigrant cohort knew French and English and there was therefore an overlapping of the language-knowledge populations, 37.1 per cent of immigrants admitted during that period can in fact be described as allophones within the meaning of the federal Official Languages Act. However, caution should be exercised in any analysis involving these statistics because the vast majority of immigrants with an acceptable level of proficiency in French and English have a different mother

Table 11.3
Knowledge of French and English among immigrants admitted
to Quebec, 2001–5 (percentages)

French only	25.4
French and English	21.6
KNOWLEDGE OF FRENCH	47.0
English only	15.9
No knowledge of French or English	37.1
KNOWLEDGE OF ENGLISH	37.5

SOURCE: Ministère de l'immigration et des communautés culturelles.

tongue and may therefore have incomplete oral and writing mastery of Canada's official languages. The fact remains that each year, before they can hope to make substantial headway on the labour market or practise a profession regulated by a professional body, almost half the immigrants admitted to Quebec must learn French for the first time, and the other half have no choice but to upgrade their French skills..

The interpretation of the 2001 data for Montreal and Quebec regarding French language trends requires some conceptual clarification. Though the opinions of some experts differ on the subject, it appears that the most important variables for measuring the vitality and durability of French in Quebec are language use and transfers from one language to another (Séguin, 2003). Even though the statistics on mother tongue are fairly significant, it goes without saying that they cannot at all reflect the fluidity and complexity of the situation on the ground and, particularly, the fact that mother tongue is a cultural variable that cannot be altered over the short or medium term. Furthermore, the act of learning a new language, the growing complexity of linguistic behaviours, and the shift from one code to another all reflect changes that can take place rather quickly and alter the cultural landscape significantly. In this sense, the substantial decline in the number of people for whom French is a first language is less important than the data regarding daily use of the language. For the first time in Quebec's relatively short linguistic history, the numbers draw a radically new picture of language use, showing a consistent, systematic increase in the use of French by newcomers (see table 11.4). This success is particularly striking with regard to allophone immigrants' transfers to French – 46 per cent of respondents in 2001, up from 39 per cent in 1996. This decisive progression over a period of only five years suggests that the shift toward French as the main language of use will probably apply to the majority of immigrants in the census of 2006 when it is analyzed.

Table 11.4
Evolution of the French language, 1996 and 2001 (percentages)

| | Province of Quebec | |
	1996	2001
French as the main language in the home	82.8	83.1

	Island of Montreal	
French as the main language in the home	55.6	56.4
Allophones who master the French language	72.9	73.1
Allophones who speak mostly French in the home environment	16.1	20.1
Allophones who adopt French as the language most often spoken at home	39	46

SOURCE: Ministère de l'immigration et des communautés culturelles, 2002; see also Office québécois de la langue française, 2005, tables 1.2, 1.6b, and 1.6c.

Similarly, the percentage of Quebecers who speak French at home[5] increased from 82.8 to 83.1 per cent in five years, while the number of allophones (people whose mother tongue is neither French nor English) also rose from 9.7 to 10.3 per cent. This increase means that enough families or households adopt French as their everyday means of communication to offset the demographic loss resulting from the aging of the population segment with French as the mother tongue. In the 2001 census, 73.1 per cent of the allophones residing on Montreal Island said that they had a command of French, compared with only 72.9 per cent five years earlier. Given the high rates of anglicization in the Montreal region more than twenty-five years ago – and, indeed, throughout the twentieth century – these numbers indicate a spectacular turnaround in the linguistic situation within the space of only a few years. The statistics are particularly significant considering the fact that some of the allophones came to Canada in a very different linguistic context from the one prevailing today. It is highly probable that the proportion of francized allophones in Montreal, which is close to three-quarters at present, will continue to grow over the next few years because, to date, francization has mainly affected immigrants belonging to the younger generation or those who have arrived recently.

The successes of the Quebec government's language policies introduced more than thirty years ago are remarkable in that they were not achieved at the expense of any of the core values concerning the promotion of bilingualism that are enshrined in the federal Official Languages Act. Even though more and more immigrants have been learning French since the Charter of the French Language was passed, the fact remains that many of them have

Table 11.5
Levels of bilingualism, 1996 and 2001 (percentages)

	Province of Quebec	
	1996	*2001*
Anglophones	62.9	67.2
Francophones	34.0	36.9
Allophones	46.8	50.5
Total	37.8	40.8
	Canada without Quebec	
	1996	*2001*
Francophones	83.6	84.8
Anglophones	7.0	7.2
Allophones	5.4	5.8

SOURCE: Census of Canada, 1996, 2001; Marmen and
Corbeil, 2004, 60, table 4.4.

made sure that they learned English too (see table 11.5). In 2001, because
of this underlying trend, almost all the indicators of bilingualism in Quebec
had gone up, particularly among allophones, whose level of bilingualism rose
by almost 4 percentage points in five years, to reach 50.5 per cent. The bilingualism rate for Quebec anglophones is even higher, at 67.2 per cent – an
increase of almost 4.5 percentage points – while the rate for francophones,
at 36.9 per cent, shows an increase of 3 percentage points over the same
period. These figures stand in stark contrast to the situation in the nine other
Canadian provinces, where only 7 per cent of anglophones and almost 6 per
cent of allophones are bilingual. In short, in Montreal, the largest metropolitan region in Quebec, French is gaining ground in all language groups,
and it remains the most bilingual region of the country by far. However, it
is important to make a distinction between, on the one hand, proficiency in
English and French for day-to-day living and, on the other, the political will
to put the two languages on an equal footing, as is the case at the Canadian
federal level. Montreal bilingualism is unique in that it thrives in a Quebec
setting where French has been the only official language since 1974. For most
francophones, the legal preponderance of French in the Montreal region is
an essential condition for maintaining harmonious relations with the English
language and anglophones.

One of the most noteworthy aspects of the data from the 2001 census on
the linguistic behaviour of the Quebec and Montreal populations is the apparent compatibility of the francization goals of the Charter of the French

Language with the bilingualization goals of the federal Official Languages Act. The relatively successful coexistence of Quebec's language management with that of Canada explains in large part why political tensions have eased in Montreal in the last twenty years or so. Immigrants do not feel that francization isolates them from the rest of Canada, and at the same time the Quebec francophone majority derives benefits from the policy. The parallel development of the two language policies will most likely continue in Montreal for some years to come, at least as long as the current constitutional situation prevails and gains can be made simultaneously on the two fronts. Yet, when the Charter of the French Language was proclaimed in 1977, there was little evidence on which to predict such an outcome, especially because of the strong, sometimes even diehard resistance of the English-speaking elites in some quarters to any acceleration in the pace of francization in Quebec (Caldwell and Waddell, 1982). Today there can be no doubt that the population group that has benefited the most from Quebec language policy is young allophones fifteen to nineteen years old, of whom 90 per cent spoke French and 71 per cent were bilingual within the meaning of the Official Languages Act in 2001, followed closely by young anglophones.

In the final analysis, the 2001 data show that the progress made by French at all levels of the Montreal allophone population has not undermined the influence of English in the city. The gains made through the Charter of the French Language have not meant losses for the anglophone community. Admittedly, there has been a significant out-migration of the English-speaking population from Montreal since 1976, when the Parti Québécois came to power (Levine, 1990, 42). However, this trend had already started in the fifties, with corporate head offices moving to Toronto, and it is largely attributable to the long-term transfer of some major economic activities to the centre of the continent. However, since the sixties the requirement for a functionally bilingual workforce has become much more widespread in Montreal, and it is hard to find employment today without being proficient in both official languages, especially in the service industry. In fact, it could be claimed with some justification, in the light of developments in Quebec over the last thirty years, that requirements for francization in the workplace have served as a springboard for asserting the primacy of the French language just as much as language policies have, if not more so. Without the constant pressure from the general public to obtain goods and services in French, the legislative framework established by successive Quebec governments would not have achieved as much success or won over as many willing participants, especially among new immigrants invited to join the demographic majority. Along with the practice of democratic values, this was one of the most important messages in the "Moral Contract between Quebec and the People Who Wish to Immigrate" released in the early 1990s by the Quebec Department of Citizen Relations and Immigration:

> In Quebec we speak French. It is the official language and the one that we use most often in everyday life: at work, in communications, and in commerce and business.

> Quebec is determined to preserve and promote its official language. French is not only an essential communication tool but also a shared symbol of membership in Quebec society. (Gouvernement du Québec, 2001, 4)

A DECISIVE TURNING POINT

Over the last thirty years, the language situation in Montreal has continued to change and be a focus of attention at all levels of society. The progress of the French language in the city has been a subject of widespread coverage in the media and of deliberation and discussion by the highest courts in the land and the political community. It has even been a key factor in the development of a contemporary Canadian identity. Without a vibrant, well-established francophone community in Montreal, Canada's official biculturalism and bilingualism policies would have been instruments with only formal and bureaucratic scope and import, with little capacity to influence the lives and values of the citizenry. A substantial decline in the use of French in Montreal in the second half of the twentieth century would no doubt have dealt a fatal blow to the long-term survival of all francophone communities in Canada. In Quebec the anglicization of Montreal would have eventually turned French, nearly four centuries after the first French settlements in the St Lawrence valley, into nothing but a cultural curiosity and attraction and confined it to marginal geographic regions. Since Montreal is the economic centre of their society, francophones would have concluded that the important transactions were made in English and that it was better to leave French at home if they wanted decent jobs. In this scenario all large-scale social or cultural ventures would have been beyond the reach of francophones, particularly since the immigrant communities would have been anglicized.

Today almost all observers agree that this scenario – disastrous for Quebec as much as for Canada – will never see the light of day. Tangible proof of a major shift in trends over the last decade in Montreal, and especially in the newer immigrant populations, was found most convincingly as of yet in the

2001 census. The primary demolinguistic indicators from the 2001 census point to a new trend confirming the francization of allophones, and this trend will likely intensify in the years to come. However, the francization of new citizens has not been at the expense of English, since, unlike the generation before them, they tend to become trilingual, not just bilingual. The result has been an unprecedented increase in the level of bilingualism in Montreal over the last few years, one that has put the city in a class of its own internationally. Many large cities boast the title of multilingual capital of the world because their streets and squares are teeming with citizens from all over the world; however, few cities have a significant majority of citizens who can speak both official languages fluently – in this case French and English, which are both important languages for international communication.

However, the steady growth of French and the continued importance of English communication in the Montreal economy and the rise of the allophone communities did not stem the steady decline in the number of anglophones of British stock in Quebec and particularly its largest city. The decline in the number of persons with English as their mother tongue in Quebec, including descendants of immigrants who arrived at the beginning of the twentieth century and who were subsequently anglicized, is a major demographic trend in Quebec and specifically in Montreal (Rudin, 1985, 28). The percentage of English-speakers has dropped in each federal census held in Quebec and Montreal since 1901, including that of 2001 (see tables 11.1 and 11.2). Only 8.3 per cent of Quebecers in 2001 stated that English was their mother tongue, compared with 8.8 per cent five years earlier. In Montreal during the same period, the decline was even more significant, from 18.9 to 17.7 per cent. These numbers suggest that English is holding its own because of its importance in North America, without a well-established, large anglophone community.

Like all minorities, Anglo-Quebecers face specific linguistic pressures, especially in mixed marriages. The 2001 census showed that 30 per cent of Quebecers with English as their mother tongue have francophone spouses. Furthermore, parents of a large proportion of children with the right, under the Charter of the French Language, to enter the English-language school system nonetheless enrolled them in French-language schools for practical reasons. Note also that, according to 2001 census data, Arabic is the language growing fastest on Montreal Island. Close to 80,000 citizens spoke Arabic, a leap of 29 per cent in five years. While 2.4 per cent of Montrealers identify themselves as Arabic-speaking, Italian is still the third most common language in the city with 127,000 speakers, or 3.8 per cent of the Greater Montreal Area. Montreal's Italian-speaking population is the result of a wave of immigration that arrived immediately after the Second World War, and its numbers should decline in the decades to come. The situation is entirely different for the Arabic-speaking population, which has accounted for a large proportion of immigrants to Quebec since 1996. Evidence of this increase is the fact that, after French and English, Arabic is currently the mother tongue most commonly spoken in the Montreal public school system, followed closely by Spanish. The difference between the Arabic- and Italian-speaking communities is that, thirty or so years ago, many Italian-speaking Montrealers were educated in English-language public schools, whereas Arabic-speaking children have studied in French-language schools as required under the Charter of the French Language. Moreover, the majority of Quebecers of Arab origins come from Lebanon, Morocco, Algeria, and Egypt, where French is still a primary language of administration and communication.

Immigrants do not make up a particularly large part of the Montreal population. According to the 2001 census, only 18.4 per cent of the city's population was born abroad, compared with 43.7 per cent in Toronto and 37.5 per cent in Vancouver. Furthermore, immigrants made up only 9.9 per cent of Quebec's population in 2001, compared with 27 per cent in Ontario and 26 per cent in British Columbia; these two provinces have had the highest influx of new immigrants over the last ten years.[6] The fact remains that the approximately 700,000 Quebecers born abroad, 88 per cent of whom live in Greater Montreal, will play a leading role in the future of the French language – a role that far exceeds their demographic weight and the role played by their counterparts in the other provinces with respect to the English language. In this context, reaching a new linguistic balance in Quebec, following up on the 2001 census data and based on recent cohorts of immigrants, will a big step forward. In the final analysis, the policies introduced in the 1960s, especially the decision in 1974 to make French the only official language under the Quebec constitutional framework, seem to have been judicious choices, given what we now know. All the changes have paved the way for a new era of maturity in language management in Montreal and in all of Quebec, one that should allow French to come into dynamic contact with other languages in a context of mutual enrichment and long-term viability.

COMPARATIVE IMPLICATIONS

The recent evolution of the French language in a context as politically charged as Montreal also points to a larger picture, that of the Canadian political environment and its unique characteristics in North America.

Although it is true that Quebec society presents features to be found nowhere else on the continent and has developed a legal culture acutely sensitive to language rights, in the last forty years Canada, too, has come into its own in this domain. In a typically Canadian fashion, and during a period of stress with regards to language use and acquisition, ways have been devised to accommodate linguistic diversity that notably favour dialogue and compromise rather than confrontation. This outcome should hardly be surprising, one must add, in a country where the French-language population of Quebec was on more than one occasion given the chance to secede from Canada altogether in a referendum. One effective way to deal with potentially disruptive linguistic clashes has been to officially transfer the responsibility of language preservation and promotion to government agencies, such as the Office of the Commissioner of Official Languages at the federal level and the Conseil supérieur de la langue française in the case of Quebec. By putting such a highly sensitive issue squarely in the hands of arm's-length civil servants with recognized competence in the field, the various governments have actually done much to blunt the edge of rancour and resentment in this field. The other tendency in Canada has been to set the consensus achieved in language affairs, no matter how fragile and tentative, into law. Once rules are defined legally and courts are entrusted with the responsibility of maintaining linguistic peace, it follows that challenges directed at the concrete application of language policies are ultimately treated with respect and patience. Canada must be one of the countries in the world with the most impressive track record in its constant promulgation and reinterpretation of language laws.

Canada has also applied the logic of a decentralized federal system to language legislation and regulation. While the federal level of jurisdiction has applied a policy of strict bilingualism evenly across the country since 1969 and promoted official language minorities, other levels of government have taken different routes without appearing to jeopardize the overall goals established in Ottawa. For instance, Quebec has declared French the only officially recognized language within its provincial jurisdiction, while New Brunswick applies a strictly bilingual policy. At the same time, Ontario, the most populated of Canadian provinces, has made no such all-encompassing declaration and, rather, offers French-language services only in certain regions where francophones are numerically important. All the other seven mainly anglophone provinces have no declared linguistic policy. In the final instance, this approach allows for a certain amount of flexibility and is perfectly legitimate in the Canadian legal system, as many judgments by the Supreme Court have shown repeatedly. Also, because provincial administrations are, as sole legal purveyors of education and health services, much more in contact with the average citizen, they also seem in a better position to adjust to the needs of specific communities at the local level. Likewise, Canadian municipalities favour vastly divergent approaches, depending on where they are situated and what official language dominates. In this sense, in the language sphere Canada appears more a superposition of different models and policies, all applied at specific junctures, than a unified and inevitably paradigmatically rigid entity.

Evidently this approach makes for a much more dynamic and complex system of linguistic governance than is found in most Western countries, notably in centralized states such as France or in places where the intervention of governments in the cultural domain is resisted as a matter of principle for ideological reasons. The Canadian solution also denotes an ability on the part of governments to evolve rapidly should public opinion shift in favour of more interventionist policies, while still promoting first and foremost an approach respectful of human rights and mindful of minority protection. Whether Canada has in the long run stemmed the tide of linguistic discontent and intolerance remains to be seen. The last few years have nonetheless shown that its citizens are more accepting than before of bilingualism in the public sphere and more attuned to the advantages of cultural pluralism, although often these attitudes do not translate into a higher level of personal fluency in both French and English. Perhaps Canadians have learned to adapt to the active presence of two official languages simply as an abstract feature of their society, while being content for the most part to live unilingual lives at home and in the workplace. The fact remains that for all its highly emotional appeal and symbolism, as played out in the media and in parliaments, only a few regions of Canada daily practise some form of bilingualism at the grassroots level, essentially those areas where the provinces of Ontario and New Brunswick share a border with francophone Quebec.

Federal and provincial linguistic and immigration policies are compared decade by decade in table 11.6. Our survey has shown that all of the policies (organized in columns) have tended to interact with one another over decades, and in recent years this interaction has increasingly become more complementary. For example, both federal and provincial linguistic and immigration policies have generally adapted to changes and been conciliatory in their implementation, while ongoing policy evaluation at both levels has tended to make for positive feedback.

Table 11.7 reinforces the conclusions derived from the text and table 11.6. Factors contributing to linguistic insecurity and political tensions are organized in columns and distinguished according to whether they have decreased or increased decade by decade (the rows). Details are important since the factors in all the columns have interacted with one another and together have shaped the flow of history across these decades. Nonetheless,

Table 11.6
The evolution of Canadian and Quebec language policies as compared to immigration policies, from the 1960s to the 1990s

	Linguistic policies of Canada	Linguistic policies of Quebec province	Immigration policies of Canada	Immigration policies of Quebec province
1960s	1969 Official Languages Act (revised in 1988): French and English are official languages in Canada	1969 Bill 63: Law promoting French as the language of instruction in Quebec's public schools		1968 Creation of a Quebec Ministry of Immigration 1968 Establishment of Centres d'orientation et de formation des immigrants (COFI)
1970s		1974 Bill 22: French declared the only official language of Quebec 1975 Quebec Charter of Human Rights and Freedoms 1978 Charter of the French Language (Bill 101)	1971 Declaration on multiculturalism 1976 Immigration Act (revised in 2002)	
1980s	1982 Repatriation of the Canadian Constitution and signing of Canadian Charter of Rights and Freedoms (without Quebec's formal consent)	1988 Ford judgment of the Supreme Court of Canada	1985 Citizenship Act 1988 Multiculturalism Act	
1990s				1990 Policy statement on immigration and interculturalism 1991 Quebec-Canada Accord relating to Immigration

Table 11.7

Factors leading to a resolution of linguistic tensions in Quebec, from the 1960s to the 1990s

	Linguistic insecurity decreasing in Quebec	Linguistic insecurity increasing in Quebec	Political tensions decreasing in Quebec	Political tensions increasing in Quebec
1960s	1969 Official Languages Act passed in Ottawa: bilingualism official in Canada	1969 Bill 63 perceived as too timid a measure to protect the French language	1960 Beginning of the Quiet Revolution with the election of Jean Lesage as premier of Quebec	1968 Pierre E. Trudeau becomes prime minister of Canada
1970s	1974 French-language signs mandatory and French the only official language in Quebec 1978 Charter of the French Language is the first consensual language law. Children of immigrants enter the French-language schools	1974 Bill 22 fails to create a consensus on language policies in Quebec society	1970 Parti Québécois wins its first seats in the Quebec legislature 1976 Parti Québécois forms the government for the first time with René Lévesque as premier	
1980s	1988 Ford judgment, Supreme Court of Canada, upholding large segments of Bill 101; Quebec language laws are constitutional		1987 Meech Lake Accord signed between Ottawa and the provinces	1980 Quebec referendum on sovereignty-association defeated 1982 Unilateral patriation of the Constitution by the federal government
1990s	1998 Linguistic school boards established in Quebec following a constitutional change		1992 Federal referendum on the Charlottetown Accord defeated	1990 Meech Lake Accord fails 1995 Quebec referendum on sovereignty-association defeated
2000s	2003 Census data on language use in Montreal demonstrate progress in francization process		2003 Liberal Party forms the government in Quebec with Jean Charest as premier	2000 Clarity Act

the overall visual impact of table 11.7 is dramatic in demonstrating the theme of this chapter, namely, the end of the language crisis in Quebec. Columns 3 and 4 reflect the continuing dialectical tension between decreasing and increasing political tensions in Quebec across decades up to the present. In contrast, column 1 documents a continuing series of events that have decreased linguistic insecurity in Quebec, while column 2 lists only factors that increased linguistic insecurity in the province in the early decades, with an absence of such factors in recent decades. The positive imbalance between columns 1 and 2 in recent decades reflects continuing progress in implementing Quebec's language policy, as well as more constructive federal-provincial interaction in linguistic affairs.

The end of the language crisis in Quebec does not mean that there will not be recurring problems for language policy in the province. The province's proactive language policy by its very nature faces, deals with, and attempts to resolve recurring problems in promoting the French language. The end of the language crisis in Quebec does mean that provincial and federal leaders together were able to work their way out of a protracted language crisis lasting at least several decades and, through concerted, sustained action, create a much more positive environment for language policy.

NOTES

This chapter was first presented as a paper at the 10th biennial Jerusalem conference in Canadian Studies, July 2004.

1 Note, for comparative purposes, that bilingual Montrealers of all ethnic backgrounds earned $32,545 in 2001, an amount that was much higher than unilingual anglophones ($24,625) and unilingual francophones ($20,334).

2 Originally, the clause applied to parents who had not studied in an English-language institution in Quebec. Since the difference in numbers between the two groups remained small, the so-called "Canada clause" has been applied since the 1984–85 school year.

3 The final challenge listed in the 1990 policy statement was: "Opening doors to the world."

4 The 2001 data on language was not strictly comparable with that obtained from the 1996 and 1991 censuses. It is possible that in geographical areas where francophones are numerically dominant, a slight overestimation of their number may have taken place.

5 These figures are subject to the same caveat as explained in note 4.

6 In 2001, immigrants accounted for 18.9 per cent of the total Canadian population.

Synthesis and Conclusion

MICHAEL A. MORRIS

MICHAEL A. MORRIS

LIMITATIONS OF THE COMPARATIVE APPROACH

While this book has presented the case for application of the comparative approach to Canadian language policies, the conclusions in this chapter are constrained by the limitations of the approach. Optimally, the approach would indicate decisively the position of a language policy at a given time and on this basis would be able to formulate precise recommendations about how to achieve policy objectives more completely. This aspiration, while laudable, has not been achieved here. For example, chapters 9 (Paillé) and 11 (Anctil) are models of a comparative approach in involving reliance on history, a careful methodology, and sustained comparisons over time. The two chapters do reflect a sizable area of consensus, but Paillé regards the position of French in Quebec as much less reassuring than does Anctil, therefore leading Paillé in his conclusion to recommend much more activist language policy measures for the province than does Anctil.

Paillé and Anctil do share a large degree of consensus in spite of their different comparative approaches, indicating that a comparative approach can make a significant contribution to the literature even if it does not reach an optimal level of consensus about policy recommendations. More broadly, the different approaches and orientations of all the contributors to this book have been compatible with a sizable area of consensus. At the same time, their progress toward forging a comparative approach has been handicapped by a lack of data for comparative analysis. There have been few previous comparative studies (see my introductory chapter) or those that would allow systematic comparisons between different language policies (this lack is evident in several chapters).

While these limitations constrain sustained comparisons between Canadian language policies, the obstacles are magnified in comparing these domestic policies with their counterparts in other countries and international bodies such as the Francophonie (Erfurt in chapter 6). Erfurt does have expertise in the language policies of both Canada and the Francophonie, but such knowledge is unusual and is practically non-existent in the case of multi-country comparisons. My introductory chapter documented, for example, that nearly all multi-country language policy comparisons required multiple authors and were only loosely comparative.

The response here to these limitations has been to recruit multiple authors who have various areas of expertise and to coordinate their analyses comparatively though a common methodology (see my introductory chapter). Comparative research in the future, it is hoped, will build on the foundation we have tried to establish.

DISTINCTIVE CONTRIBUTIONS OF THIS BOOK

My introductory chapter points toward some distinctive contributions of this book, which the intervening chapters have elaborated and reinforced. Three such contributions are synthesized here.

This book builds on and extends the literature on Canadian language policies. The existing literature has performed a major service in calling attention to the distinctiveness and importance of Canadian language policies both for the country and for other international actors involved in language policies. At the same time, the introductory chapter demonstrated that the relevant literature is diffuse, narrow, and specialized, and it is either not comparative or at most partially comparative in method and orientation. That chapter indicated more positively how the book builds on and extends that literature, and it recommended future directions for research. The introductions to the various parts of the book elaborated these themes.

The comparative framework set forth in the introductory chapter aspires to remedy the shortcomings of the literature. Most previous works, if comparative at all, address only one thematic comparison (figure I.1), while all the chapters in this book address multiple thematic comparisons, at the same time placing primary emphasis on one. Similarly, the extant literature rather vaguely addresses one or another aspect of the policy cycle (figure I.2), while the chapters here have specified which aspects of the policy cycle are under discussion and how the various components are interrelated one to another. Since the various components of both thematic and policy comparisons overlap and interact with one another, this comparative approach captures the complex, multi-faceted nature of Canadian language policies. In contrast, the emphasis of the existing literature on one element or another in isolation does not capture this complexity.

This book builds on and extends the literature on comparative language policies. Part of the Canadian literature on national language policies overlaps with the larger literature on comparative language policies. While we have faulted the existing literature on Canadian language policy in several ways, the larger literature on comparative language policies shares many of the same shortcomings. The lack of systematic comparison in the Canadian literature would have been grave had such existed in other countries. Instead, the absence of a systematic comparative approach plagues the literature at large. We have tried to take some initial steps in this book toward a systematic comparative approach without much help from the existing literature. Our approach, as documented in the introductory chapter, instead has relied primarily on the Canadian literature as well as the mainstream political science literature.

The comparative framework developed and implemented here facilitates systematic comparisons and helps generate and support conclusions. All of the contributors have relied on the comparative framework (portrayed graphically in figures I.1 on thematic perspectives and I.2 on policy comparisons) without assuming the burden of proof by giving all comparisons equal emphasis. The specific topic and logic of each chapter have led to more emphasis on some areas, although each contributor has related the part to the whole. This systematic treatment by each contributor makes chapter-specific comparisons and conclusions relevant for the whole.

Four groups of conclusions follow, each illustrated by the comparative record on which they rely. These four groups reflect recurring themes throughout this book – overall conclusions, conclusions relating to Canadian language policies, conclusions relating to the five thematic perspectives, and conclusions relating to policy comparisons.

OVERALL CONCLUSIONS

A comparative approach highlights what is distinctive and shared in a language policy and thereby provides a solid base for deriving generalizations about Canadian language policies. A comparative method is as promising for analyzing language policy in general and Canadian language policies in particular as has been the case for other disciplines. Evidence to support this conclusion includes this book and its individual chapters, recurring if scattered efforts in the existing literature assessing Canadian language policies comparatively (cited in the introductory chapter), and proposed avenues of future comparative research (see the introductory chapter as well as the introductions to the subsequent parts of the book).

The five kinds of thematic comparison (figure 1.1) in this book help to capture the complex nature and interaction of Canadian language policies. Each of these five kinds (historical, policy, international, non-linguistic, and group comparisons) has a separate identity or structure and offers distinctive insights into Canadian language policies. Each thematic comparison at the same time overlaps as well as interacts with the others. The totality of complex, multi-faceted language policies is therefore best captured by reliance on every one of the comparisons singly and in interaction with one another. This book claims originality in this regard.

Works cited in the introductory chapter assess one or at the most two of the five kinds of thematic comparison in any detail, and moreover the scope of comparisons made has been narrow. This is not to question the value of comparisons on a single dimension, and in fact the introductory chapter, as well as the introductions to the subsequent parts of the book, identified fruitful avenues of future research in each of the five thematic comparison areas. At the same time, the utility of future comparative research will be enhanced by relying on the larger context of multiple thematic comparisons of Canadian language policies as a reference point.

Similarly, both domestic and international comparisons gain from being multi-dimensional as well as focused. On the domestic front, multiple Canadian language policies are multi-faceted in nature, whether they are considered singly or as they interact with one another. Over time, these policies have increasingly interacted with one another, so that holistic comparisons complement more targeted ones. Whether the focus is on one or more Canadian language policies, multi-faceted comparisons best address a multi-faceted reality.

Cross-national comparisons provide a useful check on the efficacy of Canadian language policies as well as those of other countries. Efficacy must be judged in terms of the achievement of objectives in a rapidly changing world. Since ongoing globalization increases interaction between countries and their language policies, it follows that international comparisons need to be multi-faceted in order to capture the complex reality of each language policy on the world stage. A globalizing world also reinforces the heterogeneity of international actors, including their language policies, so that international comparisons should encompass non-state actors as well as state ones (i.e., Erfurt, chapter 6).

The six-stage policy comparison (figure I.2) in this book helps to capture the complex nature and interaction of Canadian language policies. Each of the six stages of the policy cycle represents a discrete stage in the policy process (formulation, implementation, compliance, reaction, evaluation, and modification). At the same time, each overlaps and interacts with the others. Focus on a single, static policy stage can be useful, especially when complemented by awareness of the interactive process affecting the entire policy cycle. The complex, interactive nature of policy comparisons is therefore similar to the thematic comparisons (see the conclusion immediately above) and hence need not be elaborated further.

Other comparative methods offer considerable promise as well in helping to capture the complex nature and interaction of Canadian language policies. In chapters 2 and 3 Mackey sets forth a conceptual framework for systematically comparing language policies, which relies on and extends figures I.1 and I.2. The policy components, the language components, and the evaluation of language policies are set forth and compared together with Canadian and other international examples. Subsequent chapters pick up elements of these comparisons and develop them more systematically.

Still other comparative approaches are evident. For example, Erfurt in chapter 6 and Labrie in chapter 10 rely on discourse analysis to identify the structure and evolution of complex language issues. Erfurt also makes use of the process of institutionalization to compare Canada's domestic French-speaking groups and the international Francophonie. Bilinsky in chapter 5 employs the ideal type of denial of languages as a benchmark for judging the positive and negative nature of interaction between different language policies and their consequences. Paillé in chapter 9 develops a careful methodology for demographic comparison of two Canadian provinces over time.

CONCLUSIONS RELATING TO CANADIAN LANGUAGE POLICIES

Canadian language policies have been innovative in a number of ways; however, the gap between theory and results remains substantial. This is not simply a Canadian failing but reflects larger global dilemmas. Canada stands out in global terms as an innovator in such language policy areas as bilingualism, multiculturalism, and cultural and linguistic diversity. However, practically every chapter in this book comments in one way or another on the gap between theory and reality. Canadian federal language policy is faulted (Haque, chapter 8), and Quebec's language policy is not spared from criticism either (Fontaine, chapter 7). The lack of reliable official data is a recurring concern (Paillé, chapter 9), but it is not easy to correct or lessen the gap between official claims and de facto realities. A comparative book such as this one does provide a check on official claims and can help to lessen the gap by formulating conclusions. At the same time, the process of developing lessons of language policy is necessarily protracted and incremental. The continuing pursuit of lessons learned on multiple levels suggests that no country, province, or group has cornered knowledge about language policy, all of which must continue to adapt fitfully to an increasingly complex, interdependent world.

Some shortcomings of Canadian language policies nonetheless relate more to national and provincial institutions and implementation than to generic causes. While federal and provincial language policies in Canada have reached certain accommodations over decades, it would be incorrect to regard them as complementary. For example, the Bloc Québécois has insisted that the federal government apply Bill 101 on Quebec territory instead of the federal bilingualism law. For its part, the federal government has never amended its linguistic laws to make them complementary with Quebec's language policy.

All Canadian language policies have had difficulty in achieving stated goals and retaining support of key constituencies. A case in point is how the identity of immigrants has posed a challenge for both federal and provincial language policies (Fontaine, chapters 7, and Haque, chapter 8). Similarly, federal and provincial approaches to linguistic diversity in Ontario have been inadequate (Paillé, chapter 9, and Labrie, chapter 10).

Over time, interaction among Canadian language policies has become more accommodating of respective vital interests. Anctil in chapter 11 points most directly to this conclusion, but various chapters report complementary findings. For example, Bilinsky's paradigm of denial of languages in chapter 5 shows that East European countries and Russia have continued to be dogged by the legacy of this paradigm, while Canada has evolved away from the oppressor/oppressed dichotomy implicit in the paradigm. The underlying principles of federal and Quebec language policies continue to contrast, the federal policy expressing the personality principle and Quebec's policy reflecting the territoriality principle, although this difference has not blocked some important accommodations from emerging. Quebec has been able to reverse secular trends undermining the status of French in the province and has gained control over migration into the province. The federal government has been able to maintain national unity while promoting both bilingual services and multiculturalism throughout the country. Both levels of government have been able to reach an accommodation regarding mutually acceptable participation in the international Francophonie (Erfurt, chapter 6).

Canadian language policies have broadly promoted cultural and linguistic diversity, although more specific lessons learned are still subject to debate. Federal language policy has provided bilingual services in Canada, and Quebec's language policy has enhanced the position of French in the province. There is also widespread agreement that the French language in Quebec and elsewhere in Canada, had there been neither federal nor provincial language policies, would have been much more threatened than in fact is the case at present. Also there is growing awareness that a free-market approach, whether this be the US or the Canadian variety, will tend to prejudice minority cultures and languages unless redressed or counterbalanced by language policy (Labrie, chapter 10).

Beyond these areas of agreement, there is much disagreement about the present and likely future situation of the French language in Quebec, as well as about whether and how the federal government should continue to provide bilingual services throughout the country. The federal government has not been able to reverse the steady decline of francophone communities outside Quebec (save for New Brunswick), and Quebec governments have not decided how best they should become involved in promoting French outside the province. In order to add greater specificity to the debate about what have been lessons learned and what future direction language policies ought to take, we now turn to conclusions relating to thematic and policy comparisons.

CONCLUSIONS RELATING TO THE FIVE THEMATIC PERSPECTIVES (FIGURE I.I)

Conclusions for Part One: Perspectives and Overviews

Canadian language issues are usefully considered in historical perspective, particularly since the long-standing, often tense relationship between the English and French languages has been hard to overcome. Canadian language policies all have fairly recent roots, while the often tense relationship between the English and French languages has a long history (Mackey, chapter 1). The dysfunctional historical legacy therefore must be taken into account in shaping conciliatory efforts in the present. Awareness of the importance of the historical record is a prudent first step, which also should encourage testing proposed initiatives on language policy against the historical record.

Historical perspective paired with systematic comparison provides a useful framework for assessing language issues and policy problems. Chapters 2 and 3 (Mackey) may be regarded together as developing a method or structured approach for systematically comparing language policies across time. The key components of language policy need to be assessed in historical (chapter 1) and policy (chapter 2–3) perspective. This approach is all the more important in light of the structure of the literature surveyed in the introductory chapter, which identified some partially comparative but few fully comparative studies. Even the comparative works were not systematic, were generally focused on a specific problem area, and only sporadically cast an eye on history. Mackey, in his three chapters, has raised the bar for future language policy comparisons and has set forth an approach for judging such analysis.

Conclusions for Part Two: International Perspectives

Multiple comparisons between Canada and other countries and international actors specify the complex interaction of different dimensions of Canadian language policies, thereby helping generate lessons learned for Canada as well as for others. A comparative approach is especially useful in selecting and orienting international comparisons. Criteria for international comparisons in the literature have ranged from shared ethnic and linguistic concerns (comparisons between multi-ethnic, multilingual countries) to shared problems between sovereign and subordinate political units (federal countries and states/provinces/regions). Each of the various kinds of comparison has proven useful, although a comparative approach has been applied unevenly with scattered results.

Sustained Canadian efforts of various kinds to mould language use to policy ends make Canadian language policies good candidates for other countries seeking language policy lessons. At the same time, the importance of language issues for Canada has led researchers to make a number of cross-country comparisons in search of lessons for Canada. By relying on a systematic comparative approach, this book has advanced this quest for relevant lessons by all concerned.

While various kinds of country and international comparisons with Canadian language policies offer insights, the contrast with the United States especially deserves sustained attention. Maurais in chapter 4 builds on and extends the few previous comparisons of US and Canadian language policies and approaches. Unfortunately, each country has tended to look at the other in the area of language policy as an example of how not to proceed.

Conclusions for Part Three: Non-linguistic Perspectives

Non-linguistic factors directly impact on language policy, so that their comparison highlights language policy shortcomings. Migratory patterns and population trends clearly get to the heart of language policy as evidenced in the chapters by Fontaine (7), Haque (8), and Paillé (9), although here as elsewhere the complexity of and overlap between issues makes it difficult to derive clear lessons. What is clear is that existing conceptual categories need revision (Fontaine), and more reliable data are required for demographical comparisons (Paillé). The federal government also has had difficulty in effectively balancing and relating policies on language, multiculturalism, and immigrant language training (Haque). Without these essential ingredients for sound policy, Canadian language policies have often failed to deliver sufficiently on stated policy goals. More positively, comparative issue analysis can help derive more appropriate concepts, approaches, and lessons. Each of these chapters makes such a contribution.

Non-linguistic comparisons help distinguish between language policy successes and failures, thereby allowing the formulation of more discriminating "lessons learned." As both Canada and Quebec have become more multicultural, Quebec has experienced identity problems (Fontaine), and the federal government has had difficulty balancing and relating policies on language, multiculturalism, and immigrant language training (Haque). Both authors relate these problems to specific provincial and federal contexts. From a demographic perspective via a systematic comparative approach, Paillé documents the relative success of Quebec in achieving individual bilingualism, in contrast to Ontario. (With mixed success, the federal government has promoted institutional bilingualism.)

A lesson learned from these three contributors to Part Three of the book is that issues overlap and interact, so comparisons must be cross-issue and cross-provincial in order to measure policy success and failure accurately. Language policy, for example, overlaps and interacts with other policies, just as jurisdictions responsible for language policy overlap and interact.

The dividing line between non-linguistic and group comparisons (Parts Three and Four) is increasingly blurred, so that both must be considered in interaction with one another. Chapters 7-9 were grouped together in Part Three on non-linguistic comparisons since their greatest emphasis was in that area. However, a strength of all these chapters is that they are carefully attuned to group comparisons as well (Part Four) and weave this factor into their analysis of non-linguistic comparisons. Similarly, the chapters in Part Four place most emphasis on group comparisons while also giving careful attention to non-linguistic ones.

A lesson learned is that in a globalizing world traditional boundaries are increasingly blurred, requiring that policy adapt accordingly. For example, the increasing overlap between domestic and international affairs places a premium on language policy that is active in each sphere. Similarly, the increasing overlap between linguistic and non-linguistic issues means that language policy, to be effective, must move in tandem with related policies, including education, migration, and multiculturalism. Finally, the overlap between issues (linguistic and non-linguistic) and groups gives an incentive for policy-makers to coordinate approaches to both areas.

Conclusions for Part Four: Group Perspectives

Group comparisons focus on the ultimate clients of language policy while also highlighting language policy shortcomings. Language policy is ultimately oriented toward reshaping social reality and particularly the linguistic context of target groups. A clear conclusion is that groups and their larger social reality have often been intractable to manipulation by policy-makers. Labrie in chapter 10 emphasizes that a contrasting free-market alternative may not lead to acceptable results for minority linguistic groups either.

Group comparisons can identify important "lessons learned," which can advance the goals of language policy. Comparative group analysis can help derive more effective approaches. The lesson is not that language policy is misguided in attempting to affect language group practice but, rather, that the gap between theory and reality needs to be lessened and that this process in any event is likely to be protracted. The longer the time frame, the more opportunity there is for language policy to reshape language groups. For example, over several decades Quebec's language policy has had success in promoting the gradual francization of allophones (Paillé, chapter 9, and Anctil, chapter 11). Anctil also suggests that a protracted learning curve has promoted greater public receptivity to bilingualism and that long-term provincial-federal interaction has facilitated numerous accommodations of interest.

The dividing line between private and public sector actors is increasingly blurred, so that both must be considered in interaction with the other. Erfurt, Labrie, and Anctil (chapters 6, 10, and 11) all look at private-sector actors in interaction with the public sector. In developing his methodology for language policy comparison, Mackey (chapters 2 and 3) likewise carefully examines interaction between the private and public sectors. Private–public-sector relations pose continuing problems of coordination, and all the more so since the dividing line between them is increasingly blurred. It follows that in order to promote policy ends successfully, both sectors must be managed in interaction with the other.

CONCLUSIONS RELATING TO POLICY COMPARISONS (FIGURE 1.2)

The six-stage policy cycle reflects a systemic (or political system) approach to analysis of language policy, which allows a discrete focus on each policy stage while also calling attention to interaction and overlap among all stages.

Conclusions about the Policy Cycle (All Six Stages)

The six-stage policy cycle usefully describes Canadian language policies, both individually and in interaction with one another. These language policies are both constrained and enabled by standing alone as well as being part of an interactive system. Canada's multiple language policies are all housed in the same country; so it is useful to examine them as an interactive system. Each also has its distinctive aims and jurisdiction, and the six-stage policy cycle can be applied individually to each. By adopting a comparative approach, this book has emphasized both side-by-side comparisons of Canadian language policies and interactive comparisons. The five thematic comparisons have added additional comparative perspectives to the policy cycle. This multi-tiered approach is further specified in the stage-by-stage comparisons offered below.

Systemic language policy comparisons are most productively applied to pairs and groups of countries as well as international regions and organizations, rather than in systemic global comparisons. Targeted local comparisons can be telling. Chapter 4 by Maurais is an example of a productive comparison between neighbouring countries, the Canada and the United States, and our conclusion regarding comparisons between the two called for more research in that area. Chapter 5 by Bilinsky positively contrasts the US-Canadian case with a group of countries belonging to another interactive regional language policy system (Eastern Europe).

While global comparisons may be useful selectively (i.e., the Francophonie in chapter 6), local ones may offer more promise. This conclusion follows from the popular adage "What is global is local and what is local is global." For example, Montreal has played a key role in the success of Quebec's language policy (Anctil, chapter 11). More broadly, the language trajectory of Montreal has played an important part in the Canadian language policy model, which has attracted global attention.

Conclusions about Policy Formulation (Stage One)

The historical legacy poses recurring policy challenges in the present, particularly for policy formulation (stage one). Chapter 1 by Mackey calls attention to several problems the historical legacy poses for policy formulation. It is hard to discern just when Canadian language policies began, since practices that impact on the present can be traced back centuries. The historical legacy of English-French tension has influenced the present, posing a challenge of how to overcome a diffuse, yet deeply rooted negative force. Nearly all the contributors to this volume have relied to some degree on the historical record in order to place their respective topics in perspective.

The lesson to be learned is that the policy formulation stage is more complicated than isolated formation of a new approach at a specific point in time. Tradition and legacy impose a heavy hand on the present. It therefore behooves policy-makers to be keenly aware of history when forging policy initiatives. Bilinsky shows that in their initial euphoria Eastern European authorities, in formulating new language policies, did not fully appreciate how to effectively work out of difficult language situations created by long-standing great-power denial of language.

The often-negative historical experience of Canada with First Nations (indigenous peoples and their languages and cultures) has been difficult to overcome, as discussed in several chapters. A recent case study described Canada's granting of local autonomy in 1999 to the Inuit living in the eastern part of the Northwest Territories. This Canadian initiative is recognized as "unique as a method of addressing an ethnic group's demands for self-rule," and it "can offer, if successful, a new model for other states with similar ethnic enclaves." While the authors are enthusiastic about the Canadian initiative, their qualification ("if successful") suggests the very real obstacles to be overcome. The area is vast, the Native population is small, and modernization continues to challenge this minority language and culture. The doubt expressed by the authors about the eventual outcome of this Canadian initiative after only a decade is also evident in their conclusion: "The future of the territory is yet to be told" (Kelleher and Klein, 2008, 197, 64).

Effective policy formulation is the initial stage of an ongoing policy cycle, not an end in itself. The historical legacy can be so sensitive and policy formulation so challenging that policy-makers easily succumb to inaction once a policy initiative is finally formulated and approved. In other words, the previous conclusion tends to have a negative impact on this one unless offset. Fontaine in chapter 7 documents how successive Quebec governments shifted and floundered for decades in trying to reach a satisfactory formulation of how to categorize immigrants (table 7.1). Haque in chapter 8 chronicles similar protracted policy ineffectiveness at the federal level in trying to reconcile bilingual and multicultural policies. The clear lesson is that goals set in the initial policy formulation stage need to be sufficiently specific and decisive to carry over into subsequent policy phases and that these goals need to be coordinated with goals in cognate policy areas.

There are few international success stories where the challenges of policy formulation have been clearly overcome. While the Canadian record regarding policy formulation is uneven, so too the international record is often mixed. This kind of policy dilemma is, after all, universal. While Canada has encountered recurring problems in policy formulation, the Canadian approach has been as effective, if not more so, as frequently lauded international models. This conclusion is further supported below.

Conclusions about Policy Implementation and Compliance (Stages Two and Three)

The mixed Canadian record regarding policy formulation (the first stage of the policy cycle) has contributed to the mixed record in policy implementation and compliance (the second and third stages of the policy cycle). Inasmuch as the policy cycle is a continuing process, resulting positive or negative momentum in the first three stages is hard to reverse. This conclusion applies to the policy cycle at both the federal and the provincial levels, as well as their interaction. At the federal level, the Commissioner of Official Languages has called for more effort to move from the word (goal) to the action (implementation). She has advocated building on a legacy of positive policy initiatives while addressing and correcting negative aspects (Adam, 2005).

Anctil in chapter 11 shows that serious divisions between provincial groups over Quebec's language policy goals (the first stage) contributed to the politicization of policy implementation and compliance (the second and third stages), which led to a protracted language crisis in the province. Quebec's policy cycle has subsequently been transformed from being politicized or largely negative to being positive, a shift that required a sustained conciliatory approach on all sides.

While the Canadian record in policy implementation has been mixed, the record of other countries has been no better and often worse. Canada has the advantage of being a democratic, developed country which over time has benefited from dialogue and expertise in shaping the policy cycle. Bilinsky in chapter 5 chronicles the contrasting oppressive legacy of totalitarian rule where language policy tended to be based on fiat rather than expertise. While Quebec has had success in shifting from an initial negative policy setting to a more positive one, Eastern European countries have not had such success in altering their policy setting, in spite of the language policy successes of some of the small Baltic countries. Uneven progress toward democracy in Eastern Europe has not been able to resolve underlying language policy tensions.

Conclusions about Policy Reaction and Evaluation
(Stages Four and Five)

Politicization of the policy cycle threatens to impact on policy reaction and evaluation in an especially adverse way. The language crisis in Quebec so politicized policy reaction and evaluation that reporting of figures and statistics relating to different language groups became objects of intense political discussion (Anctil, chapter 11). Policy evaluation instead needs to be objective and dispassionate in order to be able to take corrective action.

Multiple benchmarks for judging national language policy performance, including that of Canada, promote objective policy evaluation. Mackey in chapter 3 identifies and analyzes the key components in evaluation of language policy from a comparative perspective. The methodology is useful for evaluating language policies in general and Canada's in particular. Similarly, Paillé in chapter 9 develops a demographic methodology for judging the effectiveness of language policy across time. Canada's language policies are judged as having mixed results, making it all the more important to steer them reliably on the basis of multiple comparative benchmarks.

Canadian political characteristics have promoted restrained policy reaction and objective policy evaluation (the fourth and fifth stages in the policy cycle), thereby helping to improve the mixed Canadian record in the first three stages in subsequent policy iterations. Canada has a comparative advantage in being a democratic, developed country that generally emphasizes dialogue and expertise and is able to rely on ample resources to support policy. Evidence submitted reflects the positive impact of these comparative Canadian advantages in the latter policy stages.

Politicization of the language policy process has been common, thereby making objective policy evaluation difficult. Mackey in chapter 2 notes that politicization of the language policy process has been common, and he gives historical examples. Political will, even when firmly supporting language policy goals and implementation in the early policy stages, must be dispassionate in policy evaluation and feedback if necessary corrections are to be made. In the Eastern European cases (Bilinsky, chapter 5), the sensitivity of language policy has limited such a dispassionate approach, and language policy has been further undermined by lack of reliable data and resources.

Conclusions about Policy Modification (Stage Six)

The Canadian record is best with regard to the latter stages of the policy cycle, thereby helping to correct shortcomings in previous stages in subsequent policy iterations. The overall trajectory of Canadian language policies, especially in the early decades, was rocky and uneven. The Canadian comparative advantages of democratic dialogue, expertise, and resources have kicked in more effectively in recent decades to promote a more positive setting for the policy cycle. Corrective action has been taken by modifying policy goals, implementation, and evaluation, so that increasingly feedback has become important and self-correcting. Mackey in chapter 3 concludes that Quebec has done a better job with feedback than the federal government.

The international record with regard to the later stages of the policy cycle is often the worst. Strong performance in any of the previous stages can be undermined by failure to take subsequent corrective action through positive feedback. The evidence submitted supports the relationship between the six policy cycles that we have identified. That is, the more that popular and political will are focused emotionally on goals and implementation of language policy (the first four stages of the policy cycle), the more difficult it will be to have dispassionate policy evaluation and feedback (the last two stages of the policy cycle). Examples have been given from around the world where language policy is prominent in the policy arena yet policy pitfalls recur. Assertive language policies are positive in supporting cultural and linguistic diversity, yet emotional commitment has often inflamed communal/domestic rivalries. The Canadian example stands out in meeting the difficult challenges of policy evaluation and feedback (last two stages of the policy cycle), so that cultural and linguistic diversity can be harmonized with communal/domestic and regional/international relations.

Belgium and Switzerland, which have been regarded as especially pertinent cases for Canada, illustrate this conclusion as well. Failure to take constructive feedback measures over time ends up burdening the present. Fontaine in chapter 7 briefly reviews the serious language problems continuing to burden Belgium. In the context of continuing language-related problems in Switzerland, a Montreal newspaper concluded, "Our success at integrating newcomers is making us one of the most successful models in the world, without Europe's problems" (Freed, 2007).

OUTLOOK

Analyzing Canadian language policies from multiple perspectives and angles highlights the advantages of a comparative approach, including the conclusions presented here. Just as this work has relied on past research, it is hoped that our systematic comparative approach will facilitate and encourage future research on comparative language policies. More such research can further corroborate and clarify the conclusions and lessons learned here.

References

PREFACE

Corbeil, Jean-Claude. 1997. "Comment s'insère l'aménagement linguistique dans la structure et la culture politiques d'un pays: Étude d'un cas: les politiques linguistiques au Canada." In *DiversCité Langues*, vol. 1, 1–13. Online at http://www.uquebec.ca/diversite.

Mackey, William F. 1984. "Forward." In *Conflict and Language Planning in Quebec*, ed. Richard Y. Bourhis. Clevedon, UK: Multilingual Matters Ltd.

INTRODUCTION

Bourhis, Richard Y., ed. 1984. *Conflict and Language Planning in Quebec*. Clevendon, UK: Multilingual Matters Ltd.

Bourhis, Richard Y. (ed.), 1994, "French-English Language Issues in Canada," in *International Journal of the Sociology of Language* 105/106.

Burnaby, Barbara. 1996. "Language Policies in Canada." In *Language Policies in English-Dominant Countries: Six Case Studies*, ed. Michael Herriman and Barbara Burnaby, 160–219. Clevendon, UK: Multilingual Matters Ltd.

Carey, Stephen. 1997. "Language Management, Official Bilingualism, and Multiculturalism in Canada." *Annual Review of Applied Linguistics* 17: 204–23.

Commission des États généraux sur la situation et l'avenir du français au Québec. 2001. *Le français langue pour tout le monde*. Québec: Éditeur officiel.

Corbeil, Jean-Claude. 1997. "Comment s'insère l'aménagement linguistique dans la structure et la culture politiques d'un pays: Étude d'un cas: les politiques linguistiques au Canada. *DiversCité Langues* 1: 1–13. Online at http://www.uquebec.ca/diversite.

Edwards, John. 1993/94. "Language Policy and Planning in Canada." *Annual Review of Applied Linguistics* 14: 126–36.

– ed. 1998. *Language in Canada* Cambridge: Cambridge University Press.

Macmillan, C. Michael. 1998, *The Practice of Language Rights in Canada*. Toronto: University of Toronto Press.

McAndrew, Marie. 2001. *Immigration et diversité à l'école: Le débat québécois dans une perspective comparative*. Montreal: Les Presses de l'Université de Montréal.

McRae, Kenneth D. 2007. "Toward Language Equality: Four Democracies Compared." *International Journal of the Sociology of Language* 187/188: 13–34.

Royal Commission on Bilingualism and Biculturalism. 1963–70. Various volumes. Ottawa: Queen's Printer.

Slann, Martin. 2004. *Introduction to Politics: Governments and Nations in the Twenty-First Century*. 3rd ed. Cincinnati: Atomic Dog Publishers.

Woehrling, José. 1993. "Politique linguistique et libre-échange: l'incidence de l'Accord de libre-échange entre le Canada et les Etats-Unis sur la législation linguistique du Québec (à la lumière de l'expérience de la Communauté économique européenne." In *Contextes de la politique linguistique québécoise*, 79–123.

– 1995. "Convergences et divergences entre les politiques linguistiques du Québec, des autorités fédérales et des provinces anglophones: le nœud gordien des relations entre les Québécois francophones, la minorité anglo-québécoise et les minorités francophones du Canada." In *Pour un renforcement de la solidarité entre francophones au Canada*, 209-344. Quebec: Conseil de la langue française.

– 2005. "Conflits et complémentarités entre les politiques linguistiques en vigueur au Québec, au niveau fédéral et dans le reste du Canada." In *Appartenances, institutions et citoyenneté*, 295–319. Quebec: Wilson and Lafleur.

CHAPTER TWO

Ager, Dennis. 2001. *Motivation in Language Planning and Policy*. Clevedon, UK: Multilingual Matters.

Alesina, Alberto, and Enrico Spolaore. 2003. *The Size of Nations*. Cambridge, MA: The MIT Press.

Ammon, Ulrich, ed. 2000. *Sprachförderung*. Frankfurt am Main: Peter Lang.

Ammon, Ulrich, and Grant McConnell. 2002. *English as an Academic Language in Europe: A Survey of Its Use in Teaching*. Duisburg Papers on Research in Language and Culture 48. Frankfurt: Peter Lang.

Baker, Philip, and John Eversley, eds. 2000. *Multilingual Capital: The Languages of London's Schoolchildren*. London: Battlebridge.

Balbauf, Richard B., Jr, and Robert B. Kaplan. 2003. "Language Policy Decisions and Power: Who Are the Actors?" In Ryan and Terborg, 2003, 19–40.

Bédard, Édith, and Jacques Maurais, eds. 1983. *La norme linguistique*. Paris: Laffont; Québec: Conseil de la langue française.

Beebe, Von N., and William F. Mackey. 1990. *Bilingual Schooling and the Miami Experience*. Miami: Institute of Interamerican Studies.

Bendrath, Wiebke. 2003. *Ich, Region, Nation*. Tübingen: Max Niemeyer.

Blackledge, Adrian. 2005. *Discourse and Power in a Multilingual World*. Amsterdam: John Benjamins.

Blanke, Detlev, and Jürgen Scharnhorst, eds. 2007. *Sprachenpolitik und Sprachkultur*. Frankfurt: Peter Lang.

Bordieu, Pierre. 1991. *Language and Symbolic Power*. Cambridge: Polity Press.

Bouchard, Gérard, and Charles Taylor. 2008. *Building the Future: A Time for Reconciliation*. Quebec: Les Publications du Québec.

Bouchard, Pierre, and Richard Y. Bourhis, eds. 2002. *L'aménagement linguistique au Québec: 25 ans d'application de la Charte de la langue française. Revue d'aménagement linguistique*, Terminogramme, automne 2002, hors série. Quebec: Les Publications du Québec.

Breton, Roland. 1998. *Peuples et États: L'impossible équation*. Paris: Flammarion.

Calvet, Louis-Jean. 1999. *La guerre des langues et les politiques linguistiques*. 2nd ed. Paris: Hachette.

Cartwright, D.G. 1977. "The Designation of Bilingual Districts in Canada through Linguistic and Spatial Analysis." *Tijdschrift voor Econ. en Soc. Geografie* 68: 16–29.

Casad, Eugene H. 1974. *Dialect Intelligibility Testing*. SIL Publication, 38. Norman, OK: Summer Institute of Linguistics.

Clyne, Michael. 1989. "Pluricentricity: National Varieties". In *Status and Function of Languages and Language Varieties,* ed. Ulrich Ammon, 357–71. Berlin: Walter de Gruyter.

Collis, Dermot Ronán F., ed. 1990. *Arctic Languages: An Awakening*. Paris: UNESCO.

Coluzzi, Paolo. (2008). "Language Planning for Italian Regional Languages ('Dialects')." *Language Problems and Language Planning* 32: 215–36.

Cooray, L.J. Mark (1985). *Changing the Language of the Law: The Sri Lanka Experience*. CIRB Publication A-20. Quebec: Presses de l'Université Laval.

Corbeil, Jean-Claude. 1987. "Vers un aménagement linguistique comparé." In Maurais, 1987, 553–66.

Cornish, Vaughan. 1936. *Borderlands of Language and Nationality in Europe and Their Relations to the Historic Frontiers of Christendom*. London: Sifton.

Crystal, David. 2000. *Language Death*. Cambridge: Cambridge University Press.

Dalby, David. 2000. *The Linguasphere: Register of the World's Languages and Speech Communities*. 2 vols. Hebron, UK: Linguasphere Press.

Dale, E., and D. Reichert. 1957. *Bibliography of Vocabulary Studies*. Columbus: State University of Ohio.

De Certeau, Michel, D. Julia, and J. Revel. 1975. *Une politique de la langue: La Révolution française et les patois*. Paris: Gallimard.

Dedaić, Marjana, and Daniel N. Nelson, eds. 2003. *At War with Words.* Language, Power and Social Process, 10. Berlin: Mouton de Gruyter.

De Schutter, Helder (2007). "Language Policy and Political Philosophy: On the Emerging Linguistic Justice Debate." *Language Problems and Language Planning* 31: 1–24.

Djité, Paulin G. 2006. "Shifts in Linguistic Identities in a Global World." *Language Problems and Language Planning* 30: 1–20.

Domínguez, Francesc, and Núria López. 1995. *Sociolinguistic and Language Planning Organizations.* Amsterdam: John Benjamins.

Dorais, Louis-Jacques. 1994. "The Language of the Inuit: Its Survival and Development." In Fodor and Hagège, 1983–94, 6: 217–34.

Edwards, John. 2002. "Forlorne Hope?" In *Opportunities and Challenges of Bilingualism,* ed. Li Wei, Jean-Marc Dewaele, and Alex Housen, 25–44. Berlin: Mouton de Gruyter.

Fishman, Joshua A. 1991. *Yiddish: Turning to Life.* Amsterdam: John Benjamins.

Fodor, István, and Claude Hagège, eds. 1983–94. *Language Reform: History and Future.* 6 vols. Hamburg: Helmut Buske.

Fought, Carmen. 2006. *Language and Ethnicity.* Cambridge: Cambridge University Press.

Gendron, Jean-Denis. 2007. *D'où vient l'accent des Québécois? Et celui des Parisiens?* Quebec: Presses de l'Université Laval.

Gladwell, Malcolm. 2002. *The Tipping Point: How Little Things Can Make a Big Difference.* Boston: Little, Brown and Co.

Goebl, Hans. 1984. *Dialektometrische Studien.* 3 vols. Tübingen: Max Niemeyer.

González, Roseann D., and Ildikó Melis. 2001. *Language Ideologies: Critical Perspectives on the Official English Movement.* 2 vols. Urbana, IL, and Mahwah, NJ: NCTE and Lawrence Erlbaum Associates.

Grin, François. 1996. "The Economics of Language: Survey, Assessments and Prospects." *International Journal of the Sociology of Language* 121: 17–44.

Guillotte, Michel. 1987. "L'aménagement linguistique dans l'entreprise privée au Québec." In Laforge, 1987, 339–48.

Habermas, Jürgen. 1975. *Legitimization Crisis.* Boston: Beacon Press.

Hagège, Claude. 2002. *Halte à la mort des langues.* Paris: Éditions Odile Jacob.

Harvey, Louis-Georges. 2009. "Le savoir, la valeur ajoutée et les accommodements raisonnables." *Découvrir* 30: 5.

Herberts, Kjell, and Joseph Turi, eds. 1999. *Multilingual Cities and Language Policies.* Vasa: Åbo Akademi. See also the review in the *Journal of Multilingual and Multicultural Development* 24 (2003): 345–6.

Herriman, M., and B. Bernaby, eds. 1996. *Language Policies in English-Dominant Countries.* Clevedon, UK: Multilingual Matters.

Hock, Hans Henrich. 1991. *Principles of Historical Linguistics*. 2nd ed. Berlin: Mouton de Gruyter.

Hoenigswald, Henry M. 1973. "The Comparative Method." In *Current Trends in Linguistics,* ed. Thomas S. Sebeok, 11: 51–62. The Hague: Mouton.

Hoenigswald, Henry M., and Linda F. Wiener, eds. 1987. *Biological Metaphor and Cladistic Classification: An Interdisciplinary Perspective*. Philadelphia: University of Philadelphia Press.

Huebener, Thomas; and Kathryn A. Davis. 1999. *Sociolinguistic Perspectives on Language Policy and Planning in the USA*. Amsterdam: John Benjamins.

Huot, Jean-Claude. 1980. *La distance interlinguistique lexicale*. CIRB Publication B-93. Quebec: Centre international de recherche sur le bilinguisme.

Jaffe, Alexandra. 1999. *Ideologies in Action: Language Politics on Corsica*. Berlin: Mouton de Gruyter.

Jernudd, Björn, and Jírí V. Neustupný. 1987. "Language Planning: For Whom?" In Laforge, 1987, 69–84.

Joseph, John E. 2006. *Language and Politics*. Edinburgh: Edinburgh University Press.

Kallen, Evelyn. 2003. *Ethnicity and Human Rights in Canada: A Human Rights Perspective on Ethnicity, Racism and Systemic Inequality*. London: Oxford University Press.

Kaplan, Robert B., and Richard B. Baldauf. 1997. *Language Planning: From Practice to Theory*. Clevedon, UK: Multilingual Matters.

Kibbe, Douglas A. 2003. "Language Policy and Linguistic Theory." In Maurais and Morris, 2003, 47–57.

Kimball, Sara E. (2003). "The Comparative Method." In *International Encyclopaedia of Linguistics,* ed. William J.K. Frawley, 2nd ed. Oxford: Oxford University Press.

Klinkenberg, Jean-Marie. 2001. *La langue et le citoyen*. Paris: Presses universitaires de France.

Kloss, Heinz. 1965. "Territorialprinzip, Bekenntnisprinzip, Verfügungsprinzip: über die Möglichkeiten der Abgrenzung der völklichen Zugehörigkeit." *Europa Ethnica* 22: 52–73.

Kymlicka, Will, and Alan Patten, eds. 2003. *Language Rights and Political Theory*. Oxford: Oxford University Press.

Laforge, Lorne, ed. 1987. *Actes du Colloque international sur l'aménagement linguistique (Ottawa, 1986)*. CIRB Publication A-21. Quebec: Presses de l'Université Laval.

Leclerc, Jacques. 1989. *La guerre des langues dans l'affichage*. Montreal: VLB Éditeur.

– 1994. *Recueil des législations linguistiques dans le monde*. 6 vols. Quebec: CIRAL, Les Presses de l'Université Laval.

Le Grand, Julian. 2003. *Motivation, Agency and Public Policy*. London: Oxford University Press.

LePage, Robert B. 1964. *The National Language Question: Linguistic Problems of Newly Independent States.* London: Oxford University Press.

Létourneau, Jocelyn. 2000. *Passer à l'avenir.* Montreal: Boréal.

López, Manuel Triano. 2007. *The Attitudinal Factor in Language Planning: The Valencian Situation.* Lincom Studies in Romance Linguistics 54. Muechen: Lincom Europa.

López-García, Angel. 2005. *The Grammar of Genes: How the Genetic Code Resembles the Linguistic Code.* Bern: Peter Lang.

Loubier, Christiane. 2008. *Langues au pouvoir: politique et symbolique.* Paris: L'Harmattan.

Lukas, J. 1908. "Territorialitäts- und Personalitätsprinzip im österreichischen Nationalitätenrecht." *Jahrbuch des öffentlichen Rechts der Gegenwart* 2: 333–405.

Mackey, William F. 1953. "Bilingualism and Linguistic Structure." *Culture* 14: 143–9.

– 1971. *La distance interlinguistique.* CIRB Publication B-32. Quebec: Centre international de recherche sur le bilinguisme.

– 1974. "La phonologie vectorielle." *International Review of Applied Linguistics,* Special number in honour of Bertil Malmberg, 87–101.

– 1976a. *Bilinguisme et contact des langues.* Paris: Klincksieck.

– 1976b. "Las fuerzas lingüísticas y la factibilidad de las políticas del lenguaje." *Revista mexicana de sociología,* 312–39.

– 1978. "Cost-Benefit Quantification of Language Teaching Behaviour." *Die Neueren Sprachen* 1: 2–32.

– 1979a. "Language Policy and Language Planning." *Journal of Communication,* Spring, 47–53.

– 1979b. "Prolegomena to Language Policy Analysis." In *National Language Planning and Treatment,* ed. Richard E. Wood, James Marcis and T.H. Everett, *Word* 30: 5–14.

– 1985. "The Sociobiology of Ethnolinguistic Nucleation." *Politics and the Life Sciences* 4: 10–15.

– 1987. "Les paradoxes de la Francophonie: Origine, sens et directions." *Mémoires de la Société royale du Canada* 5: 107–22.

– 1988. "Geolinguistics: Its Scope and Principles." In *Language in Its Geographic Context,* ed. Colin Williams (ed.), 20–46. Clevedon, UK: Multilingual Matters.

– 1989. "Determining the Status and Function of Languages in Multinational Societies." In *Status and Function of Languages and Language Varieties,* ed. Ulrich Ammon, 3–20. Berlin: Walter de Gruyter.

– 1991. "Language Diversity, Language Policy and the Sovereign State." *Journal of the History of European Ideas* 13: 51–63.

– 1993. "Literary Diglossia, Biculturalism and Cosmopolitanism in Literature." In *Writing in Stereo: Bilingualism in the Text,* ed. Richard Hodgson and Ralph Sarkanak, *Visible Language* 27: 40–67.

– 1994a. "La politique linguistique dans l'évolution d'un État-nation." In *Langues et sociétés en contact,* ed. Pierre Martel and Jacques Maurais, *Canadiana Romanica* 8: 61–70. Tübingen: Max Niemeyer.

– 1994b. "La ecología de las sociedades plurilingües." In *¿Un estado, una lengua? La organización política de la diversidad lingüística,* ed. Albert Bastardas and Emili Boix, 25–54. Barcelona: Octaedro.

– ed. 2000a. *Espaces urbains et coexistence des langues.* Terminogramme 93–4. Montreal: Publications du Québec.

– 2000b. "Prolégomènes à l'analyse de la dynamique des langues." *DiversCité Langues* 5. Available at http://www.teluq.uquebec.ca/divercité.

– 2001. "Conflicting Languages in a United Europe." *Sociolinguistica* 15: 1–17.

– 2002. "Changing Paradigms in the Study of Bilingualism." In *Opportunities and Challenges of Bilingualism,* ed. Li Wei, Jean-Marc Dewaele, and Alex Housen, 329–45. Berlin: Mouton de Gruyter.

– 2003. "Forecasting the Fate of Languages." In Maurais and Morris, 2003, 64–84.

– 2004. "Bilingualism in North America." In *The Handbook of Bilingualism,* ed. Tej K. Bhatia and William C. Ritchie, 607–41. Oxford: Blackwell.

– 2005. "Bilingualism and Multilingualism." In *Sociolinguistics: an International Handbook of Language and Society,* ed. Ulrich Ammon, Norbert Ditmar, and Klaus S. Mattheier, 2nd ed., 699–713. Berlin: Walter de Gruyter.

– 2006. "Las dimensiones de la política del lenguaje." In *Los retos de la planificación del lenguaje en el siglo XXI,* ed. Roland Terborg and Laura García Landa, 21–58. Mexico: UNAM, Centro d'enseñanza de lenguas extranjeras.

Mackey, William F., and Donald G. Cartwright. 1979. "Geocoding Language Loss from Census Data." In *Sociolinguistic Studies in Language Contact: Methods and Cases,* ed. William F. Mackey and Jacob Ornstein. Trends in Linguistics: Monographs and Studies 6. The Hague: Mouton.

Maurais, Jacques, ed. 1987. *Politique et aménagement linguistiques.* Quebec: Conseil de la langue française; Paris: Éditions Le Robert.

– 1999. *La qualité de la langue: un projet de société.* Quebec: Conseil de la langue française.

Maurais, Jacques, and Michael Morris, eds. 2003. *Languages in a Globalising World.* Cambridge: Cambridge University Press.

McConnell, Grant D. 1991. *A Macro-sociolinguistic Analysis of Language Vitality.* CIRB Publication A-23. Quebec: Les Presses de l'Université Laval.

McConnell, Grant D., and Jean-Denis Gendron. 1993–98. *Atlas international de la vitalité linguistique.* 4 vols. CIRB Publications G13-16. Quebec: Centre international de recherche sur le bilinguisme.

McConnell, Grant D., and Brigitte Roberge. 1994. *Atlas international de la diffusion de l'anglais et du français.* Vol. 1, Éducation. Paris, Quebec: Klincksieck and PUL.

McRae, Kenneth D. 1978. "Bilingual Language Districts in Finland and Canada: Adventures in the Transplanting of an Institution." *Canadian Public Policy* 4: 333–51.

– 1983–98. *Conflict and Compromise in Multilingual Societies.* Vo1., *Switzerland*; vol. 2, *Belgium*; vol. 3, *Finland*. Waterloo, ON: Wilfrid Laurier University Press.

– 2007. "Toward Language Equality: Four Democracies Compared." *International Journal of the Sociology of Language* 187/8: 13–34.

Mühlhäusler, Peter. 2000. "Language Planning and Language Ecology." *Current Issues in Language Planning* 1: 306–67.

Myhill, John. 2006. *Language, Religion and National Identity in Europe and the Middle East: A Historical Study.* Amsterdam: John Benjamins.

Oakes, Leigh. 2001. *Language and National Identity: Comparing France and Sweden.* Impact Studies in Language and Society, 13. Amsterdam: John Benjamins.

Ostler, Nicholas, and Blair Rudes, eds. 2000. *Endangered Languages and Literacy.* Bath, UK: Foundation for Endangered Languages.

Philip, Oswald E. 1975. *Les luttes linguistiques en Alsace jusqu'en 1945.* Strasbourg: Culture alsacienne.

Piriou, Y.B. 1971. *Défense de cracher par terre et de parler breton.* Honfleur: Calvados.

Pohl, Jacques, ed. 1986–87. *Statalismes. Revue de l'Institut de sociologie*, nos. 1 and 2. Brussels: Université Libre de Bruxelles.

Ricento, Thomas, ed. 2006. *Language Policy: Theory and Method.* Oxford: Blackwell.

Rogers, Henry. 2005. *Writing Systems: A Linguistic Approach.* Oxford: Blackwell.

Ryan, Phyllis M., and Roland Terborg, eds. 2003. *Language: Issues of Inequality.* Mexico: Centro de enseñanza de lenguas extranjeras, Universidad nacional autónoma.

Sartori, G.F., W. Riggs, and H. Teune. 1975. *Tower of Babel: On the Definition and Analysis of Concepts in the Social Sciences.* Occasional Paper 6. Pittsburgh: International Studies Association.

Schieffelin, B., and R.C. Doucet. 1994. "The 'Real' Haitian Creole: Ideology, Metalinguistics and Orthographic Choice." *American Ethnologist* 21: 176–200.

Schiffman, Harold F. 2002. "French Language Policy: Centrism, Orwellian *dirigisme* or Economic Determinism?" In *Opportunities and Challenges of Bilingualism*, ed. Li Wei et al., 89–104. Berlin: Mouton de Gruyter.

Schmidt, Ronald, Sr. 2000. *Language Policy and Identity Politics in the United States.* Philadelphia: Temple University Press.

Sebba, Mark. 2006. "Ideology and Alphabets in the Former USSR." *Language Problems and Language Planning* 30: 99–126.

Sheppard, Claude-Armand. 1971. *The Law of Languages in Canada*. Ottawa: Information Canada.

Statistics Canada. 2002. *Profile of Language in Canada*. Ottawa: Ministry of Industry.

Taylor, Charles. 1994. "The Politics of Recognition." In *Multiculturalism: Examining the Politics of Recognition*, ed. A. Gutmann, 25–73. Princeton: Princeton University Press.

Trudel, François. 1996. "Aboriginal Language Policies of the Canadian and Quebec Governments." In *Quebec's Aboriginal Languages: History, Planning, Development*, ed. Jacques Maurais, 101–28. Clevedon, UK: Multilingual Matters.

Tsunoda, Minoru.. 1983. "Les langues internationales dans les publications scientifiques et techniques." *Sophia Linguistica* (Tokyo) 13: 144–55.

Ureland, P. Sture. 2001. *Global Eurolinguistics: European Languages in North America – Migration, Maintenance and Death*. Tübingen: Max Niemeyer.

Vaillancourt, François, and J. Carpentier. 1989. *Le contrôle de l'économie au Québec: La place des francophones en 1987 et son évolution depuis 1961*. Quebec: Office de la langue française.

Weinstein, Brian. 1987. "Language Planning and Interests." In Laforge, 1987, 33–59.

Woehrling, José, ed. 2001. *La protection internationale des minorités linguistiques*. Terminogramme 95–6. Montreal Publications du Québec.

Willemyns, Roland. 1983. *La convention de l'union de la langue néerlandaise*. CIRB Publication H-1. Quebec: Centre international de recherche sur le bilinguisme.

Zelinsky, Wilbur. 2001. *The Enigma of Ethnicity: Another American Dilemma*. Iowa City: University of Iowa Press.

CHAPTER THREE

Ali, Tariq. 2002. *The Clash of Fundamentalisms: Crusades, Jihads and Modernity*. London: Verso.

Bastarache, Michel. 1991. "Le principe d'égalité des langues officielles." In *Vers un aménagement linguistique de l'Acadie*, ed. Catherine Philiponneau, 37–44. Moncton: Centre de recherche en linguistique appliquée.

Bellwood, Peter, and Colin Renfrew, eds. 2002. *Examining the Farming/Language Dispersal Hypothesis*. Cambridge, UK: McDonald Institute of Archaeological Research.

Blommaert, Jan, ed. 1999. *Language Ideological Debates*. Berlin: Mouton de Gruyter.

Blouin, Jean. 1983. "Les gardiens de la langue." *Actualité*, August 1983, 49–56.

Bouchard, Pierre, and Richard Y. Bourhis, eds. 2002. *L'aménagement linguistique au Québec: 25 ans d'application de la Charte de la langue française*. In *Revue d'aménagement linguistique: Auparavant Terminogramme*, automne 2002, hors série. Quebec: Les Publications du Québec.

Caldwell, Gary. 2002. "La Charte de la langue française vue par les anglophones." In Bouchard and Bourhis, 2002, 27–36.

Caratini, Roger. 1986. *La force des faibles: Encyclopédie mondiale des minorités.* Paris: Larousse.

[Chambers, Greta]. 1992. *Report to the Minister of Education of Quebec by the Task Force on English Education.* Quebec: Ministry of Education.

Conseil supérieur de la langue française, 2005. *Le français, langue normale et habituelle du travail.* Quebec: Éditeur officiel.

Cornish, Vaughan. 1936. *Borderlands of Language and Nationality in Europe and Their Relations to the Historic Frontiers of Christendom.* London: Sifton.

Crystal, David. 2000. *Language Death.* Cambridge: Cambridge University Press.

Domenichilli, L. 1999. *Constitution et régime linguistique en Belgique et au Canada.* Brussels: Bruyant.

Dubreuil, Benoît. 2006. "Intégration des immigrants – Pour une approche basée sur les résultats." *L'Action nationale* 96, no. 8: 44–69.

Duchêne, Alexandre, and Monica Heller, eds. 2007. *Discourses of Endangerment: Ideology and Interest in the Defence of Languages.* London and New York: Continuum.

Forget, Dominique. 2004. "Immigration et racisme." *Découvrir: La revue de la recherche* 25, no. 5: 40–8.

Georgeault, Pierre, and Michel Pagé, eds. 2006. *Le français, langue de la diversité québécoise: Une réflexion pluridisciplinaire.* Montreal: CREQC (Québec Amérique).

Gouvernement du Québec. 1990. *Au Québec pour bâtir ensemble: Énoncé de politique en matière d'immigration et d'intégration.* Quebec: Publications du Québec.

Grenoble, Leonore, and Lindsay J. Whaley. 2006. *Saving Languages: An Introduction to Language Revitalization.* Cambridge: Cambridge University Press.

Jacobs, Jane. 2004. *Dark Age Ahead.* Toronto: Random House.

Kaplan, Robert B., and Richard B. Baldauf. 1997. *Language Planning: From Practice to Theory.* Clevedon, UK: Multilingual Matters.

Laforge, Lorne, ed. 1987. *Actes du Colloque international sur l'aménagement linguistique [25–29 mai 1986, Ottawa].* CIRB Publication A-21. Quebec: Presses de l'Université Laval.

Laplante, Sophie. 2005. "L'informatique en français." *Découvrir: La revue de la recherche* 26, no. 6: 19.

Laponce, Jean A. (1989). "L'aménagement linguistique et les effets pervers." In *Langue et droit,* ed. Paul Pupier and José Woehrling, 35–44. Montreal: Wilson and Lafleur.

Leclerc, Jacques. 1989. *La guerre des langues dans l'affichage.* Montreal: VLB Éditeur.

Legault, Josée. 1992. *L'invention d'une minorité: les Anglo-québécois*. Montreal: Boréal.

LePage, Robert B. 1964. *The National Language Question: Linguistic Problems of Newly Independent States*. London: Oxford University Press.

Mackey, William F. 1975. "Current Trends in Multinationalism." In Mackey and Verdoodt, 1975, 330–53.

– 1978. "Cost-Benefit Quantification of Language Teaching Behaviour." *Die Neueren Sprachen* 1: 2–32.

– 1979. "Prolegomena to Language Policy Analysis." In *National Language Planning and Treatment*, ed. Richard E. Wood, James Marcis, and T.H. Everett, *Word* 30: 5–14.

– 1989. "La modification par la loi du comportement langagier." In *Langue et droit*, ed. Paul Pupier and José Woehrling, 45–54. Montreal: Wilson and Lafleur.

– 2001. "Conflicting Languages in a United Europe." *Sociolinguistica* 15: 1–17.

– 2004. "Bilingualism in North America." In *The Handbook of Bilingualism*, ed. Tej K. Bhatia and William C. Ritchie, 607–41. Oxford: Blackwell.

Mackey, William F., and Albert Verdoodt, eds. 1975. *The Multinational Society*. Newbury House Publications. New York: Harper and Row.

Macnamara, John. 1967. *Bilingualism and Primary Education: A Study of Irish Experience*. Edinburgh: Edinburgh University Press. See also the review in *Language* 45: 225–8.]

Maurais, Jacques, ed. 1987. *Politique et aménagement linguistiques*. Quebec: Conseil de la langue française; Paris: Éditions Le Robert.

Newman, Paul. 2003. "The Endangered Language Issue as a Hopeless Cause." In *Language Death and Language Maintenance*, ed. Mark Janse and Sumen Tol. Amsterdam: John Benjamins.

Paillé, Michel. 2002. "L'enseignement au primaire et au secondaire pour les enfants d'immigrants: un dénombrement démographique." In Bouchard and Bourhis, 2002, 51–68.

Paillé, Michel, and Robert Comeau. 2005. "Libre opinion: Quand deux analystes se font une belle jambe avec le concept d'inclusion." *Le Devoir*, 25 July 2005.

Roy, Bruno. 2004. *Montréal, ville internationale de langue française*. Mémoire présenté à l'Office de consultation publique de Montréal. Montreal: Union des écrivains québécois.

Spolsky, Bernard. 2004. *Language Policy: Key Topics in Sociolinguistics*. Cambridge: Cambridge University Press.

Stefanescu, Alexandre, and Pierre Georgeault, eds. 2005. *Le français au Québec: les nouveaux défis*. Montreal: Fides.

Sunstein, Cass R. 2007. *Republic.com 2.0*. Princeton: Princeton University Press.

Thorburn, Thomas. 1971. "Cost-Benefit Analysis in Language Planning." In *Can Language Be Planned?* ed. Joan Rubin and Bjorn H. Jernudd, 253–67. Honolulu: University of Hawaii Press.

Toffler, Alvin, and Heidi Toffler. 2006. *Revolutionary Wealth*. New York: Knopf.

Wurm, Stephen. 2002. "Traditional Multilingualism and Language Endangerment." In *Language Endangerment and Language Maintenance*, ed. David Bradley and Maya Bradley. Richmond: RoutledgeCurzon, Taylor & Francis Group.

INTRODUCTION TO PART TWO

Ball, Rodney. 1997. *The French-Speaking World: A Practical Introduction to Sociolinguistic Issues*. London: Routledge.

Bourhis, Richard Y., and Marshall, D.E. 1999. "The United States and Canada." In *Handbook of Language and Ethnic Identity*, ed. J.A. Fishman, 244–64. New York and Oxford: Oxford University Press.

Cardinal, Linda, et al., eds. 2005. *Le débat sur les politiques linguistiques au Canada et en Europe/Debating Language Policies in Canada and Europe*. Ottawa. http://www.sciencessociales.uottawa.ca/crfpp/fra/textes_presentateurs.asp.

Cardinal, Linda, and Anne-Andrée Denault. 2006. "Empowering Linguistic Minorities: Neo-Liberal Governance and Language Policies in Canada and Wales." In *Territorial Governance in the 21st Century*, ed. John Loughlin and Kris Deschouwer. Brussels: Royal Flemish Academy of Belgium for Arts and Sciences.

Commission des États généraux sur la situation et l'avenir du français au Québec. 2001. *Le français, langue pour tout le monde*. Quebec: Éditeur officiel.

Courcy, Nathalie. 2008. "La diversité linguistique au Canada et au Cameroun: Deux gestions opposées?" In *Legiférer en matière linguistique*, ed. Marcel Martel and Martin Pâquet, 317–36. Quebec: Les Presses de l'Université Laval.

Covell, Maureen. 2001. "Minority Language Policy in Canada and Europe: Does Federalism Make a Difference?" In *Canadian Federalism: Performance, Effectiveness, Legitimacy*, ed. Herman Bakvis and Grace Skogstad, 238–57. Toronto: Oxford University Press.

Fréchette, Christine. 2001. *Language Issues in the Integration of the Americas*. Quebec: Conseil de la langue française.

Kalantzis, Mary, Bill Cope, and Diana Slade. 1989. *Minority Languages and Dominant Culture: Issues of Education, Assessment and Social Equity*. New York: The Falmer Press.

Mackey, William F. 1983. "U.S. Language Status Policy and the Canadian Experience." In *Progress in Language Planning: International Perspectives*, ed. Juan Cobarrubias and Joshua A. Fishman, 173–206. Berlin, New York, and Amsterdam: Mouton.

– 2003. "Bilingualism in North America." In *The Handbook of Bilingualism*, ed. Tel K. Bhatia and William C. Ritchie, 607–41. Oxford: Blackwell.

Maurais, Jacques, ed. 1987. *Politique et aménagement linguistiques*. Paris: Le Robert.

– ed. 1992. *Les langues autochtones du Québec*. Quebec: Les publications du Québec. Published in English in1996 as *Quebec's Aboriginal Languages: History, Planning, Development*., (Clevedon, UK: Multilingual Matters).

McRae, Kenneth D. 2007. "Toward Language Equality: Four Democracies Compared." *International Journal of the Sociology of Language* 187/8: 13–34.

Milian i Massana, Antoni. 1994. *Derechos lingüísticos y derecho fundamental a la educación: un estudio comparado: Italia, Bélgica, Suiza, Canadá y España*, Madrid: Generalitat de Catalunya, Editorial Civitas.

Morris, Michael A. 2003. "Linguistic Diversity in North American Integration." In *Languages in a Globalising World*, ed. Michael A. Morris and Jacques Maurais, 143–56. Cambridge: Cambridge University Press.

Ricento, Thomas, and Barbara Burnaby, eds. 1998. *Language and Politics in the United States and Canada: Myths and Realities*. Mahwah, NJ, and London: Lawrence Erlbaum Associates.

Robinson, Clinton D.W. 1994. "Is Sauce for the Goose Sauce for the Gander? Some Comparative Reflections on Minority Language Planning in North and South." *Journal of Multilingual and Multicultural Development* 15, no. 2/3: 129–45.

Rocher, Guy, and Bruno Marcotte. 1997. "Politiques linguistiques et identité nationale comparées au Québec et en Catalogne." In *La nation dans tous ses États: Le Québec en comparaison*, ed. Yvan Lamonde and Girard Bouchard, 251–67. Paris: L'Harmattan.

Tremblay, Gaétan, and Manuel Pares i Maicas, eds. 1987. *Québec – Catalogne: deux nations, deux modèles culturels*. Montreal: Université du Québec à Montréal.

Wallot, Jean-Pierre, ed. 2005. *La gouvernance linguistique: Le Canada en perspective*. Ottawa: Les Presses de l'Université d'Ottawa.

CHAPTER FOUR

Chen, E.M. 1995. "Statement of Edward M. Chen, staff counsel, American Civil Liberties Union of Northern California, on civil liberties implications of 'Official English' legislation before the United States House of Representatives Committee on economic and educational opportunities subcommittee on early childhood, youth and families." 1 November. http://www.archive.org/stream/s356language ofgooounit/s356languageofgooounit_djvu.txt.

Comité interministériel sur la situation de la langue française. 1996. *Le français langue commune, enjeu de la société québécoise*. Quebec: Ministère de la culture et des communications.

Commission des États généraux. 2001. *Le français, une langue pour tout le monde: Rapport de la Commission des États généraux sur la situation et l'avenir de la langue française au Québec, 2001.* http://www.spl.gouv.qc.ca/etatsrapport_pdf/COM1-021_Rapport_final.pdf.

Conseil des communautés culturelles et de l'immigration. 1991. Énoncé de politique en matière d'immigration et d'intégration et le niveau d'immigration pour les années 1992 à 1994: Avis présenté à la ministre des Communautés culturelles et de l'immigration. Quebec.

Crawford, J. 1992. *Hold Your Tongue : Bilingualism and the Politics of "English Only."* Reading, MA: Addison-Wesley.

Draper, J.B., and Jiménez, M., *A Chronology of the Official English Movement.* Online 24 February 2009 at http://www.ncela.gwu.edu/pubs/tesol/official/chronology.htm.

English First. 1996. *Puerto Rico & Statehood: Why Congress Must Settle the Language Issue before Puerto Rico Makes Its Choice.* Online 24 February 2009 at http://englishfirst.org/puerto/puertoeff.htm.

Grimes, B.F., 1988, *Ethnologue, Languages of the World.* 11th ed. Dallas: Summer Institute of Linguistics.

House of Representatives. 1996, *Committee Report to Accompany H.R. 123.* 104th Congress Report, 2nd Session, 104-723.

Leclerc, J. 1989. *La guerre des langues dans l'affichage.* Montreal: VLB.

– 1992. *Langue et société.* 2nd ed. Laval: Mondia.

Legault, Josée. 1992. *L'invention d'une minorité: les Anglo-québécois.* Montreal: Boréal.

Linguistic Society of America. 1996. "Statement on Language Rights." LSA *Bulletin* 151 (March).

López, R.V. 1995. *Bilingual Education: Separating Fact from Fiction.* NABE (National Association for Bilingual Education) report, 18 September.

Mackey, W.F. 1983. "U.S. Language Status Policy and the Canadian Experience." In *Progress in Language Planning: International Perspectives*, ed. Juan Cobarrubias and Joshua A. Fishman, 173–206. New York and Amsterdam: Mouton.

– 2003. "Bilingualism in North America." In *The Handbook of Bilingualism*, ed. Tel K. Bhatia and William C. Ritchie, 607–41. Oxford: Blackwell.

Marshall, D.F. 1986. "The Question of an Official Language: Language Rights and the English Language Amendment." *International Journal of the Sociology of Language* 60: 7–75.

Maurais, Jacques. 1987. "L'expérience québécoise d'aménagement linguistique." In *Politique et aménagement linguistiques*, ed. Jacques Maurais, 359–416. Quebec: Conseil de la langue française; Paris: Éditions Robert.

– ed. 1992. *Les langues autochtones du Québec.* Quebec: Conseil de la langue française.

– ed. 1996. *Quebec's Aboriginal Languages: History, Planning, Development.* Clevedon, UK: Multilingual Matters.

– 2003. "Equality, Maintenance, Globalization: Lessons from Canada." In *Language in the Twenty-First Century,* ed. Timothy Reagan and Humphrey Tonkin. London and Amsterdam: Benjamins.

National Education Association. 1996. *The Debate over English Only.* Online 27 December 1996 at http://www.nea.org/info/engonly.html.

Nunberg, G. 1989. "Linguists and the Official Language Movement." *Language* 65, no. 3: 579–87.

Office québécois de la langue française. 2005. *Les caractéristiques linguistiques de la population du Québec: profil et tendances 1991–2001.* Coll. Suivi de la situation linguistique, fascicule 1.

– 2008. *Rapport sur l'évolution de la situation linguistique 2002–2007.* Montreal.

Pullum, G.K. 1991. *The Great Eskimo Vocabulary Hoax and Other Irreverent Essays on the Study of Language.* Chicago: University of Chicago Press.

Ricento, T. 1996. *A Brief History of Language Restrictionism in the United States.* Online 24 February 2009 at http://eric.ed.gov/ERICDocs/data/ericdocs2sql/content_storage_01/0000019b/80/17/39/e7.pdf or http://www.ncela.gwu.edu/pubs/tesol/official/restrictionism.htm

Trudel, F. 1992. "La politique des gouvernements du Canada et du Québec en matière de langues autochtones." In Maurais, 1992, 151–82.

Wells, R.V. 1992. "The Population of England's Colonies in America: Old English or New Americans?" *Population Studies* 46: 85–102.

CHAPTER FIVE

Arel, Dominique. 1995. "Language Politics in Independent Ukraine: Towards One or Two State Languages?" *Nationalities Papers* 23, no. 3 (September): 597–622.

Bilinsky, Yaroslav. 1997. "Mova, natsiya i derzhava: problemy z teorii i praktyky [Language, nation and state: problems of theory and practice]." *Skhid* [East] (Donetsk, Ukraine) 2, no. 9 (April): 26–9; 4, no. 11 (June): 11–18.

– 1999. "Was the Ukrainian Famine of 1932–1933 Genocide?" *Journal of Genocide Research* 1, no. 2: 147–56.

– 2003. "On ne badine pas avec les langues vivantes: Les politiques linguistiques canadiennes d'un point de vue comparatif." In *Les politiques linguistiques canadiennes: approches comparées,* ed. Michael A. Morris, 73–82. Paris: Harmattan.

CIA. 2005. *The World Factbook for 2005.* http://www.cia.gov/cia/publication/factbook.

– 2009. *The World Factbook for 2009.* http://www.cia.gov/cia/publication/factbook.

Conquest, Robert. 1986. *The Harvest of Sorrow: Soviet Collectivization and the Terror-Famine*. New York: Oxford University Press.

Danilova, Maria. 2009. "Biden Assures Ukraine of Strong Support; VP Also Set to Visit Embattled Georgia." *News Journal* (Wilmington, DE), 22 July, A13.

Fierman, William, ed. 1995. "Implementing Language Laws: Perestroika and Its Legacy in Five Republics." Special issue, *Nationalities Papers* 23, no. 3 (September)

Hirša, Dzintra. 1998. "La politique linguistique de la Lettonie." In Maurais, 1998, 91–103.

Hryshko, Vasyl. 1983. *The Ukrainian Holocaust of 1933*. Toronto: Bahriany Foundation.

Jubulis, Mark A. 2001. *Nationalism and Democratic Transition: The Politics of Citizenship and Language in Post-Soviet Latvia*. Lanham, MD: University Press of America,

Lannin, Patrick. 2008. "Estonia Still Wrestling with Russian Speakers." *International Herald Tribune*, 25 April. http://www.iht.com.

Maurais, Jacques, ed. 1998. "Les politiques linguistiques des pays baltes." Special issue, *Terminogramme* (Bulletin de recherche et d'information en amenagement linguistique et en terminologie, Les publications du Quebec), July.

Melvin, Neil. 1995. *Russians beyond Russia: The Politics of National Identity*. Chatham House Papers. London: Pinter and Royal Institute of International Affairs.

Mikhalchenko, Vida Io., and Yulia V. Trushkova. 2003. "Russian in the Modern World." In *Languages in a Globalising World*, ed. Jacques Maurais and Michael A. Morris, 260–89. Cambridge: Cambridge University Press.

Osaulenko, O.H., ed. 2003. *Natsional'nyi sklad naselennya Ukraïny ta yoho movni oznaky za danymy Vseukrains'koho perepysu naselennya 2001 roku* [National composition of the population of Ukraine and its linguistic characteristics according to the data of the All-Ukrainian population census of 2001]. Kyiv: Derzhavnyi Komitet Statystyky Ukraïny (State Statistics Committee of Ukraine).

Pabriks, Artis. 2003. "Ethnic Limits of Civil Society: The Case of Latvia." In *Civil Society in the Baltic Sea Region*, ed. Norbert Goetz and Joerg Hackmann, 000–00[133-44]. Aldershot, UK: Ashgate.

Pettai, Vello. 1998. "L'ethnopolitique de l'integration en Estonie et en Lettonie." In Maurais, 1998, 63–89.

Raun, Toivo U. 1995. "The Estonian SSR Language Law (1989): Background and Implementation; Appendix: The Language Law (1989) of the Estonian Soviet Socialist Republic." In Fierman, 1995, 515–34.

Senkus, R[oman]. 1993. "Valuev, Petr." In *Encyclopedia of Ukraine*, ed. Danylo Husar Struk, 5: 553. Toronto: University of Toronto Press.

Toomsalu, Marju, and Leeni Simm. 1998. "Les exigences linguistiques pour obtenir la citoyenneté et occuper un emplois en Estonie." In Maurais, 1998, 37–61.

Velychenko, Stepan. 2006. "Movna polityka v hromads'komu prostori, abo Chomu anhliys'kiy movi slid buty druhoyu movoyu Ukraïny [The politics of public language use, or Why English should be Ukraine's second language]." http://www. vox.com/ua/data/osnovy?skip=10. Earlier, shorter version in *Action Ukraine Report (AUR)*, no. 653 (3 February 2006).

CHAPTER SIX

Agence de la Francophonie. 1995. *Actes de la sixième Conférence des chefs d'État et de gouvernement des pays ayant le français en partage*. December 1995. Paris: Agence de la Francophonie.

Adam, Jean-Michel. 2004. "Quand dire 'Vive le Québec libre!' c'est faire l'histoire avec des mots." In *Discours et construction identitaires*, ed. Denise Deshaies and Diane Vincent, 13–38. Quebec: Les Presses de l'Université Laval.

Ager, Dennis. 1996. *"Francophonie" in the 1990's: Problems and Opportunities.* Clevedon, Bristol: Multilingual Matters.

Augerot-Arend, Sylvie d'. 1996. "Le monde associatif comme moyen d'intervention sur le français: Diversité, dilemmes, dépendance et symphonic inachevée." In Erfurt, 1996, 253–75.

Baggioni, Daniel. 1996. "Éléments pour une histoire de la francophonie (idéologie, mouvements, institutions)." In *Le français dans l'espace francophone*. ed. Denis de Robillard and Michel Beniamino, 2: 789–806. Paris: Honoré Champion.

Bambridge, Tamatoa, Hervé Barraquand, Anne-Marie Laulan, et al., eds. 2004. *Francophonie et mondialisation*. Hermès 40. Paris: CNRS Éditions.

Bourdieu, Pierre. 2001. *Langage et pouvoir symbolique*. Paris: Seuil.

Budach, Gabriele. 2003. *Diskurse und Praxis der Alphabetisierung von Erwachsenen im frankophonen Kanada: Französisch als Minderheitensprache zwischen Ökonomie und Identität*. Frankfurt am Main: Peter Lang.

Cardinal, Linda, ed. 1993. *Une langue qui pense: La recherche en milieu minoritaire francophone au Canada*. Ottawa: Les Presses de l'Université d'Ottawa.

Centre N A Rive. 1995. *Album souvenir 1973–1995*. Montreal: MacroFormat.

Commission des États généraux sur la situation et l'avenir de la langue français au Québec. 2001. *Le français, une langue pour tout le monde: Une nouvelle approche stratégique et citoyenne*. Gouvernement du Québec.

Erfurt, Jürgen, ed. 1996. *De la polyphonie à la symphonie: Méthodes, théories et faits de la recherche pluridisciplinaire sur le français au Canada*. Leipzig: Leipziger Universitätsverlag.

– 1997. "Ma langue maternelle c'est l'anglais – oui, well, mon père était anglais, pis ma mère était française." In *Languages and Lives*, ed. James R. Dow and Michèle Wolff, 155–70. New York: P. Lang.

– 1998. "Politiques linguistiques du monde associatif francophone en Ontario." *Études canadiennes/Canadian Studies* 45: 163–77.

– 1999. "Le changement de l'identité linguistique chez les Franco-Ontariens: Résultats d'une étude de cas." In *L'enjeu de la langue en Ontario français*, ed. Normand Labrie and Gilles Forlot, 59–77. Sudbury: Prise de parole.

– 2000a. "Unilinguismus versus Bilinguismus. Sprachpolitische Diskurse frankophoner Assoziationen in Ontario, Kanada." In *Frankophone Sprachvarietäten: Hommage à Daniel Baggioni de la part de ses "dalons,"* ed. Peter Stein, 191–209. Tübingen: Stauffenburg.

– 2000b. "Frankophone Minderheiten, Migration und *mixité* in Kanada." *Zeitschrift der Gesellschaft für Kanadastudien* 37: 97–112.

– 2005a. *Frankophonie: Sprache, Diskurs, Politik.* Tübingen/Basel: Francke/UTB.

– 2005b. "De *même I hope j'te bother pas*: Transkulturalität und Hybridität in der Frankophonie." In *Transkulturalität und Hybridität: L'espace francophone als Grenzerfahrung des Sprechens und Schreibens*, ed. Jürgen Erfurt, 9–36. Frankfurt/M.: Peter Lang; Europäischer Verlag der Wissenschaften.

– 2007. "'Alpha-francisation' haitianischer Migranten in Montréal." In *Montréal – Toronto. Stadtkultur und Migration in Literatur, Film und Musik*, ed. Verena Berger, Fritz Peter Kirsch, and Daniel Winkler, 129–42. Berlin: Weidler Buchverlag.

– 2009. "Multiculturalisme canadien vs. interculturalisme québécois: Les défis pour l'immigration et la nouvelle francophonie au Québec." RANAM *(Recherches anglaises et nord-américaines)* (Strasbourg), no. 42: 131–48.

Erfurt, Jürgen, Monica Heller, and Normand Labrie. 2001. "Sprache, Macht und Identität im französischsprachigen Kanada. Ein Forschungsbericht." *Zeitschrift für Kanadastudien* 39: 44–67.

Fraser, Graham. 2007. *Sorry, I don't speak French; Ou pourquoi quarante ans de politiques linguistiques au Canada n'ont rien réglé … ou presque.* Montreal: Boréal.

Geertz, Clifford. 1987. *Dichte Beschreibung. Beiträge zum Verstehen kultureller Systeme.* Frankfurt am Main: Suhrkamp.

Georgeault, Pierre, and Michel Page, eds. 2006. *Le français, langue de la diversité québécoise: Une réflexion pluridisciplinaire.* Montreal: Québec Amérique.

Gouvernement du Québec. 1998. *Programme d'intégration sociolinguistique pour les populations immigrantes peu alphabétisées ou peu scolarisées: Version en vigueur (février 1998).* Quebec: Direction des politiques et programmes de francisation, Module de la formation linguistique, Ministère des Relations avec les citoyens et de l'Immigration.

– 2000. *Niveaux de competence en français langue seconde pour les immigrants adultes.* Ministère des Relations avec les citoyens et de l'Immigration.

– 2005. *Plan stratégique, 2005–2007.* Ministère des Relations internationales

Guespin, Louis, and Jean-Baptiste Marcellesi. 1986. "Pour la glottopolitique." *Langages* 83: 3–34.

Heller, Monica, and Normand Labrie, eds. 2003. *Discours et identités: La francité canadienne entre modernité et mondialisation*. Cortil-Wodon: Les Éditions Modulaires Européennes.

Hymes, Dell. 1996. *Ethnography, Linguistics, Narrative Inequality: Toward an Understanding of Voice*. London: Taylor and Francis.

Juteau, Danielle. 1994. "Multiples francophonies minoritaires: multiples citoyennetés (Etats-Unis, Canada)." *Sociologie et sociétés* 26: 33–45.

Le Scouarnec, François-Pierre. 1997. *La Francophonie*. Montreal: Boréal.

Kolboom, Ingo. 2002a. "Die Frankophonie als internationales System." In *Handbuch Französisch. Sprache-Literatur-Kultur-Gesellschaft*, ed. Ingo Kolboom, Thomas Kotschi, and Edward Reichel, Edward, 462–8. Berlin: Erich Schmidt Verlag.

– 2002b. "Die Internationale Frankophonie – Kulturelle Makro-Region und politischer Akteur in der globalen Welt." In *Frankophonie – nationale und internationale Dimensionen*, ed. Ingo Kolboom and Bernd Rill, 7–20. München: H.-Seidel-Stiftung.

Kymlicka, Will. 2001. *La citoyenneté multiculturelle*. Montreal: Boréal.

Labrie, Normand, Marcel Grimard, Roger Lozon, and Carsten Quell. 2003. "Rencontre provinciale de 1998: de la fragmentation à l'éclatement?" In Heller and Labrie, 2003, 229–67.

Laurier, Michel D. 2005. "La maîtrise du français dans la formation des immigrants adults." In Stefanescu and Georgeault, 2005, 567–87.

Maclure, Jocelyn, and Alain-G. Gagnon, eds. 2001. *Repères en mutation: Identité et citoyenneté dans le Québec contemporain*. Montreal: Éditions Québec Amérique.

McAndrew, Marie. 2001, *Immigration et diversité à l'école: Le débat québécois dans une perspective comparative*. Montreal: Les Presses de l'Université de Montréal.

Pagé, Michel. 2006. "Proposition pour une approche dynamique de la situation du français dans l'espace linguistique québécois." In Georgeault and Pagé, 2006, 27–76.

Riesz, János. 2003. "'Frankophonie' – Überlegungen zur Geschichte ihrer Anfänge und der Narration ihrer frühen Entwicklung." *Grenzgänge. Beiträge zu einer modernen Romanistik* 19: 100–29.

Senghor, Léopold S. 1980, *La poésie de l'action: Conversations avec Mohamed Aziza*. Paris: Stock.

Stefanescu, Alexandre, and Pierre Georgeault, eds. 2005. *Le français au Québec: Les nouveaux défis*. Quebec: Fides.

Tétu, Michel. 1996. "Le français au Canada et le monde francophone." In Erfurt, 1996, 351–63.

Thériault, Joseph-Yvon, ed. 1999. *Francophonies minoritaires au Canada: L'état des lieux*. Moncton, NB: Éditions d'Acadie.

– 2005. "L'institution en Ontario français." *Mens* 6: 11–21.

United Nations. 2005. *Human Development Report, 2005*. Online 28 December 2005 at http://hdr.undp.org/reports/global/2005/.

Vallières, Pierre. 1994. *Nègres blancs d'Amérique*. Montreal: Typo.

Venne, Michel, ed. 2000. *Penser la nation québécoise*. Montreal: Québec Amérique.

Weinmann, Heinz. 2002. "Geschichte des frankophonen Nordamerika." In *Handbuch Französisch: Sprache Literatur Kultur Gesellschaft*, ed. Ingo Kolboom, Thomas Kotschi, and Edward Reichel, 432–9. Berlin: E. Schmidt Verlag.

Woehrling, José. 2005. "Conflits et complémentarités entre les politiques linguistiques en vigueur au Québec, au niveau fédéral et dans le reste du Canada." In *Appartenances, institutions et citoyenneté*, ed. Pierre Noreau and José Woehrling, 295–319. Montreal: Wilson & Lafleur.

INTRODUCTION TO PART THREE

Chiswick, Barry R., ed. 1992. *Immigration, Language, and Ethnicity: Canada and the United States*. Washington, DC: The AEI Press.

Demolinguistic Trends and the Evolution of Canadian Institutions. 1989. Montreal: Department of the Secretary of State, the Office of the Commissioner for Official Languages, and the Association for Canadian Studies.

Duchesne, L. 1980. "Quelques données démographiques sur un Québec aussi français que l'Ontario est anglais." In *La situation démolinguistique au Québec et la Charte de la langue française*, ed. M. Amyot, 41–50. Quebec: Conseil de la langue française.

Lachapelle, Réjean, and Jacques Henripin. 1982. *The Demolinguistic Situation in Canada: Past Trends and Future Prospects*. Montreal: The Institute for Research on Public Policy.

Pal, Leslie A. 1993. *Interests of State: The Politics of Language, Multiculturalism, and Feminism in Canada*. Montreal and Kingston: McGill-Queen's University Press.

Paillé, Michel. 1988. "Le Québec anglophone: Une comparaison sommaire avec les Franco-Ontariens." *Bulletin du Conseil de la langue française* 5, no. 2: 4–5.

– 1991. "Choix linguistiques des immigrants dans les trois provinces canadiennes les plus populeuses." *Revue internationale d'études canadiennes/International Journal of Canadian Studies* 3: 185–93.

– 1997. "La communauté anglophone du Québec et les minorités francophones du Canada anglais: Une comparaison démographique." *Bulletin d'histoire politique* 5, no. 2: 66–79.

– 2002. "Les groupes linguistiques anglais et français au Canada." Special issue on Canada, *Le Rotarien* 588: 20–4.

Wardhaugh, Ronald. 1987. *Languages in Competition: Dominance, Diversity, and Decline*. London: Basil Blackwell. See especially chapter 10, "Old States, New Pressures," 230–64.

CHAPTER SEVEN

Ambroise, A. 1987. "Modernisation politique et administrative au Québec (1960–1985)." *Revue internationale des sciences administratives* 8, no. 2 : 175–202.

Babie, B. 1993. "Flux migratoires et relations internationales." In *Migrations et relations transnationales*, special issue, *Études internationales* 24, no 1: 7–16.

Balthazar, L. 1986. *Bilan du nationalisme au Québec*. Montreal: Éditions de l'Hexagone.

Bergeron, G. 1984. *Pratique de l'État au Québec*. Montreal: Québec-Amérique.

Bergheim, K. 1997. "'We are Québécois': Dimensions of National Identity in Quebec in the 1990's." Thesis for master's degree in the Department and Museum of Social Anthropology, University of Oslo.

Bill 63. 1969. *Loi pour promouvoir l'enseignement de la langue française au Québec*. 4ième session, 28ième législature. Quebec.

Bill 101. 1977. *Charte de la langue française*. Lois refondues du Québec, chapitres C-1 à C-24. Quebec: Éditeur officiel.

Boileau, J. 2005. "Si peu visible." *Le Devoir*, 7 December.

Bourdieu, P. 1982. *Ce que parler veut dire: L'économie des échanges linguistiques*. Paris: Fayard.

Burdeau, G. 1980. *Traïté de science politique*. Vol. 2, *L'État*. Paris: Librairie générale de droit et de jurisprudence.

Burnet, J. 1987. "Le multiculturalisme." In *Encyclopédie du Canada*, 2: 1289–90. Montreal: Stanké.

Canada. House of Commons. 1971. *Debates*. Vol. 8, 13 September–19 October, 7737–8852.

– 1984. *Equality Now! Report of the Special Committee on Participation of Visible Minorities in Canadian Society*. Ottawa: Supply and Services Canada.

Carens, J.H. 1995. "Immigration, Political Community, and the Transformation of Identity: Quebec's Immigration Policies in Critical Perspective." In *Is Quebec Nationalism Just? Perspectives from Anglophone Canada*, ed. Joseph H. Carens, 20–81. Montreal and Kingston: McGill-Queen's University Press.

Chercheurs de l'Observatoire de l'administration publique de l'ENAP. 2006. "Le Québec dans le monde (12): Immigration: équilibre entre contrôle et insertion." *Le Soleil*, 18 April. www.observatoire.enap.ca/observatoire/docs/Presse/Soleil05-06/Soleil-18-04-06.pdf; accessed 8 August 2006.

Crépeau, F. 1986. "Catégories d'immigrants et niveaux d'immigration au Canada: une politique volontariste." *Revue européenne des migrations internationales* 2, no. 2: 145–64.

Crête, J., and J. Zylberberg. 1991. "Une problématique floue: l'autoreprésentation du citoyen au Québec." In *Citoyenneté et nationalité en France et au Québec,* ed. D. Colas, C. Emeri, and J. Zylberberg, 423–33. Paris: Presses universitaires de France.

De Coorebyter, Vincent. 2007. "Wallons et Flamands condamnés à s'entendre: Un fédéralisme belge en perpétuel chantier." *Le Monde diplomatique*, November, 4–5. http://www.monde-diplomatique.fr/2007/11/DE_COOREBYTER/15321; accessed 13 February 2009.

Delwit, Pascal, Andrea Rea, and Mark Swyngedouw, eds. 2007. *Bruxelles, ville ouverte: Immigration et diversité culturelle au coeur de l'Europe.* Paris: L'Harmattan.

Dyer, Gwynne. 1998. "How the 'New' Francophones Will Save Canada." *Globe and Mail*, 28 March, D3.

Etzioni, A. 1971. *Les organisations modernes.* Collection Sociologie nouvelles théories. Gembloux: Éditions J. Duculot.

Fontaine, L. 1990. "L'organisation étatique de l'inclusion et de l'exclusion: Le cas du Québec (1976–1988)." Doctoral thesis in political science, Université Laval.

– 1992. "Immigration et politique dans la communauté française de Belgique: des liens de connivences entre différents acteurs d'autorité." *Canadian Ethnic Studies/ Études ethniques au Canada* 24, no.2: 46–59.

– 1993a. "Portrait ethnographique d'un groupe ethnique à Montréal: Une étude de deux associations irlandaises." *Cahiers pour l'analyse concrète* 32–3: 121–32.

– 1993b. *Un labyrinthe carré comme un cercle.* Montreal, Paris: L'Étincelle.

– 1995a. "Immigration and citizenship in Canada and Belgium: Is the Canadian Model of Citizenship Useful for the European Union?" In *Migration, Citizenship and National Identities in the European Union*, ed. M. Martiniello, 93–102. Research in Ethnic Relations Series. Aldershot: Avebury.

– 1995b. "Immigration and Cultural Policies: A Bone of Contention between the Province of Quebec and the Canadian Federal Government." *International Migration Review* 29, no. 4: 1041–8.

– 1996. "Entre l'officiel et l'officieux: Le cas de la Corporation de développement économique communautaire Côte-des-Neiges/Notre-Dame-de-Grâce." Unpublished paper.

– 1999a. "Les 'communautés culturelles': L'évolution d'une catégorie politico-administrative." In *Identité collective et altérité: Diversité des espaces/spécificité des pratiques,* ed. Marie-Antoinette Hily and Marie Louise Lefebvre, 149–60. Collection Espaces interculturels. Paris, Montréal: Les Éditions l'Harmattan.

– 1999b. "Le quadrillage ethnique de Bruxelles." *Recherches sociologiques* 30, no.1: 117–29.

– 2004. "Les multiples mirages de l'identité québécoise." In *La francophonie: enjeux et identités*, ed. Marta Tordesillas, Margarita Alfaro, André Bénit, Carmen Mata, and Gema Sanz, 23–42. Madrid: Universidad Autónoma de Madrid and IMA Ibérica Asistencia.

Goffman, E. 1975. *Stigmate: Les usages sociaux des handicaps*. Paris: Les Éditions de Minuit.

Govaert, Serge. 1998. "Belgium in the Balance: Flemish Far Right Sets Its Sights on Brussels." Trans. Barry Smerin. *Le monde diplomatique*, English ed., January. http://mondediplo.com/1998/01/06brussels; accessed 26 February 2009.

Gouvernement du Québec. 1972. *Rapport de la commission d'enquête sur la situation de la langue française et sur les droits linguistiques au Québec*. 3 vols. Quebec: Éditeur officiel.

– 1976. *La Charte des droits et libertés de la personne et la Commission de la personne: Vous avez le droit. Les autres aussi*. Assemblée nationale du Québec, Law adopted 27 June 1975, chapter 4, "Droits économiques et sociaux," article 43.

– 1978. *La politique québécoise du développement culturel*. 2 vols. Quebec: Éditeur officiel.

– 1979. *L'État et les communautés culturelles: pour une action concertée: Rapport et recommandations du colloque de Montréal, 3–4 novembre 1979*.

– 1981. *Autant de façons d'être québécois: Plan d'action du gouvernement du Québec à l'intention des communautés culturelles*. 1st ed. Ministère des communautés culturelles et de l'immigration.

– 1990. *L'énoncé de politique en matière d'immigration et d'intégration: Pour bâtir ensemble*. Montreal: Ministère des communautés culturelles et de l'immigration.

– 1997a, *Entre-nous*. Bulletin d'information à l'intention des employés du Ministère des relations avec les citoyens et de l'immigration, numéro spécial, October.

– 1997b. *Le MRCI en chiffres*. Bulletin statistique trimestriel du Ministère des relations avec les citoyens et de l'immigration, vol. 1, no. 2 (Summer).

– 2000. *Rapprochement interculturel*. http://www.mrci.gouv.qc.ca/civiques/fr/290_2.asp; accessed 18 May 2000.

– 2007a. *Mandate [of the Consultation Commission on Accommodation Practices Related to Cultural Differences]*. http://www.accommodements.qc.ca/commission/mandat-en.html; accessed 20 January 2008.

– 2007b. *Work Plan [of the Consultation Commission on Accommodation Practices Related to Cultural Differences]*. http://www.accommodements.qc.ca/commission/plan-de-travail-en.html; accessed 20 January 2008.

Henderson, A. 2007. *Hierarchies of Belonging: National Identity and Political Culture in Scotland and Quebec*. Montreal: McGill-Queen's University Press.

Hollifield, J.F. 1993. "Immigration et logiques d'États dans les relations internationales." *Migrations et relations transnationales*, special issue, *Études internationales* 24, no 1: 31–50.

Jacobs, Dick, and Andrea Rea. 2007. "Open Forum: The End of National Models? Integration Courses and Citizenship Trajectories in Europe." *International Journal on Multiculturalism Societies* 9, no. 2: 264–83. www.unesco.org/shs/ijms/vol9/issue2/art8; accessed 25 February 2009.

Kallen, E. 1982. "Multiculturalism: Ideology, Policy and Reality." *Journal of Canadian Studies/Revue d'études canadiennes* 17, no. 1: 51–63.

Lacroix, B. 1985. "Ordre politique et ordre social." In *Traité de science politique*, vol. 1, *La science politique, science sociale. L'ordre politique*, ed. M. Grawitz and J. Leca, 469–565. Paris: Presses universitaires de France.

L'Allier, J.-P. 1976. *Pour l'évolution de la politique culturelle*. Document de travail. Quebec: Bibliothèque nationale du Québec.

Lapointe, G. 1980. *Les communautés culturelles et la fonction publique québécoise: Rapport du groupe de travail interministériel formé par le C.I.P.D.C.* Quebec: Conseil de la langue française.

Larue, J. 1977. *La philosophie de la politique québécoise d'immigration: Rapport de l'atelier du 16 août 1977*. Ministère de l'immigration du Québec.

Lévesque, Kathleen. 2007. "L'immigration, terrain miné?" *Le Devoir*, 15–16 September. http://www.ledevoir.com/2007/09/15/156934.html; accessed 25 July 2007.

Linteau, P.-A., R. Durocher, J.-C. Robert, and F. Ricard. 1986. *Histoire du Québec contemporain*. Vol. 2, *Le Québec depuis 1930*. Montreal: Les Éditions du Boréal Express.

Lochak, D. 1985. *Étrangers: de quel droit?* Collection Politique d'aujourd'hui. Paris: Presses universitaires de France.

McRoberts, K., and D. Postgate, D. 1983. *Développement et modernisation du Québec* Montmagny: Boréal Express.

Molinaro, I. 1999. "Contexte et intégration: Les communautés allophones au Québec." *Globe: Revue internationale d'études québécoises* 2, no. 2: 101–24.

Office québécois de la langue française. 2005. *Grand Dictionnaire terminologique*. www.granddictionnaire.com; accessed 22 February 2005.

Pelletier, C. 1985. *Les communautés culturelles au Québec: Un monde à découvrir*. Quebec: Direction générale de la recherche et du développement, Bureau de l'égalité en emploi, Office des ressources humaines.

Pelletier, R. 1992. "La Révolution tranquille" In *Le Québec en jeu: Comprendre les grands défis*, ed. G. Daigle and G. Rocher, 609–24. Montreal: Les Presses de l'Université de Montréal.

Projet de loi 1. 1977. *Charte de la langue française*. 1st reading, 2nd session, 31st legislature, 1–50.

Projet de loi 22. 1974. *Loi sur la langue officielle*. 2nd session, 30th legislature, 31 July. Quebec.

Quell, Carsten. 2000. "Caught between Bilinguism and Multiculturalism: African and Caribbean Francophones in English Canada." Paper presented at the 8th World Congress of the International Political Science Association, Quebec, 1–5 August.

Ramirez, B. 1991. "Les rapports entre les études ethniques et le multiculturalisme au Canada: Vers de nouvelles perspectives." *International Journal of Canadian Studies/Revue internationale d'études canadiennes* 3: 171–81.

Rioux, Marcel. 1974. *Les Québécois*. Collection "Le temps qui court." Paris: Seuil.

Rocher, F. 1993. "Pluralisme et multiculturalisme: Le rôle des langues dans la quête des identités." In *Les droits linguistiques au Canada: collusions ou collisions?/ Linguistic Rights in Canada: Collusions or collisions?* Centre canadien des droits linguistiques/Centre for Linguistic Rights, Colloque/Conference. Ottawa: Faculté de droit, Université d'Ottawa.

Shiose, Y., and L. Fontaine. 1995. "La construction des figures de l''autre': Les communautés culturelles au Québec." *Canadian Review of Sociology and Anthropology/ Revue canadienne de sociologie et d'anthropologie* 32, no. 1: 91–110.

Simard, C. 2001. "La politique québécoise d'immigration et d'intégration: Perceptions des fonctionnaires en matière de francisation." In *Enjeux de l'administration publique*, ed. M. Charih and P. Tremblay, 111–37. [Sainte-Foy]: École nationale d'administration publique.

Tajfel, H. 1981. *Human Groups and Social Categories*. Cambridge: University Press.

Vicière, S.-H. 1994. "La structuration de l'autre: La politique des communautés culturelles 1976–1981." Thesis for master's degree in political science, Université Laval.

Werly, Richard. 2008. "Le poison linguistique." In *Encyclopédie de l'état du monde*. http://edm.etatdumonde.com/EDMweb/navigation/pays/EURBENELBEL.html; accessed 25 February 2009.

CHAPTER EIGHT

Bannerji, Himani. 2000. *The Dark Side of the Nation: Essays on Multiculturalism, Nationalism and Gender*. Toronto: Canadian Scholars' Press.

Brunet, Jean. 1978. "The Policy of Multiculturalism within a Bilingual Framework: A Stock- taking." *Canadian Ethnic Studies* 10: 107–13.

Burnaby, Barbara. 2002. "Reflections on Language Policies in Canada: Three Examples." In *Language Policies in Education*, ed. James Tollefson, 65–82. Mahwah, NJ: Lawrence Erlbaum Associates.

Canada. Department of Manpower and Immigration. 1966. *Canadian Immigration Policy*. White Paper on Immigration. Ottawa.

Canada. House of Commons. 1962. *Debates*. 1st Session, 25th Parliament, vol. 1, 19 January. Ottawa: Queen's Printer.

– 1971a. *Debates*. 3rd Session, 28th Parliament, vol. 8, 8 October. Ottawa: Queen's Printer.

– 1971b. "Federal Government's Response to Book IV of the Report of the Royal Commission on Bilingualism and Biculturalism: Document Tabled in the House of Commons." In *Sessional Papers*, 283-4/101B, Appendix, 8583–4.

Canadian Mennonite Association. 1965. *Brief to the Royal Commission on Bilingualism and Biculturalism*. Winnipeg.

Citizenship and Immigration Canada. 2001. *Performance Report*. Ottawa: Minister of Public Works.

Frith, Royce. 2003. "Integration." In *Canadian Issues/Thèmes canadiens: Immigration and the Intersections of Diversity*, ed. M. Burstein, 35–6. Montreal: Association of Canadian Studies.

Haque, Eve. 2005. "Multiculturalism within a Bilingual Framework: Language and the Racial Ordering of Difference and Belonging in Canada." PhD dissertation, University of Toronto.

Haque, Eve, and Ellen Cray. 2006. "Putting Them in their Place: Language Policies and Newcomers in Canada." In *The Poetics of Anti-Racism*, ed. Nuzhat Amin and George Seifa Dei. Halifax: Fernwood Press.

Hawkins, Freda. 1988. *Canada and Immigration: Public Policy and Public Concern*. 2nd ed. Montreal and Kingston: McGill-Queen's University Press.

Immigrant Policy and Program Development Branch. 1991. *New Immigrant Language Training Policy (NILTP)*. Ottawa: Employment and Immigration Canada.

Imperial Order Daughters of the Empire. 1964. *Presentation by the Imperial Order Daughters of the Empire (I.O.D.E.) to the Royal Commission on Bilingualism and Biculturalism*. Toronto.

Jenson, J. 1994. "Commissioning Ideas: Representation and Royal Commissions." In *How Ottawa Spends, 1994–95*, ed. Susan D. Phillips. Ottawa: Carleton University Press.

Laurendeau, André. 1991. *The Diary of André Laurendeau: Written during the Royal Commission on Bilingualism and Biculturalism, 1964–1967*. Selected and with an introd. by Patricia Smart. Trans. Patricia Smart and Dorothy Howard. Toronto: James Lorimer and Co.

Lupul, Manoly R. 1983. "Multiculturalism and Canada's White Ethnics." *Canadian Ethnic Studies* 15: 99–107.

Mutual Co-operation League of Canada. 1964. *Brief to the Royal Commission on Bilingualism and Biculturalism*. Toronto.

Rassool, Naz. 1998. "Postmodernity, Cultural Pluralism and the Nation-State: Problems of Language Rights, Human Rights, Identity and Power." *Language Sciences* 20: 89–99.

Royal Commission on Bilingualism and Biculturalism. 1963. *Preliminary Hearing* [Transcript]. 7 and 8 November. Ottawa.

– 1965a. *Transcripts of Public Hearings.* Microfilm; 7 reels. Ottawa.

– 1965b. *A Preliminary Report of the Royal Commission on Bilingualism and Biculturalism.* Ottawa: Queen's Printer.

– 1967. *Report.* Vol. 1, *General Introduction; Book 1, The Official Languages.* Ottawa: Queen's Printer.

– 1969. *Report.* Vol. 4, *Book IV, The Cultural Contribution of the Other Ethnic Groups.* Ottawa: Queen's Printer.

Social Study Club of Edmonton. 1964. *Brief to the Royal Commission on Bilingualism and Biculturalism.* Edmonton.

Taylor, K.W. 1991. "Racism in Canadian Immigration Policy." *Canadian Ethnic Studies* 23: 1–20.

Wardaugh, Ronald. 1983. *Language and Nationhood: The Canadian Experience.* Vancouver: New Star Books.

CHAPTER NINE

Amyot, Michel. ed. 1980. *La situation démolinguistique au Québec et la Charte de la langue française.* Quebec: Conseil de la langue française.

Beaulieu, Mario. 2005. "Le cégep français: pour faire du français la langue nationale." Mouvement estrien pour le français, Sherbrooke, 27 May. http://www.mef. qc.ca/cegep-francais-langue-nationale.htm.

Castonguay, Charles. 1974a. "La domination de l'anglais au Québec." *Le Droit,* 22 May, 7.

– 1974b. "Les dangers du district fédéral: Le français décroît, l'anglais progresse." *Le Jour,* 23 May, 6.

– 1994. *L'assimilation linguistique: Mesure et évolution, 1971–1986.* Quebec: Conseil de la langue française.

– 1999a. "Déclaration de l'origine ethnique lors des recensements: 'Call me Canadian!'" *Le Devoir,* 30 April, A9.

– 1999b. "French Is on the Ropes: Why Won't Ottawa Admit It?" *Policy Options* 20, no. 8: 39–50.

– 2003. "Politiques linguistiques et avenirs des populations de langue anglaise et de langue française au Canada." In Morris, 2003, 174–234.

– 2005. "Les indicateurs généraux de vitalité des langues au Québec: Comparabilité et tendances 1971–2001." Montréal: Office québécois de la langue française.

Churchill, Stacey. 1998. *Official Languages in Canada: Changing the Language Landscape.* Ottawa: Canadian Heritage.

Courtois, Charles-Philippe. 2009. "Se soumettre à l'anglais: Option Louisiane." *L'Action nationale* 99, no. 2: 15–41.

Dominion Bureau of Statistics. 1971. "1971 Census of Canada, [Questionnaire] 2B." Ottawa.

Duchesne, Louis. 1977. "Quelques données démographiques sur un Québec aussi français que l'Ontario est anglais." In Amyot, 1980, 41–50.

Dufour, Christian. 2008. *Les Québécois et l'anglais: Le retour du mouton*. Montreal: Les Éditions réunis.

Dupré, Ruth. 1993. "Was the Quebec Government Spending So Little? A Comparison with Ontario, 1867–1969." *Journal of Canadian Studies* 28, no. 3: 45–61.

Dutrisac, Robert. 2008. "Québec aide les immigrants à parler l'anglais." *Le Devoir*, 1 May.

Grenier, Gilles. 1989. "Bilingualism among Anglophones and Francophones in Canada." In *Demolinguistic Trends and the Evolution of Canadian Institutions*, 35–45. Montreal: Association for Canadian Studies.

Groupe de travail ministériel. 2000. *Les défis de la langue française à Montréal et au Québec au XXIe siècle: Constats et enjeux*. Quebec: Government of Québec.

Guilbault, Louise. 1999. "Les retraités: une comparaison entre le Québec, l'Ontario et le Canada." Institut de la statistique du Québec, *Bulletin* 3, no. 3: 5–6.

Henripin, Jacques. 1974. *L'immigration et le déséquilibre linguistique*. Ottawa: Main d'œuvre et immigration.

Institut de la statistique du Québec (ISQ). 2004. "Immigrants, émigrants et résidents non-permanents, Québec, Ontario et Canada, 1951–2003." 6 March. http://www. stat.gouv.qc.ca/donstat/societe/demographie/migrt_poplt_imigr/index.htm.

– 2008. "Taux de fécondité selon le groupe d'âge de la mère, indice synthétique de fécondité et âge moyen à la maternité, Québec, 1951-2007." Demographical data: births and deaths. http://www.stat.gouv.qc.ca/.

Journal de Montréal. 2009. "L'économie et le français en déroute." 18 February, 9.

Lachapelle, Réjean, and Jacques Henripin. 1980. *La situation démolinguistique au Canada: Évolution passée et prospective*. Montreal: L'Institut de recherches politiques.

Laurin, Camille. 1977. *Le français, langue du Québec*. Montreal: Éditions du jour.

Marmen, Louise, and Jean-Pierre Corbeil. 2004. *New Canadian Perspective: Languages in Canada, 2001 Census*. Ottawa: Minister of Public Works and Government Services Canada.

Ministère de l'Immigration et des Communautés culturelles (MICC). 2008. *Pour enrichir le Québec: franciser plus, intégrer mieux*. Montreal: Gouvernement du Québec.

Morris, Michael A., ed. 2003. *Les politiques linguistiques canadiennes: Une approche comparée*. Collection Espaces discursifs. Paris: L'Harmattan.

Mouvement Montréal français (MMF). 2007. "Des centaines de citoyens se rassemblent pour le français au travail. Press release, 29 April. http://www.montrealfrancais.info/ node/209.

– 2008. "Le gouvernement libéral doit appliquer la Loi 101 dans ses communications avec les entreprises au Québec." Press release, 10 October. http://www.montrealfrancais.info/node/937.

Office québécois de la langue française (OQLF). 2005. *Les caractéristiques linguistiques de la population du Québec: Profil et tendances*. Montreal.

Paillé, Michel. 1988. "Le Québec anglophone, une comparaison sommaire avec les Franco-Ontariens." *Bulletin du Conseil de la langue française* 5, no. 2: 4–5.

– 1989. *Nouvelles tendances démolinguistiques dans l'île de Montréal, 1981–1996* Quebec: Conseil de la langue française.

– 1991a. *Les écoliers du Canada admissibles à recevoir leur instruction en français ou en anglais.* Quebec: Conseil de la langue française.

– 1991b. "Choix linguistiques des immigrants dans les trois provinces canadiennes les plus populeuses." *International Journal of Canadian Studies* 3 (Spring): 185–93.

– 1997. "La communauté anglophone du Québec et les minorités francophones du Canada anglais: Une comparaison démographique." *Bulletin d'histoire politique* 5, no. 2: 66–79.

– 1998. "La population québécoise francophone: un constat de diversité." *Collectif interculturel: La revue de l'Institut de recherche et de formation interculturelles de Québec* 4, no. 1: 71–80.

– 2003a. "Les langues officielles du Canada dans les provinces de Québec et d'Ontario: Une comparaison démographique." In Morris, 2003, 111–51.

– 2003b. "Démolinguistique 101: Pertinence et légitimité de la démographie dans le domaine linguistique." *L'Action nationale* 93, no. 7: 170–204.

– 2003c. "Portrait des minorités francophones et acadiennes au Canada: Un bilan démographique." In *Actes du colloque pancanadien sur la recherche en éducation en milieu francophone minoritaire: Bilan et prospectives, Moncton 1er-4 novembre 2000*, ed. Centre de recherche et de développement en éducation, 21–9. Moncton: Faculté des sciences de l'éducation, Université de Moncton.

– 2007. "L'immigration et la question linguistique." *L'Action nationale* 97, no. 3: 89–100.

– 2008a. "Un progrès continu." *La Presse*, 29 February, A17.

– 2008b. "Pour une 'Agence de la francisation.'" *La Presse*, 17 March, A18.

– 2008c. "L'incontournable francisation des immigrants adultes." *L'Action nationale* 98, nos. 9 and 10: 36–43.

Paillé, Michel, and Robert Comeau. 2005. "Quand deux analystes se font une belle jambe avec le concept d''inclusion.'" *Le Devoir*, 25 July, A6.

Polèse, Mario. 1996. "Impact régional de la mondialisation de l'économie canadienne: Question et éléments d'analyse." *Canadian Journal of Regional Science* 19, no. 3: 283–301.

Pressat, Roland. 1969. *L'analyse démographique: Concepts – Méthodes – Résultats.* Paris: Presses universitaires de France.

Statistique Canada. 1989. *Rétention et transfert linguistiques: Dimensions*. Ottawa: Ministre des approvisionnements et services Canada. Catalogue no. 93-153.

− 1993. *Rétention et transfert linguistiques, 1991: Dimensions*. Ottawa: Ministre de l'industrie, des sciences et de la technologie. Catalogue no. 94-319.

− 2001. *Statistiques démographiques trimestrielles* 14, no. 4. Ottawa: Ministre de l'Industrie. Catalogue no. 91-002-XPB.

− 2002. "Detailed Mother Tongue, Sex, Knowledge of Official Languages and Age Groups for Population, for Canada, Provinces, Territories, Census Metropolitan Areas and Census Agglomerations, 1996 and 2001 Censuses." Ottawa: Minister of Public Works and Government Services Canada. Catalogue no. 97F0007 XCB2001009; released 10 December.

− 2003. "Detailed Mother Tongue, Language Spoken Most Often at Home and Language Spoken at Home on a Regular Basis for Population, for Canada, Provinces, Territories, Census Metropolitan Areas and Census Agglomerations, 2001 Census." Ottawa: Minister of Public Works and Government Services Canada. Catalogue no. 95F0336XCB2001004; released 13 March.

− 2005. "Age and Sex for Population, for Canada, Provinces, Territories, Census Metropolitan Areas and Census Agglomerations, 2001 Census." Catalogue no. 95F0300XCB2001004, 17 August. http://www12.statcan.ca/francais/census01.

− 2007. "Le portrait linguistique en évolution, Recensement de 2006 : Évolution de la situation linguistique au Québec. Ottawa, 4 December. http://www12.statcan. ca/francais/census06/analysis/language/anglo_franco.cfm.

Termote, Marc. 1991. "L'évolution démolinguistique du Québec et du Canada." In *Éléments d'analyse institutionnelle, juridique et démolinguistique pertinents à la révision du statut politique et constitutionnel du Québec*, ed. Commission sur l'avenir politique et constitutionnel du Québec, 239–329. Document de travail no. 2. Quebec: Assemblée nationale du Québec.

− 1994. *L'avenir démolinguistique du Québec et de ses régions*. Quebec: Conseil de la langue française.

− 1999. *Perspectives démolinguistiques du Québec et de la région de Montréal à l'aube du XXIe siècle: Implications pour le français langue d'usage public*. Quebec: Conseil de la langue française.

− 2008. *Nouvelles perspectives démolinguistiques du Québec et de la région de Montréal, 2001–2051*. Quebec: Office québécois de la langue française.

INTRODUCTION TO PART FOUR

Demolinguistic Trends and the Evolution of Canadian Institutions. 1989. Montreal: Department of the Secretary of State, the Office of the Commissioner for Official Languages, and the Association for Canadian Studies.

Edwards, John, ed. 1984. *Linguistic Minorities: Policies and Pluralism*. Burlington, MA: Academic Press.

– ed. 1998. *Language in Canada*. Cambridge: Cambridge University Press.

Georgeault, Pierre. 2006. "Langue et diversité: un défi à relever." In *Le français, langue de la diversité québécoise: Une réflexion plurisdisciplinaire*, ed. Michel Pagé and Pierre Georgeault, 283–325. Quebec: Québec Amérique.

Landry, Rodrigue, and Éric Forgues. 2007. "Official Language Minorities in Canada: An Introduction." *International Journal of the Sociology of Language* 185: 1–9.

Laponce, Jean. 1984. *Langue et territoire*. Quebec: Presses de l'Université Laval. Published in English as *Languages and Their Territories* (Toronto: University of Toronto Press).

– 2006. *Loi de Babel et autres regularités des rapports entre langues et politique*. Quebec: Les Presses de l'Université Laval.

McRae, Kenneth. 1978. "Bilingual Language Districts in Finland and Canada: Adventures in the Transplanting of an Institution." *Canadian Public Policy/ Analyse de politiques* 4: 331–51.

– 1983–98. *Conflict and Compromise in Multilingual Societies*. Vol. 1, *Switzerland*; vol. 2, *Belgium*; vol. 3, *Finland*. Waterloo: Wilfrid Laurier University Press.

Maurais, Jacques, ed. 1992. *Les langues autochtones du Québec*. Quebec: Les publications du Québec. Published in English as *Quebec's Aboriginal Languages: History, Planning, Development* (Clevedon, UK: Multilingual Matters, 1996).

Schneiderman, David, ed. 1991. *Language and the State: The Law and Politics of Identity*. Cowansville, PQ: Les Éditions Yvon Blais. See especially Part 5: "Sociétes multilingues: Structures et stratégies / Multilingual Societies: Structures and Strategies" (151–207), particularly the texts by Kenneth McRae and Jean Laponce.

Thériault, Joseph Yvon. 2007. "Ethnolinguistic Minorities and National Integration in Canada." *International Journal of the Sociology of Language* 185: 255–63.

Wardhaugh, Ronald. 1983. *Language and Nationhood: The Canadian Experience*. Vancouver: New Star Books.

CHAPTER TEN

Blommaert, Jan. 1996a. "Language Planning as a Discourse on Language and Society: The Linguistic Ideology as a Scholarly Tradition." *Language Problems and Language Planning* 20, no. 3: 199–222.

– ed. 1996b. "The Politics of Multilingualism and Language Planning." Proceedings of the Language Planning workshop held at the Political Linguistics Conference, Antwerp, December 1995. *Antwerp Papers in Linguistics* 87.

– *Language Ideological Debates*. Berlin: Mouton de Gruyter.

Bokhorst, Wendy. 1998. "Language, Mass Media, and the Nationalist Project." PhD dissertation, University of Toronto.

Bourhis, Richard Y. 1994. "Introduction and Overview of Language Events in Canada." "French-English Language Issues in Canada," special issue, *International Journal of the Sociology of Language* 105/106: 5–36.

Breton, Raymond. 1968. "Institutional Completeness of Ethnic Communities and the Personal Relations of Immigrants." In *Canadian Society: Sociological Perspectives,* ed. B.R. Blishen, 77–94. Toronto: Macmillan of Canada.

Calvet, Louis-Jean. 1996. *Les politiques linguistiques, Que sais-je ? 3075.* Paris: Les Presses universitaires de France.

Cooper, Robert L. 1989. *Language Planning and Social Change.* Cambridge: Cambridge University Press.

Coulombe, Pierre A. 1995. "Language Rights in French Canada." In *Francophone Cultures and Literatures,* ed. Tamara Alvarez-Detrell and Michael G. Paulson. Berlin: Peter Lang.

Erfurt, Jürgen. 2003. "L'Église catholique: entre conservatisme et mondialisation." In *Discours et identité: La francité canadienne entre modernité et mondialisation,* ed. M. Heller and N. Labrie, 117–46. Cortil-Wodon: Éditions modulaires européennes.

Fairclough, Norman. 1992. *Discourse and Social Change.* Cambridge: Polity Press.

Farmer, Diane. 1996. *Artisans de la modernité: Les centres culturels en Ontario français.* Ottawa: Les Presses de l'Université d'Ottawa.

Foucault, Michel. 1969. *L'archéologie du savoir.* Bibliothèque des sciences humaines. Paris: Les Éditions Gallimard.

Foucher, Pierre. 1993. "Fédéralisme et droit des minorités: Tension ou complémentarité?" In *L'État et les minorités,* ed. Jean Lafontant, 201–29. Saint-Boniface: Les Éditions du Blé, Les Presses de l'Université de Saint-Boniface.

Guespin, L., and Jean-Baptiste Marcellesi. 1986. "Pour la glottopolitique." *Langages,* no. 83: 5–34.

Heller, Monica. 2003. "La Patente: l'embryon de la modernisation." In *Discours et identité: La francité canadienne entre modernité et mondialisation,* ed. M. Heller and N. Labrie, 147–76. Cortil-Wodon: Éditions modulaires européennes.

Heller, Monica, and Gabriele Budach. 1999. "Prise de parole: La mondialisation et la transformation des discours identitaires chez une minorité linguistique." *Bulletin suisse de linguistique appliquée* 69, no. 2: 155–66.

Heller, Monica, and Normand Labrie. 2003. "Langue, pouvoir et identité: Une étude de cas, une approche théorique, une méthodologie." In *Discours et identité: La francité canadienne entre modernité et mondialisation,* ed. M. Heller and N. Labrie, 9–39. Cortil-Wodon: Éditions modulaires européennes.

Joy, Richard J. 1992. *Canada's Official Languages: The Progress of Bilingualism*. Toronto: University of Toronto Press.

Labrie, Normand. 1995. "Complémentarité et concurrence des politiques linguistiques au Canada: Le choix du médium d'instruction au Québec et en Ontario." *Bulletin suisse de linguistique appliquée* 62: 9–33.

– 1999. "Vers une nouvelle conception de la politique linguistique?" In *Contact + Confli(c)t: Language Planning and Minorities / Sprachplanung und Minderheiten / L'aménagement linguistique / Tallbeleid en minderheden*, ed. P.H. Weber, 201–22. Bonn: Dümmler.

Labrie, Normand, Marcel Grimard, Roger Lozon, and Carsten Quell. 2003. "La Rencontre provinciale de 1998: De la fragmentation à l'éclatement?" In *Discours et identité: La francité canadienne entre modernité et mondialisation*, ed. M. Heller and N. Labrie, 229–67. Cortil-Wodon: Éditions modulaires européennes.

Mougeon, Raymond. 1994. "Interventions gouvernementales en faveur du français au Québec et en Ontario. *Langage et société* 67: 37–52.

Patrimoine canadien. 1995. "Les langues officielles, un trait d'union." Ottawa: Ministre des approvisionnements et services Canada.

Quell, Carsten. 2000. "Speaking the Languages of Citizenship." PhD dissertation, University of Toronto.

Skutnabb-Kangas, Tove, and Robert Phillipson, eds. 1995. *Linguistic Human Rights: Overcoming Linguistic Discrimination*. Berlin: Mouton de Gruyter.

Statistique Canada. 2002. *Recensement de 2001: "Série analyses," Profil des langues au Canada: l'anglais, le français et bien d'autres langues*. Ottawa.

Tabouret-Keller, Andrée. 1988. "La nocivité mentale du bilinguisme, cent ans d'errance." In *Euskara Biltzarra*, 155–69. Vitoria-Gasteiz: Eusko Jaurlaritzaren Argitalpen-Zerbitzu Nagusia.

Van Dijk, Teun A. 1993. "Principles of Critical Discourse Analysis." *Discourse and Society* 4, no. 2: 249–83.

CHAPTER ELEVEN

Abella, Irving, and Harold Troper. 1983. *None Is Too Many*. Toronto: Lester & Orpen Dennys.

Anctil, Pierre. 1988. Le Devoir, *les Juifs et l'immigration: De Bourassa à Laurendeau*. Quebec: Institut québécois de recherche sur la culture.

– 1996. "La trajectoire interculturelle du Québec: La société distincte vue à travers le prisme de l'immigration." In *Language, Culture and Values in Canada at the Dawn of the 21st Century / Langues, cultures et valeurs au Canada à l'aube du XXIᵉ siècle,* ed. André Lapierre, Patricia Smart, and Pierre Savard, 133–54.

Ottawa: International Council for Canadian Studies / Conseil international d'études canadiennes and Carleton University Press.

– 1997. "En quête d'un partenariat fructueux: Les Juifs de Montréal face à la législation linguistique québécoise." In *Tur Malka: Flâneries sur les cimes de l'histoire juive*, 171–99. Sillery: Éditions du Septentrion.

– 1999. "À la recherche du paradigme de base de la culture francophone d'Amérique." In *Le dialogue avec les cultures minoritaires*, ed. Eric Waddell, 3–26. Collection Culture française d'Amérique. Sainte-Foy: Presses de l'Université Laval.

Boissevain, Jeremy. 1971. *The Italians of Montreal: Social Adjustment in a Plural Society*. Royal Commission on Bilingualism and Biculturalism, no. 7. Ottawa.

Caldwell, Gary, and Eric Waddell. 1982. *Les anglophones du Québec: De majoritaires à minoritaires*. Quebec: Institut québécois de recherche sur la culture.

Charbonneau, Hubert, and Robert Maheu. 1973. *Les aspects démographiques de la question linguistique*. Quebec: Éditeur officiel.

Corcos, Arlette. 1997. *Montréal, les Juifs et l'école*. Sillery: Éditions du Septentrion.

Gouvernement du Québec. 1977. *La politique québécoise de la langue française*.

– 1978. *La politique québécoise du développement culturel*. Vol. 1. Quebec.

– 1990. Ministère des communautés culturelles et de l'immigration. *Au Québec pour bâtir ensemble: Énoncé de politique en matière d'immigration et d'intégration*.

– 1991. Ministère des communautés culturelles et de l'immigration. *Accord Canada-Québec relatif à l'immigration et à l'admission temporaire des aubains / Quebec-Canada Accord Relating to Immigration and Temporary Admission of Aliens*.

– 2001. Ministère des relations avec les citoyens et de l'immigration. *Le Québec est une société ouverte: Contrat moral entre le Québec et les personnes qui désirent y immigrer*.

Jedwab, Jack, and Chris Baker. 2003. *Perceived Threat to the French Language and Culture and Support for Bilingualism in Canada*. Available on the website of the Association for Canadian Studies at www.acs-aec.ca under "Research"; accessed June 2004.

Joly, Jacques. 1996. *Sondage d'opinion publique québécoise sur l'immigration et les relations interculturelles*. Quebec: Ministère des relations avec les citoyens et de l'immigration.

Knowles, Valerie. 1992. *Strangers at Our Gates: Canadian Immigration and Immigration Policy, 1540–1990*. Toronto: Dundurn Press.

Levine, Marc V. 1990. *The Reconquest of Montreal: Language Policy and Social Change in a Bilingual City*. Philadelphia: Temple University Press.

Linteau, Paul-André. 1982. "La montée du cosmopolitisme montréalais." In *Question de culture*: *Migrations et communautés culturelles*, 23–53. Quebec: Institut québécois de recherche sur la culture.

Linteau, Paul-André. 2000. *Histoire de Montréal depuis la Confédération*. Montreal: Éditions du Boréal.

Louder, Dean, Jean Morrisset, and Eric Waddell, eds. 2001. *Vision et visages de la Franco-Amérique*. Sillery: Septentrion.

Marmen, Louise, and Jean-Pierre Corbeil. 2004. *New Canadian Perspectives: Languages in Canada: 2001 Census*. Ottawa: Canadian Heritage and Statistics Canada.

McRoberts, Kenneth, and Dale Postgate. 1988. *Quebec: Social Change and Political Crisis*. 3rd ed. Toronto: McClelland and Stewart.

Morin, Rosaire. 1966. *L'immigration au Canada*. Montreal: Les Éditions de l'Action nationale.

Morrisset, Jean, and Eric Waddell. 2000. *Amériques: deux parcours au départ de la Grande Rivière de Canada: Essais et trajectoires*. Montreal: L'Hexagone.

Office québécois de la langue française. 2005. *Les caractéristiques linguistiques de la population du Québec: Profil et tendances*. Collection Suivi de la situation linguistique, fasc. no. 1. Montreal.

Rudin, Ronald. 1985. *The Forgotten Quebecers: A History of English-Speaking Quebec, 1759–1980*. Quebec: Institut québécois de recherche sur la culture.

Séguin, Rhéal. 2003. "'English Overtaking French in Montréal,' Experts Warn. Math Professor Cites Statistics Showing a Net Anglicization of Francophones." *Globe and Mail*, 24 November, A4.

Taddeo, Donat J., and Raymond C. Taras. 1987. *Le débat linguistique au Québec: La communauté italienne et la langue d'enseignement*. Montreal: Presses de l'Université de Montréal.

SYNTHESIS AND CONCLUSION

Adam, Dyane. 2005. "De la parole à l'action: Les nouveaux défis de la gouvernance linguistique canadienne." In *La gouvernance linguistique: Le Canada en perspective,*" ed. Jean-Pierre Wallot, xvii–xxvi. Ottawa: Les Presses de l'Université d'Ottawa.

Freed, Josh. 2007. "Newcomers Should Have to Wash Down Their Pâté Chinois with Quebec Wine." *Gazette* (Montreal), 27 October, A2.

Kelleher, Ann, and Klein, Laura. 2008. *Global Perspectives: A Handbook for Understanding Global Issues*. 3rd ed. Upper Saddle River, NJ: Pearson Prentice Hall.

Index

aboriginal languages, 86
aboriginal languages of Canada. *See*
 First Nations of Canada
Académie française, 22
Acadian settlements, 27–9, 53, 64n21
Action catholique, 28
Act of Union, 32, 34
actors in Canadian language policies.
 See groups (or actors) in Canadian
 language policies
African languages, 107–8
Air Canada, 31
Alberta, 35, 53; French settlements in, 27
Alexander ii, Czar of Russia, 34
Alliance for the Preservation of English
 in Canada, 171–2
allophones: compared in Ontario and
 Quebec, 310–12, 315, 321. *See also*
 Montreal; Quebec; Quebec language
 policy; *and other ethnic groups*
Alpha-francisation, 224
American War of Independence, 28
anglophone groups: attitudes to lan-
 guage issues, 6–7; in Quebec, 9
Anglo-Saxon language, 20
Assemblée de la francophonie de
 l'Ontario, 220–1, 236

Association canadienne-française
 de l'Ontario. *See* Assemblée de la
 francophonie de l'Ontario
Australia: language policy, 330
Austria: and European language preferences, 22

Baltic states: language policies, 179–0,
 182–90, 197–8. *See also* Estonia;
 Latvia; Lithuania
Basque language policy, 125, 134
Belgian language policy, 78; compared
 to Canada, 123, 162, 164, 208, 262–
 3, 265, 329–30, 384
Bibeau Report, 41, 47–9, 148
Bill 22 (Quebec), 37, 252, 350
Bill 63 (Quebec), 37, 252, 350
Bill 101 (Quebec). *See* Charter of the
 French Language
Bill 178 (Quebec), 38
bilingual countries: institutional bilingualism in, 8; language policies, 5–6, 42
bilingual districts, 6, 89; in Canada, 6,
 40, 43–6, 104, 114n3, 130, 147
bilingualism in Canada, 42–3, 168–9;
 and individual bilingualism, 280–1;
 and institutional bilingualism, 280–1

bilingualizing the Canadian public service, 40, 43, 46–9, 123–5, 138. *See also* Coulombe Report
Bouchard, Gérard, 39
Bouchard-Taylor Commission, 88, 249
Bourassa, Robert, 37, 350–1
British citizenship: and language, 90
British Columbia, 35, 52
British language policy, 330
British North America Act, 29, 32, 35, 346
Brunet, Jean, 289, 291

Calvin, Jean, 25
Cameroon language policy: and Canada, 163
Canadian Charter of Rights and Freedoms, 41, 56, 288, 338
Canadian language policies: conclusions about, 373–5; ethnic component, 33, 110–11; Europe and, 161–2; evolution of, 32–5, 75–6, 92; and federation, 77–8; groups in, 330–1; importance of, xi; interaction between, 10–14, 372, 374–5; legislation, 8–9; literature, 5–7; mother tongue and home language compared, 309–15, 321; and nationhood, 119n33; number of, xi; and promotion of French, 6; religious component, 33; territorial component, 33; US distortions of, xi–xii. *See also* comparative approach; federal language policy of Canada; provincial language policies of Canada; territorial language policies in Canada; *and under names of provinces*
Canning Instructions, 23, 130
Catalan language: in France, 91; in Spain, 99

Catalan language policy, 125, 161–2, 164
Catholics in Canada, 28, 30–1
Centre N a Rive, 223
Charles V, King of Spain, 21–2
Charter of the French Language (Bill 101), 7–9, 37–8, 60, 101; aboriginal languages in, 76, 169; contrasts with US language practice, 172–5; and demographical contrasts, 297–8; English language rights in, 171–2; and French language promotion in Montreal, 351–4; implementation of, 142–3, 145–8; Parti Québécois and, 252; and Quebec identity, 252–3; recommended improvements in, 321–4; and the Supreme Court of Canada, 169
Chrétien, Jean, 47
Clemenceau, Georges, 23
Comité catholique du Conseil de l'instruction publique, 36
Comité protestant du Conseil de l'instruction publique, 36
Commissioner of Official Languages (Canada), 43, 49–50, 141–2, 364, 381
comparative approach, xi–xii, 3–6, 10–13, 70–1; contributions of, 370–1; diachronic comparisons, 74–5; limitations, 369–70; synchronic comparisons, 74. *See also* policy comparisons; thematic comparisons
comparative issue analysis, 10–11, 377. *See also* comparative approach
comparison of federal and provincial Canadian language policies, 6–7. *See also* federal language policy of Canada; provincial language policies of Canada

Confederation debates, 33
Congress of Vienna, 22
Conseil de la vie française en Amérique, 27
Conseil supérieur de la langue française, 364
Constitutional Act, 32–4
Coulombe Report, 40, 46–7, 148
Covenant of the League of Nations, 24
Creole language, 223, 336

Dade County, Fla: language policy, 79
demography: impact on Canadian language policies, 8, 35, 38, 297–8; and overview of Canada, 298–300
Department of Canadian Heritage, 226
Department of Foreign Affairs, 227
Department of International Cooperation, Francophonie and Official Languages, 225
discourse analysis, 334–5
Drury Declaration, 40, 46
Duhamel Commission, 44
Dunton, Davidson, 42
Duplessis, Maurice, 36, 218, 346
Durham Report, 33–4, 39, 233; aftermath, 53
Dutch language treaty, 78; *See also* Netherlands

Eastern European language policies, 164–5
Eastern Townships, Que., 29
England: and the English language, 18–19; and the French language, 20; literacy in, 25
English language: in Canada, 29, 31–2; in Europe, 19–21, 83; and the Industrial Revolution, 26; international status of, 22–4, 26; national identities and, 117n24; national status of, 20–1, 24–6, 58–9; in North America, 26–9, 59; rivalry with French language, 18–19, 57
English First, 166, 172–4, 176
English Only, 166, 172
Erasmus Commission, 41. *See also* First Nations of Canada
Estates-General report, 39, 149
Estonia: language policy, 184–90
European Federation of National Institutions for Language, 83
European Union: languages in, 82–2; and language minorities, 91, 104–5; and subsidiarity, 78
evaluation. *See* policy evaluation

Federalist Papers, 78
federal language policy of Canada, 5–6; and bilingual services, 8, 101; comparison with provincial language policies, 6–7, 9, 19, 93–4, 127–8, 130, 294–5, 364–6, 368, 379–84; cost of, 136–7; in eastern Canada, 75; evolution of, 40–1, 75–6, 125–6; and feedback, 149; and Franco-Ontarians, 337–8, 340–1; and francophone groups, 224–6; and the Francophonie, 218–19; implementation, 47–9, 141–2, 147–8; and institutional bilingualism, 8, 52, 126; jurisdiction, 8; and minority languages, 76; and multiculturalism, 8, 19, 56–7, 107; origins, 31–4; and other ethnic groups, 294–5; and Quebec language policy, 226–8, 359–60; and relation to non-linguistic issues, 243–4; in western Canada, 30, 75. *See also* Canadian language policies; Quebec language policy

Fédération des communautés franco-
    phones et acadiennes, 221–2, 232
Fédération des francophones hors
    Québec, 36, 53
Federation of Saskatchewan Indian
    Nations, 55
federations: language policy of, 116n16,
    122
Finland: bilingual districts, 6, 104; lan-
    guage policy, 93, 164, 329
First Nations of Canada, 41; and bi-
    lingualism,169; comparison of lan-
    guages of, 76, 117n20; corpus, 100;
    and language development, 94, 133,
    154–5; and language policy, 19, 54–
    6, 59, 95, 149, 380; language rights
    in, 116n14; language script of, 96–7;
    lexicon, 99; and the two founding
    nations, 238n3
founding races. *See* two founding races
    in Canada
Fox, Paul, 44
France: and the French language,
    18–19; and global trade, 215; and
    the Treaty of Amity with the United
    States, 23
Francis I, King of France, 21–2
Franco-Ontarians, 6
francophone groups of Canada: atti-
    tudes to language issues, 7, 234
francophones de souche, 234, 298
Francophonie, 208–9, 211–17, 237;
    Algeria and, 210; Canada in, 208–19,
    225–6, 234–5, 237–8; France and,
    226, 238; New Brunswick in, 208,
    213, 237–8; Quebec in, 208, 211,
    214, 216 , 218–19, 237–8
"French fact in America," 30
French language: in Europe, 19-21; and
    the French Revolution, 25–6, 33, 91;

and the Industrial Revolution, 26;
    international status of, 20, 21–4, 26,
    93, 101; literacy in, 25–6; national
    status, 24–6, 58–9, 84; in North
    America, 26–8, 59; rivalry with
    English, 18–19, 57. *See also* French
    language in Canada
French language in Canada, 18, 31–2,
    39, 152; and British conquest, 28;
    policy, 330
French Revolution, 25–6, 33; and lan-
    guage policy, 85
French immersion classes, 50
Front de libération du Québec, 37
functional bilingualism, 9. *See also*
    Quebec language policy

Gagnon-Tremblay-McDougall
    Agreement, 352
Gaspé Peninsula, 29
Gendron Commission, 36–7, 130, 252
Gens de l'air crisis, 41
Grégoire, Abbé Henri, 25
groups (or actors) in Canadian lan-
    guage policies, 10–11, 17, 329–32,
    377–9; anglophone groups, 6–7,
    9; and change in language policy,
    12–13; francophone groups, 6–7, 9.
    See also comparative approach

Habsburg Empire: language policies,
    111, 116n13
Haut Comité de la langue française, 99
Hayakawa, S.I., 166
Herder, Johann, 108
historical perspectives: on Canadian
    language policy, 10–11, 17–19, 376–
    7 (*see also* comparative approach);
    on language policy, 10–11, 17
Holy Roman Empire, 21–2

Hundred Years War, 21
Hungarian language policy, 92

immigration policy: and language
    policy, 19
immigration to Canada, 28, 30, 209,
    344–6; and Canadian policy, 289–91,
    381; and English-language training,
    291–4; and language, 276; literature,
    243–4; and marginalization of new-
    comers, 293–4; and multiculturalism,
    289–91
India: language policy, 94–5, 97, 103
indigenous languages of Canada. *See*
    First Nations of Canada
individual bilingualism: Ontario and
    Quebec compared, 320–1, 377
Indonesia: language policy, 132
institutional bilingualism, 8, 52, 377
institutionalization: as a methodology,
    206–7, 235–6
interculturalism, 234, 239n18
international perspectives on language
    policy, 10–11, 376. *See also* com-
    parative approach
Inuit Cultural Institute, 99
Inuit Tapirisat, 55, 97
Inuktitut language, 55, 75
Ireland: language policy, 78, 125,
    132–3, 136
irredentism: and language, 92
Israel: language policy, 132
Italian language policy: and Canada, 162

James Bay Agreement, 54–5

Kurdish language, 83, 116n16

language academies, 117n21
language commissions, 69

language development, 131–2
language diversity, 119n35
language identities, 106–8
Language Instruction for Newcomers to
    Canada (LINC), 292–4, 296
language minorities, 118n28, 129–31
language planning, 72–3, 76
language policy: and the Canadian
    policy process, 59–60; and dialects,
    94; and diasporas, 105–6; challen-
    ges to, 4–6, 68–9, 71–2; changes in,
    83–4; and economic factors, 86–7;
    and education, 79, 86; and ethnicity,
    89, 109–11; evaluation of, 120–1;
    and identity, 118n26; and intercom-
    munication, 151–5; measurement of,
    79–82; nature of, 6, 67–8; and non-
    linguistic perspectives, 10–11; and
    orthography, 97–8; and the policy
    process, 12–13; and religion, 90,
    120–1; in small and large countries,
    102–3; and thematic perspectives,
    10–11
language preservation, 85–6, 134
language revival, 132–4, 155
language rights: in Canada, 7, 9, 123–4
language training, 48–9. *See also* bilin-
    gualizing the Canadian public service
language vitality, 80
Latin language: status in Europe, 21–2,
    101–2, 116n15, 117n19
Latvia: language policy, 184–90
Laurendeau, André, 42
Laurendeau-Dunton Commission. *See*
    Royal Commission on Bilingualism
    and Biculturalism
Lesage, Jean, 217–18
Lévesque, René, 37, 218
Lithuania: language policy, 184–90
Lloyd-George, David, 23

Louisiana Purchase, 27
Lower Canada, 34–5

Maison d'Haïti, 223
Manitoba, 35, 41, 54; French settlement
    of, 27, 30, 64n21; language policy,
    51–2, 168–9, 232
Marxist regimes: and ethnic and lin-
    guistic identity, 109
Maritime provinces, 34–5
McRae, Kenneth, 11, 42
Meech Lake Accord, 41
methodology: and the interactive policy
    process, 12–13; and other methodol-
    ogies, 13–14; and thematic perspec-
    tives, 10–11. *See also* comparative
    approach; discourse analysis; stan-
    dard population method
Métis, 30, 51
Métis National Council, 55
Miami, Fla. *See* Dade County, Fla
minority language groups, 6, 81, 91,
    102–3; education of, 7; status of,
    269–70
Montreal: allophones, 355–8; English-
    speaking groups, 29, 104, 362;
    English-French divide, 30, 127;
    French language in, 38; immigrants,
    344–5, 347–52; importance, 361–2,
    380; language distribution in, 323–4;
    language of education in, 37; minor-
    ities, 39, 146; settlement of, 27
multiculturalism in Canada, 8, 19,
    55–7, 150–1; background, 267–9;
    within bilingual framework, 286–8;
    and language, 273–6; Quebec and,
    234, 239n18, 250–1. *See also* federal
    language policy of Canada
multilingual countries: comparison with
    Quebec, 7

Napoleonic empire: and status of
    French, 22–3
nation-states: and languages, 166–7
Netherlands: language policy, 78
New Brunswick, 28, 45; language
    policy, 6, 50–3, 165, 169, 210, 232;
    and non-governmental organizations,
    220; population characteristics, 8
Newfoundland, 41, 45, 53
New France, 27–8, 32
New Zealand: language policy, 110
non-linguistic perspectives on language
    policy. *See* comparative approach;
    comparative issue analysis
North American Free Trade Agreement
    (NAFTA): and Canadian language
    policies, 7, 163, 197
North American language area, 104
Northern Coordination Research
    Centre, 95
North-West Territories (pre-1905),
    51–2
Northwest Territories, 55
Nova Scotia, 53; language policy, 262–
    3; settlement of, 28
Nunavut, 55, 75

October Crisis, 37
Office de la langue française, 36
Official Languages Act (Canada, 1969),
    6, 8, 40, 43–4
Official Languages Act (Canada, 1988),
    41, 49–50
Official Languages Law (New
    Brunswick), 9
Oliver, Michael, 42
Ontario French Language Services Act,
    51
Ontario language policy, 6, 50–3, 165,
    169, 210, 232; and demographic

trends, 297–8; and demolinguistic contrast with Quebec, 301–4; francophones in, 333, 335–6, 341–2; groups in, 331; and non-governmental organizations, 220–4
Ordre de Jacques Cartier, 337
Organisation internationale de la Francophonie. *See* Francophonie
Organization for Security and Cooperation in Europe, 91
"other ethnic groups." *See* Royal Commission on Bilingualism and Biculturalism
Ottoman Empire, 89; language policies, 111

Pacific Coast: French settlement on, 27
Pakistan: and English language, 92
Parti Québécois, 36–8, 40, 222, 229, 233, 350–1. *See also* Quebec
patriation of Canadian Constitution, 41, 147
Pearson, Lester, 41
Pearson Declaration, 40, 46
Pépin-Robarts Task Force on Canadian Unity, 41
personality principle, 26, 45, 50, 53, 89, 105, 374; criticism of, 329; contrasted with Eastern Europe, 199
Pitt, William, 34
Plains of Abraham, battle of, 28, 33, 64n22
policy. *See* language policy
policy comparisons, 12–13, 379–84. *See also* comparative approach
policy evaluation, 12–13, 120–1, 382–3. *See also* comparative approach
population trends in Canada: literature, 243
Port-Royal, 27

Prince Edward Island, 35, 53
Protestants in Canada, 28, 30
Protestant Reformation: and European languages, 25
provincial language policies of Canada: characteristics, 50–3; comparison with federal language policy, 6–7, 9, 14, 51; jurisdiction, 8. *See also under names of provinces*
Public Service Alliance, 46
Puerto Rico: language policy, 168, 176–7

Quebec: cultural communities, 255–7, 260–1; English-speaking minority, 29–31, 118n32, 119n34; and France, 218; and francophone minorities in other provinces, 222; identity, 108, 110, 224, 228–32, 246–7, 249, 254; immigration policy, 146, 228–32, 323, 352; language and religion in, 29–31, 33; political change in, 346–52; referendum (1995), 258; Secrétariat aux affaires autochtones, 55; separatism, 35–7, 41, 222, 260. *See also* Parti Québécois
Quebec Act, 32–4
Quebec City: settlement of, 27
Quebec institutions: religious representation in, 28
Quebec language policy, 6–7, 332; and aboriginal communities, 149, 164, 169; and the anglophone minority, 306–7, 309; and comparison with federal language policy, 6–7, 9, 19, 93–4, 114n3, 127–8, 130, 144–5, 147–8, 150, 226–8, 379–84; contrast with francophone areas and countries, 163–4; contrast with other provincial language policies, 36,

231–2; contrast with Puerto Rico,
176–7; contrast with the US, 173;
and demographic concerns, 8, 35,
38, 297–8; and demolinguistic comparison with Ontario, 301–4; and
economic factors, 87; and education
of immigrants, 347–52; and English
competency, 307, 309; evolution, 35–
9, 75–6, 84–5; and feedback, 149;
groups in, 330–2; and immigrants,
37–8, 149–50, 173, 209, 263–5,
378; implementation, 142–4, 147–8,
381–2; and language minorities, 76,
102, 145–6, 149–50; and language
planning, 73, 76; and language
rights, 88; and language training of
immigrants, 229–31; and the lexicon, 99; and Montreal, 323–4, 380;
and municipalities, 105; and policy
process, 12–13, 32; before the Quiet
Revolution, 84; scope, 139–40. *See
also* Charter of the French Language
(Bill 101); Montreal
Quebec Ministry of Immigration and
Cultural Communities, 247–50,
263–4
Québécois de souche, 39
Quiet Revolution, 33, 36, 39–40, 217–
18, 251–2, 347

religion in Canada, 29
Riel, Louis, 30, 51
Rowell-Sirois Commission, 41
Royal Commission on Aboriginal
Peoples, 54
Royal Commission on Bilingualism and
Biculturalism: background, 5–6, 33,
40–3, 54–6, 267–8; and bilingualism
and biculturalism, 267–8, 281–2,
286–8; language and, 278–80; and

"other ethnic groups," 269–72,
276–9, 281–5, 287–9, 291, 294; on
public servants, 131; and Quebec,
172, 219–20. *See also* multiculturalism: within a bilingual framework;
two founding races in Canada
Russia: language policy, 165, 183;
status of the French language, 22. *See
also* Soviet Union
Russian Empire: language policies, 111,
179–80
Russian language: status of, 24

Sainte-Foy, battle of, 28
St Lawrence river: English settlements
on North Shore, 29
Saskatchewan, 35, 52, 55; French settle-
ment of, 27, 30
Secretariat of State (Canada), 49
Seven Years War, 22
Singapore: language policy, 334
Société Saint-Jean-Baptiste de Montréal,
222–3, 235, 237
Soviet Union: language policy, 164,
179–80, 182–3
Spanish Empire: language policy,
116n15, 117n18
Spanish language: international status,
22, 24; status in the US, 79
Spanish language policy: and Canada,
162, 330
standard population method, 304. *See
also* methodology
Switzerland: language policy, 329–30,
384

Taylor, Charles, 39
territorial approach to language policy,
9, 26, 89, 374; Augsburg principle of
territoriality, 22

territorial language policies in Canada, 6, 34, 36, 45, 53, 105; contrasted with Eastern Europe, 199; support for, 329–30. *See also* Quebec language policy

thematic comparisons, 10–11, 372, 375–9. *See also* comparative approach

Thirty Years War, 34

Toronto: and immigrants, 344, 360

Treasury Board: and implementation of bilingual public service, 44, 46–9

Trudeau, Pierre Elliot, 37, 45, 286–9

Trudeau Declaration, 40

Turkey: and Kurdish language, 83, 116n16

two founding races in Canada, 33, 38, 41–2, 150, 251, 268–9, 276–81; in Ontario, 336–9; and other two solitudes, 30

Ukraine: language policy, 182–3, 185, 191–6, 198–200

United Nations: official languages, 24

United Nations Human Rights Commission: on linguistic minorities, 128, 174

United States: and aboriginal languages, 169; and Alaska, 34; bilingual education in, 175–6; contrast with Quebec, 173; cultural impact on Canada, 31; Dade County, Fla, 79, 111–12, 170–1; English as official language, 111–12, 167; federalism and language practice in, 115n10; French settlement of, 27; and immigrant languages, 107, 111; and immigration policy of Canada, 295; and international status of English, 23–4; language policies of states, 167–8; and language policies of Canada, 162–3, 330; language practices, 72–3, 78; and linguistic diversity, 91; and Puerto Rico, 168, 176–7

Upper Canada, 28, 34–5

Utrecht, Treaty of, 28

Versailles, Treaty of, 24

Vienna, Treaty of: and language preferences, 23

visible minorities, 39, 291

Welsh language, 91

Western Canada, 34, 64n21; settlements in, 30

Westphalia, Treaty of, 22, 62n10

Wilson, Woodrow, 23

Yukon, 55